JE

To the Janes,
May the Lord continue
to bless your family! And use
you all to grow His Kingdom!

L. E. Start

OTHER BOOKS BY L. E. STARK

JOURNEY: A Collection of Poetry

Tales of the Soul: JOPLIN May 22

Letters to Aaron

Sasquatch for Dinner And Other Short Stories

10 Topics which the CHURCH Needs to Talk About

JESUS

By

L. E. Stark

STARK
PUBLISHING®

Createspace website: http://www.createspace.com

ISBN 978-1539675549

DEDICATED TO THE
ROLLA CHURCH OF CHRIST

"I am an historian, I am not a believer, but I must confess as a historian that this penniless preacher from Nazareth is irrevocably the very center of history. Jesus Christ is easily the most dominant figure in all history."

—H. G. Wells

Contents

PROLOGUE

Jesus, give me strength, I thought to myself.

My throat was tight, as I sat on my stool in front of my Sunday school class of teenagers. I had seen each of their faces before and they had yet to transform into an angry mob equipped with torches and pitchforks. But just like every time before, I felt nervous. I did have my class prepared, but what if I messed up? What if I missaid something? What if I made myself look like a fool . . . again. Or had misinterpreted the Bible in such a way, that I would lead a teen down the wrong path to the fires of Hell? 'What if's' clouded my mind, before I finally reopened my mouth: "Who remembers what the theme is for this summer?"

"Jesus," answered several. Of course, this would be the typical Sunday morning answer which you would expect. Yet in this case, it was more. Different.

***

DURING THE SUMMER of 2016, I was blessed to serve the Rolla Church of Christ as their summer intern. It was an *amazing* experience which I truly treasure within my heart. One that I will never forget and full of irreplaceable memories. Some involving things, like: tarantulas, squirrels, Batman, and pancakes. This book, stems from that summer.

"WHAT ARE YOU going to be talking about?" asked a teen's mom on my first Wednesday night.

"Well, Jesus . . ." I began to answer.

I guess I accidently sounded sarcastic or joking, for she then replied, "I hope so."

I chuckled. "But yeah, Jesus. We're going to look into the Bible and see what it says who Jesus is. We're going to be studying Jesus in the Old Testament, or how the Old Testament points toward Jesus on Sundays. And Jesus in the New Testament on Wednesdays."

"Oh, awesome. Mind if I sit in?" she asked.

"No, not at all."

Jesus, who is he? I mean, when you hear the name 'Jesus,' what is the first thing you think of? A white guy with a beard, long hair, and blue eyes? Why? Because it's the image he's often depicted as, isn't it? At least in the U.S. So much so, that I once heard a long-haired, agnostic comedian tell of a time, when a stranger had walked up to him and said, "You look like a chubby Jesus."

"Thanks?" The crowd laughed. "What do you say to that? . . . I decided then I wasn't going to forgive him. I'd leave that for the skinny Jesus."

We have been conditioned to think of Jesus as this white man with a beard and long hair. Not saying that this is wrong or sinful, and we're not the only ones who imagine him looking like us either. I've

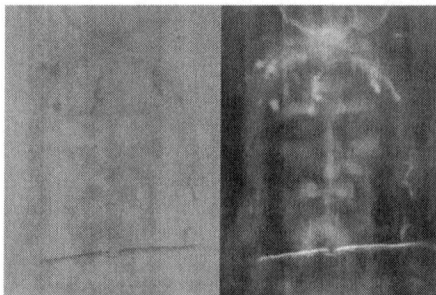 also seen images of him being black, Asian, even Apache. In fact, did you know—honestly, I didn't until moments just before writing this—that before

our image of Jesus became popular, there were many depictions of him from the third century up to the twelfth of him being beardless? (Arguably, because they too may have been reflecting the culture which they were painted by, Jesus, perhaps, given features similar to that of a Roman Emperor.)

In fact, our modern illustrations of Jesus have been influenced by the Shroud of Turin, (a one-piece burial cloth with the imprint of a man who may have been crucified. Those who believe it is Jesus, reason the image was burned into the cloth by his resurrection, while others argue that it's a medieval forgery). However, a problem with this shroud, as pointed out by John Calvin in his *Treatise on Relics*, is that Jesus was not wrapped with a single cloth, but by two. One around his head and another around his body. (John 20:6-7).

With that said, Jesus was probably not white. No, I wasn't alive 2,000 years ago; I'm not that old yet. But from what I know of ancient Israel and her culture, he most likely had olive skin with a beard, short hair (1 Corinthians 11:14-15), and either brown or hazel eyes. And unlike his great-granddaddy David, Jesus was just average looking, not one to stick out of a crowd solely by his looks (Isaiah 53:2); though, he was

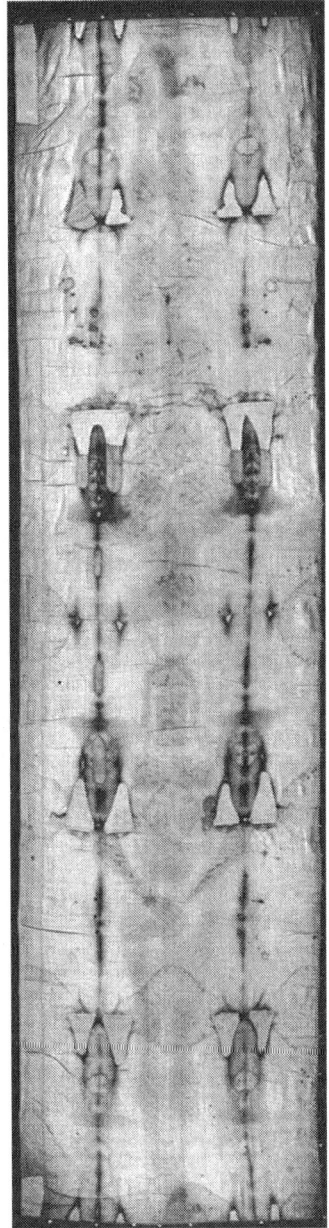

probably pretty well-built from being a carpenter. Now, I could be completely wrong with this description, and I'm okay with that. The point is though, what is the foundation of our image of Jesus? Is it tradition? Television/movies? Society? Pop culture? Bumper stickers? Or the Bible?

We *all* have preconceived notions who we believe Jesus is. The Vintage21 Church in Raleigh, North Carolina demonstrates this very clearly in a satirical manner, with their dubbing of four clips from an old Jesus film. They used these vids in 2003 for a four-week series in discovering more of what Jesus said and did. And thank goodness he's *not* who many believe him to be: "Rule number two. You're not allowed to have any fun unless you're laughing at how dumb the Devil is."[3]

Another modern depiction of Jesus, comes from the mind of WM. Paul Young in his Bestselling novel, *The Shack*. Young provides a proposed description of what Jesus could look like if he was living within our culture in the flesh today. And though his depiction is spot on, in my opinion, it's not typically what you would first imagine if nonchalantly conjuring an image of him:

> He appeared Middle Eastern and was dressed like a laborer, complete with tool belt and gloves. He stood easily, leaning against the door-jamb with arms crossed in front of him, wearing jeans covered in wood dust and a plaid shirt with sleeves rolled just above the elbows, revealing well-muscled forearms. His features were pleasant enough, but he was not particularly handsome—not a man who could stick out in a crowd. But his eyes and smile lit up his face, and Mack found it difficult to look away. . . .
>
> "You look as if you're from the Middle East, maybe Arab?" Mack

guessed.

"Actually, I'm a stepbrother of that great family. I am Hebrew, to be exact, from the house of Judah."

"Then . . ." Mack was suddenly staggered by his own realization. "Then, you are . . ."

"Jesus? Yes. And you may call me that if you like. After all, it has become my common name. My mother called me Yeshua, but I have also been known to respond to Joshua or even Jesse."

Mack stood dumbfounded and mute.[4]

In the summer of 2016, both me and the youth group made our own dive into the Bible to discover what the Scriptures say who Jesus was. I would be naïve indeed if I said I could cover this topic in one book. For even the Bible gives us just a glimpse of this awesome man (John 20:30-31, 21:25); however, I do hope this book gives a peek at who we know as Jesus—the real Jesus. Not homeboy, hippie, or overly tolerant Jesus, but Jesus.

"JESUS ISN'T UNDER every stone in the Old Testament," reminded a mentor of mine, recalling a friend of his who had tried to show Jesus verse by verse.

His statement is one which I agree with. The stones which David chose to fight Goliath with have nothing to do with the stone that closed the mouth of the tomb. However, the Old Testament as a whole points to Jesus, for he is without any doubt the crux of the Bible. Without Jesus, there is no Bible. For without him, what would be the point of it? The Bible is HIS-story. Yes, there's a lot of other stories in it too, but they direct us to him. Therefore, it shouldn't be surprising that he is indeed in the Old Testament more than what we normally think that he is. Though the opposite is also true, we can very easily over Christianize the Old Testament. Therefore, we need a balance.

However, I want to also point out that Jesus is *everywhere*. Not just in the Bible, but everywhere. For example, we are surrounded by natural metaphors of him. Such as we can see the Son in the sun, which sets (or dies) every night, yet resurrects with the morning. Or the caterpillar, who falls into a deep sleep before emerging as a beautiful butterfly. Just as Jesus spent three days sleeping in the belly of the earth, before he too emerged as something beautiful.

I MUST ALSO inform you, that much of the artwork within this book was illustrated by the romanticist, William Blake. Now, know culturally/historically, Blake's art is not the most accurate, and his style is very . . . different. But that is exactly why I chose Blake. No, I do not agree with all of his teachings, such I believe as C. S. Lewis does that Heaven and Hell should remain divorced. And I admit he may have been a little outlandish. However, he was not afraid to speak up against the hypocrisy of the church. His work is different, but my hope is that his perspectives will aid in opening ourselves up, in seeing Jesus in another light.

Additionally, Blake is not the sole illustrator of this publication, for the works of other painters have also been used, and many modern artists have *graciously* allowed me to use their work, too. Personally, I believe the ministry of art within the protestant church is often over-looked. For as a famous cliché clearly states, "A picture is worth a thousand words."

Lastly, I had the brief idea for *JESUS* being the beginning of a trilogy during a long car ride, each book being about one of the members of the Trinity. But, as Jesus told Philip, "Whoever has seen me has seen the Father. How can you say, 'Show us the Father'?" (John 14:9).

I do encourage you, however, to conduct your own study of the Godhead, and to find connections between the three. To get you started, notice some of the roles that the Spirit plays in the Old Testament (Genesis 1:2, Judges 14:6, I Samuel 16:13). And notice when you read, that the Father is just as gracious in the Old Testament, as He is in the New. For does He not spare the lives of Adam and Eve when they eat the fruit? Or what about the 120 years of grace He gives before the Flood? And how many times does He call out, "Repent, and come back to Me," in the midst of His promises of wrath through His prophets like Isaiah and Jeremiah?

THE THEME THAT summer for the Rolla youth group, was Jesus. We even made T-shirts for the occasion. To remind us that he is *much*, much more than a theme for VBS, a little kid song, or a flannel board character, having more layers to him than any onion:

EXPRESSIONS OF JESUS

ANGRY   **HAPPY**   **SAD**

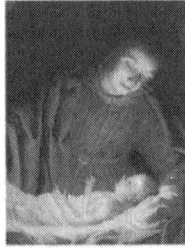  

HUMAN   **TEACHER**   **KING**

  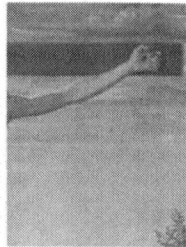

LOVE   **MERCY**   **GRACE**

That is the backstory, to this story. And so, I invite you into this dialogue. As we explore the Bible together to see what the Word says, about Jesus.

***

AS WE READ and as I spoke, the nervousness quickly vanished, as we discussed and discovered what the Gospel said about the Son of God.

NOTES

1. Fig. 1: Georgoudis, Dianelos. "Shroud of Turin." 2014. *Photograph*. The image is enhanced with digital filters.
2. Fig. 2: Enrie, Giuseppe. "Full-length image of the Turin Shroud." 1931. *Photograph*. Cathedral of Saint John the Baptist: Turin, Italy.
3. Vintage Church. "Vintage Church-Jesus Video #1." *Youtube.com*. 10 March, 2008. Web. 21 August, 2016.
4. Young, WM. Paul, Wayne Jacobsen, and Brad Cummings. *The Shack: Where Tragedy Confronts Eternity*. Newbury Park, CA: Windblown Media, 2007. Print. p. 86, 88-89.
5. Fig. 3: Milošević, Petar, *The Good Shepherd*. *Photograph*. 5th century. The Mausoleum of Galla Placidia: Ravenna, Italy.
6. Fig. 4: Ribeiro, José Luiz Bernardes. *Christ Trampling The Beasts*. *Photograph*. 6th century. The Archbishop's Chapel: Ravenna, Italy.

JESUS:

IN THE OLD TESTAMENT

CHAPTER 1

CREATION: A CHANCE TO PLAY WITH MUD

A rizona's Painted Desert. Beautiful forests of the Ozarks. Speed-racing lizards, frightening snakes, and cows, were some of the aspects of Creation which I witnessed that summer. Not even a handful of the amazing things which were created by our Maker, yet each one just as awing.

***

"LOGAN, THERE'S JUST one problem with that theme," countered one of the young men in the youth group, after I had told him the plan for the summer, "Jesus isn't in the Old Testament."

He was smiling, so I couldn't tell if he was joking or not, yet I replied, "Or is he?"

Of course, it can be easy to forget, but we do know that Jesus is indeed in the Old Testament—with all of those prophecies of the coming Messiah. Though I could fill an entire book alone about the forecasts of Christ, which are much more reliable than the local

---

*This was a lesson which I did not directly discuss in class; however, in my defense, I've included it, because there were a few times which I did mention the story of Creation that summer. And I couldn't possibly just leave out the very first instance which Jesus is hinted at either, now could I? There will also be other chapters included within this book that are additions to that summer. As well as *expanded* material to the lessons that I did teach. I feel these will add more depth to this discussion, as well as interesting thoughts from chasing rabbits and seeing where they lead . . . many rabbits. Honestly, there's only so much which you can cram into ten weeks. Each of these additional chapters will be marked with a star at the beginning of them.

weather station, they are not the focus of this book. For Jesus is in-volved much more deeply than passively being mentioned.

Additionally, we can also know that Jesus is in the Old Testament, for he says so himself in John 5: "You search the Scriptures because you think that in them you have eternal life; and it is they that bear witness about me. . . . For if you believed Moses, you would believe me; for he wrote of me. But if you do not believe his writings, how will you believe my words?" (39, 46)*

Now, Jesus could be referring to himself as the Word, the Lógos, as John introduces him as at the beginning of his Gospel. Or, Jesus may be revealing another thing, that he himself was more active within the Old Testament than what we normally think or believe.

For example, from the very beginning of the Bible, we are given hints of Jesus being a hands-on potter during creation:

> Then God said, "Let us make man in our image, after our likeness. And let them have dominion over the fish of the sea and over the birds of the heavens and over the livestock and over all the earth and over every creeping thing that creeps on the earth."
>
> So God created man in his own image,
>
> in the image of God he created him;
>
> male and female he created them. (Genesis 1:26-27)†

Wait?! Jesus can't be in Genesis 1, can he? That's the kickoff of

---

*Yes, in this first section, I will be talking about how Jesus is in the Old Testament, but I will throughout need to use the New Testament to defend/connect these thoughts with the New, just as I'll later use the Old Testament to support the New Testament. That's one of the beauties of the Bible being so beautifully and connectively written.

†There's a very good reason why I began in the middle of the Creation Story instead of from the beginning of it. The reason being, that since it's my favorite Bible story, I've read and studied so much about it, that this chapter could be a book in itself. And yet, there's so much which I don't know about these two chapters in Genesis—that I still need to read and study upon.

the Bible?

Oh, but he is, my friend. Let me nerd out with some Hebrew for a second to explain. In Genesis 1 in the Hebrew, God is known as אֱלֹהִם (Elohim). What's interesting about this name for God, is that it's the *plural* of אֱלוֹהַ (Eloah). Meaning that 'Elohim' can actually be translated as 'God' or 'gods.' The ending '-im' is the equivalent as adding an 's' to most words in English (with the exception of the weird ones, like deer, oxen, geese, and fungi). This can be seen by other words transliterated as well, such as Nephilim, cherubim, and seraphim. Yet, though the noun 'Elohim' in its nature is plural, giving hint to the Trinity,* the verbs which express the actions of God up to this point have been singular, such as וַיֹּאמֶר (va-yomer) translating as, "And said" or as, "And he said" in the Hebrew. 'He' not 'they.' However, there's an abrupt change in verse 26. In this one verse as God is talking to the Holy Community (or perhaps the Divine Council†), the plural markers are seen, both in the Hebrew and in the English: "Let *us* make man in *our* image, after *our* likeness." Wow! And notice that it comes up in the discussion of creating man. Doesn't that just give you goosebumps?

I'm not making this up either. For we know Christ was involved in Creation from other passages in the Bible as well. Paul himself states

---

*But to the Jews, they would have understood that 'Elohim' being plural meant that He was superior than the other gods. That He was the "Power of powers," or in other terms, the "God of gods."

†The Jews would have understood this passage differently, for the concept of the Trinity had not yet been revealed to them. I mean, it's a concept which we struggle to grasp. And trying to explain it to a nation who constantly struggled to worship one God because of their polytheistic neighbors would have been *disastrous*. Therefore, the Jews might have understood this passage as God addressing the Divine Council instead of Himself, which the Trinity most definitely is the figurehead of. For in Jewish tradition, the angels were created on the fourth day, the same as the stars. Yet, and this is my opinion, I personally believe He's specifically addressing the Trinity here, for it sounds weird that he would say to the angels, "Let us create man in our image." Unless, both angels and humanity poses the *imago Dei*? (The Image of God).

so in Colossians 1:15-17:

> He is the image of the invisible God, the firstborn of all creation. For
> by him all things were created, in heaven and on earth, visible and
> invisible, whether thrones or dominions or rulers or authorities—all
> things were created through him and for him. And he is before all
> things, and in him all things hold together.

Paul uses the argument that since Jesus was actively involved in Creation, it makes him the rightful ruler over it, just as he is the head of
the Church since it was established by his blood.

John also states this truth in the beginning of his Gospel, as he provides evidence of Jesus' being divine as well as man: "In the beginning
was the Word, and the Word was with God, and the Word was God.
He was in the beginning with God. All things were made through him,
and without him was not any thing made that was made. In him was
life, and the life was the light of men." No, John's not just spouting out
philosophy after tripping on some mushrooms; he's trying to describe something deep and spiritual within the limits of words.

In his defense, probably against rising Gnostic ideas, John mentions that Jesus was an active participant of Creation in the beginning,
and he uses very Genesis-like language to do so, providing evidence
that Jesus was, before he was a man (John 1:30).

Even from the get-go, Jesus had a special connection with humanity. Normally, we only think that before the Fall, man had a relationship with solely the Father, don't we? Since it was 'YHWH God' who
walked in the garden with Adam and Eve. Yet, this is clearly not the
case. For Jesus is Lord, and Lord over all of Creation.

***

AS THE LYRICS of "As the Deer" echoed around the amber flames, I looked up above the swaying pines into the dark sky. Looking up at the twinkling stars. While taking note how they were so beautifully, and wonderfully made.

NOTE

1. Fig. 1: Peel, Mike. "The Flood Tablet." 2010. *Photograph.* British Museum: London. This is the eleventh tablet of the Epic of Gilgamesh.
2. Matthews, Victor Harold, and Don C. Benjamin. *Old Testament Parallels: Laws and Stories from the Ancient Near East.* New York: Paulist Press, 1991. Print. p. 8.

Shared Myths

There are *many* stories that are not only found within the Bible, for they can be found within other cultures and religions as well. Therefore I wonder, is this because man shares a common ancestor; therefore, the same stories based on actual events were passed down from one generation to the next, but changed? Or is it because man shares the same Creator? Or is it because as humans, no matter where we live or where we come from, we share something beyond just physical similarities? Or is it because there are only so many stories within this world, each sharing the same basic building blocks?

- **A MIGHTY HERO** who exhibits supernatural strength and performs miraculous deeds, though he is also usually not too bright:
    - Samson (Judges 13-16)
    - Hercules (Greek)
    - Gilgamesh (Mesopotamian)
    - Beowulf (Anglo-Saxon)
    - Thor (Norse)
    - Hulk (Marvel)

- **A WOMAN TEMPTED BY FRUIT**/a woman who is tempted, and then brings chaos into the world:
    - Eve (Genesis 3)
    - Pandora (Greek)
    - Persephone (Greek)
    - Snow White (German)

- **A GREAT FLOOD STORY:**
    - Tales involving a great flood, usually caused by a deity and usually global, are shared across the world. For example, Genesis 6-9, The Epic of Gilgamesh, Cherokee legends, Chinese myths, and Maasi oral traditions are only a *few* examples of this shared story.

- **A CREATION MYTH:**
    - This is a common myth shared by *everyone*. For every person, I believe, has a natural wonder where he or she came from. There are *numerous* versions of this myth, and each with their own spin. Such as (to name only a *few*): Elohim purposefully and personally creating the universe and man from out of chaos (*Genesis 1-2*). Chaos being in the beginning, before gods arise and the universe is created as a result of a war amongst themselves

(*Egyptian, Greek, Mesopotamian, Babylonian, Canaanite*). (The Egyptians also have another myth, that the universe was created by Ra, such as he made the wind and the rain by masturbating.[2]) The gods and giants melting from out of ice, such as the giant Ymir and the cow Auðumbla—who then frees Búri, Odin's grandfather, from licking him out of his icicle prison. Odin and his brothers will then later rise up against Ymir, creating the world from out of his corpse (*Norse*). Pan Gu hatching from a cosmic egg floating in the midst of chaos, whose shell is composed of Yin and Yang. Pan Gu separating the two before he later dies, and his body is used to create the world—such as humans from the fleas that were on his skin (*Chinese*). The great Father of All Spirits awakening Mother Sun, who awakes all the totemic ancestors from their caves. The world being populated and ruled by animals for a time, before the Father later creates man (*Australian Aborigines*). And the explosion of one particle in a moment, which results in the accidental creation of everything, occurring about 13.8 billion years ago (*The Big Bang Theory*).

With all of that said, here is one last question for us to meditate upon, and research well, "What makes the Bible different, from these other sources?"

CHAPTER 2

ADAM & EVE:

BEWARE OF FRUIT AND STONED BREAD

It was my first Sunday morning teaching of Jesus being in the Old Testament. There was a mixture of looks from the teens of curiosity and disbelief, hopefully none of them thinking I was on crack. For it's so easy to neglect the Old Testament, believing that it's obsolete since we now have the New. But that was one reason which I wanted to pursue this study, for the Old Testament is more important than what we give it credit. There's a reason it makes up 70% of the Christian canon.

"Turn with me, to Genesis chapter three," I announced.

***

AFTER GOD HAD created man, He made for them a beautiful garden in which to dwell in, the paradise of Eden. A place to call home and a responsibility to care after. Yet, when he created man and woman, He did not want an animatronic race. And so He planted two trees in the garden. The first, the Tree of Life. And the second, the Tree of the Knowledge of Good and Evil—planted in the *midst* of the garden so that it would not be snacked on by mistake. For He had said that the man and the woman could eat from *any* other tree in the garden— perhaps apples, and bananas, and oranges, and pineapples (though they don't grow on trees), and maybe even fruits which we've never even heard of?! But that one tree was the only one, the *only one*, which they were not allowed to eat from, or they would surely die. God wanted a genuine relationship with humanity. He wanted us to choose to love Him. Meaning, in order to freely love, there must also be the choice to freely not love. God did not want a race of robots; therefore, He blessed mankind with the gift of free will.

And so, Adam and Eve dwelt in the garden for a time. For how long, I dare not say. Yet, there was one who wished to deceive them, to separate the creation from their Creator:

Now the serpent was more crafty than any other beast of the field that the LORD God had made.

He said to the woman, "Did God actually say, 'You shall not eat of any tree in the garden'?" And the woman said to the serpent, "We may eat of the fruit of the trees in the garden, but God said, 'You shall not eat of the fruit of the tree that is in the midst of the garden, neither shall you touch it, lest you die.'" But the serpent said to the woman, "You will not surely die. For God knows that when you eat of it your eyes will be opened, and you will be like God, knowing good and evil." So when the woman saw that the tree was good for food, and that it was a delight to the eyes, and that the tree was to be desired to make one wise, she took of its fruit and ate, and she also gave some to her husband *who was with her*, and he ate. Then the eyes of both were opened, and they knew that they were naked. And they sewed fig leaves together and made themselves loincloths. (Genesis 3:1-7)

Wow!

. . . This, is one of the most *tragic* moments of human history (man crucifying Christ on the cross, the Crusades, and World War II I argue as others). God had molded mankind, setting us apart from His other creations. He created a very special place for us, gave us a plethora of

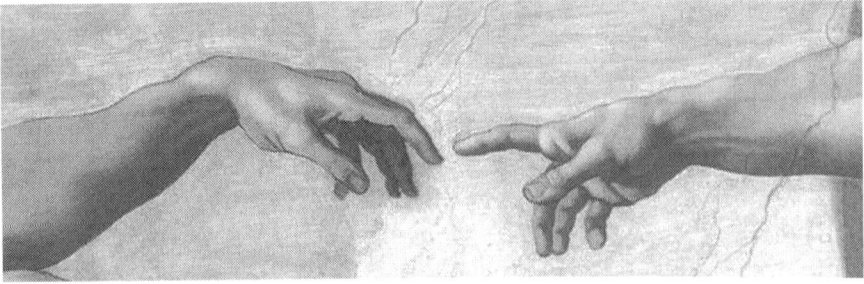

choices, and yet we still chose to disobey Him, and to take from the tree which we should not have. And I say 'we,' because how often are we guilty of making the same mistake as Adam and Eve?

The serpent came to Eve and tempted her to eat the fruit. He did *not* force her, did not hinder her free will, but tempted her to make the choice herself to disobey God. For just as Jesus said to the Pharisees in John 8:44, "You are of your father the devil, and your will is to do your father's desires. He was a murderer from the beginning, and does not stand in the truth, because there is no truth in him. When he lies, he speaks out of his own character, for he is a liar and the father of lies." The serpent was a deceiver, twisting the very words of God to tempt the woman to disobey Him. For the 'best lies,' are always wrapped in truth.

He lured the woman into the conversation with a general question for her to answer, before snaring her by adding just one word to God's warning, *one word*, "not." Yet, it was enough to get Eve to consider his proposal. Notice the process of her thinking: "So when the woman saw that the tree was good for food, and that it was a delight to the eyes, and that the tree was to be desired to make one wise, she took of its fruit and ate." First, the desire of the flesh. Second, the desire of the eyes. And third, the pride of life, just as John warns in 1 John 2:16, "For all that is in the world—the desires of the flesh and the desires of the eyes and pride of life—is not from the Father but is from the world."

Eve saw that the fruit was חֹף (toph [good]). So she reached out for it and took it. Sadly, this motif of the Fall can be seen replayed again and again throughout the Old Testament: Lot sees that the land was "toph," so he reaches out for it and loses the promise. David sees that Bathsheba is "toph," so he reaches out for her, before he is later expelled from Jerusalem and suffers the turmoil within his family. And Jerusalem sees that the gods of Canaan are "toph," so they reach out for them, before being expelled from the Promise Land by means of the Exile. Again and again man falls prey to the lust of their eyes. That is why we must stand ever diligent, so we ourselves do not fall prey to such sins, such as pornography.

THEN NOTICE THAT Eve gave some of the fruit to Adam, "*who was with her.*" It appears that Adam was there the whole time as Eve was being tempted, and yet he did not man up to protect his woman. So many times we're guilty of giving Eve all the flak of falling under the spell of temptation, yet Adam was just as guilty as his wife. *Both* male and female being held responsible for introducing us to sin.

So he took the fruit from her and ate it.

"We're naked!!" they then realized. For never before had Adam nor Eve thought of streaking in their birthday suits as an oddity, having the innocence of a child. (Though samely, they weren't children. For it appears that they were created as adults, just as the plants weren't created as seeds nor the birds and fish as eggs. They had the innocence of children, yet they were still man and wife. Meaning, they could do things with their bodies [sex] which children wouldn't think of.)

They then noticed they were stark naked, for never before had

13

there ever been lust nor shame within the world.* They felt shame of the bodies which God had created for them, which I'm sometimes guilty of when I look into the mirror. They felt shame of their bodies, because they had fallen into the desire of their temptation and had sinned against Him.

Speaking of temptation, notice that the two do not notice their nudity until *after* they ate the fruit. For temptation in itself is not a sin, but giving into it is. It is when they take a bite that they shatter their relationship with God and usher in the Age of Sin. It is then that they attempt to cover themselves and even hide from God when He comes into the garden.

Yet, as we know, no one can win a game of hide-and-go-seek with God (or sardines), even though sometimes we think that we can. He calls out, just as He calls out to us in the midst of our sin, "Where are you?" Adam answers, and as God questions him—for a second time instead of manning up, he tries to cast the blame upon Eve, who in turn tries to pass it on to the serpent, playing a deadly game of hot potato.

God, there and then, could have wiped out mankind for their disobedience. He could have acted as He had promised and condemned the man and the woman to not only a spiritual death, as they had already brought upon themselves, but a physical one as well—be done with mankind once and for all. Or even, wipe the slate clean and start all over again.

Yet, the Father showed mercy. Instead, he cursed the serpent, the woman, and the man, and casted them out from the garden; however, He spared their lives.† Perhaps even, at the cost of proving the ser-

*Though, isn't it strange, that this couple is worried about their nudity, while, as far as the Bible mentions, they're the only ones within the garden?

†But before God casted them out, He clothed them. Adam and Eve had tried to clothe

pent right to a point? He spared the punishment which they so right-fully deserved, just as He so too spares us from eternal death, if we accept the blood of His Son.

He cursed them:[‡]

> The LORD God said to the serpent,
> "Because you have done this,
>> cursed are you above all livestock
>> and above all beasts of the field;
> on your belly you shall go,
>> and dust you shall eat
>> all the days of your life." (Genesis 3:14)

Wait, time out. Did snakes have legs before the Fall?

Possibly. Both pythons and boas have vestigial hind bones near the end of their tales, which could be remnants from legs. Possible evidence that they may have once walked, which evolutionists use to prove that they evolved from lizards. So, this curse could have been a physical limitation which God had placed upon snakes as a punish-ment.

Or, this passage could have a metaphorical meaning. It may mean that the serpent could never again lift itself into a striking position,

---

themselves but epically *failed*. Hastily making loincloths by strapping on veggies, to, most likely, only cover what makes a man a man and a woman a woman. Just as we fail to clothe ourselves. But God clothed them with garments made from animal skins. Just as He clothes us in righteousness when we're saved, weaved from the blood of Christ. And again one day with a white robe, when we're finally with Him in heaven.

[‡]I personally believe particular things were created by God to further punish man at the Fall, such as: mosquitos, chiggers, ticks, flies, wasps, and poison ivy, along with the thorns and thistles in 3:18. True, mosquitos could have been around before sin, sucking juices from fruit, only corrupted by sin like the earth who now suffers from earthquakes and tornados as it cries out to be refined. But they're way too *evil* for this to be the case; therefore, I believe God specifically created them in this moment as torture because of sin. The monsters which were spawned, like the Furies and Giants from Uranus' blood.

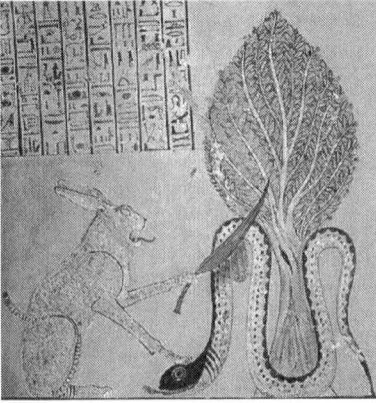

cursed to remain grounded, as one of my Harding instructors (we'll call him 'the Professor') has speculated. Explaining that there are Egyptian paintings of snakes depicted together in both striking and nonstriking positions. Or similarly, how there are depictions of Ra [or Bastet], holding down the head of Apep, keeping the snake from being able to strike as he slays it. In fact, priests daily could go to the temple and chant spells from the *Books of Overthrowing Apep*, while spitting, burning, and mutilating wax snake images to help Ra defeat his foe each day. The title of the second chapter of this book being, "Defiling Apep with the Left Foot."

YET, IN THE midst of these curses, God again shows His love by making a prophecy of redemption in verse 15:

"'I will put enmity between you and the woman,

and between your offspring and her offspring;

he shall bruise your head,

and you shall bruise his heel."

In the midst of punishment, God makes a promise that Jesus will come and redeem His creation. That he will crush the serpent, and reverse the sin of man. Which he did exactly that when he sacrificed himself upon the cross. One tree bringing death, but his tree through death, bringing life. The cross reversing the sin from the tree in the midst of the garden.

At first glance, it appears that the offspring of the woman won't suffer much, just a bite to the heel. When compared to a head wound, it's not as severe. This is true, for Jesus' victory was absolute and a fatal blow to the Devil; however, it is also false.

"Most people believe, that the woman's seed will be inflicted with just a bite to the heel, while he will crush the head of the serpent. However, they're both fatal wounds," I remembered the voice of Dr. Hunt echo, seeing flashbacks from his mythology class that I had taken earlier that summer. "Interestingly enough, this is one example of the motif of the wounded foot." He then continued by explaining the findings of Erich Auerbach, the author of *Mimesis*.

Auerbach noticed a trend in many stories of a mighty hero being slain or crippled by a wound to the foot, such as the Greek's Achilles, the Egyptian's Ra, the Hindu's Krishna, the Celt's Bran, and even the Arthurian Fisher King.* Ironically, Auerbach was also struck by a serpent—receiving a bite to his heel at the time of his research.† Totally serious! A weird/cool fact.

Fortunately, he survived his wound. But time and time again he noticed that a hero would be destroyed by a wound to the heel. Perhaps inspired by this story in Genesis? And in reverse, perhaps revealing how fatal this promise is? For Jesus does crush the serpent on the cross, but he does so by facing death himself.

What's also amazing about this prophecy, is that it was made *millenniums* before crucifixion was even invented. And yet, even then, it

---

*He who inspired Ransom's wound, the protagonist in C. S. Lewis' *Space Trilogy*.

†Auerbach's incident is just as ironic as Brad Pitt's, who, as Achilles, tore his left Achilles tendon while filming a fight scene for the movie *Troy*.[4]

17

describes an aspect of Jesus' death. In many pictures of the Crucifixion, we often see a nail piercing the top of Jesus' feet, which could be how it happened. However, another common method of crucifixion which was around during the time of Christ, would be to drive nails through each heel of the criminal, fastening them securely to each side of the cross. Jesus may have literally had his heels bruised. Struck by that cowardly serpent cursed to crawl on its belly, unable to strike any higher than his feet.

Do also take notice the Bible says that Adam and Eve ate the "*fruit,*" not an apple. I mean, it could have been an apple. Or an orange, or a grapple, or some kind of yellow orb, or maybe even a fruit which no longer exists. The point is, the Bible says a "fruit" (פְּרִי [peri]), while tradition has made it commonly an apple. A prime example of *knowing* what the Bible says, vs. what we *believe* it says. Knowing 'why' we believe what we believe. Another example of this, is that throughout Genesis 3, the tempter is known as the "serpent." Never once does it call him "Satan." Therefore, how do we know that the snake was the Devil?

One possible hint is found in Ezekiel 28:13. That is, if Ezekiel is both describing a literal prince of Tyre, while also alluding to the fall of Satan, "You were in Eden, the garden of God." If so, this would be a direct connection between Satan and the garden.

However, to find further evidence, we must look in the New Testament for answers. For it's not until the revelations of Paul that we know the serpent in the garden was indeed the Devil. Before then, the Jews would have just known the serpent as an agent of chaos. For snakes were symbols of both wisdom and chaos, which the serpent in Genesis 3 displays both of these qualities, using his craftiness to trick Eve and ushering chaos into the world. This can also be seen by the Egyptian god, Apep (or Apophis in Greek). His appearance was that of a giant serpent, and he was the embodiment of chaos. Additionally, he religiously tried to disrupt the balance of Ma'at and to devour the sun god Ra, daily (this being the Egyptian's explanation of why the sun rose and set). With Israel's 400+ years of experience with Egyptian culture, and if Moses is indeed the author of Genesis, it's easy to see how the Jews may have associated the serpent with the attributes of Apep.

Snakes were also known to be mysterious, for they did not move with legs. And *dangerous*, which is not surprising, since there are (in present day) thirty-five known species of venomous snakes in the Middle East.[6] Also interestingly, in another story known as The Epic of Gilgamesh,* a snake prevents the hero Gilgamesh from obtaining eternal life.†

---

*An ancient Sumerian epic poem, which is believed to have been recorded even before the book of Genesis. It also features a flood story in the midst of it.

†"There he saw the plant growing; although it pricked him he took it in his hands; then he cut the heavy stones from his feet, and the sea carried him and threw him on to the shore. Gilgamesh said to Urshanabi the ferryman, `Come here, and see this marvelous plant. By its virtue a man may win back all his former strength. I will take it to Uruk of the strong walls; there I will give it to the old men to eat. Its name shall be "The Old Men Are Young Again"; and at last I shall eat it myself and have back all my lost youth.' So Gilgamesh returned by the gate through which he had come, Gilgamesh and Urshanabi went together. They travelled their twenty leagues and then they broke their fast; after thirty leagues they stopped for the night.
Gilgamesh saw a well of cool water and he went down and bathed; but deep in

However, Paul later reveals the true identity of the snake. In 2 Corinthians 11 he writes:

> But I am afraid that as the serpent deceived Eve by his cunning, your thoughts will be led astray from a sincere and pure devotion to Christ. For if someone comes and proclaims another Jesus than the one we proclaimed, or if you receive a different spirit from the one you received, or if you accept a different gospel from the one you accepted, you put up with it readily enough. . . .

> And what I am doing I will continue to do, in order to undermine the claim of those who would like to claim that in their boasted mission they work on the same terms as we do. For such men are false apostles, deceitful workmen, disguising themselves as apostles of Christ. And no wonder, for even Satan disguises himself as an angel of light. So it is no surprise if his servants, also, disguise themselves as servants of righteousness. Their end will correspond to their deeds. (3-4;12-15)

Paul issues a warning to the Church to be aware of false apostles, alerting that they use the very same techniques as their master, the Devil, in order to deceive. Paul also writes a similar warning to the church in Rome in Romans 16, while also delivering a promise of the Lord's victory, drawing upon the prophecy of Genesis 3:15:

> I appeal to you, brothers, to watch out for those who cause divisions

---

the pool there was lying a serpent, and the serpent sensed the sweetness of the flower. It rose out of the water and snatched it away, and immediately it sloughed its skin and returned to the well. Then Gilgamesh sat down and wept, the tears ran down his face, and he took the hand of Urshanabi; 'O Urshanabi, was it for this that I toiled with my hands, is it for this I have wrung out my heart's blood? For myself I have gained nothing; not I, but the beast of the earth has joy of it now. Already the stream has carried it twenty leagues back to the channels where I found it. I found a sign and now I have lost it. Let us leave the boat on the bank and go.'"[7]

and create obstacles contrary to the doctrine that you have been taught; avoid them. For such persons do not serve our Lord Christ, but their own appetites, and by smooth talk and flattery they deceive the hearts of the naive. For your obedience is known to all, so that I rejoice over you, but I want you to be wise as to what is good and innocent as to what is evil. The God of peace will soon *crush Satan under your feet.* The grace of our Lord Jesus Christ be with you. (17-20)

The Apostle Paul is the one who reveals that the serpent in the garden was indeed the Devil, the enemy of the Church. Additionally, the Apostle John also alludes to Satan being this snake, as he describes Satan as the red dragon in Revelation[*] 12:

---

[*]Notice, it's "Revelation" not "Revelation**S**."

And a great sign appeared in heaven: a woman clothed with the sun, with the moon under her feet, and on her head a crown of twelve stars. She was pregnant and was crying out in birth pains and the agony of giving birth. And another sign appeared in heaven: behold, a great red dragon . . . And the dragon stood before the woman who was about to give birth, so that when she bore her child he might devour it. She gave birth to a male child, one who is to rule all the nations with a rod of iron, but her child was caught up to God and to his throne, and the woman fled into the wilderness, where she has a place prepared by God, in which she is to be nourished for 1,260 days.

Now war arose in heaven, Michael and his angels fighting against the dragon. And the dragon and his angels fought back, but he was defeated, and there was no longer any place for them in heaven. And the great dragon was thrown down, *that ancient serpent, who is called the devil and Satan, the deceiver of the whole world*—he was thrown down to the earth, and his angels were thrown down with him. And I heard a loud voice in heaven, saying, "Now the salvation and the power and the kingdom of our God and the authority of his Christ have come, for the accuser of our brothers has been thrown down, who accuses them day and night before our God. And they have conquered him by the blood of the Lamb and by the word of their testimony, for they loved not their lives even unto death. Therefore, rejoice, O heavens and you who dwell in them! But woe to you, O earth and sea, for the devil has come down to you in great wrath, because he knows that his time is short!"

And when the dragon saw that he had been thrown down to the earth, he pursued the woman who had given birth to the male child. But the woman was given the two wings of the great eagle so that she might fly from the serpent into the wilderness, to the place where she is to be nourished for a time, and times, and half a time. The serpent poured water like a river out of his mouth after the woman, to sweep her away with a flood. But the earth came to the help of the woman, and the earth opened its mouth and swallowed the river that the dragon had poured from his mouth. Then the dragon became furious with the woman and went off to make war on the rest of her offspring, on those who keep the commandments of God and hold to the testimony of Jesus. And he stood on the sand of the sea.

Whoa! What just happened?! What's with the crazy, voodoo language? Is this the weird Apocalypse stuff that's going to happen in the future?

I don't believe so, for I personally believe that Revelation is much more symbolic than what we were led to believe, and that a lot of Revelation has already come to pass or we're living in the midst of it. I could be very wrong, and I'm okay with that. But here is how I believe this passage can be interpreted:

The woman symbolizes God's people. She's adorned with twelve stars, which I believe connects her with the twelve tribes of Israel and the twelve apostles. For the woman symbolizes Israel before the birth of her child, Jesus, and the Church after his birth. The dragon attempts to destroy the child, just as Satan did through Herod when he was born; and how he constantly tried to do so by causing Jesus to fall, such as by tempting him to sin in the wilderness. Yet, Jesus did not succumb, he was not devoured by the dragon, and he ascended into heaven until the appointed day which he'll return. Sometime after the symbolic, not literal, 1,260 days.

I then believe that John describes the time when Satan was casted out of heaven, his vision not being seen in chronological order. He then describes Satan's desperate attempt to prevail against God's people and to try and to devour as many as he can, to make them fall and to worship their sin rather than the Lord.

John later describes in chapter 20, the dragon being bound and thrown into a bottomless pit for a thousand years, before being released for a short time, and then thrown into the lake of fire. Just like Martin Luther, I believe that Satan is bounded now, that we are in the thousand years. Not a literal time, but the time when Satan's power has greatly diminished. That he was bounded from the victory on the cross and is now like a dog on a chain. That he can only bite you, if you draw close enough for him to do so.[10]

SO WE'VE ESTABLISHED that the serpent is indeed Satan. This is most needed to make a comparison, for the fall in Eden is not the end of the story. There's another which is very similar to the temptation of Adam and Eve, yet it's also very different:

After being baptized by John the Baptist, Jesus then sought solitude in the wilderness, "And Jesus, full of the Holy Spirit, returned from the Jordan and was led by the Spirit in the wilderness for forty days being tempted by the devil. And he ate nothing during those days. And when they ended, he was hungry." (All three synoptic Gospels record the story of Jesus being tempted in the wilderness, yet we're going to mostly focus upon Luke's account of this event, which is found within Luke chapter 4.)

Jesus endured a *forty day* fast within the wilderness. (My longest fast has only been twenty-four hours, and I *barely* survived that.) The wilderness being a place of few plants and "wild animals" according to Mark's account (1:13), a contrast to the garden full of life and benevolent animals in which Adam failed. It was after this fast, when Jesus was tired, weak, and hungry, when the cowering Devil revealed himself to Jesus.

Satan then plays off Jesus' hunger and tempts him by saying, "If you are the Son of God, command this stone to become bread." Satan first tempts Jesus with a desire of the flesh. Just as Eve was tempted by the fruit, so too was Jesus tempted by bread.

But wait, how is turning rocks into food a sin? I mean there isn't a commandment which states, "Thou shall not turn thine stones to bread."

Eve sinned because God specifically told her and Adam to not eat the fruit of the Tree of the Knowledge of Good and Evil. Therefore, eating it was a sin, because it was disobeying God. (*That* fruit, not all fruit, for those who think they can use this verse against their moms to not eat healthy. For remember, they could eat from the other trees in the garden, just not that one.) But why would performing the magic trick of turning this rock in the desert, not dessert, into a loaf of bread be disobedient?

Growing up, I simply heard that the temptation was coming from Satan; therefore, it was wrong. Period. But that answer was *not* satisfying.

It would be years later in which I would hear an answer that provided better closure/understanding. During my very first semester at Harding University in Dr. Cloer's class "New Testament Survey," this very question was brought up, and his answer was much more satisfying. Satan tempts Jesus to solve a problem of humanity with a divine solution. BOOM! Mind blown!

Normal people get hungry (some more often than others), but normal people cannot transform rocks into bread. (But that would be so cool if we could! I've always wanted to have supernatural abilities. Sadly, the only two superpowers I currently possess, are the abilities to tell twins apart and to turn invisible when nobody's looking.)

As fleshed out by the first four Ecumenical Councils, Jesus was fully God, but He was also fully man. Though this theology is fully supported by the Bible, it is not stated as outright within Scripture as it's defined within the creed crafted during the fourth council, the Chalce-

donian Definition: "We, then, following the holy Fathers, all with one consent, teach men to confess one and the same Son, our Lord Jesus Christ, the same perfect in Godhead and also perfect in manhood; truly God and truly man . . ."

The simplest way to explain this phenomena, is that Jesus emptied himself, *kenosis* (Philippians 2:7), giving up some of his godly aspects in order to also be a man. Such as taking on one body that could only exist in one spot, instead of being omnipresent. Furthermore, he didn't just look like a man, he was a man. Meaning, he got hungry, that his body would need food in order for him to live. But he would have to obtain that food in the same ways as we do, such as hunting, shopping, or being given food, instead of just simply creating some for himself from out of the air. Yes, Jesus did indeed perform miracles, but not once did he perform a miracle for himself. It was always for others, such as when he fed over 5,000 with both bread and fish.

JESUS WAS TEMPTED:

For surely it is not angels that he helps, but he helps the offspring of Abraham. Therefore he had to be made like his brothers in every respect, so that he might become a merciful and faithful high priest in the service of God, to make propitiation for the sins of the people. For because he himself has suffered when tempted, he is able to help those who are being tempted. (Hebrews 2:16-18)

Jesus was tempted, meaning again that temptation itself is not a sin. For if it was, Jesus would not have been our perfect sacrifice. However, embracing his humanity, Jesus responded to Satan by quoting from Scripture instead of falling prey to sin, from Deuteronomy 8:3 to be exact. Defending himself with the sword of the Spirit as he

battled not a fleshly enemy, but a spiritual one (Ephesians 6:12).

Foiled, Satan then tempts the Son of Man a second time with the desire of the eyes, by showing him all the kingdoms of the world and offering Jesus, "This authority and their glory, for it has been delivered to me, and I give it to whom I will," all for the price of Jesus' worship. What Satan is offering is an easy way out. If Jesus accepted Satan's offer, he would not have had to die on the cross. He would have already been the king of the world, but an earthly king. If he wanted to, Jesus could have been king, yet his mission was not to establish an earthly kingdom, but a spiritual one. So he rebuttals with Deuteronomy 6:13, responding by quoting Moses' warning of being attracted to Canaanite cults, again rejecting Satan's lure by embracing Scripture (quoting from the *Old Testament* at that).

Satan then makes one last attempt by attacking Jesus' pride, bringing him to the pinnacle of the temple and challenging, "If you are the

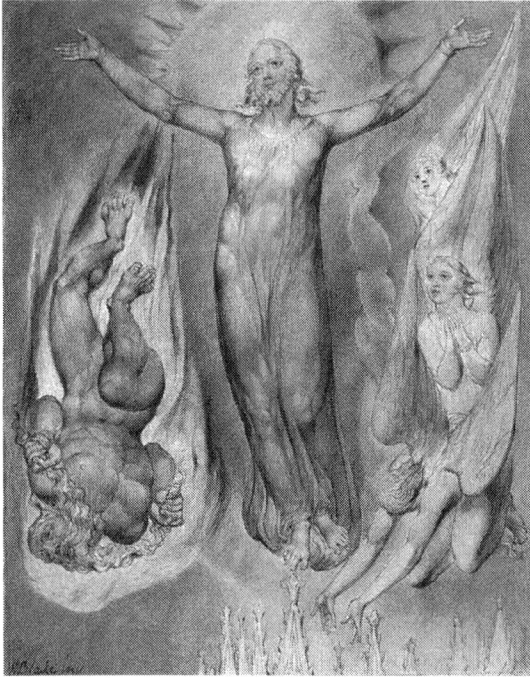

Son of God, throw yourself down from here." He then quotes from Psalms 91:11-12 in defense of his taunt, attempting to twist Scripture against Jesus, just as he had twisted God's words against Eve. Attempting to use Jesus' own weapon against him. He does so unsuccessfully, for just as he had defended himself before, Jesus counters with another passage from Deuteronomy (6:16), and refuses to give into the desires of his flesh.

Verse 13 then says the Devil left him, "until an opportune time," evidence that this was *not* the only time in which Satan tempted Jesus. For he was also tempted to become an earthly king again in John 6:15, tempted to lust after a woman caught in adultery in John 8:1-13, and was more than likely tempted to not go through with the Father's plan, as can be seen by his prayers of grief in the Garden of Gethsemane the night before his crucifixion. Him praying, "Father, if you are willing, remove this cup from me," . . . before concluding faithfully,

"Nevertheless, not my will, but yours be done." Being fully man, like us, Jesus would have also been tempted daily, and perhaps even more relentlessly than we. For if the Devil could have gotten Jesus to fail, there would have been *no* hope for us. Game Over.

But Jesus prevailed! In the wilderness, by denying the desires of his flesh, Jesus reversed the fall of Adam and Eve, remaining untainted by Satan's attacks. Where the first Adam failed, the second Adam triumphed!

***

I DID NOT present this lesson that Sunday as beautifully as it's written within these pages. And I believed I could chalk up my first failure. I mean, I presented most of the information which is here, but I stumbled a lot, backtracked to cover points that I missed, and I did a *lot* of sweating. Yet, it was comforting to hear a couple of days later from a parent, that their teen had enjoyed my class.

Really?! I literally thought. For I am my *worst* critic—and being a perfectionist does *not* help. Though surprised, I was even more pleased that God had taught. And that Jesus and been seen despite the failures which I had seen in myself.

NOTES

1. Fig. 1: Simoni, Michelangelo di Lodovico Buonarroti. *The Creation of Adam*. 1511. Sistine Chapel: Vatican City.
2. Fig. 2: A wall painting from the Thebes' tomb of Inherkha.
3. Fig. 3: A detail from the papyrus of Hunefer.
4. Morales, Tatiana. "Brad Pitt On 'Troy' And The DVD." *CBSNews.com*. 6 January, 2005. Web. 24 August, 2016.
5. Fig. 4: A display in the Linda Byrd Smith Museum of Biblical Archaeology at Harding University. Above the orthopaedic foot, is an "authorized reproduction (from the Israel Antiquities Authority) of the only piece of archeological evidence of a crucifixion found. It is the right heel bone (calcaneus) of the person with a nail preserved in it. The artifact dates from the 1st century AD and was found beyond the northern wall of 1st century Jerusalem," as stated by an informational sheet within the display.
6. Shupe, Scott. *Venomous Snakes of the World: A Manuel for use by U.S. Amphibious Forces*. NY: Skyhorse Publishing, 2013. Print. p. 141-161.

7. Sandars, N. K. *The Epic of Gilgamesh*. Harmondsworth: Penguin, 1972. Print. p. 116-117.

8. Fig. 5: Blake, William. *The Great Red Dragon and the Woman Clothed in Sun*. 1803-1805. Brooklyn Museum: New York.

9. Fig. 6: Blake, William. *The Great Red Dragon and the Woman Clothed with the Sun*. 1805. National Gallery of Art: Washington, D.C.

10. Plass Ewald. *What Luther Says An Anthology*, Volume 1. Saint Louis: Concordia Pub. House, 1959. Print. p. 402

11. Fig. 7: Blake, William. *The First Temptation* from Milton's "Paradise Regained." 1816-1820.

12. Fig. 8: Blake, William. *The Second Temptation* from Milton's "Paradise Regained." 1816-1820.

13. Fig. 9: Blake, William. *The Third Temptation* from Milton's "Paradise Regained." 1816-1820.

CHAPTER 3

*NOAH: TOY BOAT, TOY BOAT, TOY BOAT

"**H**ey Logan, would you like to do a devo for the kids at camp?"

"Sure!" I beamishly replied to an elder, looking forward in having the opportunity to speak to the 5-year-olds—2nd graders. I've done plenty of devos in the past, why not another?

THE NIGHT BEFORE, I kept racking my brain, trying to still come up with an idea of what I was going to talk about.

Come on Logan, think! Song of Solomon is out of the question, so only 65 books to choose from. . . . Haha, could talk about Lamentations, that would be a downer. No, come on Logan, you need a story . . .

(Okay, this may not be the exact conversation which I had with myself, but it was something like it. It can be truly scary what goes on in my brain sometimes.)

. . . The theme for camp this year is Nahum 1:7, the Lord is our refuge. . . . Like how the ark was a refuge for Noah during the Flood! Brilliant!

I felt like a rock star from this epiphany which the Spirit had blessed me with. I almost even broke out the air-guitar. Not knowing that it would lead to something . . . much deeper.

***

LIKE ANY GOOD Christian boy raised in the Church, I know the story of Noah's Ark, having read it and heard it more times than I can count. Yet, there is always something new to learn, which is *easy* to forget. But that's one of the amazing things about the Bible. That no man can fully know it. And that summer, I saw something in the story of Noah, which I had never seen before:

When man began to multiply on the face of the land and daughters were born to them, the sons of God saw that the daughters of man were attractive. And they took as their wives any they chose. Then the LORD said, "My Spirit shall not abide in man forever, for he is flesh: his days shall be 120 years."* The Nephilim were on the earth in those days, and also afterward, when the sons of God came in to the daughters of man and they bore children to them. These were the mighty men who were of old, the men of renown.

The LORD saw that the wickedness of man was great in the earth, and that every intention of the thoughts of his heart was only evil continually. And the LORD regretted that he had made man on the earth, and it grieved him to his heart. So the LORD said, "I will blot out man whom I have created from the face of the land, man and animals and creeping things and birds of the heavens, for I am sorry that I have made them." But Noah found favor in the eyes of the LORD. (Genesis 6:1-8)

Wait, this is the prologue of the events which led up to the Flood? So the Flood happened because angels were having sex with men?

---

*What is the "120 years" spoken here? 1. Is it a gradual capstone for the lifespan of man? I say gradual, for though man lived considerably shorter after the Flood compared to before it, Abraham still lived to be 175-years-old, Isaac lived to be 180, and Jacob 147.

2. Is it a countdown for the Flood? An act of mercy by God to give humanity a chance to repent? Or 3. It's both.

This is one popular interpretation of this passage; however, it is one which I disagree with. Firstly, because of Jesus' response to the Sadducees who were trying to trap him with the question, 'if a woman had seven husbands, who would be her husband in the afterlife?'

"You are wrong, because you know neither the Scriptures nor the power of God. For in the resurrection they neither marry nor are given in marriage, but are like angels in heaven," said Jesus in Matthew 22:29-30, and also in Mark 12:24-25. Therefore, if angels do not marry, why would God make them as sexual creatures, since God (outside of the animal kingdom) created sex to be solely holy *only* within the context of marriage? (Unless, you want to make the case that God created the angels to be more like the animals?)

Yeah, but Logan, what about The Book of Enoch? It tells of how the angel Samyaza led others to interbreed with humanity, and goes into great detail of what happened because of this, such as the emergence of the Nephilim and how man became so wicked:

And it came to pass when the children of men had multiplied that in those days were born unto them beautiful and comely daughters. And the angels, the children of the heaven, saw and lusted after them, and said to one another: 'Come, let us choose us wives from among the children of men and beget us children.' And Semjaza, who was their leader, said unto them: 'I fear ye will not indeed agree to do this deed, and I alone shall have to pay the penalty of a great sin.' And they all answered him and said: 'Let us all swear an oath, and all bind ourselves by mutual imprecations not to abandon this plan but to do this thing.' Then sware they all together and bound themselves by mutual imprecations upon it. And they were in all two hundred; who descended in the days of Jared on the summit of Mount Hermon, and they called it Mount Hermon, because they had sworn and bound themselves by mutual imprecations upon it. . . .

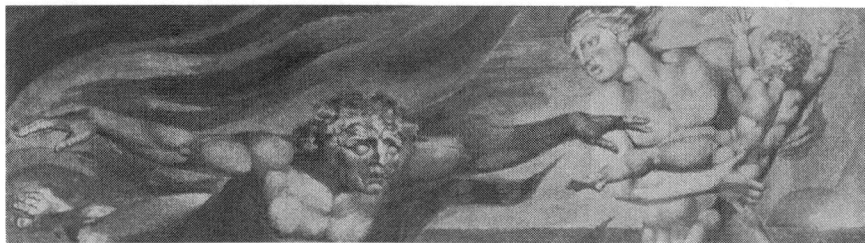

And all the others together with them took unto themselves wives, and each chose for himself one, and they began to go in unto them and to defile themselves with them, and they taught them charms and enchantments, and the cutting of roots, and made them acquainted with plants. And they became pregnant, and they bare great giants, whose height was three thousand ells: Who consumed all the acquisitions of men. And when men could no longer sustain them, the giants turned against them and devoured mankind. And they began to sin against birds, and beasts, and reptiles, and fish, and to devour one another's flesh, and drink the blood. Then the earth laid accusation against the lawless ones.

And Azazel taught men to make swords, and knives, and shields, and breastplates, and made known to them the metals of the earth and the art of working them, and bracelets, and ornaments, and the use of antimony, and the beautifying of the eyelids, and all kinds of costly stones, and all colouring tinctures. And there arose much godlessness, and they committed fornication, and they were led astray, and became corrupt in all their ways. Semjaza taught enchantments, and root-cuttings, 'Armaros the resolving of enchantments, Baraqijal (taught) astrology, Kokabel the constellations, Ezeqeel the knowledge of the clouds, Araqiel the signs of the earth, Shamsiel the signs of the sun, and Sariel the course of the moon. And as men perished, they cried, and their cry went up to heaven . . . (Chapters 6-8)

Your statement is true; nevertheless, scholars believe that The

Book of Enoch is a collection of pseudepigrapha manuscripts. Meaning that the book itself claims to be written by Enoch; however, the evidence points to the book being written under a pseudo name only 300-200 years before Christ—*long* after Enoch was taken up to heaven before the Flood. It was also written in a time when other similar documents were appearing as well, such as the Apocalypse of Zephaniah. Jewish writers were taking on names from those who had lived in the past, and were writing these texts, which were believed to be read as popular literature at the time (like our fads of wizards, vampires, and dystopias). This phenomenon is also similar, in how others forged documents under false names during the time of the New Testament church.

Additionally, the oldest copies of Enoch which have been found, were the fragments in Qumran. These were mostly scribed in Aramaic, the language the Jews began to dominantly use over Hebrew as a result of the Exile, starting in 586 BCE.

1 Enoch has also never been used as Scripture within the Jewish canon, apart from Beta Israel, nor the Christian canon, with the *only* exceptions being the Ethiopian Orthodox Tewahedo Church and the Eritrean Orthodox Tewahedo Church.

Okay, but then why does Jude quote from Enoch in verses 14-15, if we shouldn't think of it as Scripture? Is our Bible missing a book?

It was also about these that Enoch, the seventh from Adam, prophesied, saying, "Behold, the Lord comes with ten thousands of his holy ones, to execute judgment on all and to convict all the ungodly of all their deeds of ungodliness that they have committed in such an ungodly way, and of all the harsh things that ungodly sinners have spoken against him."

I cannot deny the fact that Jude does draw from Enoch (as well as possibly the *Assumption of Moses* in verse 9); however, that doesn't mean we should look at it as Scripture. For Paul quotes from Epimenides' *Cretica* in Titus 1:12, which is also quoted from in Acts 17:28, and Proverbs 22:17-24:22 borrows wisdom from the Egyptian *Wisdom of Amenemope*. The Bible does draw from other texts, but that doesn't mean these other texts were inspired by the Spirit.

I believe Jude, like Paul, was using material at the time to support his points, sort of like using a movie clip in a sermon illustration. It is also a possibility, he may have been operating within the worldview of the time. Jude knowing that 1 Enoch was not Scripture, but drawing from that text to help others to understand the message he was wanting to convey, such how the Bible (though it does have many verses alluding to the Earth being a sphere) also talks of the world being flat, "He will raise a signal for the nations and will assemble the banished of Israel, and gather the dispersed of Judah from the *four corners* of the earth" (Isaiah 11:12). Or how both Jesus and Paul don't try to abolish slavery within the Roman Empire, and even use slavery as allusions within their messages, such as serving two masters or being a slave to sin.

With that said, I do also believe that the Christian canon is *complete*. And if it were not, then something would have happened since the Council of Carthage to change the Bible which we currently have, some sort of Divine Intervention, which has not occurred. Yes, the Catholic Bible does indeed include more books than the Protestant Bible. But—and if you are Catholic, please know I say this most compassionately, with no intentions to offended; though, I do know this upcoming statement will be like poking something sensitive with something sharp—I personally believe that they should not be elevated to the status of Scripture.

Now firstly, I could be very wrong. And if I am, thank God there is grace. I do admit I have been raised with a bias, and a bias I have had to come to defend in order for my own faith and theology to make sense to myself—not saying my theology is flawless, for indeed it is not. Which is why it's ever growing and changing, for I am just a man. However, it is what makes sense to me. We all have our own theologies, but only a few of us are daring or foolish enough to print them. But just as C. S. Lewis made known in the preface of his *Mere Christianity*, I too do not intend to divide the Church any more than what it has already been splintered.*

Now, concerning these other books. I believe they do possess material which they can offer, and they shouldn't just be ignored/cast aside, such as the historical value of the Maccabees. However, I don't believe they're Scripture. Such as in how Lewis is an excellent author to learn from and even reference in a Bible class or from the pulpit, but his writings aren't considered Scripture. Therefore, I do not believe we're missing a book of the Bible, which is still floating around somewhere out there.

Now, these other texts are not some secret documents being hidden either. You can even read some of them if you want to, and decide for yourself. Many of them can even be found by using Google.

PERSONALLY, I BELIVE that "the sons of God" are the descendants of Seth, and that "the daughters of man" are the descendants of Cain. That the descendants of Seth were righteous, but they became corrupt by the offspring of Cain as they continued to have relations with

---

*Please note this book does have my opinions littered throughout it, since it has been written by my hand. But I pray I have made enough distinction between what is my opinions—using such words as 'possibly,' 'maybe,' and 'perhaps,' which can be questioned and argued—and what is said by the Bible.

them. This being one of the reasons why God later warns his people to not intermarry with other nations in Deuteronomy 7, and why Paul warns Christians to not be unequally yoked with nonbelievers in 2 Corinthians 6:14. For it's far easier to pull someone down, than it is to pull them up.

Alright, but what about the Nephilim? Why were they giants?

Were they?

We know there were giants in Canaan, both because of the story of David and Goliath and the report of the spies in Numbers 13:32-33:

> So they brought to the people of Israel a bad report of the land that they had spied out, saying, "The land, through which we have gone to spy it out, is a land that devours its inhabitants, and all the people that we saw in it are of great height. And there we saw the Nephilim (the sons of Anak, who come from the Nephilim), and we seemed to ourselves like grasshoppers, and so we seemed to them."

However, this report comes *after* the Flood. How then could these be the descendants of the same Nephilim?

. . . Maybe some of them survived it? Knew how to swim better than the others. You know, backstroke, backstroke, backstroke.

But then what would be the point of the Flood? Would the Flood have mattered if there were others than Noah and his family who had survived? Weren't the Nephilim the catalysts for the Flood in the first place?

. . . Okay Logan, you know. What's the answer?

Well, I think I know. Like I've said before, I could be wrong, but I'm okay with that. However, I believe what I do, not just because two mentors of mine also believe similarly, but because I have also tried to dive into the Bible and see what it says.

'Nephilim' comes from the Hebrew word נָפַל (naphal) which means "to fall." And remember the '-im' ending in Hebrew is just the plural. So if we translate 'Nephilim' instead of transliterating it, it reads: "The Fallen Ones were on the earth in those days." Therefore, the Fallen Ones weren't necessarily giants, since they were most likely a separate group than the Canaanites. For many assume the Nephilim in Genesis were giants since the ones in Canaan were. Yet, like the Canaanites, they were a people of sin, hence being labeled the 'Fallen Ones,' which is why both these Nephilim and the Nephilim in Canaan can both be called, "The Fallen Ones," without necessarily being related.

DURING THE TIME of Noah, sin had become rampant. So corrupt and so evil, that the Bible says God "regretted" ever making humanity. A world of violence, greed, selfishness, rape, murder, blood. Yet, in the midst of all this sin, was Noah.

"Noah was a righteous man, blameless in his generation. Noah walked with God" (Genesis 6:9). That is a testimony in itself. During such a time of wickedness, Noah was able to walk with God like his great grandfather, Enoch. An encouragement to us today. For though we live in a world of sin, we do *not* have to succumb to the negative peer pressures of it. That we can stand firm against it and remain righteous. If Noah did it, so can we. For Noah put up with this corruption for over *600 years*. 600 years before he stepped foot on the ark. (600 years, in the 2nd month, on the 17th day of that month to be exact, according to Genesis 7:11.)

God is *patient*. Much more patient than us. I don't know about you, but when I want something, I want it now. And when I pray to our Lord, usually I'm praying with instant results in mind. Such as for a healing or for suffering to stop. Yet God . . . such a patient Father who has put up with the mess of humanity for so, so long. And we're still here.

God revealed His plan of both destruction and salvation to Noah. Now Noah, could have chosen to ignore Him and to live out the rest of his days as he had before. Yet he chose to obey, "By faith Noah, being warned by God concerning events as yet unseen, in reverent fear constructed an ark for the saving of his household. By this he condemned the world and became an heir of the righteousness that comes by faith" (Hebrews 11:7). Noah accepted his mission from the Lord, just as Jesus chose the cross for our salvation. For God doesn't force us to act, doesn't take away our free will. He allows us to make the choice to either choose Him, or to not.

So Noah spent approximately the next *20-120 years* building this ark that God had commanded him to construct. Talk about dedication. I mean this thing was HUGE!

Make yourself an ark* of gopher wood. Make rooms in the ark, and cover it inside and out with pitch. This is how you are to make it: the length of the ark 300 cubits [450 or 510ft.†], its breadth 50 cubits [75

---

*The Hebrew word for "ark" which is used here, is תֵּבָה (tabat), which can mean a box or a chest. What's interesting/cool about this word, is that it's only used to reference *two* things within the whole Bible. The first being Noah's ark, and the second being Moses' basket: "When she could hide him no longer, she took for him a basket [a tabat] made of bulrushes and daubed it with bitumen and pitch. She put the child in it and placed it among the reeds by the river bank" (Exodus 2:3). Amazingly, Moses too was saved by the means of both a tabat and water. For Pharaoh had commanded all the Hebrew male babies to be thrown into the Nile, which Jochebed faithfully obeys. She just gives her son a little protection before he goes swimming with the crocodiles. (However, another word is used for "ark" when referencing the Ark of the Covenant (made with acacia wood), אֲרוֹן (aron [aw-rone']), not to be confused with אַהֲרוֹן (Aharon [Aaron]).

†These two approximate, rounded lengths, come from using two different types of measurements—the short Hebrew cubit (17.5in.) and the long Hebrew cubit (20.4in). Though it's uncertain which of the two was used by Noah, that is, assuming he used Hebrew measurements. For the cubit varied from group to group, such as the

or 85ft.], and its height 30 cubits [45 or 51ft.]. Make a roof for the ark, and finish it to a cubit above, and set the door of the ark in its side. Make it with lower, second, and third decks. (Genesis 6:14-16).

To bring this construction project into perspective, the ark was anywhere from about the length of a football field, to a football field and a half. If NASA wanted to, they would be able to land three space shuttles nose to tail on the ark's deck. It would be large enough to house 15 blue whales within it. And, if flipped upright, the ark's length would make it almost as tall as the Great Pyramid. Again, HUGE! It's no wonder it took Noah and his family so long to construct this ship. Especially if it was just the eight of them, with no outside aid from others, such as servants or hired help.[†]

Additionally, not only did Noah build this wonder, but it sounds like he was also acting as a missionary as he did so. 2 Peter 2:5 calls

Egyptian royal cubit was 20.6in., and the Babylonian royal cubit was 19.8in.[2]

[†]Opened since July 7, 2016, a full-size Noah's ark can currently be found and experienced in Williamstown, Kentucky. Two other life-size replicas can be located in Dordrecht, Netherlands and Ma Wan Island, Hong Kong.

Noah "a herald of righteousness" or "a preacher of righteousness" in some translations. It sounds like Noah was the crazy guy saying: "The end of the world is here! Death by water! All will drown! Repent, for the judgment of God is here!" Noah was God's servant offering these men who had sinned so greatly His grace, yet sadly, it appears none listened. Possibly not even his 969-year-old grandfather, Methuselah, which the math says died either right before or during the Flood.

For around 20-120 years, Noah made himself look like a fool. For as far as we know, rain may have never fallen on the earth before, only increasing the possible faith Noah had in his Maker. Genesis 2:5-6 mentions a mist that watered the earth:

> When no bush of the field was yet in the land and no small plant of the field had yet sprung up—for the LORD God had not caused it to rain on the land, and there was no man to work the ground, and a mist was going up from the land and was watering the whole face of the ground—

If true, can you imagine what Noah's neighbors must have thought of him? A crazy Chicken Little building a boat in the middle of nowhere, and ranting about, "The sky is falling!"*

---

*There is also the possibility, that Genesis 2:5-6 may not be describing an alternate system than the water cycle, but evidence that Genesis 2 is a separate creation account than Genesis 1. Chapter 2, not just describing man being sculpted before the Garden, but before all plants. Genesis 1 not being a step by step process of God creating the universe, but a narrative with poetic elements of Him creating order to a world of water, and Genesis 2 describing Him bringing order to a world of desert. Both being separate stories of God creating the universe, being the Creator, while also bringing order to chaos, no matter the most extreme. Sea nor desert, which so happened to be two of the most dangerous forces to the peoples of the ancient world. This would not be an abnormality either, for the Egyptians also had multiple creation accounts. Nor would it be strange to find two accounts of one event in the Bible. For it houses both Kings and Chronicles, and not one, but four Gospels accounting Jesus' time here on earth.

AFTER THE ARK was built, God sent the animals. Lions, and tigers, and bears, oh my! Sadly, the unicorns didn't get the memo.

But what about the dinosaurs? Were there dinosaurs on the ark?

Maybe. I want to say yes, really I do. I mean I *love* dinosaurs. There's a reason I keep watching the *Jurassic Parks* (well, I guess the *Jurassic Worlds* now) though they're all the same. I love seeing dinosaurs, especially on the big screen. But biblically, I can only confidently say maybe. For the Bible does not tell us everything—it tells us everything we need to know to follow God, yes. But it doesn't talk about lightbulbs, or cars, cell phones, youth ministers, or even church buildings. And when it comes to the issue of dinosaurs, the Bible is super vague.

The Behemoth and the Leviathan could be two dinosaurs which are mentioned in the book of Job, or they could be something completely different entirely. Such as demons, which Gregory A. Boyd speculates in his book, *God at War*, one of the many books on my shelf which I still need to read . . . (The Behemoth is *not* a hippo though, as some theorize. Hippos do *not* have "tails stiff like a cedar." Nor do elephants, which others think it may be.*) Or, maybe what we call 'dinosaurs,' the Bible calls 'dragons?' For the word "dinosaur" wasn't even around, until the biologist/paleontologist Sir Richard Owen

---

*Though some do defend this theory, pointing out that (in other translations) the comparison isn't the size of the tail, but the movement of it. That a hippo's tail can sway just like a branch or even a twig of a cedar. The biologist Michael Bright makes another suggestion, that instead of comparing the size of the tail to the size of the flora, that the reference to the cedar tree could be a comparison of its needle-like leaves to the bristles of the hippo's tail.[4] Still others suggest that זְנָבוֹ (zenabow), though its root is translated as 'tail' in other passages (such as Exodus 4:4, Deuteronomy 28:13, and Judges 15:4), could, in this instance, be translated as another appendage instead. Such as an elephant's trunk, or the Behemoth's uh . . . manhood. For the Hebrew verb associated with zenabow, יַחְפֹּץ (yahpos), is most often translated as "moveth" (*KJV*), "sways" (NIV), "stiff" (ESV), or "bends" (NASB). And the second part of the verse does talk of the sinew around his "stones," in the Hebrew that is. Most modern English translations translate פַחֲדָיו (pahadaw) as loins.

coined "Dinosauria" in 1941.

However, if dinosaurs existed, I believe they were on the ark.

'If?'

Yes. For what if when God created the world, he created the earth with a history already within it? like a prologue in a book? Adam and Eve were created as adults, and it sounds like the animals (and stars) were too, so why not the earth? However, some don't like this theory, because they see it as God creating intentional lies to trick man, instead of as another opportunity to express our creativity. Allowing us to create the history of the earth, similarly in how He allowed Adam to name the animals (Genesis 2:19-20). (It would explain why the earth can appear as 4.543 billion years-old, instead of around 6,000.)

Like I said, I really, really, really hope dinosaurs are real, really. I plan to talk to God about having a velociraptor as a pet when heaven is here. It's one of my two requests which I would like to make, if we get requests. The other may involve something about angel wings. Yet, if He does say, "No," I hope not, but if He does, no big. I mean it'll still be heaven.

But . . . there is a tragic possibility we may need to be prepared to embrace, that dinosaurs may have never been. (And this is just one out of the many, many theories of how God created the universe. For there are some mysteries of the Bible we *won't* know, until we get to heaven. However, they're still fun to think about and attempt to figure out.)

But, if dinosaurs were real, they may indeed have been on the ark.*

---

*One theory, presented by paleontologist Dr. Marcus Ross, is that the fossil record gives us a glimpse into a violent world. Not a world at Creation, but at the Flood. A world that had been warped by sin, creating *terrifying* monsters with sharp teeth and claws, like the *Tyrannosaurus rex* or the Mosasaurs. Therefore, it's possible that not only was God giving man a clean slate, but the whole earth as well. Meaning, that the dinosaurs may have not been allowed onto the ark, but sentenced to death by the Flood. Allowing the possibility that when God told Noah, "And of every living thing of all flesh, you shall bring two of every sort into the ark to keep them alive with you.

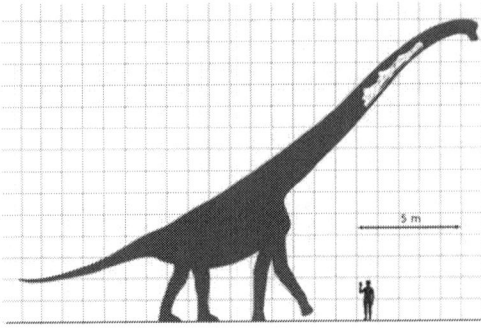

True, but how? I mean, how would the ark house all of them and all the other animals, too? The *Sauroposeidon proteles*, the tallest known dinosaur, is believed to have been able to grow to 60.7ft.! And the Argentinosaurus, the heaviest known dinosaur, is estimated to have weighed anywhere from 60 to 100 tonnes! Not to mention that currently, there's a believed estimate of 8.7 million species living on planet earth! (give or take 1.3 million),[7] though this number is constantly in flux, with over 15,000 new species being discovered *yearly*. And that's not even considering all the food it would take to keep all of these animals fed for a year! keeping Noah safe from becoming lunch.

Well, there's *a lot* of theories about that. Some, such as:

1. The dinosaurs were brought on as eggs instead of adults. (And perhaps, all the animals were babies, which would save *a lot* of space and food.) Makes you wonder, if Noah and his wife had the ultimate Easter egg hunt? Or if the other animals brought the dino eggs with them. Such as the birds carrying them in their talons, the monkeys having loaded armfuls, and the kangaroo having her pouch stuffed with them. Or maybe, Noah just woke up one morning and *poof!* was surprised at the sight of thousands of eggs sitting in his front yard, a little more intimidating than finding a puppy on your porch, don't you think? Or, similar to the rolling Stone in the wilderness, maybe the eggs rolled onto the ark, two by two?

2. There were less species then, then what are alive today. Both

---

They shall be male and female" (Genesis 6:19), that God could have been using a hyperbole. That there may have been things living before the Flood, like unicorns, that were not allowed to exist after it. Again, this is a possible theory, for we weren't alive before the Flood; therefore, we can only speculate about it.[5]

because of natural selection and adaption, and because God is still creating, still tinkering with His creation. (Such as only one pair of dogs (or wolves) came on to the ark. Instead of two poodles, two German shepherds, two schnauzers, etc.).

3. God shrunk all of the animals so they could fit on the ark. (Why not? I mean, He is God).

4. The ark was like a Harry Potter tent, looking smaller on the outside, while having a much larger interior.

Though we don't know how—somehow, some way, all of the different animals did cram onto the ark with Noah and his family.*

And I don't believe food would be an issue, for a God who could make bread fall out of the sky for over 40 years (Exodus 16), who could keep a jar of flour and a jug of oil from ever emptying during a three-year drought (1 Kings 17:1-16), or the God who could feed a crowd of over 5,000, with five loaves of bread and two fish (Matthew 14:13-21; Mark 6:30-44; Luke 9:10-17; John 6:1-15). Now poop, that would be the real issue. Not only in how to get rid of it all, but I don't believe air fresheners were invented yet.

THEN THE RAINS came.

For as were the days of Noah, so will be the coming of the Son of Man. For as in those days before the flood they were eating and drinking, marrying and giving in marriage, until the day when Noah entered the ark, and they were unaware until the flood came and swept them all away, so will be the coming of the Son of Man. (Matthew 24:37-39)

---

*It appears that Noah didn't have to worry about aquatic animals though, which no whales would save *a lot* of room. For Noah takes beasts, livestock, creeping things, and birds, but Genesis doesn't specifically mention the fish of the sea.

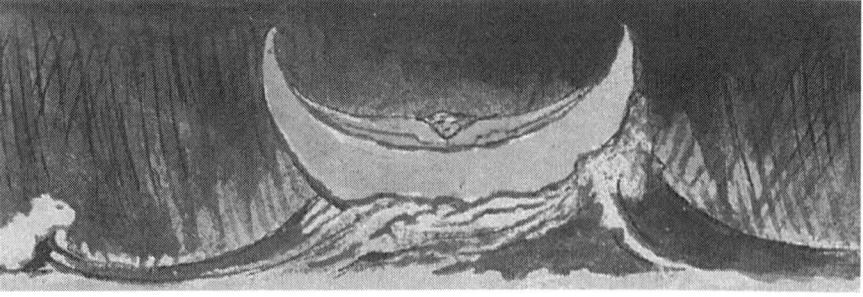

For forty days and forty nights, it stormed. Can you imagine what it must have been like for Noah and his family? Being rocked back and forth by the monstrous waves which covered the mountains? Hearing the roaring thunder and the heavy rain pouring all around you? It must have been scary! And sometimes, we go through storms in our own lives, don't we? We get rocked around by the waves, see the lightning, hear the thunder, we go through storms like Noah. Yet, if we trust God, He will protect us. Noah still endured the storms of the Flood, but he was not drowned by them, because of his faith.

The waters cleansed the earth. It washed away all the evil and wickedness of the Fallen Ones, causing such destruction. Yet, the waters were also the salvation for Noah and his family. This was the revelation that hit me that summer: Noah and his family were saved by water, like baptism. And the ark, well, it's like the cross. Through faith, Noah built the ark which provided his salvation, as the Flood cleansed the earth from its sin through water. Just as Jesus through faith, sacrificed himself upon the cross, which provided salvation to us by cleansing us from our sins through his blood.*

And notice that Noah and his family were not alone, all the animals were with them, too. Just as I believe that Jesus' blood is to purify *all*

*When the world was void and dark, the Spirit of God hovered over the waters (Genesis 1:2). When the ark had landed, Noah released a dove, which hovered over the waters of the Flood, bringing back to Noah an olive branch during its second release, yet never returning when released a third time (Genesis 8:6-12). And it was in the form of a dove, that the Spirit descended and rested upon Jesus at his baptism (Luke 3:22, John 1:32).

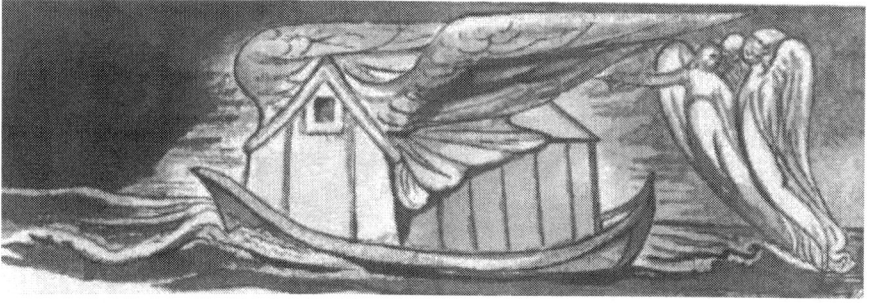

of creation. For the Bible talks about the second Flood, not of water, but of fire, as Peter makes known in 2 Peter 3:10. Yet, earlier he wrote of a refining fire, that the fire will not just merely destroy, but refine like gold. Meaning, that heaven may be very different than what we imagine—a place high in the clouds with us wearing togas and playing harps. That it may be the purified version of all of creation. Perhaps being a lot like the Garden of Eden? For is this why Revelation 21 talks of a "new heaven" and a "new earth," and the "new Jerusalem" which comes down from the sky?

Nevertheless, the ark-revelation is nothing new, for the Bible says the very same thing. Connecting Jesus and the Flood, to Noah and Baptism:

> For Christ also suffered once for sins, the righteous for the unrighteous, that he might bring us to God, being put to death in the flesh but made alive in the spirit, in which he went and proclaimed to the spirits in prison, because they formerly did not obey, when God's patience waited in the days of Noah, while the ark was being prepared, in which a few, that is, eight persons, were brought safely through water. Baptism, which corresponds to this, now saves you, not as a removal of dirt from the body but as an appeal to God for a good conscience, through the resurrection of Jesus Christ, who has gone into heaven and is at the right hand of God, with angels, authorities, and powers having been subjected to him. (1 Peter 3:18-22)

49

So wait, did Jesus time travel back to before the Flood to minister to the Fallen Ones? Or, was he ministering to their souls in Sheol, during the three days which he was in the grave?

I have to answer with, "I don't know."

This passage is very unclear in that aspect, leaving scholars to only scratch their heads and speculate. However, it is very clear in another aspect—the connection between Noah and Jesus. How through faith, they obeyed the Father. How Noah used gopher wood to build an ark, how Jesus was nailed to a tree. How they both, were the salvation of mankind. One physically, the other spiritually.

Alright. And concerning baptism, why did Jesus get baptized? According to Mark 1:4, John the Baptist was baptizing for the repentance of sins. Yet, Jesus didn't sin, right? So why did he get baptized?

That, is an *excellent* question. Truthfully, no one knows for certain; however, here are four speculations of why Jesus may have chose to be dunked under the water (Note: Jesus' reason for doing so, doesn't have to be one or the other. Perhaps he had multiple reasons to be baptized?):

1. *Example:* Jesus allowed himself to be baptized, though he had no need of it, so that all of his disciples would follow him into the water. For Jesus both began his ministry with baptism, and ended his ministry by commissioning his disciples to baptize others (Matthew 28:18-20).

2. *Confirmation*: Jesus' identity was confirmed at his baptism. What's amazing about this event, is that all three members of the Trinity were present, marking this moment as a *special* occasion. The Son who was baptized, the Spirit who came down and rested upon him, and the Father who said, "This is my beloved Son, with whom I

am well pleased" (Matthew 3:17). Perhaps, the Father was confirming Jesus' identity to the witnesses who were present. Or perhaps, it was confirmation for Jesus himself? Maybe, he had known there was something special about him, had feelings of who he was, and had heard the narrative of his birth on multiple occasions. But, it wasn't until this moment, in which he *knew* without any doubt, that he was truly the Son of God?

3. *Affirmation:* Similar to the theory of confirmation, but different. For affirmation is the idea that Jesus was baptized, so that the onlookers present (that we), would know he was truly the Son of God. That when the Father said, "This is my beloved Son, with whom I am well pleased," that it was for our benefit, rather than for Jesus'. That he was baptized so there would be no doubt who he was, where he had come from, what kind of message he was preaching, or what kind of prophet he was.

4. *Initiation:* Jesus' baptism was perhaps the beginning of his ministry. It wasn't long after his baptism, in which he called his first disciples, began to travel—ministering and preaching, and when he began

to perform miracles. Additionally, it may have been in this moment in which Jesus received the Spirit (or perhaps a greater portion of it. For he, like his cousin, may have been filled with the Spirit even within his mother's womb (Luke 1:15)). Shortly after Jesus is baptized in Luke's Gospel, we are told that he was "full of the Holy Spirit" (4:1). And as far as we know according to the Bible, Jesus hadn't performed any miracles until after his baptism. And maybe, as part of Jesus limiting himself, he didn't perform signs through his own power, but like his apostles, through the power of the Spirit: "you yourselves know what happened throughout all Judea, beginning from Galilee after the baptism that John proclaimed: how God anointed Jesus of Nazareth with the Holy Spirit and with power. He went about doing good and healing all who were oppressed by the devil, for God was with him" (Acts 10:37-38).

You can also add the thought that Jesus joins us in our humanity in baptism, suggested my mentor. Mark [1:5] says that all of Israel was getting baptized (a clear exaggeration) maybe declaring that everyone needs remission. Then Jesus who has not sinned, gets baptized like everyone else needs. God joins us. We then join Him in His Godliness in baptism as he joined us in our humanity.

(Other theories of why Jesus was baptized include the foreshadowing of his death, burial, and resurrection, and him performing a ritual in preparation in becoming our Great High Priest.)

Nevertheless, if Jesus, he who committed no sin was baptized, how much more should we who are sinners, follow him through the practice of this sacrament? No, it is not the water itself that saves us, for it is only water—a compound made up of two hydrogen atoms and one oxygen, nothing special. For *only* the blood of Christ saves us. Yet, we accept his sacrifice, accept God's forgiveness (Acts 22:16), His salvation (Mark 16:16), and His Spirit (Acts 2:38), and join the fellowship of the Church (1 Corinthians 12:13), by faithfully dying to our sins through the baptism of water and Spirit (Mark 1:8), "in the name of the Father, the Son, and the Holy Spirit" (Matthew 28:19), and raising again as a new creation.*

***

AS THE KIDS sat down after singing the "Hippo Song," I began to animate the story of Noah and the Flood. Describing the evilness of the world, how the people were bad and didn't listen to their mommies and daddies, and how they were mean to their brothers and sisters. How in the midst of sin was the righteous man, Noah. Who obeyed God and built an ark to save him, his family, and all the animals (giving the kids a chance to yell out some of their favorites).

Then the Flood came, and though Noah and his family were in the storm, they were safe. And how the water had saved them, just as it (through the blood of Christ) saves us, when we follow Jesus through baptism.

I then concluded with Noah and the animals leaving the ark, and the rainbow. Stopping before having to explain to five-year-old's why getting drunk is not okay.

We said a quick prayer after that, before it was time for games and crafts.

NOTES

1. Fig. 1: Blake, William. *The Good and Evil Angels.* 1805. Tate Britain: London.
2. "How Long is a Cubit." *ArkEncounter.com.* 2017. Web. 4 February, 2017.

---

*I remember my youth minister telling me once, of a story he had heard during his time at Harding:

There was a village in an arid area of Africa, who, sadly, were familiar with digging graves, because of a high mortality rate due to HIV. However, when they had heard the Gospel, they were so convicted, that they dug a grave to baptize their tribe members in, filling it with water they had in their village. How much more literal can you get, to dying to your sins?

3. Fig. 2: Kampschaefer, Keith. *Superboat XLVIII. Elijah1757.wordpress.com.* 2014. Web. 13 Feb. 2017.
4. Bright, Michael. *Beasts of the Field: The Revealing Natural History of Animals in the Bible.* London: Robson, 2006. Print. p. 346.
5. *Is Genesis History?* Dir. Thomas Purifoy. Fathom Events, 2017. DVD.
6. Fig. 3: Steveoc 86. *Sauroposeidon Scale Diagram.* 2009.
7. Zimmer, Carl. "How Many Species? A Study Says 8.7 Million, but It's Tricky." 23 August, 2011. Web. 4 February, 2017.
8. Fig. 4: Blake, William. *Jerusalem: The Emanation of The Giant Albion*, copy E , Plate 24. 1820. Yale Center for British Art: New Haven, Connecticut.
9. Fig. 5: Blake, William. *Jerusalem: The Emanation of The Giant Albion*, copy E , Plate 44. 1820. Yale Center for British Art: New Haven, Connecticut.
10. Fig. 6: Blake, William. *The Baptism of Christ.* (1799-1803). Rhode Island School of Design Museum of Art .

CHAPTER 4

ABRAHAM & ISAAC:

BRING YOUR KID TO WORK DAY

Many times that summer, I remember looking up into the sky at the stars. Remembering how truly beautiful they were. Seeing them twinkle above the wilderness of Show Low, Arizona, and above the pine forests of Little Prairie Bible Camp,* (even some shooting ones at Meramec State Park, maybe, if I was allowed to talk about Man Camp. For, "What happens at Man Camp, stays at Man Camp"). Living in a city (well, a small town) all my life, I don't always have a great view of them because of the light pollution. But that's not a problem out in the country. One of the reasons, besides seeing wildlife, and not hearing the constant hum of cars, why I enjoy being out in nature. I'll gladly risk ticks, mosquitos, and poison ivy, in order to view Orion, Monoceros, and the Big Dipper. The very same stars, which smiled down upon Abraham many years ago.

***

ABRAMHAM LINCOLN, I mean, Abram, (for he was alive way, *way* before "four score and seven years ago"), was at first a foreigner of Canaan. He had lived in Ur and then Haran when the Lord had came to him:

---

*LPBC

55

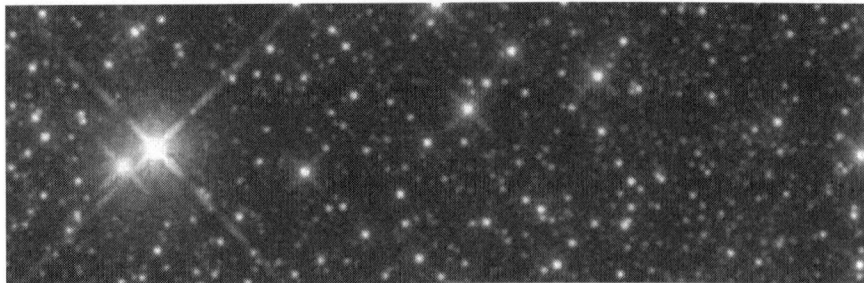

Now the LORD said to Abram, "Go from your country and your kindred and your father's house to the land that I will show you. And I will make of you a great nation, and I will bless you and make your name great, so that you will be a blessing. I will bless those who bless you, and him who dishonors you I will curse, and in you all the families of the earth shall be blessed." (Genesis 12:1-3)

Abram was to begin his life a second time as a foreigner when the Lord had came to him. Telling him to pack up, to leave his home and his kin, and to go to a strange land. To give up everything to follow His plan. And perhaps maybe, these were even instructions from a strange God? For Abram could have been a worshipper of Nanna (or Šin [S-ee-n]) , the moon goddess, before Yahweh had come to him and sent him on his mission. For she was the popular deity of that region.

Like Abram, like Rahab, and like Ruth, Jesus was also a foreigner. Like some of his greatest known ancestors, Jesus was a stranger to the world which he was born to. True, his human-self was Jewish, born in the Promise Land in the little town of Bethlehem. Yet his God-self was a stranger. An alien from heaven above, sent on a mission from the Father to come into a strange land. To give up everything, to leave the splendors of the throne room, so to follow His plan. For Jesus was a part of two worlds, like Superman, being part human, and part something else. (Yes, I know, Kal-El is a Kryptonian; however, he

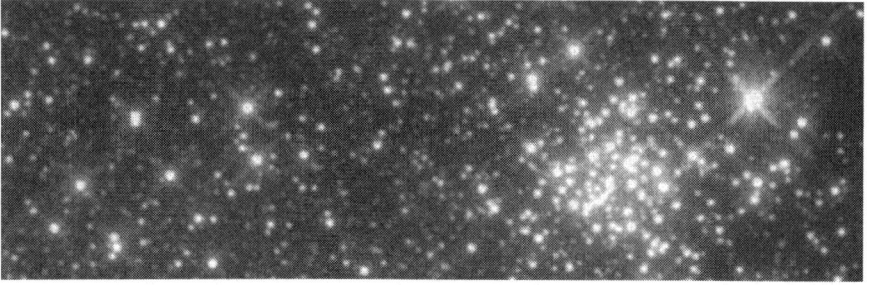

was raised as a human, given human values, and was a part of the human world. Yet he was also a super powered alien from another planet, providing a perfect parallel between the Son of Krypton and the Son of God. Just one of many similarities which they share, actually. Can you think of others?)

And as Yahweh announced to Abram his mission, He also delivered to him the first of His promises, the most important being, "and in you all the families of the earth shall be blessed." For it was through the seed of Abram, through Jesus, in which this promise was fulfilled. For all the families of the world were blessed by the blood shed upon his cross. The freedom which came from it to shake off the shackles of sin.

Abram was 75 when he left Haran and journeyed to the Land of Canaan. Some time would pass before Yahweh would again come to him, with even more promises:

After these things the word of the LORD came to Abram in a vision: "Fear not, Abram, I am your shield; your reward shall be very great." But Abram said, "O Lord GOD, what will you give me, for I continue childless, and the heir of my house is Eliezer of Damascus?" And Abram said, "Behold, you have given me no offspring, and a member of my household will be my heir." And behold, the word of the LORD came to him: "This man shall not be your heir; your very own son shall be your heir." And he brought him outside and said, "Look to-

ward heaven, and number the stars, if you are able to number them."
Then he said to him, "So shall your offspring be." And he believed the
LORD, and he counted it to him as righteousness. (Genesis 15:1-6)

God promises to Abram that he would have a son from his own body,
and that his descendants will be as numerous as the stars. He then
makes a covenant with Abram.

As was the custom, Abram was to take an animal to sacrifice and
to cut it in half. He would כָּרַת (karat) a covenant; he would 'cut a
covenant' as the Israelites would say. In this case, he took a heifer and
a she-goat and cut them in half, and he also sacrificed a turtledove
and a pigeon, arranging the animal halves opposite of one another.
For when cutting a covenant, an animal would be cut in half and both
parties would walk in between the two halves, as symbolism, 'if one
of us breaks this covenant, let us end up like this animal or worse.'
Covenants were a *serious* business, and marriage was one such covenant which would be made under this manner.

Such *powerful* symbolism. Which is why if I get married, I'll want a
plastic cow cut in half on opposite sides of the stage, with me and my
bride in between them. (For some reason, I think people would frown
upon us if we stood in between an actual cow.)

So in Genesis 15, you have this weird scene of an old guy hanging
around a bloody circle of animal pieces, with buzzing flies, while
keeping away vultures from eating the carcasses. This may be a crazy
image for us to imagine, but things get stranger.

Abram keeps away the buzzards until the sun begins to set, before
he passes out and has a vision. During which, God reveals that his descendants will serve as slaves for a time to another nation, before
plundering it and inheriting the Land of Promise. But He also promis-

es Abram that he himself will die in peace.

When the sun has set, Abram then witnesses God pass through the animal pieces. As I said, when making a covenant, both parties would walk in-between the carcasses, but not this time. God fulfills both parts of the covenant, as He passes through the bodies in the forms a smoking pot and a flaming torch. Perhaps symbolizing a covenant which God makes with Himself as the Father and the Son. Jesus, per-forming the role as a mediator for Abram, so that he would not have to do anything to receive the blessing of this covenant, for Jesus would fulfill the role for him.*

This idea is an abstract one; however, it does revolve around a vi-sion, an unclear one at that. The flaming torch may have been Jesus, the Light of the world, who mediated for sinful man in a covenant made with the righteous Father, the smoking pot. Jesus is the Light of the world (John 8:12), our guide to the Father. Just as he may have been a literal light and associated with fire again in Exodus 13. For Jesus may have also been the pillar of fire which would guide Israel by night in the wilderness, and the Spirit the Glory Cloud which would lead them by day. (The cloud which would cover and fill the Tent of Meeting when the Israelites pitched camp (Exodus 40:34-38), and it was in the form of a cloud in which the Spirit of God filled Solo mon's temple (I Kings 8:10-11). Though the Spirit is also associated with fire in Acts 2, when it comes upon the apostles in the form of tongues of flames, while rushing upon them like a mighty wind, filling its new temple.) Just as Jesus and the Spirit may have guided/led the

---

*This would also not be the only covenant which God would fulfill both sides of. He did so again through Jesus to fulfill the covenant which He had made with Moses and Israel at Mount Sinai. For Israel did *not* remain faithful and holy as they had prom-ised. They worshipped other gods, and they never fully cleared the land of the Ca-naanites. Yet Jesus was righteous, and he made a way to cleanse not just the Promise Land, but the whole world of sin. Jesus would also fulfill the covenant which God would make with King David. Jesus being David's descendant who will sit upon the throne for all eternity.

Israelites, so too do they guide us in our daily lives. If we so choose to follow them that is.

Now, do remember this is a theory; there's not really much more proof to back up this speculation. I mean, I believe Jesus could have been the pillar of fire, but I could be very wrong. Maybe the Spirit is both pillars of cloud and flame, while Jesus is just the Rock that follows the Israelites,* who knows. We'll find out one day.

AFTER THIS RITUAL is performed, Yahweh promises to Abram that his descendants will inherit the land of Canaan. God makes all these grand promises to Abram, and yet in his old age, he had yet to see any of them fulfilled. For God's timing is not our own. Just as Moses prayed in Psalm 90:4:

"For a thousand years in your sight

　are but as yesterday when it is past,

　or as a watch in the night."

The Lord is *patient*. He sees time much differently than what we do, making it so difficult for us to wait. But that is where faith comes in. For God is the Promise Keeper; He always fulfills His promises.

Sadly though, being like us so many times, Abram's patience was not as long as the Lord's, and he took matters into his own hands. He had a much shorter nose than God. (The Jews have an interesting idiom. If you have a lot of patience, instead of having a long fuse, you

---

*"The Rock?" Stay tuned and find out. All will be explained in a later chapter.

have a long nose. This is because the Hebrew word for 'nose,' אַף

(aph), is also the very same word for 'anger.' And it also references the action of flaring your nostrils when mad. Therefore, they thought of God as having a long nose, "Like Pinocchio!" exclaimed a friend of mine.

"Yes, but for good. Not lying," I replied.)

Abram and Sarai took matters into their own hands. Sarai gave her Egyptian maid servant to Abram to sleep with, so he could have a son through her servant since she was barren. So Abram and Hagar had sex, and she became pregnant. Giving birth to Ishmael nine months later and creating an *elephant load* of problems. Sarai's jealousy for one (even though it was *her* idea), which is why she later has Abraham get rid of Hagar and Ishmael (Genesis 21:8-21). And the conflict between the Jews and Muslims as another, which is later inherited as a conflict between Christians and Muslims. For we are the adopted sons of Abraham, and as the angel of the LORD told Hagar concerning Ishmael in Genesis 16:12:

"He shall be a wild donkey of a man,

his hand against everyone

and everyone's hand against him,

and he shall dwell over against all his kinsmen."

When Abram was *99*, God again appears to him and promises that he will be a "father of a multitude of nations," that Canaan shall be the

61

Land of Promise, and that Sarah shall give birth to Isaac, the heir of the covenant which the Lord makes with Abraham. All he has to do as a sign of this covenant, is to circumcise himself and his entire household . . . Abraham obeys. He does ask, 'how can a man of a 100 and a woman of 90 bear a son?' Yet he still obeys Yahweh's instructions, and circumcises . . . ouch! (If you don't know what circumcising is . . . it's the removal of the foreskin from a guy's manhood. In Abraham's case, probably with a flint knife.)

Chapter 18 then takes an interesting turn, for it begins as: "And the LORD appeared to him," but then it mentions Abraham lifting his head and seeing "three men." At first, it sounds if God is appearing to Abraham, yet the Bible then mentions these three men, whom we usually think of as angels. Even more confusing, when they speak for a first and second time, the Bible says, "they spoke," yet when they speak for a third time, it's God speaking, "The LORD said, 'I will surely return to you about this time next year, and Sarah your wife shall have a son.'" So who are they? Angels or God?

Yes.

The Bible can be very ambiguous when it comes to the spiritual, for we see this same kind of language in Exodus 3 when God speaks to Moses through the fiery bush. For the passage begins as: "And the angel of the LORD appeared to him in a flame of fire out of the midst of a bush." Yet, when the bush starts talking, it speaks in first person, "God called to him out of the bush, 'Moses, Moses!' And he said, 'Here I am.' Then he said, 'Do not come near; take your sandals off your feet, for the place on which you are standing is holy ground.' And he said, 'I am the God of your father, the God of Abraham, the God of Isaac, and the God of Jacob.' And Moses hid his face, for he was afraid to look at God."

One explanation for this, is that God could be speaking directly through the angels, kind of like a holy possession, being opposite of what we see in horror movies. The men see the angels' body, but they hear God's voice. Another, is that the angel could be acting as a translator, simply repeating the message which God is speaking to it. Or, these could be instances of theophanies, which can also be seen when Jacob wrestles a man in Genesis 32 and is renamed 'Israel,' for he had striven with God and prevailed? and by the man who confronts Joshua and gives him the battle plans to defeat Jericho in Joshua 5, for he is known as the "commander of the LORD's army," and who other than the LORD, is the commander of His army?

A *theophany* is a visible manifestation of God to a man, which is why perhaps there are three men who appear to Abraham, each being a member of the Trinity—the Father, the Holy Spirit, and *Jesus.* This *isn't* a fact, but it is a possibility. (Which if true, there's no wonder Sodom was destroyed—annihilated—gone! For the men of Sodom wanted to have a homosexual encounter with two of these men when they come to Lot in the next chapter. It's also amazing, that God could come down in the form of a man (*not* as a man, yet) in the form of a man, in the midst of a city renowned even today for its sin. Just as He's also beside us in this world of sin today.) However, these three men could very well be three angels, or the Father and two angels (being an Old Testament allusion to the Trinity), there's no way to know for certain.

And so Abraham sees these men and invites them to rest under a tree, have their feet washed, and gives them some food to eat, providing excellent hospitality to them. For as the writer of Hebrews wrote in 13:2, "Do not neglect to show hospitality to strangers, for thereby some have entertained angels unawares." Hospitality was an important custom to the Jews, and it shows from the kindness which Abraham displays to these strangers. They then reveal that in a year, Sarah would give birth to a son. She laughs of course, for she is *old* and barren. But God then asks, "Is anything too hard for the LORD?" Of course the answer is 'no,' yet how easy is it to doubt Him? How easy is it to pray, yet do we really believe what we are saying, the words that are coming from out of our mouths? Like the church, who was praying for Peter's release from prison in Acts 12, yet they didn't believe the servant girl when she told them that Peter was knocking at the door. So let us pray like the man with the demon possessed son in Mark 9, "I believe; help my unbelief!"

Additionally, John 8 may be further evidence that Jesus may have convened with Abraham in this moment. For in this passage, Jesus talks as if he personally knew Abraham. Which even confuses the Jews:

> Jesus answered, "If I glorify myself, my glory is nothing. It is my Father who glorifies me, of whom you say, 'He is our God.' But you have not known him. I know him. If I were to say that I do not know him, I would be a liar like you, but I do know him and I keep his word. Your father Abraham rejoiced that he would see my day. He saw it and was glad." So the Jews said to him, "You are not yet fifty years old, and have you seen Abraham?" Jesus said to them, "Truly, truly, I say to you, before Abraham was, I am." (54-58)

This language of companionship which Jesus uses may be because he is a member of the Trinity, therefore knowing Abraham since he and the Father are one—which is a theme throughout the Gospel of John. Or, it may be a hint that Jesus on a more one-on-one level communed with Abraham under a shade tree. Which shouldn't be too strange, since we do see him in conversation with two other Old Testament figures on the Mount of Transfiguration: Moses and Elijah.

AND SO, JUST as Yahweh promised, finally, after *years* of waiting—when Abraham was 100 years-old—Isaac is born! Kind of like another baby which was promised, yet he didn't come until years and *years* of waiting. A baby which was wrapped in swaddling clothes and lain in a manger, for God's timing is not our own. Let us try to remember this when we pray. For God, like His promises, *always* answers prayer. It may be "Yes," or "No," or "Yes, but not yet. Wait." And believe me when I say it can be *hard* to know which answer He gives. Sometimes it is clear, but others *not* so much. But let us have faith in our Father. After all, He did create the whole universe, which I believe are credentials for being an omnipotent being. If not, I don't know what is. Yes, it's *hard*, difficult, challenging to be patient. Yet if we are to be His people, we must learn to be. For is patience not a portion of the fruit of the Spirit, along with love, joy, and peace?

Isaac, the Promise Child, is finally born! Yet, Abraham will again be tested, beyond than just being patient. A test to see how much he is willing to sacrifice to serve his God:

"After these things God tested Abraham and said to him, 'Abraham!' And he said, 'Here I am.' He said, 'Take your son, your *only son* Isaac, *whom you love*, and go to the land of Moriah,* and *offer* him

---

*Though spelled a little differently, it is revealed in J. R. R. Tolkien's *The Two Towers*, that it was above the mines of Moria, on top of the mountain Silvertine, where Gandalf the Grey sacrificed himself to slay the demonic Balrog.

Tolkien himself made it very clear that his trilogy is not an allegory. Nevertheless, as gleamed by many, there is still much Christian influence and symbology present within his works. Such as the elves who were corrupted and became orcs, as the angels who became demons, and the small but heavy Ring that can represent sin. Jonathan and Kenneth Padley make the convincing argument in their article, "'From Mirrored Truth the Likeness of the True': J. R. R. Tolkien and Reflections of Jesus Christ in Middle-Earth," that Tolkien represented Christ as three personas within his trilogy, unlike his contemporary, C. S. Lewis, who represented Jesus as the lion Aslan in

there as a burnt offering on one of the mountains of which I shall tell you.'" Yahweh again comes to Abraham, and asks him to sacrifice his 'only son' to Him. Words which sound very much like another verse: "For God so loved the world, that he gave his only begotten Son, that whosoever believeth in him should not perish, but have everlasting life" (John 3:16 *KJV*). God was asking Abraham, to do the very thing which He was planning to do for us.

HOW OLD WAS Isaac when this episode happened?

I do not know. Personally, I believe he was a teenager. There are several guesses out there, many amongst the Jews alone. Some believing he was two, three, five, ten, twelve, eighteen or twenty, or even thirty-seven. According to the historian, Flavivus Josephus, "Now Isaac was twenty-five years old,"[4] so he writes/believes. Though we don't know his exact age, we do know from the text he was old enough to carry the wood for the offering, aware enough to know how sacrifices worked, and keen enough to notice that there was no lamb with them.

They make it up the mountain, before Abraham builds the altar and binds Isaac to it. (Can you even imagine what Isaac must have been thinking?! "My dad's crazy!" This experience would have most definitely put strain on their relationship, even if he knew these instructions came from God. I mean, I would have *major* doubts in my dad, and would definitely need a therapist to talk to about the day my

his *Chronicles of Narnia*: Gandalf, "Christ's divine nature;" Frodo, "Christ's humanity;" and Aragon, "Christ's quality of kingliness."[3] (Arguably, Samwise may also be included within this list, the *faithful* companion who carries us up mountains.

About a thousand years later, King David would build an altar to the Lord on top of Mount Moriah, to offer unto Him a sacrifice as atonement and to save Israel from a plague (2 Samuel 24:18-25). The very same location, where King Solomon would later construct the Temple (2 Chronicles 3:1), the Jewish pinnacle of worship and sacrifice. As for today, it is the site of the Islamic shrine Qubbat as-Sakhrah (Dome of the Rock).

dad tried to kill me. And can you imagine Sarah's reaction when she found out? "Your father did what?! ABRAHAM! You're *never* allowed to be alone with our son again! You hear me?! *Never!*" Sadly, some rabbis believe it was the shock of this instance which led to Sarah's death, for she does pass away in the next chapter. . . . Also, how do you think Isaac looked at God, after this experience?)

Then Abraham reached out his hand and took the knife to slaughter his son. But the angel of the LORD called to him from heaven and said, "Abraham, Abraham!" And he said, "Here I am." He said, "Do not lay your hand on the boy or do anything to him, for now I know that you fear God, seeing you have not withheld your son, your only son, from me." And Abraham lifted up his eyes and looked, and behold, behind him was a ram, caught in a thicket by his horns. And Abraham went and took the ram and offered it up as a burnt offering instead of his son. So Abraham called the name of that place, ["Yahweh-yir'eh"] "The LORD will provide"); as it is said to this day, "On the mount of the LORD it shall be provided." (Genesis 22:10-14)*

*The text of the Qur'an varies very differently from this biblical account. For the Muslims believe Ishmael to be the son of promise, instead of Isaac:
[Following the destruction of his father's and tribesmen's idols, Abraham prays:]
"O Lord give me *a son*, of the righteous."
We announced to him a youth of meekness.
And when he became a full-grown youth,
His father said to him, "My son, I have seen in a dream that I should sacrifice thee; therefore, consider what thou seest *right*."
He said, "My father, do what thou art bidden; of the patient, if [Allah] please, shalt thou find me."

What thoughts, were going through Abraham's mind?! He was about to sacrifice his son—his *son*. Ishmael was gone. Isaac was his only son he had left. The son he had been promised. The son who was to be his heir. The son who was to give him grandkids, and great grandkids, and great-great grandkids. The son he loved. The son he had waited *thirty-five* years for. . . . Yet, he still had the faith to obey God.

And his faith was rewarded:

By faith Abraham, when he was tested, offered up Isaac, and he who had received the promises was in the act of offering up his only son, of whom it was said, "Through Isaac shall your offspring be named." He considered that God was able even to raise him from the dead, from

---

And when they had surrendered them to the will of [Allah], he laid him down upon
   his forehead:
We cried unto him, "O Abraham!
Now hast thou satisfied the vision." See how We recompense the righteous.
This was indeed a decisive test.
And We ransomed his *son* with a costly victim,
And We left this for him among posterity,
"PEACE BE ON ABRAHAM!"
Thus do We reward the well doers,
For he was of Our believing servants.
And We announced Isaac to him—a righteous prophet—
And on him and on Isaac We bestowed Our blessing. And among their offspring were
   well doers, and others, to their own hurt undoubted sinners. (37:98-113)[6]

which, figuratively speaking, he did receive him back. (Hebrews 11:17 -19)

Abraham was stopped, and God provided a ram* to be sacrificed instead. . . . Just as He provided the Lamb to be sacrificed on the altar of the cross. Just as Isaac had an altar built for his blood, so too have we built our own altars, constructed from our sins. Yet, though we were the rightful sacrifices, another was sacrificed in our stead—Jesus. For the Lord will provide.†

And yet, though Abraham did have *great* faith, it was not his faith alone which was shown on that day, but also his actions. Him acting out his faith. For just as it is written in James 2:20-24:

Do you want to be shown, you foolish person, that faith apart from works is useless? Was not Abraham our father justified by works when he offered up his son Isaac on the altar? You see that faith was active along with his works, and faith was completed by his works; and the Scripture was fulfilled that says, "Abraham believed God, and it was counted to him as righteousness"—and he was called a friend of God. You see that a person is justified by works and not by

---

*The image of a sacrificial ram, is not solely unique to the Jewish culture. In Greek mythology, Athamas, the king of Orchomenus, married the nymph Nephele as his first wife. They knew each other and had two children, Phrixus and his sister Helle. At a later time, Athamas was also enchanted by the beauty of the mortal Ino, and married her as well. Ino, however, hated her stepchildren, and devised a plot to kill them both. But Zeus took pity on the innocent Phrixus and his sister, saving them while they were being led to their deaths with a winged ram clothed in a golden fleece. Sadly, Helle fell off the ram while they were flying above the Euxine Sea, while Phrixus was safely taken to the country of Colchis. He then sacrificed the ram on an altar to Zeus, in gratefulness for his rescue, and hung its golden fleece in a tree. The same Golden Fleece, within the tale of Jason and the Argonauts.

†"I would add that in Muslim Morocco, under the name of 'Abraham's Sacrifice' a feast is still celebrated which includes the slaughter of a ram under a tent located two or three minutes from the mosque; as soon as the victim has received the death blow it is thrown onto the saddle of a horseman who dashes off at a gallop to the mosque: if the ram is still alive when it arrives, the people of the Maghreb say it is a sign of good fortune for the coming year."[8]

faith alone.

Not only did Abraham have faith in God, but he also used his actions to express his faith. Not only did he believe God's words, but he *did* what God had told him to do.

For Faith without works is dead.

Faith without works is dead. Which is why we should not only believe, but also be baptized. And not only should we be baptized, but also live an active life as if we're Jesus ourselves. Loving others just as he loved us. Not trying to meet the bare minimum to get into heaven, but living a lifestyle. For "Christian" means "mini-Christ." No, our works will not save us, grace does. But are not our works the fruit of what has been planted within our hearts?

YAHWEH HAD MADE many promises to Abraham. Yet, it's interesting how he only saw *one* fully fulfilled. The birth of a son from his own body, Isaac. True, he lived in the Promise Land, but so did the Canaanites—the land was not yet his. He was not yet a father of a nation, or many nations, nor were his descendants more numerous than the stars in the sky or the sand on the seashore. He had waited *years* for one promise, while not fully seeing the others fulfilled. And yet, Abraham was faithful to the very end, as we should be. For there are still promises which the Lord has made that have yet to be fulfilled.

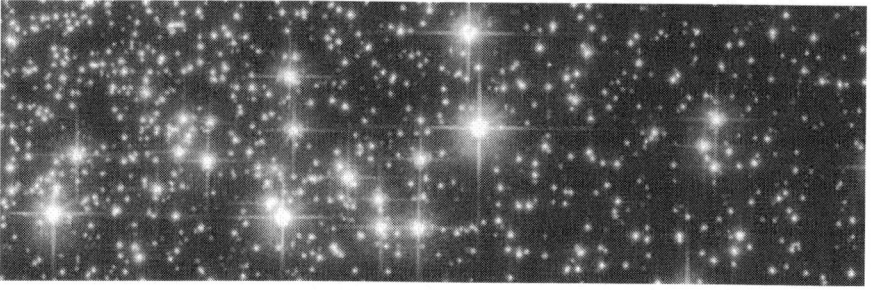

Promises made to the apostles, which they did not see fulfilled before their graves. Yet they were still faithful. Even as they suffered *excruciating* deaths—crucifixion, beheading, impalement, stoning, etc. The promise of Jesus' return, and the promise of heaven.

Though we are still waiting, one day, we will wait no more! For the Promise Keeper *always* fulfills His promises. Until then, we must have faith, like those who came before us.

And the angel of the LORD called to Abraham a second time from heaven and said, "By myself I have sworn, declares the LORD, because you have done this and have not withheld your son, your only son, I will surely bless you, and I will surely multiply your offspring as the stars of heaven and as the sand that is on the seashore. And your offspring shall possess the gate of his enemies, and in your offspring shall all the nations of the earth be blessed, because you have obeyed my voice." So Abraham returned to his young men, and they arose and went together to Beersheba. And Abraham lived at Beersheba. (Genesis 22:15-19)

***

AS I WAS stargazing, I heard footsteps—before a flashlight blinded my eyes. "Logan, we found you!" said Hal, discovering me behind a tree in our game of flashlight tag.

"About time," I joked, rubbing my poor irises which had been assaulted, then picking myself up from the ground. I took one last glance at the sky above, before refocusing my mind to the fun at the moment. "You better be ready to hide real good," I warned. Most eager to get my playful revenge.

"No worries there," replied Hal. Before he and Dalton bolted to find a good spot to hide.

NOTES

1. Fig. 1: *NASA/ESA. Hubble Peers into the Most Crowded Place in the Milky Way.* 2015. *Photograph.*
2. Fig. 2: *NASA/ESA. Hubble Sweeps Scattered Stars in Sagittarius.* 2016. *Photograph.*
3. Padley, Jonathan, and Kenneth Padley. "'From Mirrored Truth The Likeness Of The True': J. R. R. Tolkien And Reflections Of Jesus Christ In Middle-Earth." *English: The Journal Of The English Association* 59.224 (2010): 70-92. *Humanities International Complete.* Web. 18 Apr. 2017.
4. Josephus, Flavius, transl. William Whiston. "Antiquities of the Jews," *The Life and Works of Flavius Josephus,* 1974 reprint. Grand Rapids, MI: Baker. (1.13.2).
5. Fig. 3: Blake, William. *Abraham Preparing to Sacrifice Isaac (Genesis, XXII, 9-12).* 1783. Museum of Fine Arts: Boston.
6. Rodwell, John Medows. *The Koran.* NY: Bantam Dell, 2004. Print.
7. Fig. 4: Blake, William. *Abraham and Isaac.* 1799-1800. Yale Center for British Art: New Haven, Connecticut.
8. Charbonneau-Lassay, Louis, and D. M. Dooling. *The Bestiary of Christ.* New York: Parabola , 1991. Print. p. 70-71.
9. Fig. 5: *NASA/ESA. Field of Stars.* 2012. *Photograph.*

CHAPTER 5

JOB: GIANT ZITS FROM HEAD TO TOE

rap! What am I going to do? I thought to myself, rocking back and forth in my office chair. I kept glancing around the room, hoping something was willing to jump out and bail me out of my predicament. Nothing did. Not Dr. Seuss, C. S. Lewis, nor Donald Miller, who all sat quietly upon the bookcase in front of me. Not the cooler full of pops left over from Tuesday night. Nor the snakeskin which Mamma Brunner had found on the church grounds. Everything reminded silent. *Thanks*, I thought. *So much for being a team.*

I thought I had prepared so perfectly for that summer, all the topics for my classes picked out . . . but I had missed one. *One.* One stupid week which I had somehow overlooked when planning the summer of Jesus. And now I was in a pickle of trying to figure out what the topic of that week should be.

The week before had been Daniel, meaning I couldn't just jump back to someone before him or my mistake would be totally obvious. . . . Unless I went far enough to make it look intentional. But who?

. . . My peripherals caught sight of the Jonah commentary upon my desk, recalling the words of my moreh (teacher): "Christianity, is not a vending machine religion."

That's it! I exclaimed, as I tore into the book of Job.

***

TECHNICALLY, THIS WAS the last lesson we discussed of Jesus in the Old Testament that summer; however, I thought it would best serve placed here, within these pages of this book, in an attempt of keeping things chronological. For many believe that Job may have been a contemporary of Abraham's. And Job appears to be the oldest book of the Bible ever written, even predating Genesis—though Genesis does cover older material.

Another note before we get started, the book is pronounced 'Jobe,' rhymes with robe. It's not job, that's something you work at. . . .

Anyways, the book of Job begins as: "There was a man in the land of Uz whose name was Job, and that man was blameless and upright, one who feared God and turned away from evil" (1:1). Notice that Job lived in the Land of Oz, I mean Uz. He was *not* an Israelite, already making this story pretty interesting. Yet, he was still a *faithful* man of God, "blameless and upright," the Bible says. For now, this is important, because it shows that God can have an intimate relationship with Gentiles—those who were not His people, especially one as faithful as Job. This is important for another reason as well, but we'll talk about that later. For now, remember that Job was one awesome dude.

The passage then begins to describe all the material blessings that Yahweh had blessed him with: "There were born to him seven sons and three daughters. He possessed 7,000 sheep, 3,000 camels, 500 yoke of oxen, and 500 female donkeys, and very many servants, so that this man was the greatest of all the people of the east" (1:2-3). Job was *rich*, possessing the bling-bling of sheep and camels.

If he was alive today, it's estimated he would have anywhere from $5.3 million to $21 million—and that is both before the Lord doubles his possessions [spoiler alert], and only estimating the value of his livestock. That's not even adding up the worth of his houses, land, servants, or other possessions. Just think of Job as a Bill Gates character, living in a Malibu mansion with a whole parking garage full of sports cars. And perhaps even owning a flying iron suit, which he uses to fight crime with.*

However, Job's wealth did not go unnoticed:

Now there was a day when the sons of God came to present themselves before the LORD, and Satan also came among them. The LORD said to Satan, "From where have you come?" Satan answered the LORD and said, "From going to and fro on the earth, and from walking up and down on it." And the LORD said to Satan, "Have you considered my servant Job, that there is none like him on the earth, a blameless and upright man, who fears God and turns away from evil?" Then Satan answered the LORD and said, "Does Job fear God for no reason? Have you not put a hedge around him and his house and all that he has, on every side? You have blessed the work of his hands, and his

---

*Not only was Job stinkin' rich, but he was a righteous man of character. For the Bible then tells us, that whenever his children would have a party, Job would make a sacrifice for each of them to the Lord, in case they had sinned against Him.

75

possessions have increased in the land. But stretch out your hand and touch all that he has, and he will curse you to your face." And the LORD said to Satan, "Behold, all that he has is in your hand. Only against him do not stretch out your hand." So Satan went out from the presence of the LORD.

Whoa, whoa, whoa, back up. What is Satan doing in heaven? Isn't he the enemy of God? And wasn't he casted out of heaven?

There are two explanations which I know of for this predicament:

The first, is the more traditional. That this is Satan, whom God for some reason has allowed to come before Him with the other angels. And He points out one of his most beloved servants, Job. A righteous man who adores Him. Yet Satan doesn't believe so, believing that Job only loves God for the stuff He has blessed him with. "Take that away, and Job will turn away," claims the Devil. And so the Lord allows Satan to test Job to prove his loyalty, that Satan may take anything from Job, but cannot lay a finger upon Job himself.

So you're saying that God and Satan make bets, and gamble with the souls of men?

Great question, but here's another: can it truly be called 'gambling,' if one can look into the future and know the outcome?

There is another explanation, though. In the Hebrew, 'Satan' is written as הַשָּׂטָן (ha-satan [saw-tawn]) which translates as "the adversary" or "the accuser." This could be translated as *the* Satan, *the* Devil, meaning the one and only. Or it could be less personal, the satan, meaning the accuser in the throne room, the accuser of the Divine Council.

Wait? The satan may be one of God's angels?! How does that work?

Think of it this way, there is a lot of legal verbiage within Job, like a trial. What if the satan is like a prosecutor? He's not evil. He's been watching Job, and truly believes Job is only faithful to God because of his stuff, so he puts Job on trial. Testing Job's heart to see if he genuinely loves his Creator, or if only obeys because of His blessings. Both explanations do have questions which must be explained, but they both bring something unique to the table.

Whether the satan is the Devil or not, the book of Job does revolve around an important theme—the disproof of retribution theology.

Retribution theology, is the belief that if you obey God, good things will happen to you, but if you disobey God, bad things will happen to you. Sort of like holy karma. Jesus himself speaks against this thinking in his Sermon on the Mount, in Matthew 5:45, "For he makes his sun rise on the evil and on the good, and sends rain on the just and on the unjust." Jesus teaches that sometimes good things do happen to bad people, and sometimes bad things happen to good people. This is one reason why God's people have cried out to Him asking, "How long shall the wicked triumph?" (Psalm 94:3).

But wait, doesn't the Bible contradict itself? For Deuteronomy 28 is filled with blessings which the Israelites will receive if they obey Him:

> "And if you faithfully obey the voice of the LORD your God, being careful to do all his commandments that I command you today, the LORD your God will set you high above all the nations of the earth. And all these blessings shall come upon you and overtake you, if you obey the voice of the LORD your God. Blessed shall you be in the city, and blessed shall you be in the field. Blessed shall be the fruit of your womb and the fruit of your ground and the fruit of your cattle, the increase of your herds and the young of your flock. Blessed shall be your basket and your kneading bowl. Blessed shall you be when you come in, and blessed shall you be when you

go out. . . ."

And if they don't, then there's whole a list of curses that'll come upon them:

> "But if you will not obey the voice of the LORD your God or be care-
> ful to do all his commandments and his statutes that I command
> you today, then all these curses shall come upon you and overtake
> you. Cursed shall you be in the city, and cursed shall you be in the
> field. Cursed shall be your basket and your kneading bowl. Cursed
> shall be the fruit of your womb and the fruit of your ground, the in-
> crease of your herds and the young of your flock. Cursed shall you
> be when you come in, and cursed shall you be when you go out. . .
> ."

We must look at Deuteronomy as a special circumstance. For if retribution theology was true, why should Paul have been stoned, bitten by a snake, or shipwrecked while he was serving God? Or why should King Ahab have been allowed to rule for twenty-two years, being as wicked as he was? Or why should Jesus have been hung upon the cross?

Deuteronomy is a promise to the Israelites under the Mosaic Law, a part of the covenant which Yahweh makes with them. If they follow Him, they will be blessed. And if they don't, they will be punished. (This can be seen very noticeably in the book Judges.) Yet, there are times when Israel is unfaithful to God, and He holds back or delays His punishment, such as during the time of King Solomon. For God allows peace, just as he had promised his father David there would be (1 Chronicles 22:9), even though Solomon builds *numerous* high plac-es of adultery for his foreign wives. Or the Babylonian Captivity, which God delivered warnings time and time again through His prophets like Jeremiah. Asking His people to repent, while giving them ample time to do so, yet they never did. Even within his Deuteronomic covenant, God still exhibits mercy and grace when dealing with man.

Retribution theology, as can be seen in both the book of Job and other sections of the Bible, is false. For God wants a relationship with us, which is why Judaism, and now Christianity, are not vending machine religions.

Which means . . . that we can't pray to God about Coke?

Haha, no. What I mean is, is that we participate in a religion that does not work like a vending machine. Think of how a vending machine works for a second. You insert your money, pick the product that you want, and once you click the button, the desired product comes out (if the machine is working properly, and you don't almost smash yourself by shaking the machine to try and get your pop or snack out). The point is, put your money in, pick what you want, it comes out.

Back in the day, if you were a Pagan, and you wanted a good harvest, you would make a sacrifice or another form of appeasement to the god or goddess of the harvest to get good crops. You would then make another sacrifice to the god or goddess of war to win a great victory. If you wanted something, you would pick the god who was over what you wanted, and would bribe him or her to obtain that said object.

Christianity is not like that, however. God isn't some magical genie, a jolly Santa Claus, or a lucky Buddha. God is GOD. He doesn't want us to serve Him so we can get things. He wants us to serve Him because of our love. That is one reason why the Professor believes the satan in Job is not Satan. For Satan would *want* us to believe that

"God is our 'Sugar Daddy' in the sky."

Christianity is not a vending machine religion. That's why I don't like the last verse of the song, "The Wise Man Built His House." The blessings don't necessarily come down as the prayers go up. Good people can still die from cancer or have their homes blown away from tornadoes, while greedy politicians and vanity-driven movie stars can live such gluttonous lives. We still live in a broken world. But there is a God who still loves us, and He wants us to love Him too. Not for blessings, not for promises, not for heaven, or crowns, or mansions, or streets of gold, not to escape hell. He wants us to love Him for Him. Just as we want Him to love us for being us, despite our scars, mistakes, and brokenness.

SO THE SATAN tests Job. He takes away all of his sheep, his donkeys, and his children. Servants come and deliver these news to their master. But after Job hears their words . . . he *praises* the Lord: "Then Job arose and tore his robe and shaved his head and fell on the ground and worshiped. And he said, 'Naked I came from my mother's womb, and naked shall I return. The LORD gave, and the LORD has taken away; blessed be the name of the LORD'" (1:20-21). Although Job praises the One who gives and takes away, notice that he still "tore his robes and shaved his head," which was a common practice then for mourning. Job was still upset. He wasn't happy. Not only did he lose all of his wealth in an *instant*, (which is why our faith should be in God and not in things), but he just lost his ten children whom he loved. They were his children who he made sacrifices for. His flesh and bone. Of course Job would be upset. . . . Yet, even in the midst of the storm, in loss, he could still worship the Almighty.

"In all this Job did not sin or charge God with wrong" (1:22). Despite *all* that Job had lost, he still chose to praise God *during* the trial. . . . All I can say . . . is, 'Wow!'

THE SATAN AGAIN comes to the Lord, believing his first test had only failed because he had not been allowed to inflict Job directly, "Skin for skin! All that a man has he will give for his life. But stretch out your hand and touch his bone and his flesh, and he will curse you to your face" (2:4-5). God again allows for the satan to test Job, only he may not take his life. And so Job is struck with *massive* zits all along his body. From the soles of his feet to the crown of his head bud these painful, pussy sores *covering* him. Job then sits in ash and scrapes himself with shards of broken pottery, in a pitiful attempt in relieving himself from this misery.

His wife then comes to him and says, "'Do you still hold fast your integrity? Curse God and die.' [Gotta love her.] But he said to her, 'You speak as one of the foolish women would speak. Shall we receive good from God, and shall we not receive evil?' In all this Job did not sin with his lips" (2:9-10).

Again, Job stays faithful to his Lord, even after he believes that God was the one who had afflicted him with this pain.

James, the same James who tells us to, "Count it all joy,* my brothers, when you meet trials of various kinds," (James 1:2) commends

---

*"Joy' not 'happiness.' Not even Jesus was happy all the time (John 11:35, John 2:14-17, Luke 22:41-44).

Job, and tells us in chapter 5 of his epistle, that we need to stand as steadfast and as patient as Job in times of suffering.

THREE FRIENDS OF JOB come and mourn with him. They sit with him for seven days and seven nights, just being there with their friend in his time of need. Not a word was spoken. But there didn't need to be any. For through their actions, these three friends demonstrated what Job meant to them.

After these seven days, Job cries out in lament. Cursing the day of his birth, wishing that he had never been born. Never had been allowed to endure such misery. For he is not afraid to speak his mind, and neither should we. We do not have to like the storms which we go through; we can tell God. He knows we're thinking it anyways, and He wants to have an honest relationship with us. No, we don't curse God, but if we are to be honest with Him, we can ask Him 'why?' For Job didn't understand why he was suffering, and neither did his friends.

They believed it was because of retribution theology, and so they engage Job in a long debate of trying to figure out what sin Job had

committed to deserve such distress. They spout out proverbs to him, trying to find one that sticks to his situation, yet none of them do the trick. For proverbs, though they can be wise, are but Band-Aids. They cannot be a solution to a problem. Spouting, "The early bird gets the worm," doesn't silence the alarm in the morning. Besides, "The second mouse gets the cheese."

In the midst of this debate, Job makes a case for himself in chapter 9:

"But how can a man be in the right before God?
If one wished to contend with him,
　one could not answer him once in a thousand times.
He is wise in heart and mighty in strength
　—who has hardened himself against him,
　　and succeeded?—
he who removes mountains, and they know it not,
　when he overturns them in his anger,
who shakes the earth out of its place,
　and its pillars tremble;
who commands the sun, and it does not rise;

who seals up the stars;

who alone stretched out the heavens

and trampled the waves of the sea . . .

Though I am in the right, I cannot answer him;

I must appeal for mercy to my accuser.

If I summoned him and he answered me,

I would not believe that he was listening to my voice . . .

If it is a contest of strength, behold, he is mighty!

If it is a matter of justice, who can summon him?

Though I am in the right, my own mouth would condemn me;

though I am blameless, he would prove me perverse.

I am blameless; I regard not myself;

I loathe my life.

It is all one; therefore I say,

'He destroys both the blameless and the wicked.'

When disaster brings sudden death,

he mocks at the calamity of the innocent.

The earth is given into the hand of the wicked;

he covers the faces of its judges—

if it is not he, who then is it? . . .

If I wash myself with snow

and cleanse my hands with lye,

yet you will plunge me into a pit,

and my own clothes will abhor me.

For he is not a man, as I am, that I might answer him,

that we should come to trial together.

There is no arbiter between us,

who might lay his hand on us both.

Let him take his rod away from me,

and let not dread of him terrify me.

Then I would speak without fear of him,

for I am not so in myself." (9:1-8, 15-16, 19-24, 30-35)

Do you remember how the book of Job began?

The Bible described him as a "blameless and upright" man. Yet Job admits himself, if he went up against God, he would lose. That God is *greater*. That there is *no* way that a man can stand against God, for God is God. Heartbroken, Job cries out for an "arbiter" (or a mediator) to plead his case to God. "Who is that arbiter?" I asked the class. "Who mediates between us and God?"

"The Holy Spirit?" answered a teen. (Not what I was expecting). *Come on, we've been talking about him all summer.*

"A good guess, but no. The Holy Spirit does intercede for us as we pray [Romans 8:26], but that's not the right answer. He helps us pray to the Father, but he does not make us righteous so that we can talk to God." (I wish my answer came out like this. Instead, it was something more along the lines of: "Uhhhh . . . no. Does anyone have another guess?")

". . . Jesus?" asked another.

"Yes! Jesus. For he is the mediator between us and God. He was the one who died for our sins, making reconciliation possible with God.

85

He was the Atoner, and he mediates for the forgiveness of our sins."

Job knew he was innocent, so he wished there was one who could plead his case before the throne of God. He cried out for Jesus. As Paul wrote in I Timothy 2:5, "For there is one God, and there is one mediator between God and men, the man Christ Jesus."

Mankind is guilty. We are guilty of sin and therefore cannot pardon ourselves. No amount of good works or rule following can ransom us from the charge of sin. We deserve to face the death penalty. That is why, as Job knows, we need a mediator. One who is righteous who can plead our case before God. One who can redeem us, take the punishment for us. That arbiter, that man, was Jesus. Unknowing, Job cries out for the Son of God to represent him in God's court, for he knew he himself was unworthy to do so. He knew he was righteous in his case, yet he also knew he was just a man, but Yahweh was God.

THOUGH JOB LAMENTS and cries out, he does not sin and stays faithful to God. After many more debates between Job and his friends, Yahweh Himself confronts Job, and reminds him Who He is. That *He* is God, and Job is a man. He tells Job, "Dress for action like a man [or to "gird up your loins"]; I will question you, and you make it known to me" (38:3), before He delivers His speech:

He asks Job if he was the one who laid the foundations of the earth? Did he tell the sea, "Thus far shall you come, and no farther?" Had he commanded the mornings since time began? Could Job cast down lightning? Or did he give understanding to the mind? Have the ability to number the clouds? Could he feed the mouths of the lion's cubs or the chicks of the raven? Did he know when the mountain goat would give birth? Or made the ostrich a foolish mother? And strangely, in the midst of this interrogation, God reveals how much He takes pride in one of His special creations, horses:

> "Do you give the horse his might?
>> Do you clothe his neck with a mane?
> Do you make him leap like the locust?
>> His majestic snorting is terrifying.
> He paws in the valley and exults in his strength;
>> he goes out to meet the weapons.
> He laughs at fear and is not dismayed;
>> he does not turn back from the sword.
> Upon him rattle the quiver,
>> the flashing spear, and the javelin.
> With fierceness and rage he swallows the ground;
>> he cannot stand still at the sound of the trumpet.
> When the trumpet sounds, he says 'Aha!'
>> He smells the battle from afar,
>> the thunder of the captains, and the shouting." (39:19-25)

The way the Lord describes horses, it sounds like He truly takes exceptional pleasure in them. The one animal that can weirdly be loved by both little girls who watch *My Little Pony* and bull riding cowboys. Or by a teen girl in our youth group who rides her rescue horses almost daily, saving them from the fate of being shipped to a glue factory.

God then continues by asking Job, if it was because of him that the hawk soars? Or did he tell the eagle where to build her nest? Or was it him who created the mighty Behemoth?:*

---

*בְּהֵמוֹת (Behemot) is believed to be the plural form of 'behemah,' translating as "beasts" in Hebrew. For it is believed to be the 'Beast of beasts.' Additionally, this word may come from the Egyptian "Pehemout," which means "water-ox." However, it is unclear what the Behemoth and Leviathan are, though there are several theories of what they could be. Such as:

"Behold, Behemoth,

which I made as I made you;

he eats grass like an ox.

Behold, his strength in his loins,

and his power in the muscles of his belly.

He makes his tail stiff like a cedar;

the sinews of his thighs are knit together.

His bones are tubes of bronze,

his limbs like bars of iron. . . .

For the mountains yield food for him

where all the wild beasts play. . . .

Can one take him by his eyes,

or pierce his nose with a snare?" (40:15-18, 20, 24).

Or finally, could he fish out the Leviathan† with a hook?

"Can you draw out Leviathan with a fishhook

or press down his tongue with a cord?

Can you put a rope in his nose

or pierce his jaw with a hook? . . .

Will you play with him as with a bird,

or will you put him on a leash for your girls? . . .

Can you fill his skin with harpoons

or his head with fishing spears?

Lay your hands on him;

BEHEMOTH: Hippopotamus, Elephant, Rhinoceros, Water Buffalo[1], *Nigersaurus, Apatosaurus, Ultrasaurus, Brachiosaurs,* or a Giant Cow-like thing.

LEVIATHAN: Crocodile, Whale, Shark, SuperCroc, *Plesiosaurus, Kronosaurus, Tyrannosaurus rex,* Hadrosaur, or a Dragon.

†לִוְיָתָן (Livyatan) literally translates as "twisted" or "coiled," or can also be translated as "sea serpent" or "dragon." In modern Hebrew, it means "whale." However, I haven't seen too many whales who can huff out smoke or breathe fire (Job 41:19-21).

---

[1]"Everybody's got a water buffalo."[6]

remember the battle—you will not do it again! ...

I will not keep silence concerning his limbs,

or his mighty strength, or his goodly frame.

Who can strip off his outer garment?

Who would come near him with a bridle?

Who can open the doors of his face?

Around his teeth is terror.

His back is made of rows of shields,

shut up closely as with a seal. ...

His sneezings flash forth light,

and his eyes are like the eyelids of the dawn.

Out of his mouth go flaming torches;

sparks of fire leap forth.

Out of his nostrils comes forth smoke,

as from a boiling pot and burning rushes.

His breath kindles coals,

and a flame comes forth from his mouth.

In his neck abides strength,

and terror dances before him. ...

His heart is hard as a stone,

hard as the lower millstone. ...

On earth there is not his like,

a creature without fear.

He sees everything that is high;

he is king over all the sons of pride."* (41:1-2, 5, 7-8, 12-15, 18-22,

24, 33-34)

---

*I believe not only did Tolkien take inspiration from the book of Revelation in creating his red dragon, but also from these descriptions in Job of the Leviathan. For compare its description to how the dragon Smaug describes himself to Bilbo:

"I kill where I wish and none dare resist. I laid low the warriors of old and their like is not in the world today. Then I was but young and tender. Now I am old and strong, strong, strong. Thief in the Shadows!" he gloated. "My armour is like tenfold shields, my teeth are swords, my claws spears, the shock of my tail a thunderbolt, my wings a hurricane, and my breath death!"[7]

Now, the Lord's monologue may sound *harsh* to us, especially compared to *everything* Job had just gone through. . . . But perhaps it was a preemptive measure to discourage Job from sinning in the near future, steering him away from evil? God may have also been reminding Job, that though he was righteous in this case, he was *not* God, not perfect, still sinful flesh. Additionally, Yahweh had to also reverse the curse which Job had casted in chapter 3, when he had tried to undo the day of his birth.

Nevertheless, after the Lord delivers this speech, He doubles Job's blessings—making him even more wealthy than what he was before. (Meaning, he could build another parking garage filled with even more sports cars.) Yet, though this may sound good to us, just remember how much Job had suffered. And the payback, the things he got, don't sound like they equal all that Job had lost . . . Neither a mansion nor a sports car can replace a child. Nor can a child be replaced by another. And Job had lost *ten*. . . .

***

"DO YOU GUYS have any other questions? Or any other comments you would like to say?" I asked, as class was coming to a close. I was surprised when there were none, for we had covered some pretty heavy material. *Hopefully I wasn't too confusing*, I prayed. While also secretly hoping I wouldn't be burned at the stake as a heretic, for saying that Satan may have not been the adversary of Job.

I then made a few announcements of the upcoming Man Camp and Chicks and Chocolate, before one of the young men ended us in prayer. "Heavenly Father . . ." he addressed, as we approached the throne room of God.

NOTES

1. Fig. 1: Blake, William. *Thus did Job continually*. 1805-1810. The Morgan Library and Museum: New York.
2. Fig. 2: Blake, William. *Thy Sons & thy Daughters were eating & drinking Wine in their eldest Brothers house & behold there came a great wind from the Wilderness & smote upon the four faces of the house & it fell upon the young Men & they are Dead*. 1805-1810. The Morgan Library and Museum: New York.
3. Fig. 3: Blake, William. *And when they lifted up their eyes afar off & knew him not they lifted up their voice & wept, and rent every Man his mantle & sprinkled dust upon their heads towards heaven*. 1805-1810. The Morgan Library and Museum: New York.
4. Fig. 4: Blake, William. *The Just Upright Man is laughed to scorn*. 1805-1810. The Morgan Library and Museum: New York.
5. Fig. 5: Blake, William. *Let the Day perish wherin I was Born*. 1805-1810. The Morgan Library and Museum: New York.
6. *Where's God When I'm S-Scared?*. Dir. Phil Vischer. Big Idea Productions, 1993. DVD.
7. Tolkien, J. R. R. *The Hobbit: Or There and Back Again*. NY: Random House Publishing Group, 1997. Print. p. 226.
8. Fig. 6: Blake, William. *So the Lord blessed the latter end of Job more than the beginning*. 1805-1810. The Morgan Library and Museum: New York.
9. Fig. 7: Blake, William. *Behold now Behemoth which I made with thee*. 1805-1810. The Morgan Library and Museum: New York.

CHAPTER 6

MOSES, AARON, & JOSHUA:

WHY IT'S OKAY TO DRINK SHEEP'S BLOOD

"**A**men," I repeated before lifting my head. A reverent silence then took hold of the auditorium.

Patiently, I waited for the silver communion tray to be passed to me, so that I could participate in the remembrance of the Crucifixion. Waiting to break off a piece of the cracker that symbolized Christ's body which was broken for us. That communion was a little more . . . I don't want to say 'special,' but it sort of was. For just earlier that morning in Sunday school, we had talked about the event which had been the launch pad for the Eucharist—the Passover.

***

"TURN WITH ME, to Exodus chapter 12," I began. Once everyone was there, we began to read of the first Passover. Of the instructions which God had given to Moses and to Aaron to share with His people. A feast of remembrance, to remember when they were freed:

> Tell all the congregation of Israel that on the tenth day of this month every man shall take a lamb according to their fathers' houses, a lamb for a household. And if the household is too small for a lamb, then he and his nearest neighbor shall take according to the number of persons; according to what each can eat you shall make your count for the lamb. Your lamb shall be without blemish, a male a year old. You

93

may take it from the sheep or from the goats, and you shall keep it until the fourteenth day of this month, when the whole assembly of the congregation of Israel shall kill their lambs at twilight. (Exodus 12:3-6)

The Hebrews were told how each household was to take a lamb, and to sacrifice it. They were then commanded to take some of its blood and to smear it on their doorposts with hyssop branches, before eating its cooked meat with bitter herbs and unleavened bread. The herbs to remind them of the bitterness of slavery. And the unleavened bread, because they were to be ready to leave at *any* moment—to finally leave Egypt, to be free from their bondage; therefore, they didn't have time to wait for it to rise. Which is also why they were to eat fully dressed with their sandals on their feet and their walking sticks in their hands. (Just as we should be prepared to leave at *any* moment, for Jesus to free us from the world, from our bondage:

"Therefore, stay awake, for you do not know on what day your Lord is coming. But know this, that if the master of the house had known in what part of the night the thief was coming, he would have stayed awake and would not have let his house be broken into. Therefore you also must be ready, for the Son of Man is coming at an hour you do not expect." (Matthew 24:42-44))

The Lord had prepared one final plague against Egypt, to demonstrate His power, that *He* is God. This was Round 10 in the match Yahweh vs. the gods of Egypt. For in each plague, God had demonstrated that He was more powerful than any of the Egyptian deities. That He is the Master of the Nile, not Hapi (which made Hapi, very unhappy).

That He is the God of the Sun, not Ra. That He is the King of Egypt—not Pharaoh. Pharaoh was the last god that Yahweh had to conquer, for the Egyptians believed that the pharaoh was the embodiment of Horus, a sky god.

Just as Pharaoh had killed the children of the Hebrews, so too had God planned to slaughter the children of the Egyptians, for the Lord is an Avenger. That is why the Israelites were to slaughter lambs and to smear their blood upon their doorposts. For if *Yahweh* saw the blood upon the door, He would 'passover' to the next, sparing death.* Similarly, in how Rahab the prostitute was later spared through faith, saved from the judgment of Jericho by displaying a scarlet cord from her window. Scarlet being the color of blood (Joshua 2, 6:22-25). Or similarly, how if the doorposts of our hearts are covered by the Holy Spirit, will He passover us on the Day of Judgement, sparing death. The Israelites were to sacrifice a lamb to save the lives of their households, just as Jesus was the Lamb who was slaughtered to save us. Paul makes reference to this in 1 Corinthians 5:6-8, as he encourages the church in Corinth to get rid of the old leaven, and feast on "the unleavened bread of sincerity and truth." For Jesus is our Passover Lamb.

So Yahweh stretched out His hand against Egypt. I can't help but to

---

*Notice in Exodus 11:4-7, 12:12-13 and 29, that Yahweh is the one who strikes down the firstborns, not an angel of death. The concept of an angel of death or Grim Reaper character is found within many religions; however, there is no support for such a being in the Bible. True, sometimes God does use angels for killing (the angel of the LORD in Number 22:22-41, 2 Samuel 24:15-25, 2 Kings 19:35, 1 Chronicles 21:14-30, Acts 12:21-23; "a company of destroying angels" in Psalms 78:49, and four angels in Revelation 9:14-15); however, this is not the case in Exodus. Nor is there one angel within the Bible whom is specifically bestowed the title, 'the angel of death.' Arguably, one could say that Yahweh may have used an angel to strike down the firstborns, since sometimes God and angels are difficult to distinguish from one another within ambiguous language; however, it would not be known as the angel of death, but 'the destroyer,' who the LORD would not allow to enter into a home with blood on its doorpost (Exodus 12:23). Though Exodus itself does not mention if the destroyer is an angel or not.

think of the creepy scene in *The Prince of Egypt* when I imagine this plague. Seeing the white wisp that stole life in the sound of a breath. [Goodness, gave myself chills when I wrote that.] But that night . . . was *devastating*. So devastating indeed, that it wasn't the Nile turned to blood, the locusts which devoured the crops, or the boils which convinced Pharaoh to release the Israelites. It was the loss of his firstborn. And more than likely, not only did he lose his heir, but *several* children too. For like the Jews, the Egyptians believed their bloodline was passed on through the mother, not the father.* Meaning that the Pharaoh's many concubines could have born to Pharaoh many firstborns.

Firstborn plays an important theme in this section. It is the firstborns who were killed if there was no blood on the doorpost, and at the start of Chapter 13, God tells His people to consecrate their firstborns to Him. Just as it was His firstborn whom He sacrificed for

---

*This is most likely because back in the day, before there was DNA testing, you could prove who the mother was (whom the baby comes out of), but not necessarily who the father was. This is why Timothy was still a Jew though his father was a Greek, because his mother was a Jew (which is the very reason why Paul circumcises him . . .).

us.

Finally, Pharaoh lets God's people go. They are free! Free from slavery! Free to embark on their adventure to the Promise Land! Just as we are free when we're baptized in the blood of Christ! Free from slavery! Free from sin! Free to embark on our adventure to the Promise Land! Heaven!

———

IN THE WILDERNESS, we get another glimpse of Jesus. In Exodus 16, the people are grumbling for they are hungry. Though they have steak and lamb chops all around them, they gripe to Moses that they don't have any food: "Waa, Moses I'm hungry. I wish I would have died in Egypt. Waa, get me something to eat. Waa, you brought us out here to die." "Hey, if you're taking orders, can I get a McDouble, please? Hold the pickles."

And it's easy for us to point fingers, yet I don't know about you, but I'm guilty of the very same thing: "God, I know you just gave me some scholarships, but I really need a new car too. One which I can roll down the left window without it trying to come out of the door, and with working air-conditioning. And with tires that don't pop in the driveway. And I need a better phone with a battery which doesn't die so fast when I play my games."

Griping is easy. Contenting, not so much. Just because Thanksgiving is in November, doesn't mean it's only in November which we need to remember to be thankful, to praise God for His gifts and blessings. Just as we shouldn't just think of Jesus' birth on Christmas, or the Crucifixion and the Resurrection only on Easter and on Sundays.

God heard the grumbling of His people, and so He opened the storehouses of heaven and gave to them bread:

And when the dew had gone up, there was on the face of the wilderness a fine, flake-like thing, fine as frost on the ground. When the people of Israel saw it, they said to one another, "What is it?" For they did not know what it was. And Moses said to them, 'It is the bread that the LORD has given you to eat. (Exodus 16:14-15)

Haha, so imagine you're an Israelite. You go to bed one night in your tent. You roll around a little, trying to find a spot that's not so rocky, before you finally get to sleep. You wake up in the morning, most in likely because your bladder tells you it's time to go. And as you open the flap of your tent, you see this weird white stuff everywhere. "What is it?" asked the Israelites, or מָ֣ן ה֔וּא ("Man-hu?") in Hebrew, which is where manna gets its name from.

But you see this stuff that looks like snow. I don't know about you, but I think my first instinct would probably be to roll around in it. Make some manna angels, maybe even make a manna-man named Olaf who likes warm hugs.

But Logan, you're not supposed to play with your food.

. . . Anyways, so Moses explains to them about this food. And exactly what to do with it:

"This is what the LORD has commanded: 'Gather of it, each one of you, as much as he can eat. You shall each take an omer, according to the number of the persons that each of you has in his tent.'" And the people of Israel did so. They gathered, some more, some less. But when they measured it with an omer, whoever gathered much had nothing left over, and whoever gathered little had no lack. Each of them gathered as much as he could eat. And Moses said to them, "Let no one leave any of it over till the morning." But they did not listen to Moses.

Some left part of it till the morning, and it bred worms and stank. And Moses was angry with them. Morning by morning they gathered it, each as much as he could eat; but when the sun grew hot, it melted [like snowmen].

On the sixth day they gathered twice as much bread, two omers each. And when all the leaders of the congregation came and told Moses, he said to them, "This is what the LORD has commanded: 'Tomorrow is a day of solemn rest, a holy Sabbath to the LORD; bake what you will bake and boil what you will boil, and all that is left over lay aside to be kept till the morning.'" So they laid it aside till the morning, as Moses commanded them, and it did not stink, and there were no worms in it. Moses said, "Eat it today, for today is a Sabbath to the LORD; today you will not find it in the field. Six days you shall gather it, but on the seventh day, which is a Sabbath, there will be none."...

Now the house of Israel called its name manna. It was like coriander seed, white, and the taste of it was like wafers made with honey. (Exodus 16:16-26, 31).

Moses explains to the people they are only to gather a day's portion (with the exception of the sixth day) and eat it. For the expiration date for manna is *much* sooner than for Twinkies, since it goes bad before the next day. This was a daily reminder to the Israelites that God was their Provider. The Father who would bless them with bread instead of stones. Just as He would later send another kind of bread from heaven.

O THE LITTLE town of Bethlehem. The name for this town is a compound word formed by two words. 'Bet,' which comes from the word בַּיִת (bayit) and means 'house,' and לֶחֶם (leḥem) which means 'bread.' בֵּית לֶחֶם (Beṭleḥem) literally means, the 'house of bread.' Is it any coincidence, that the Bread of Life was born in the House of Bread?

> Lifting up his eyes, then, and seeing that a large crowd was coming toward him, Jesus said to Philip, "Where are we to buy bread, so that these people may eat?" He said this to test him, for he himself knew what he would do. Philip answered him, "Two hundred denarii worth of bread would not be enough for each of them to get a little." (John 6:5-7)

Jesus puts Philip in a difficult situation, as he does and still does to all of his disciples. John tells us that Jesus was "testing" him; he already knew what he was going to do. You have to wonder then if he asked this question with a smile. I think too often we picture Jesus as being this reverent character, and his humor almost never leaves the pages of the Gospel. He is God, and God has a sense of humor. After all, He invented it. He is the one who created the duck-billed platypus and the noise that farts make. And Jesus was also human, for if he didn't have a sense of humor, he would have been a robot. Honestly, was Jesus 100% serious when he told Peter and Andrew, "Follow me, and I will make you fishers of men" (Matthew 4:19)? Or, was he being punny, using their lingo to relate to them, "I'm gonna help you fishermen catch men."

There's a scene in *The Passion of the Christ* that I love. It's of Jesus interacting with his mother. She's coming outside, calling him in for dinner, and they joke about the tall table that he's making for a rich man. "Does he like to eat standing up?" Mary asks. Which Jesus responds, "No. He prefers to eat like . . . so." Jesus then pretends to sit in the air, talking about how a tall table needs tall chairs, but he hasn't made them yet. Mary mimics him, she too sitting in the air. She then pretends to pour herself a cup of water, with Jesus back on his feet, smiling, chuckling at her. "This will never catch on!" she exclaims, before telling Jesus to take off his dirty apron before coming into the house, and to wash his hands. Jesus of course obeys his mother, but he also playfully throws some of the water she poured into his hands at her face, before giving his mom a loving kiss.

No, this scene is nowhere to be found in the Bible, but I love it because it depicts how human Jesus was. A man who could joke, tease, and have fun. Yes, he was also blunt and honest, but he was always loving.

SO PHILIP WAS sweating bullets, probably baffled how his rabbi expected him to feed all these people. "It would take more than 200 days wages to feed all them!" he exclaims. Then Andrew brings a small boy to Jesus, with five dinner rolls and two anchovies, and Jesus uses that small portion, to feed the crowd:

Jesus then took the loaves, and when he had given thanks, he distributed them to those who were seated. So also the fish, as much as they

101

wanted. And when they had eaten their fill, he told his disciples, "Gather up the leftover fragments, that nothing may be lost." So they gathered them up and filled twelve baskets with fragments from the five barley loaves left by those who had eaten. (John 6:11-13)*

No one left that day hungry, everyone eating their fill with twelve baskets left over. And if Jesus' bread was anything like his wine, it was only the best.

Jesus then said to them, "Truly, truly, I say to you, it was not Moses who gave you the bread from heaven, but my Father gives you the true bread from heaven. For the bread of God is he who comes down from heaven and gives life to the world." They said to him, "Sir, give us this bread always."

Jesus said to them, "I am the bread of life; whoever comes to me shall not hunger, and whoever believes in me shall never thirst." (John 6:32-35)

*Another king who provided bread to others, was David. The man who brought ten loaves to his three older brothers when they were out on the battlefield against the Philistines (1 Samuel 17:17-22), and the king who gave a cake of bread, meat, and raisins to the people of Jerusalem, while he was dancing in his underwear—celebrating the Ark of the Covenant being brought into the city (2 Samuel 6:18-19).

Jesus himself reveals that he is the bread of life. A truth he makes known the day after he fed the 5,000 with bread and fish. That just as manna came from the heavens, so too did he come from heaven to accomplish the Father's will. That whosoever eats of his flesh and drinks of his blood will have eternal life. (A comparison he will again make at the Last Supper.) And he purposefully sounds like he is talking literally of cannibalism* too, to weed out those who will truly follow him, and those who will only follow him because of free food. For Jesus wanted genuine followers, a desire shared by his Father. Not those he would have to bribe, like those who called out, "Caesar is Lord!" because of the free bread the emperor would hand out to the citizens of Rome. As Harding's president, Dr. Bruce McLarty, points out in his book, *Journey of Faith: Walking with Jesus Through the Gospel of John*:

> His words must have sounded like the ravings of a madman to many in the crowd, but Jesus was emphasizing that the only proper relationship with the Son of Man is a consuming one. Jesus wanted more than mere acquaintances, friends, soldiers, or subjects. Jesus insisted that each true follower "abides in Me, and I in him" (6:56). He had to be closer to His followers than a king to his people, a general to his army, or a rabbi to his students. Jesus insisted on being like bread digested and absorbed by every cell in their bodies. In other words, Jesus was saying, "You must let Me into your innermost being."
>
> This message of Jesus is as shocking and threatening today as it

---

*Three of the most common crimes which the First Century Church were accused of, were cannibalism, incest, and atheism. The charges of cannibalism and incest came from the misunderstanding of outsiders not knowing the lingo of the Church, believing that these Christians were actually eating and drinking human flesh and blood, and that they were actually marrying their brothers and sisters. And the Church was accused to be atheists, because she refused to participate in communal ceremonies to worship the Roman gods and emperors.

was two thousand years ago. He still rejects a casual relationship with those who wish to be His followers. He still wants to be as close to us as the blood in our veins, the breath in our lungs, or the marrow in our bones. He demands to be allowed into the secret places of our lives, whether it is our bank accounts, our marriages, or our ambitions. As the Bread of Life, He will accept nothing less than a 100 percent intimate relationship with us.[4]

Jesus wants a CLOSE relationship with us. I'm sure he was heartbroken seeing this crowd disperse from him after hearing these challenging words. Yet, he did not chase after them with a softer or watered down message. For what he asks is *not* facile. He wants *all* of us. Heart, soul, strength, and mind (Matthew 22:37, Luke 10:27).*

And just as manna had a short expiration date, so too was the Son of Man, who was here for only a little while. I mean his ministry was only about three years long, yet, he made such a *huge* difference, the biggest mark in all of history. And one day, he'll descend from heaven again!†

JESUS ALSO REVEALS that not only is he the bread of life, but he is also the living water, just as he tells the woman at the well, "Everyone

---

*Following Jesus is *not* easy. There are many other harsh teachings Jesus also speaks of, as the cost that comes in choosing him. Such as Jesus telling the rich young ruler to sell all of his possessions (Matthew 19:16-30, Mark 10:17-31), him teaching that he brought not peace but a sword (Matthew 10:34-39), or saying, "Leave the dead to bury their own dead" (Luke 9:57-62).

†In Judges, Gideon hears an interesting dream that involves God's salvation for the Israelites, coming in the form of a barley loaf: "When Gideon came, behold, a man was telling a dream to his comrade. And he said, 'Behold, I dreamed a dream, and behold, a cake of barley bread tumbled into the camp of Midian and came to the tent and struck it so that it fell and turned it upside down, so that the tent lay flat.' And his comrade answered, 'This is no other than the sword of Gideon the son of Joash, a man of Israel; God has given into his hand Midian and all the camp.'

As soon as Gideon heard the telling of the dream and its interpretation, he worshiped. And he returned to the camp of Israel and said, 'Arise, for the LORD has given the host of Midian into your hand.'" (7:13-15)

who drinks of this water will be thirsty again, but whoever drinks of the water that I will give him will never be thirsty again. The water that I will give him will become in him a spring of water welling up to eternal life" (John 4:13-14).

Jesus is the living water. The one who if we drink his blood, we will gain eternal life. Now no, Jesus is not trying to create a coven of vampires, but he reveals in an intimate way that eternal life comes from his blood which was shed upon the cross. This theme in John is perhaps most prevalent when Jesus' heart is pierced: "But one of the soldiers pierced his side with a spear, and at once there came out blood and water" (John 19:34). John is the only one who records this event in the Gospels. Medically, the explanation of both water and blood pouring out from Jesus' body separately is believed to be pleural effusion. Symbolically, this event is so much more. Because of his blood, a river of life pours out from Jesus' body, just like the river of life which flows out from the temple in Ezekiel (47:1-2) and from the throne of God in Revelation (22:1-5).

In one of his letters, Paul also makes an allusion to Jesus being the source of living water for the Israelites, during their wandering in the wilderness:

> For I do not want you to be unaware, brothers, that our fathers were all under the cloud, and all passed through the sea, and all were baptized into Moses in the cloud and in the sea, and all ate the same spiritual food, and all drank the same spiritual drink. For they drank from the spiritual Rock that followed them, and the Rock was Christ. (I Corinthians 10:1-4)

It is believed, that the apostle is drawing from an extra biblical tradition that was contemporary to him, in which the stone that Moses struck followed the Israelites in their wandering, this rolling stone being the source of their water.* If this is truly an accurate detail and not merely a metaphor instead, this would explain why there are two events in which Moses strikes the rock (Exodus 17:1-7, Numbers 20:2 -13). True, this is a weird concept to consider, that Jesus may have been a moving rock tailing the Hebrews; however, is it any more bizarre than them following a pillar of cloud and fire?

(It also wouldn't be the first time, for Jesus to be represented as a

---

*Known sources of this tradition roughly date from around the New Testament era to the medieval period. Three of these sources have been included below:

Pseudo-Philo's Book of Biblical Antiquities
Now he led his people out into the wilderness; for forty years he rained down for them bread from heaven and brought quail to them from the sea and brought forth *a well of water to follow them.*

And there [in the desert] he commanded him [Moses] many things and showed him the tree of life, from which he cut off and took and threw into Marah, and the water of Marah became sweet. *And it [the water] followed them in the wilderness forty years and went up to the mountain with them and went down into the plains.*

And after Moses died, the manna stopped descending upon the sons of Israel, and they began to eat from the fruits of the land. And these are the three things that God gave to his people on account of the three persons; that is the well of the water of Marah for Miriam and the pillar of cloud for Aaron and the manna for Moses. And when these came to their end [i.e., died], these three things were taken away from them. (10:7, 11:15, 20:8)[5]

Tosephta Sukka
And so the well which was with the Israelites in the wilderness was a rock, the size of a large round vessel, surging and gurgling upward, as from the mouth of its little flask, *rising with them up onto the mountains, and going down with them into the valleys. Wherever the Israelites would encamp, it made camp with them*, on a high place, opposite the entry of the Tent of Meeting. The princes of Israel come and surround it with their staffs, and they sing a song concerning it: *Spring up, O Well! Sing to it; [the well which the princes dug, which the nobles of the people delved with the scepter and with their staves]* (3:11)[6]

Targum Onqelos to Num 21:16-20
At that time the well was *given* to them, that is the well about which the Lord told Moses, "Gather the people together, and I *will give* them water." So Israel offered this praise, "Rise O well, sing to it." The well which the princes dug, the leaders of the people dug, the scribes, with their staffs, and *it was given to them*, since wilderness <times>. Now since *it was given to them, it went down with them to the valleys*, and from the valleys it went up with them to the high country. And from the high country to the descents of the Moabite fields, at the summit of the height, which looks out towards Beth Yeshimon.[7]

rock:*

"As you looked, a stone was cut out by no human hand, and it struck the image on its feet of iron and clay, and broke them in pieces. Then the iron, the clay, the bronze, the silver, and the gold, all together were broken in pieces, and became like the chaff of the summer threshing floors; and the wind carried them away, so that not a trace of them could be found. But the stone that struck the image became a great mountain and filled the whole earth. . . .

"As you saw the iron mixed with soft clay, so they will mix with one another in marriage, but they will not hold together, just as iron does not mix with clay. And in the days of those kings the God of heaven will set up a kingdom that shall never be destroyed, nor shall the kingdom be left to another people. It shall break in pieces all these kingdoms and bring them to an end, and it shall stand forever, just as you saw that a stone was cut from a mountain by no human hand, and that it broke in pieces the iron, the bronze, the clay, the silver, and

---

*In his song in Deuteronomy 32, Moses both calls God "Rock" again and again, and equates Him to some rocky metaphors: "He made him ride on the high places of the land, and he ate the produce of the field, and he suckled him with honey out of the rock, and oil out of the flinty rock." (13)

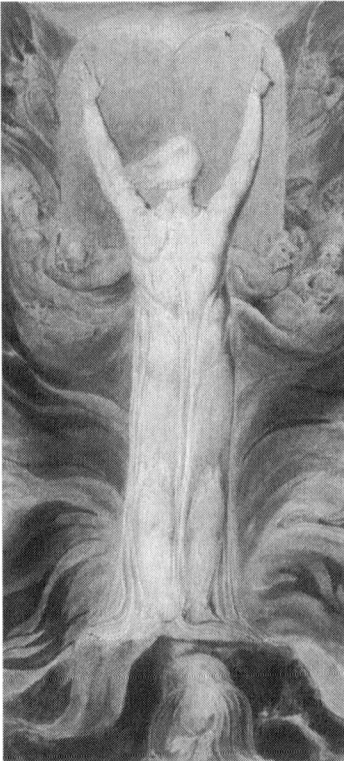

the gold. A great God has made known to the king what shall be after this. The dream is certain, and its interpretation sure." (Daniel 2:34-35, 43-45))

———

FOR QUITE SOME time, I've playfully threatened each time I've heard a teen joke about stealing another's hat, or crossing your fingers isn't lying, or threatening to kill the other (without the love of the Lord), of giving a devo over the Ten Commandments. Years of empty threats were finally fulfilled in a camp devo that summer, which went something like this:

"Three months after leaving Egypt. After being saved from the Egyptians by the Red Sea, by water, just as we're saved through water at baptism, the Israelites arrive at Mount Sinai. It is here where Yahweh says He will reveal Himself to His people. And it is here where He intends to begin to forge them into a nation.

"So the people prepare themselves. They wash their clothes, take their baths, abstain from sex, three days of preparation to meet their God. He said He would appear to them on the mountain, but *no* one was to touch it. No person, no animal, nothing. The consequence for doing so—death. To be stoned or shot.

"The people consecrated themselves, and the Lord came. It was crazy! There was thunder and lightning, a trumpet blast. And the mountain

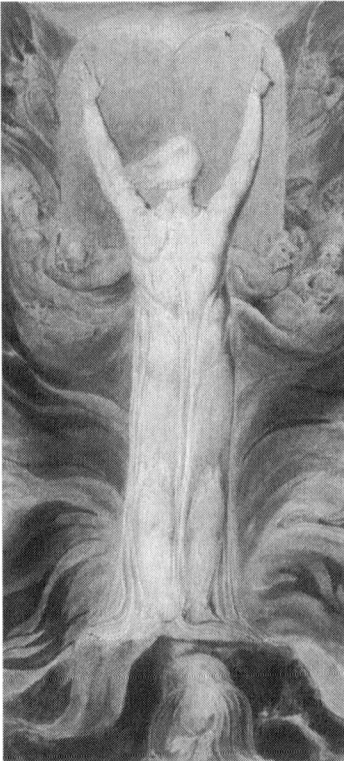

was wrapped in smoke and God came down in fire! The mountain was wrapped in darkness, yet it was in this very darkness where the Lord was. Which is funny. For don't we usually think of Him wrapped in light?

"And the people were *afraid* of God. They told Moses to speak for them. They didn't want God to speak to them. The Bible even says in Exodus 20:21, that 'The people stood far off, while Moses drew near to the thick darkness where God was.'

"The Lord descended to the top of the mountain which *no* one was supposed to touch. And He called out to Moses to come up to the top of the mountain, to join Him. And it is from the top of this mountain, where God delivers the Ten Commandments to His people. If you have your Bibles, please turn with me to Exodus 20. Exodus 20 verses 1-17:

"And God spoke all these words, saying,

I. "'I am the LORD your God, who brought you out of the land of Egypt, out of the house of slavery.

'You shall have no other gods before me.

II. 'You shall not make for yourself a carved image, or any likeness of anything that is in heaven above, or that is in the earth beneath, or that is in the water under the earth. You shall not bow down to them or serve them, for I the LORD your God am a jealous God, visiting the iniquity of the fathers on the children to the third and the fourth

generation of those who hate me, but showing steadfast love to thousands of those who love me and keep my commandments.

III. 'You shall not take the name of the LORD your God in vain, for the LORD will not hold him guiltless who takes his name in vain.

IV. 'Remember the Sabbath day, to keep it holy. Six days you shall labor, and do all your work, but the seventh day is a Sabbath to the LORD your God. On it you shall not do any work, you, or your son, or your daughter, your male servant, or your female servant, or your livestock, or the sojourner who is within your gates. For in six days the LORD made heaven and earth, the sea, and all that is in them, and rested on the seventh day. Therefore the LORD blessed the Sabbath day and made it holy.

V. 'Honor your father and your mother, that your days may be long in the land that the LORD your God is giving you.*

VI. 'You shall not murder.

VII. 'You shall not commit adultery.

VIII. "You shall not steal.

IX. 'You shall not bear false witness against your neighbor.

X. 'You shall not covet your neighbor's house; you shall not covet your neighbor's wife, or his male servant, or his female servant, or his ox, or his donkey, or anything that is your neighbor's.'"

After I read these words, I then closed my Bible and asked the question: "The Ten Commandments, were a pretty big deal to the Israelites. I mean God gave them these rules Himself. So my question for you guys, are we still supposed to follow these commandments today?"

The chapel became quite, before one brave soul answered, ". . . No?"

---

*Notice, how this is the only commandment which comes with a blessing. It was also given to adults, something which we often overlook when parenting. For kids and teens are not the only ones who are supposed to honor their parents.

"No? So, it's okay to murder, then?" I asked.

"No. But . . . they're in the Old Law . . ."

"It was a trick question," I quickly stated, throwing out a lifesaver. "Kind of like the trick question Jesus received in Matthew 22. You see, the Pharisees and the Sadducees were asking Jesus questions, trying to trip him up and trap him. They had already asked if they should pay taxes to Rome and what marriage would be like after the resurrection, before a lawyer, of all people, asked Jesus,

> "'Teacher, which is the great commandment in the Law?' And he said to him, 'You shall love the Lord your God with all your heart and with all your soul and with all your mind. This is the great and first commandment. And a second is like it: You shall love your neighbor as yourself. On these two commandments depend all the Law and the Prophets.'" (36-40)

Jesus answers by first quoting the Shema, which is found in Deuteronomy 6:4-9. 'Shema' is just the Hebrew word, 'to hear,' for it begins, "Hear O Israel." And secondly, with Leviticus 19:18*, which is now known as the Golden Rule. Jesus summarizes all Ten Commandments into two. Love God, and love your fellow man.

"So the answer to my earlier question, is 'Yes.' But not because we have too since they're commandments. But because we should want to. We should not murder people not because we're not supposed to, but because we love God and want to do what is holy. If we truly love God, we'll want to do what's right. Yes, as Christians we'll still make some stupid mistakes. But if we truly love Him we'll strive to make

---

*Haha, so in an earlier draft, I had accidentally typed "Leviticus 18:19," which in the words of my proofer, "Says something totally different!": "You shall not approach a woman to uncover her nakedness while she is in her menstrual uncleanness." I'm definitely *grateful* she caught this typo, though this mistake was too funny not to share.

those mistakes less and less because we love Him and don't want to hurt our relationship with Him.

"God gave to Moses the Ten Commandments. He also gave to him other laws for the people to live by: laws for the Sabbath and other festivals, how to construct the Tabernacle* and the Ark of the Covenant, and the duties of the priests and how they should dress, how they should wash themselves before entering the Tabernacle (just as we wash ourselves before entering the Church)—for God was establishing a nation. He gave to them something much more than a rule book of, Da Rules. He gave to them the Law. Gave to them insight how to establish their identity, how to be His people, and how to be like Yahweh.

[God established the priesthood of His people through the bloodline of the Levites. Aaron was to be the first high priest. A representative of the people to God, who would make the sacrifices on their behalf for the forgiveness of their sins. Yet, there was one high priest who was greater than Aaron, greater than the clan of Levi. That priest being—Jesus:

Since then we have a great high priest who has passed through the heavens, Jesus, the Son of God, let us hold fast our confession. For we do not have a high priest who is unable to sympathize with our weak-

*In Hebrew, 'tabernacle' is translated from the noun מִשְׁכָּן (mishkan), which means "a dwelling place." Both the Tabernacle and the Ark of the Covenant were taken with the Israelites wherever they went. And when this tent was pitched, it was to be set up in the very middle of the Israelite's camp (Numbers 2:17). For Yahweh doesn't want to be in the outskirts of our lives, but in the very center of everything we do. He wants more than Sunday, but Sunday—Sunday. Not to only be with us in the church building, but even when we go home, or school, or work—*wherever* we go.

And in the New Testament, John even uses 'tabernacle' once as a verb to describe the coming of Christ: "And the Word became flesh and dwelt [ἐσκήνωσεν (eskenosen)] among us . . ." (1:14). Literally, Jesus "pitched a tent" to be with us. Metaphorically, he decided to leave the comforts of the camper to come out and camp in the woods with us. To be with us, experience what it's like to be bitten by a mosquito or suffer the pain of poison ivy. . . . He dwelt amongst us, suffered pain, trials, even death, to experience what it's like to be human.

nesses, but one who in every respect has been tempted as we are, yet without sin. Let us then with confidence draw near to the throne of grace, that we may receive mercy and find grace to help in time of need.

For every high priest chosen from among men is appointed to act on behalf of men in relation to God, to offer gifts and sacrifices for sins. He can deal gently with the ignorant and wayward, since he himself is beset with weakness. Because of this he is obligated to offer sacrifice for his own sins just as he does for those of the people. And no one takes this honor for himself, but only when called by God, just as Aaron was.

So also Christ did not exalt himself to be made a high priest, but was appointed by him who said to him,

"You are my Son,

today I have begotten you";

as he says also in another place,

"You are a priest forever,

after the order of Melchizedek."

In the days of his flesh, Jesus offered up prayers and supplications, with loud cries and tears, to him who was able to save him from death, and he was heard because of his reverence. Although he was a son, he learned obedience through what he suffered. And being made perfect, he became the source of eternal salvation to all who obey him, being designated by God a high priest after the order of Melchizedek. (Hebrews 4:14-16; 5:1-10)

The writer of Hebrews lets us know how fortunate we are to have a High Priest who can sympathize with us. Not only does he represent us before God, but Jesus knows what it's like to live as a man, to live in a world of sin. For he became one of us, so that he could bring his sacrifice before the Father to rid us of our sins once and for all.

AND WITH THE establishment of the priesthood, came the demand for blood (and fat, for the Lord knows the best part of a steak, that where all the flavor is kept (Leviticus 3:16)). This demand for blood was *steep*. Blood being required for sin, being spilt during festivals, *22,000 oxen* and *120,000 sheep* being sacrificed in the dedication of Solomon's Temple. Gallons upon gallons of blood were split for the people of Israel. To either push back their sins, or arguably, to give advance forgiveness because of Jesus' future sacrifice, kind of like having and driving a car before you've paid it off.[*]

Sheep, goats, doves, and oxen were victims of a holocaust, for no matter how much blood was spilled, "it [was] impossible for the blood of bulls and goats to take away sins" (Hebrews 10:4). The blood of animals was not the solution to man's chronic illness, we *needed* Jesus. And when he finally sacrificed himself upon the altar of the cross, he ended this demand for blood. He became the ultimate sacrifice, his blood finally appeasing the thirst for redemption. Becoming the final sacrifice to appease all sins (Hebrews 10:12-14), putting an end to the demand of the blood of bulls once and for all. . . . That was, until McDonald's came around.]

"**SADLY, AS MOSES** was having this amazing mountaintop experience with God, the people were falling into sin. Moses had been gone for forty days, *forty days*. Which is a long time to be away. Yet it was only

[*]Nowhere does the Bible specifically say, that the sins of man were pushback, or rolled over due to the sacrifices. This is the lingo of man. The lingo of the Bible states many times throughout Leviticus, that after a sacrifice was made, ". . . the priest shall make atonement for them, and they shall be *forgiven*" (Leviticus 4:20). I believe, even in the Old Testament, there was forgiveness. No, it did *not* come from the blood of the bulls or lambs, only from God. But He gave it, because His people were faithful and obeyed His command by sacrificing the bull, knowing too that Jesus' blood would be spilt upon the cross. This same concept can be seen in baptism. Forgiveness does not come from the water, it comes from God alone, and it's made possible because of the blood of Christ. But, I believe, He gives it at baptism, because of the faithfulness of the Christian following His command through the action of being dunked.

forty days ago when the Israelites had seen Yahweh descend upon the mountain. And they were already so eager to worship another. I mean these were the same people who saw the plagues of Egypt, saw the parting of the Red Sea, saw the manna from heaven. . . . Just as their descendants would be the ones to cry out, "Hosanna," at the beginning of a week. Before crying out, "Crucify!" at the end of it. . . . It just, amazes me. Yet, how often are we guilty of doing the same? How often do we worship God on Sundays, but we indulge ourselves in sin on Monday morning or Saturday night? Or how easy is it for us to forget what it's like to be on the mountaintop during church camp or a youth rally, and fall back into a routine of sin when we step off of it?

"And so they come to Aaron, the guy who's supposed to be the first high priest for Yahweh, they come to him and say, 'Aaron, your brother's dead. So we want an idol. This Moses who led us out of Egypt just disappeared, so make us gods. Oh, and we want a calf.' You know, something to this effect. And Aaron does it! Like us so many times, he falls under the negative peer pressure and he makes for the Israelites an idol. Now, we may not be tempted to make golden statues, but how often do we do things to please others? To say things we shouldn't, or to see movies which we should not have, or take a drink or sniff of this?

"So Aaron collects gold from the people, and he makes this golden calf. Now, my question for you all, why a calf?"

It was a question which I had not thought of before until the beginning of that summer, when my own youth minister had brought it up in a devo. Why a calf? I mean, bulls were a common animal to worship, but this wasn't a bull. Nor was it a cow, a heifer, or a steer—it was a calf. So why a calf?

"Because calves, are easy to control," my youth minister had said. He

then elaborated by giving the example of when we had worked cattle earlier that summer. How it was easier to get the calves in the shoots than the cows, because they were smaller, and if they didn't want to go, you could just grab their back legs and drag them in. You can't do that with a cow or a bull. He then talked about how he felt bad for the little bull calves, and had prayed for each one as we had castrated them (he left out the part when we were offered to try rocky mountain oysters . . . ew!). And he couldn't help but to tell his bull riding story. That there had been a little bull calf which had got itself turned around and had charged him. He had safely jumped up the corral and thought the calf had ran past him. So he eased his way back down, only to find his butt on top of the little calf's back—for like a second or two. But he did have the glory to now say he had ridden a bull.

"Why a calf?" I had asked again. ". . . Because calves are easy to control. The Israelites wanted a god which they could control and manipulate. They wanted a god which they didn't have to fear. I mean I don't fear a little calf the way I do a bull. They knew they couldn't put Yahweh in a box, but they could this golden calf. . . . And how often, are we guilty of doing the same? How often do we want something which we can control, or think we can. We each have our own golden calves, our Ba'als, our Asherahs. We have our idols or our things we'd rather do instead of serving God, such as drinking, pornography, or drugs. But we *got* to get rid of them.

"When Moses came down that mountain, he was *furious*. He had already interceded for them to God, Who had wanted just to wipe them out and to start again through Moses. But just as Jesus interceded for us, saved us from the wrath of God, so did Moses intercede for the Israelites.

"So he came down the mountain and was so horrified, that he

threw. He didn't gently toss, he threw the stone tablets with the Ten Commandments written on them, you know like, 'Don't have any another gods before me?' He threw them and they broke. He then, oh this is great, took the golden calf, used the fire to ground it into powder, scattered the powder in the water, and made the people drink it. Doesn't that just sound tasty? I mean who doesn't want golden calf Kool-Aid?

"He then talks to Aaron, asking how he had allowed this to happen. And Aaron blames the people. 'The people came to me and you were gone, and they wanted a god, so I just collected some gold and threw it in the fire and out pops this calf.' Then Moses and the Levites kill a bunch a people.

"After all of this, Moses goes back up the mountain. He first makes atonement for the people's sin. He then cuts new tablets so the Lord can write the Ten Commandments again. And he gets a glowing, holy sunburn on his face from seeing the Shekinah glory, the back of God! Wow! And just think that one day, we won't only get to see the back of God, but we'll get to see Him face to face! Wow!

"Let's pray . . ."

———

IN NUMBERS 21, we find another episode of the Israelites complaining to God:

From Mount Hor they set out by the way to the Red Sea, to go around the land of Edom. And the people became impatient on the way. And the people spoke against God and against Moses, "Why have you brought us up out of Egypt to die in the wilderness? For there is no food and no water, and we loathe this worthless food." (Number 21:4-5)

For *years* the Israelites have been wandering in the wilderness, as punishment for them not having faith in their God to enter into the Promise Land. In their wandering, they gripe about the manna which they have been eating day after day. The food that God has freely provided them with. And they have the audacity to call it '*worthless.*' Yes, I too would grow tired of eating the same thing again and again and again. And who knows how many recipes you can invent to use manna in: manna stew, manna tacos, manna pizza. But they call God's food 'worthless.' And God is *not* happy:

Then the LORD sent fiery serpents among the people, and they bit the people, so that many people of Israel died. And the people came to Moses and said, "We have sinned, for we have spoken against the LORD and against you. Pray to the LORD, that he take away the serpents from us." So Moses prayed for the people. And the LORD said to Moses, "Make a fiery serpent and set it on a pole, and everyone who is bitten, when he sees it, shall live." So Moses made a bronze serpent and set it on a pole. And if a serpent bit anyone, he would look at the bronze serpent and live.* (Number 21:6-9)

Just as God had plagued the Egyptians with frogs, flies, and locusts,

---

*Sadly, this very serpent, this symbol of salvation, would later become an idol worshipped by Judah, as discovered in 2 Kings 18:4, "He [Hezekiah] removed the high places and broke the pillars and cut down the Asherah. And he broke in pieces the bronze serpent that Moses had made, for until those days the people of Israel had made offerings to it (it was called Nehushtan)."

He plagues His people with venomous snakes. The Israelites felt the burn of the venom in their veins, and many of them even died from these serpents, before they came to Moses. They confessed their sins and asked God's prophet for salvation. And so Moses prays for them, and the Lord provides grace. He has Moses forge a bronze snake and place it on a pole, sounding like it was something which looked similar to the Rod of Asclepius or a caduceus (Hermes' staff), both of which are used as medical symbols today. And if the people looked upon this serpent, they would be saved. God used, no, not St. Patrick, but Moses to deliver His people from the hissing reptiles that He had sent.

We have been plagued by sin. We all have been effected by its venom, the poison coursing through our veins, and some have even died because of it. However, if we confess our sins and cry out for salvation, and look upon the man who was stretched upon a cross, we can be saved from it. Just as Jesus told Nicodemus in John 3:14-15: "And as Moses lifted up the serpent in the wilderness, so must the Son of

Man be lifted up, that whoever believes in him may have eternal life." It's ironic, that the people were saved by a bronze snake, when it had been a snake that had tempted man to fall. Almost as ironic, as a God becoming a man.

———

"AND WHO LED the Israelites into the Promise Land?" I asked my Sunday school class.

"Moses," answered a few.

"Wait, who?" I asked again.

They looked at me confused for a moment, before clarity overcame their brain farts, "Oh, Joshua."

"Yes, Joshua. And check this out. This is cool! And it's something we really can't see in the English translations." I uncapped a dry erase marker and scribbled two scarlet words up on the board:

יְהוֹשֻׁ֫עַ

יֵשׁ֫וּעַ

"The first, you pronounce as 'Yehoshua,' and the second is 'Yeshua.' Now, I know you can't read Hebrew, but what do you notice about these two words?"

"They're similar," came an answer.

"True. But not only are they similar, but they're in fact the same name. See, if I erase these two letters in Yehoshua here, [the hei and the ḥolam-vav] and change these dots . . ."

יֵ שׁ֫וּעַ

"We get Yeshua. Isn't that cool?! This is because Joshua and Jesus, in Hebrew, is the same name, just a little different spelling. Kind of like spelling Kaleb with either a 'C' or a 'K.' It's the same name, but spelled differently. And they both mean, 'Yahweh saves,' or 'Yahweh is salvation.'"

"Then why do we pronounce his name 'Jesus?'" asked a teen.

"Great question. This is because 'Jesus' in English, evolved from the Latin form of his name, 'Iesus.' And this Latin form stemmed from the Greek 'Iésous,'* instead of the Hebrew, 'Yeshua,' since that was the language which the New Testament was written in."

"Okay," he said, nodding his head.

"And just as Joshua led the Israelites into the Promise Land, so will Jesus lead us into the Promise Land, to heaven!" I exclaimed, finally connecting the dots. "For Jesus is our salvation!"

***

THANK YOU, I THOUGHT, as I took the cup and drank the grape juice. The symbolic remembrance of the Lamb who had given up his life, to cleanse the doorposts of my heart. *"Drink of it, all of you, for this is my blood of the covenant, which is poured out for many for the forgiveness of sins,"* Jesus' words echoed within my head. Before I passed the tray to the friend beside me.

NOTES

1. Fig. 1: Blake, William. *Pestilence: Death of The First Born.* 1805. Museum of Fine Arts: Boston.
2. Fig. 2: Eric Feather. *Christ Feeding the Five Thousand.*
3. Fig. 3: *The Miracle of the Loaves and the Fishes.* 6th century. Basilica di Sant'Apollinare Nuovo: Ravenna, Italy.
4. McLarty, Bruce. *Journey of Faith: Walking with Jesus Through the Gospel of John.* Searcy, AR: Resource Publications, 2015. Print. p. 133.
5. Harrington, D. J., ed. James H. Charlesworth. *The Old Testament* Pseudepigrapha. 2 vols. Garden City, NY: Doubleday, 1983. Print. p. 2.317, 319, 329.
6. Neusner, Jacob. *The Tosefta, Translated from the Hebrew.* 6 vols. New York: Ktav

---

*Ἰησοῦς

Publ. House, 1981. Print. p. 2.220.

7. Grossfeld, Bernard. *The Aramaic Bible: The Targum Onqelos to Leviticus and the Targum Onqelos to Numbers*, vol. 8. Wilmington, DE: Michael Glazier, 1988. p. 126.

8. Fig. 4: Blake, William. *Moses Striking the Rock*. 1805. Philadelphia Museum of Art.

9. Fig. 5: Blake, William. *God Writing Upon the Tables of the Covenant*. 1805. Scottish National Gallery.

10. Fig. 6: Blake, William. *Moses Receiving the Law*. 1780. Yale Center for British Art: New Haven, Connecticut.

11. Fig. 7: Blake, William. *Moses Indignant at the Golden Calf*. 1799-1800. Tate Britain: London.

12. Fig. 8: Blake, William. *Moses Erecting the Brazen Serpent*. 1801-1803. Museum of Fine Arts: Boston.

Chapter 7

Ruth & Boaz:

How to Get a Wife 101

Should I get a plant? I debated with myself. *I can't get a dog. And I do love to see things grow . . .*

What time do you have to take care of it?

True. It would be awkward asking someone to house sit it. Or the teens would laugh and make fun of me if I took it with me to camp and kept it in the cabin. . . . Maybe next year, (if you come back).

Though I have yet to have a garden of my own, I love messing with plants (excluding poison ivy). There's just something cool about planting something, taking care of it, and seeing it grow—like pumpkins. Pumpkins are fun! Because after they get big enough, you don't even have to weed them. They strangle any plant that's around them.

However, there is a small difference between pruning roses for older ladies (which is a rewarding experience), and gleaning wheat for them.

***

RUTH, IS A very short book. But it's a book compacted with amazing love.

It begins with a prologue, explaining that this story was during the time of the judges. A time before there was a human king on the throne in Israel. And there was a *famine*. Meaning, that it was during a time which the Israelites were being punished for their sin. So since there was little food, a man by the name of My God is King (Elimelech),* from the House of Bread (Bethlehem), took his family to the foreign country of Moab. Taking his wife, Pleasant (Naomi), and their two sons, Sickness (Mahlon) and Consumption (Chilion), which is ironic, because they are leaving since there is no bread in the House of Bread.

And who wouldn't want parents like Elimelech and Naomi? You're going through a rough season in life, so you name your kids "Sickness" and "Consumption." That's like naming a child "Cancer" or "Bankrupt" during a pretty rough year. I mean, can you imagine that conversation? Dad's sitting on the couch watching the news, and his little girl comes up and asks him, "Daddy, why did you name me 'Cancer?'"

"Because Pumpkin, you were born in the year your mom was diagnosed with leukemia."

Just like if Chilion had walked up to Elimelech, "Dad, why did you name me, 'Consumption?'"

"Because son, when we were starving, you were born. And began to eat what little food we had. I mean, both me and your mom had to cut our rations in half just to feed ya." Goodness, just terrible.

Seriously, what were the Israelites thinking sometimes when naming their kids? I mean, Lo-ammi ("Not My People")—though in Hosea's defense, God did tell him to name his son that self-confidence booster: "Hey, Dad."

"Yes, Not My People?"

". . . Never mind."

"Okay. Hey, go call your sister in for dinner."

"Yes, Dad. Hey No Mercy, it's time to eat."

---

*Names play an important role in the story of Ruth.

But I guess we don't really have room to talk either. After all, Michael Jackson did name one of his kids Blanket. Or there is the commonality in America of choosing names from characters in movies, videogames, and romance novels . . .

So anyways, the Elimelech family packs up and moves to Moab. As they settle into their new home, My God is King kicks the bucket. Sickness and Consumption marry Neck (Orpah) and Companion (Ruth), but ten years later, Sickness and Consumption die too. Now, it's unclear if this trilogy of men die from natural causes, or as punishment for leaving Israel. Nevertheless, three husbands pass away, leaving three widows to fend for themselves in a very patriarchal society.

Pleasant then gets word while in the fields of Moab, that Yahweh had given Israel food—that the famine was now over. So she makes plans to return to her home, but not before demonstrating her ḥesed. Ḥesed (חֶסֶד), is one of the key themes in the book of Ruth. Ḥesed is a covenantal love, or mercy,* and Pleasant shows her ḥesed at this mo-

*In the *ESV* 'ḥesed' is translated as 'kindness;' however, ḥesed is much more than that. Think of it more as a type of love which is given, but it's not deserved/earned.

ment. She tells her daughters-in-law's that they should both return to their families, that they're young and can still find good husbands for themselves. They weep together, and both Neck and Companion try to convince Pleasant that they should come with her. But Pleasant tells them:

> "Turn back, my daughters; why will you go with me? Have I yet sons in my womb that they may become your husbands? Turn back, my daughters; go your way, for I am too old to have a husband. If I should say I have hope, even if I should have a husband this night and should bear sons, would you therefore wait till they were grown? Would you therefore refrain from marrying? No, my daughters, for it is exceedingly *bitter* to me for your sake that the hand of the LORD has gone out against me." (1:12-13)

And so they cry together again after Pleasant's speech. And Neck, turns her neck on her mother-in-law and leaves. But Companion refuses and clings to Pleasant, before she breaks into Chris Tomlin:

> But Ruth said, "Do not urge me to leave you or to return from following you. For where you go I will go, and where you lodge I will lodge. Your people shall be my people, and your God my God. Where you die I will die, and there will I be buried. May the LORD do so to me and more also if anything but death parts me from you." (1:16-17)

Well, I guess Chris Tomlin breaks into Ruth; anyways, Ruth makes an oath to her mother-in-law which demonstrates her ḥesed. "Where you go, I'll go. Where you stay, I'll stay. Your people shall be my people, and your God my God." "Your God my God," is perhaps the most important part of this oath. For Chemosh was the god of Moab (2

Kings 23:13), not Yahweh. Not only is Ruth willing to leave her home and family to go to a strange land, but she's willing to give up even her religion—to give up *everything* to take care of her mother-in-law. That, is ḥesed indeed. And it shows the *amazing* heart that Ruth possessed within her.

I THINK THIS would be the perfect time to point out, that women, are *amazing*! A truth that is seen more than once within the Bible. Such as the love and courage Jochebed showed in harboring her baby boy from the Pharaoh. *The* Pharaoh. The ruler who could take her life with but a word. Raising him for three months in her home, before smuggling him to the Nile in a basket (Exodus 2:1-10). Or the love and sacrifice Mary of Bethany showed, by the gift she gave to her Lord and Savior:

> Six days before the Passover, Jesus therefore came to Bethany, where

Lazarus was, whom Jesus had raised from the dead. So they gave a dinner for him there. Martha served, and Lazarus was one of those reclining with him at table. Mary therefore took a pound of expensive ointment made from pure nard, and anointed the feet of Jesus and wiped his feet with her hair. The house was filled with the fragrance of the perfume. But Judas Iscariot, one of his disciples (he who was about to betray him), said, "Why was this ointment not sold for three hundred denarii and given to the poor?" He said this, not because he cared about the poor, but because he was a thief, and having charge of the moneybag he used to help himself to what was put into it. Jesus said, "Leave her alone, so that she may keep it for the day of my burial. For the poor you always have with you, but you do not always have me." (John 12:1-8)

In this passage, Martha showed her love for Christ through her hands, through service. And Mary . . . she took a year's wages to buy a bottle of pure* nard, and anointed her Lord's feet with it. Think of that for a moment . . . she took a *year's* wages. If comparing this with a modern example, let's say the average wage in the U.S. in 2015, that would be an alabaster bottle† worth roughly around $48,098.63. And what does she do with this very expensive gift? She pours it all out in a moment, to wash the stinky feet of a man.

A professor of mine believes, that Mary was even sacrificing much more than this. What if this gift, was her dowry? What if Mary, in a patriarchal society, was giving away any chance she had of marriage, in order to show her love for Jesus?

---

*The Greek word used here, is πιστικῆς (pistikes). It can be translated as "pure," but it can also be translated as "faith." I believe John chose this word, for not only does it describe the extravagance of the gift, but what type of gift it was. It was a faith gift.

†There are parallel stories to this one within the Synoptic Gospels: Matthew 26:6-13 and Mark 14:1-10. However, Mary is not the same woman, who performs a similar action in Luke 7.

... Before the cross is revealed in John's Gospel, this would be the ultimate act of love shown within it. And Mary, didn't stop there. She took her hair, the glory of her head (1 Corinthians 11:1-16), and used it to wash the feet of Jesus. The feet, being one of the most disgusting parts of the body—especially in a sandal-wearing society. Yet Mary, humbled herself, displaying an act of pure love. An act that is later mirrored by Jesus in the next chapter, when he humbles himself and washes the feet of his disciples. An act that is criticized by a thief, a hypocrite. Perhaps by a disciple pretending to love this same man? For no man can love both God and money (Matthew 6:24). And Jesus quickly defends Mary, for she gave to him such a precious gift.

Yes, there are many acts of love shown by men throughout the Bible too, but women ... there's just something special about them.

SO BOTH PLEASANT and Companion the Moabite return to Bethlehem. And as gossip in any small town goes, news spread quickly that Pleasant was back. In their surprise they asked, "Is this Pleasant?" Now Pleasant was grieving. She had lost her husband and her two sons. She believed that God was against her, and had left her alone. And so she tells the women, "No, do not call me Pleasant, call me Bitter (Mara), for the Almighty has dealt bitterly with me. I went away full, and the LORD has brought me back empty. Why call me Pleasant, when the LORD has testified against me and the Almighty has brought calamity upon me?"

Pleasant and Companion return to the House of Bread at the beginning of the barley* harvest. So Companion asks permission from her mother-in-law to go glean from the fields, and her mother says, "Go my daughter" (2:2). Companion goes to a field, which happens to

---

*Just as a cool side note, John let's us know in his Gospel, that the five loaves which were used to feed the crowd of over 5,000, were barley loaves (6:9).

be the field of Quickness (Boaz), and begins to collect food left behind by the reapers—*not* the Grim Reaper.

"Does anyone know why she could do this? Why she could gather the grain after the reapers?" I asked the class.

"Wasn't it because God told them not to harvest it all?" asked a teen.

"Correct. God makes a law for His people to leave a portion of their field so to feed the poor and travelers. Think of it like a tithe, only with food instead of money. This can be found in Leviticus of all places. Leviticus 19:9-10, one of the many reasons why this book is important, though many see it as boring. Which I do admit, it can be at times. However, as can be seen, it does have a purpose. Let's keep reading." (I didn't read the verse in class, there isn't time when you try to cram the whole book of Ruth into one session, but I thought I would include it here for you:

"When you reap the harvest of your land, you shall not reap your field right up to its edge, neither shall you gather the gleanings after your harvest. And you shall not strip your vineyard bare, neither shall you gather the fallen grapes of your vineyard. You shall leave them for the poor and for the sojourner: I am the LORD your God.")

While Companion is collecting grain, she catches the eyes of Quickness, who thinks she's smoking *hot*. He asks his workers, "Who is that woman?" and discovers that she's a Moabite who had come back to the House of Bread with Pleasant, and that she is also a hard worker. *Not* wanting Companion to leave, Quickness quickly confronts her and tells her to not go to any other field, that she is welcomed here. He tells her he has commanded all his men to not touch her, letting her know that she is safe and protected. And when she's thirsty, she can go to the vessels to get a drink.

"Then she fell on her face, bowing to the ground, and said to him, 'Why have I found favor in your eyes, that you should take notice of me, since I am a *foreigner*?' (2:10). Quickness tells her it's because of her ḥesed to her mother-in-law. She had given everything, left her father and mother, her home, everything, to serve her mother. Because of this, Quickness tells her that the Lord will bless her.

Quickness shows his ḥesed by taking care of Companion. At the next meal, he asks Companion to eat some bread and dip it into the wine (which sounds like the Lord's Supper, does it not?). She eats until she's satisfied, though probably not as much as devouring a *giant* pancake in a LPBC food challenge . . . before upchucking it.

Companion eats until she is satisfied, and even has food leftover. (Only if she had some fish, then it would indeed be even more similar to another story which I know.) Quickness then hooks Companion up, by having his workers leave extra grain for her to collect. "You taking notes guys?" I asked the class. "This is great dating advice right here. Free of charge, too."

After such an amazing day, Companion returns to Bitter with her leftovers and all the grain she'd collected, and then tells her about her day. "Whose field did you glean from?" asks Bitter.

"The field belonged to Quickness," Companion replies.

"May he be blessed by the LORD, whose ḥesed has not forsaken the living or the dead!" Bitter is overjoyed, and then tells Companion that Quickness is one of their kinsman redeemers. Kinsman redeemer or גָּאַל (ga'al) in Hebrew, is another important theme within this book. The kinsman redeemer is a *significant* figure in the Jewish culture, having three main duties:

1. A redeemer of property (Leviticus 25:25-55).

2. An avenger if a family member was murdered (Numbers 35:9-34).

3. A giver of a son (Genesis 38). If a husband left a widow with no children, the kinsman redeemer's job would be to marry her and to give to her children, most desirably, a son. This custom may sound strange to us, but remember, the Jews believed their bloodline was passed on through the mother. Also, they lived in a very patriarchal society. A son would be needed to look after his mother's physical needs, to protect her, and to take care of the property.

Bitter ends their conversation by telling Companion, "It is good, my daughter, that you go out with the young women, lest in another field you be assaulted" (2:22). In other words: "Glad you went to that field, honey. If you went to another, you might have been raped." Yes, this was a real danger. Still, at the same time in my opinion, it's a weird way to end a conversation.

COMPANION STAYS IN the field of Quickness through the barley and the wheat harvests, while living with her mother-in-law. Just as she cares for her mother, so too does Bitter care for her daughter. Like any good mother, she wants to see Companion taken care of and married to a good man. So like any good mother, Bitter offers dating advice. With the faith of Mary, Companion follows her mother-in-law's wisdom. She takes a bath, does her makeup, anoints herself with oil, and waits for Quickness to fall asleep before she uncovers his feet and lies down beside them. Isn't that romantic? I mean, who doesn't want to lay next to smelly man feet?*

Do notice that Companion lies at his *feet*, not beside him. She comes to Quickness modestly. And he takes notice: "At midnight the man was startled and turned over, and behold, a woman lay at his feet!" (3:8). Haha, this is one of the most humorous verses I have found in the Bible. Quickness wakes up, "and behold a woman lay at his feet!" Haha.

And Quickness finds out that it's not just any woman, it's Companion: "He said, 'Who are you?' And she answered, 'I am Ruth, your servant. Spread your wings over your servant, for you are a redeemer'" (3:9). How's that for a proposal? Companion makes it known that she wants Quickness to be her husband, a desire which he too wishes. However, he tells her that though he is a redeemer, there is a redeemer nearer in kin than he. But Quickness doesn't stop there, he reveals that he will quickly take care of the matter, *tomorrow*.

So Companion lay at his feet till morning. And with the character of Joseph, Quickness tells Companion to not let anyone know she spent the night, so no one would think she was immoral and had sexual relations with him (remember, word travels fast in a small town). He then gives her more food, and Quickness tells her that he will settle the matter *that* day, for Quickness is quick to act. And he also real-

---

*Maybe this romantic encounter was even an inspiration for Dan Brown's *The Da Vinci Code*, or at least provides some support for the romantic aspect of it. A story revolving around the conspiracy theory of Mary Magdalene mistakenly being believed to have been involved in a romantic relationship with Jesus, even marrying him, and giving birth to a daughter, which became known as the Holy Grail. Christ's child being the Grail instead the cup from the Last Supper as in Arthurian legend. A relationship which was sparked by Mary being the woman who anointed and washed Jesus' feet in Luke 7:36-50.

ly, really wants to marry this cute girl.

Quickness quickly goes to the town's gate, the place where business matters were taken care of back in the day, and discusses the situation with the other redeemer. Quickness is smart, too. Firstly, he has with him ten elders as witnesses. In ancient Israel, all you needed were two men to bear witness (Deuteronomy 19:15), but Quickness wanted there to be no doubt in the terms of their agreement. Secondly, he begins by telling the other redeemer about Bitter—how she's selling land, which peaks the other redeemer's interest; he's all for it. But then Quickness quickly adds in the part, that if he redeems the land, then he will also have to marry Companion as his second duty as a redeemer. This quickly turns the other redeemer off to the proposal:

> Then the redeemer said, "I cannot redeem it for myself, lest I impair my own inheritance. Take my right of redemption yourself, for I cannot redeem it."
>
> Now this was the custom in former times in Israel concerning redeeming and exchanging: to confirm a transaction, the one drew off his sandal and gave it to the other, and this was the manner of attesting in Israel. So when the redeemer said to Boaz, "Buy it for yourself," he drew off his sandal. Then Boaz said to the elders and all the people, "You are witnesses this day that I have bought from the hand of Naomi all that belonged to Elimelech and all that belonged to Chilion and to Mahlon. Also Ruth the Moabite, the widow of Mahlon, I have bought to be my wife, to perpetuate the name of the dead in his inheritance, that the name of the dead may not be cut off from among his brothers and from the gate of his native place. You are witnesses this day." (4:6 -10)

As a kinsman redeemer, Quickness redeems the land of My God is

King. He redeems Bitter and Companion by taking Companion as his wife and giving to her a son, Worshipper* (Obed) (who was the father of Yahweh Exists (Jesse), who was the father of Beloved One (King David)). And Quickness also became the redeemer for Moab. In Deuteronomy 23:3-4, God had cursed the Moabites. He had cursed them, because they did not feed the Israelites and had tried to lead Israel astray with their women. But Ruth does the opposite. She is fed by Israel and is known for being righteous instead of a prostitute, and is even a great grandmother of Jesus! (Well, ~great x 40.)†

A "law" abiding Jew would miss the grace proclaimed here, my youth minister had texted me one night. The night when he had brought this very passage to my attention.

Quickness had redeemed the foreigner, just as our own kinsman redeemer redeemed us while we were still foreigners, living in the Nation of Sin instead of the Kingdom of Heaven. "Who is our kinsman redeemer?" I asked the class.

"Jesus," answered a teen.

"Yes, Jesus. Just at Boaz redeemed Ruth and Naomi, so too did Jesus redeem us."

***

WHEN OUR MISSION group had been returning from Arizona, we drove through the town of Roswell, New Mexico—and there were

---

*Or Servant.

†Ruth is also one of the four women mentioned within Matthew's genealogy of Christ (1:5), along with: Tamar (1:3), Rahab (1:5), and [sort of] Bathsheba (1:6). Not only were women often left out of Jewish genealogies, but look at what women are mentioned within Jesus': Tamar, who disguised herself as a prostitute for Judah to sleep with her; Rahab, who was a prostitute and a foreigner; Ruth, who was also a foreigner, and Bathsheba, the woman who David had an affair with and murdered her husband. In an average family, these would be four women whom their relatives would be ashamed to be related to, and may even try to hide such relations. Yet, within Jesus', they are given branches of honor. I believe being more proof that Jesus was truly the Messiah, and not just some fictional character.

aliens *everywhere*. Hotels, restaurants, gift shops—the little green men had invaded the city. I felt like I was in an episode of *The X-files*.

Well, I guess not all of them were so little; we took a picture with one who was at least twelve foot. We didn't have time to visit the UFO Museum, but we did make a quick stop at Domino's to get a pic with this jolly green giant. A foreigner.

Ruth was probably a whole lot prettier. I don't think Boaz would have thought one of these extraterrestrials were hot. But she was a Moabite. A foreigner of Israel, who was adopted into the family of Jesus. Just as we all were once foreigners, before we are adopted into the family of Christ through his blood (Romans 8:14-19).

"Say cheese," said chaperon Dan, before he snapped the evidence we needed to prove that aliens do exist! . . . At least they do in Roswell.

NOTES

1. Fig. 1: Blake, William. *Naomi entreating Ruth and Orpah to return to the land of Moab*. 1795. Fitzwilliam Museum: Cambridge, England.
2. Fig. 2: Blake, William. *Ruth the Dutiful Daughter-in-law*. 1803. Southampton City Art, England.
3. Fig. 3: Wilkinson, Charles K. *Sennedjem and Iineferti in the Fields of Iaru*. 1922. The Metropolitan Museum of Art: New York. A painting based on original artwork found on the east wall of Sennedjem's tomb in Deir el-Medina. A village opposite of Thebes, where those who excavated and decorated the royal tombs were allowed to reside. It is believed, this nonroyal was allowed to decorate his own tomb in his free time, painting him and his wife reaping a field in the next life, 1295–1213 B.C.

CHAPTER 8

*DAVID: WE'RE DUMB AS SHEEP

"Awe," echoed almost the entire auditorium. Kyler was giving a sermon over the 23rd Psalm. A picture of two little lambs had just flashed upon the screen. He then began to talk about how dumb sheep can be. "Sheep on their own, I mean there's no nice way to put it, are well, pitiful. You do some research and they're not the smartest animals in the world." Sheep *need* something to follow, for if left to their own devices, will fall into foolishness, such as grazing a field to nothingness.

Sheep need something to follow, even if it be a leader who leads them off a cliff (which happened to a herd in Turkey; 450 fell to their deaths, providing cushioning for another 1,100 who survived), they tend to wander and get lost, and they're defenseless (which is why they make great snacks for lions and wolves). "Is there any wonder why the Bible constantly compares us to sheep?" asked Kyler, referencing what he had read in preparation for that Sunday, W. Phillip Keller's book, *A Shepherd's Look At Psalm 23*. There were laughs throughout the auditorium, but it was the truth. Without a shepherd, sheep have no hope. Without the Good Shepherd, we have no hope.

***

IN THE FIELDS outside of the little town of Bethlehem, was a shepherd boy, David. According to 1 Samuel 16:12, this son of Jesse—the

137

youngest even—was a pretty boy; he was "ruddy and had beautiful eyes and was handsome." He was also skillful with the harp, and he may have wrote some of his psalms while tending his sheep, instead of trolling the Bethlehemites by crying out, "Wolf! Wolf!", such as this one:

A Psalm of David.*

The LORD is my shepherd; I shall not want.

    He makes me lie down in green pastures.

He leads† me beside still waters.

    He restores my soul.

He leads† me in paths of righteousness

    for his name's sake.

  Even though I walk through the valley of

      the shadow of death,

---

*Something which I found interesting when I took Hebrew, was that this tagline at the front of most of the Psalms which tells who wrote it, in the Hebrew Bible, is actually the first verse of the Psalm. While in the English translation, we just include them as a subheading.

†Notice, He "leads me," He doesn't "drive me." You can't drive sheep like you can cattle. You must lead them.

I will fear no evil,

for you are with me;

your rod and your staff,

they comfort me.

You prepare a table before me

in the presence of my enemies;

you anoint my head with oil;

my cup overflows.

Surely goodness and mercy shall follow* me

all the days of my life,

and I shall dwell in the house of the LORD

forever.†

---

*The root of the Hebrew verb used here, is רָדַף (radaph). It shouldn't be translated as 'follow' but as, "goodness and mercy shall 'chase' or 'pursue' me all the days of my life." 'Goodness' and 'mercy,' are "Not a little poodle," that walks beside us, said the Professor. But more like a hunter, *actively* pursuing his prey.

†In the midst of the arrangement of Psalms 15-24, Psalms 23 shares many similarities with Psalms 16, such in how they both are confessions of trust in Yahweh:[2]

A Miktam of David.
Preserve me, O God, for in you I take refuge.
I say to the LORD, "You are my Lord;
    I have no good apart from you."
As for the saints in the land, they are the excellent ones,
    in whom is all my delight.
The sorrows of those who run after another god shall multiply;
    their drink offerings of blood I will not pour out
    or take their names on my lips.
The LORD is my chosen portion and my cup;
    you hold my lot.
The lines have fallen for me in pleasant places;
    indeed, I have a beautiful inheritance.
I bless the LORD who gives me counsel;
    in the night also my heart instructs me.
I have set the LORD always before me;
    because he is at my right hand, I shall not be shaken.
Therefore my heart is glad, and my whole being rejoices;
    my flesh also dwells secure.
For you will not abandon my soul to Sheol,
    or let your holy one see corruption.
You make known to me the path of life;
    in your presence there is fullness of joy;
    at your right hand are pleasures forevermore.

Such a beautiful Psalm, which has become well renowned. For though simple, it holds such great importance. It is a beautifully written poem of how God cares for each of us. And even though it's written in the first person, it's not from the point of view of the shepherd, but a sheep. For though David himself was a shepherd, he also understood he needed a shepherd—that being the Lord.* For there were many times when David cried out to his Shepherd. Many times when he needed God to lead him:

Make me to know your ways, O LORD;
  teach me your paths.
Lead me in your truth and teach me,
  for you are the God of my salvation;
  for you I wait all the day long. (Psalm 25:4-5)

When he became lost and needed found:

Create in me a clean heart, O God,
  and renew a right spirit within me.
Cast me not away from your presence,
  and take not your Holy Spirit from me.

---

*It's also interesting, that the 23rd Psalm comes after the 22nd in the Bible, which begins with, "My God, my God, why have you forsaken me?" A Psalm which begins with woe, yet ends with praise, in contrast to the 23rd which is praise throughout. This Psalm was probably what Jesus was quoting while he was hanging on the cross, when he cried, "My God, my God, why have you forsaken me?" Most likely, he was not lamenting how God had turned His back on him, but was offering his Father praise though he was in woe. In Jesus' time, the Jews had more of the Scriptures memorized than the average modern Christian. Therefore, a rabbi could quote one verse, and those listening would know what he was referencing without him quoting the whole Scripture. Jesus could have been quoting this Psalm, for he may have felt very alone, while still giving praise to his Father. For how can a member of the Trinity turn His back on Himself? Yes, they are separate, but they are also *one*. And if the Father could turn His back on His Son during his darkest moment, what would stop Him from turning His back on us? True, Jesus did embody *all* of sin in that moment; however, that was his very purpose for coming to earth, and never did he stop being the Son within the Holy Trinity.

Restore to me the joy of your salvation,

and uphold me with a willing spirit. (Psalm 51:10-12)

When he was in danger and needed rescued:

Be not silent, O God of my praise!

For wicked and deceitful mouths are opened against me,

speaking against me with lying tongues.

They encircle me with words of hate,

and attack me without cause.

In return for my love they accuse me,

but I give myself to prayer.

So they reward me evil for good,

and hatred for my love. (Psalm 109:1-5)

And when he was in anguish:

For mine iniquities are gone over mine head: as an heavy burden they are too heavy for me.

My wounds stink and are corrupt because of my foolishness.

I am troubled; I am bowed down greatly; I go mourning all the day long.

For my loins are filled with a loathsome disease: and there is no soundness in my flesh. (Psalm 38:4-7 *KJV*)

David was both a shepherd and a psalmist. And, according to his credentials, he was also a warrior. When he had come before King Saul to explain why he should be the one to face Goliath,* he described to the king how keeping sheep is not always an easy task:

---

*"Fee-fi-fo-fum," did you know that "goliath" in English today, means "giant," because of the influence of this biblical story? However, in Hebrew, it is believed that "Goliath" comes from the verb גָּלָה (galah), which means to "uncover" or "reveal."

"Your servant used to keep sheep for his father. And when there came a lion, or a bear, and took a lamb from the flock, I went after him and struck him and delivered it out of his mouth. And if he arose against me, I caught him by his beard and struck him and killed him. Your servant has struck down both lions and bears, and this uncircumcised Philistine shall be like one of them, for he has defied the armies of the living God." (1 Samuel 17:34-36)

David explains to Saul that he is more than a pretty face. That when his sheep were threatened, he defended them. That if a predator took one lamb, he would hunt it down and rescue that lamb. A lot like the Good Shepherd in the parable found in Luke 15:

"What man of you, having a hundred sheep, if he has lost one of them, does not leave the ninety-nine in the open country, and go after the one that is lost, until he finds it? And when he has found it, he lays it on his shoulders, rejoicing. And when he comes home, he calls together his friends and his neighbors, saying to them, 'Rejoice with me, for I have found my sheep that was lost.' Just so, I tell you, there will be more joy in heaven over one sinner who repents than over ninety-nine righteous persons who need no repentance. (4-7)

Unlike a bad shepherd who only cares for himself (Ezekiel 34:1-10), David had explained to Saul that he would protect his sheep when threatened. And the sheep of Israel were threatened by the Philistine bear, Goliath. David was *ready* to defend the sheep he had been anointed king over. He was a shepherd of Israel anointed by God, just as later would Peter be anointed a shepherd of the church by Jesus, who commanded him, to, "Feed my sheep" (John 21:17).

And defended his flock he did—for David struck down Goliath and beheaded the giant with his own sword.*

However, when we read this story, about how a shepherd boy defeated a mighty giant, don't we usually put ourselves into it as David—taking away the lesson that with God on our side, we can conquer giants? Which isn't a bad lesson, but it would be better with Jesus—who defeated the giants of sin and death. For what if instead of putting ourselves in the story, we try putting Jesus into it? A suggestion made by David Bowden, while on stage of the 2017 Jumpstart youth rally. "A story about Jesus, is much better than a story about you," he said. "All offense intended."

This is an exercise that Bowden got from the book, *Jesus on Every Page*, and a challenge which I also issue to you.

JUST LIKE HIS great grandfather, so too is Jesus a shepherd who

---

*One of my friends once shared with me, that he had learned from a rabbi that the Israelites would have looked at David as an important figure from this moment on. Not just because he had won a great victory for them against the Philistines, but because he had struck Goliath in the *head* before cutting it off. Them associating that moment with the promise given in Genesis 3:15,"he shall bruise your head." For they saw similarities between the serpent and Goliath, and saw David's deed as a symbol that he had indeed been chosen by God.

cares after his sheep. The Good Shepherd who knows each of his sheep by name, and whose voice the sheep *know* (John 10). So too is he the warrior on the white horse in Revelation, just as David was the warrior who had slain 200 Philistines for their foreskins (1 Samuel 18:27), had fought in many battles, and had even shed too much blood to be the one to build the Temple (1 Chronicles 22:8). And just as David was anointed king, so too is Christ. "And the LORD said, 'Arise, anoint him, for this is he.' Then Samuel took the horn of oil and anointed him in the midst of his brothers . . . " (1 Samuel 16:12-13). He was King David, one of the most renowned kings of all of Israel. He was the king who unified the country under one banner, as one kingdom. He was the one, who conquered Jerusalem, established it as the country's capital, and who had the Ark of the Covenant brought into its walls. The one, who gathered the materials to build the Temple. The one who's bloodline was to sit upon the throne, "And your house and your kingdom shall be made sure forever before me. Your throne shall be established forever'" (2 Samuel 7:16).

But Logan, a descendant of David doesn't sit on a throne in Israel today. In fact, the decline of the Davidic Dynasty is the main theme of Book III in Psalms. Additionally, the State of Israel doesn't even have a monarchy anymore. It's ruled by a prime minister.

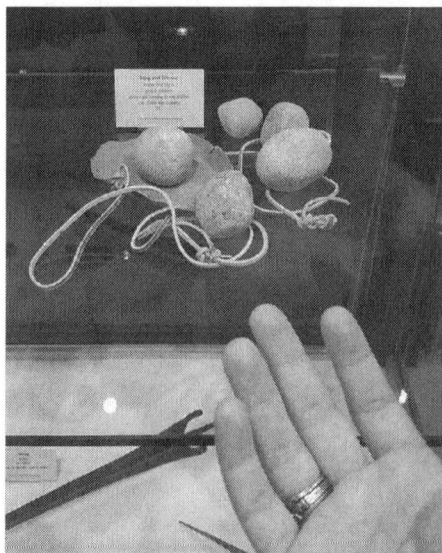

True, Israel the country does not. But God's promise was more than any earthly kingdom. For the Son of David sits at the right hand of God, on a throne of the Kingdom which will last forever. Israel may have lost its earthly king, but it's had a King before David, before Saul even. And He still sits on His throne today, with His Son right beside Him. (Get it, "right" beside Him? . . .)

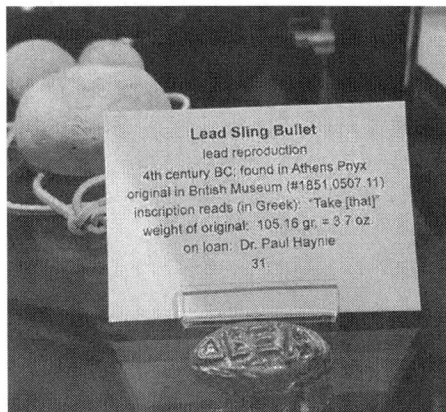

Stephen himself, the first martyr, reported seeing Jesus in a vision just before he was stoned, "Behold, I see the heavens opened, and the Son of Man standing at the right hand of God," (Acts 7:56). (Though he doesn't see Jesus sitting but standing. Perhaps greeting him as he comes home?)

Just like the son of Jesse, Jesus is both shepherd and king. Like David, Jesus is the Shepherd King, for as the Lord had said to David, "You shall be shepherd of my people Israel, and you shall be prince over Israel" (2 Samuel 5:2). Though notice, that the *ESV* does not say 'king' here before David is crowned, but "prince." For he is not *the* king of Israel, but a servant to the King of kings and the Good Shepherd.

Sadly, though David was a great man, he made some *dumb* mistakes as king: committing adultery with Bathsheba, murdering Uriah, her husband; and remaining passive instead of dealing with both of his sons: Amnon, who raped his sister, and Absalom, who murdered his brother and raised a rebellion against David. David made some stupid, stupid decisions, yet he was still the king whom God had chosen. A man after 'His own mind.'* Jesus though is the perfect king, who

---

*The way the Jews thought of the heart, is different than how we think of it. They, like their contemporary neighbors, saw the heart as the equivalent to how we see the brain. So when the Bible says in 1 Samuel 13:14 that David was a man after 'His own heart,' it really means David was a man after 'His own mind.' David was the king whom God wanted, while Saul had been the king who Israel had wanted. The Hebrew word in question is לֵבָב (lebab), which does mean heart, but again, the Jews thought

redeemed the throne of David, cleansing it of the sin of his ancestors. He did so, not by wearing a crown of gold, but of thorns.

> And they brought the colt to Jesus and threw their cloaks on it, and he sat on it. And many spread their cloaks on the road, and others spread leafy branches that they had cut from the fields. And those who went before and those who followed were shouting, "Hosanna! Blessed is he who comes in the name of the Lord! Blessed is the coming kingdom of our father David! Hosanna in the highest!" (Mark 11:7-10)

Jesus, is not like those who came and claimed to be the 'Messiah' before him. He rode into Jerusalem, not in a war chariot, but a donkey. Not a symbol of war but of peace. Nevertheless, he was greeted as a victor. The Jews crying out, "Hosanna!" "Hosanna!" which translates: "Save us! Save us, Son of David!" His people crying out for rescue, from the Roman Empire.

When Jesus first came, he did not establish an earthly kingdom as many believed the Messiah would. But, he did indeed begin the age of the Kingdom upon his cross. For the Kingdom is here, but not in its entirety. It's here but not yet. Nevertheless, that will change, on the

of the heart as a organ of thought, not of love. This slight flaw in our English translations is perhaps due to tradition; however, what's interesting, is that labab is translated as 'mind' instead of 'heart' in other passages, such as in Daniel 5:21 and 7:4.

day he returns as a conquering king. On *that* day, Jesus will fully establish his Kingdom. He will be seen in his full glory, and will be known as the king that he is. For on that day, "at the name of Jesus every knee should bow, in heaven and on earth and under the earth, and every tongue confess that Jesus Christ is Lord, to the glory of God the Father" (Philippians 2:10-11).

Jesus is King! The King of kings and the Lord of lords. For he is the Alpha and the Omega, the Beginning and the End. *Both* the Good Shepherd, and the Conquering King.*

ONE LAST CORRELATION between David and Jesus, is the Temple. In 2 Samuel 7 (and in 1 Chronicles 17), we read that David wished to build a house for the Lord, which he receives permission to do so from the prophet Nathan. However, it appears that Nathan spoke without first consulting God, for that very night, he is approached by Yahweh, Who tells him to tell David to not build Him a house. For never had He rebuked His people for not building Him a Temple. And it sounds as if God is content to be amongst His people and to move with them while dwelling in the portable Tabernacle. However, He does make this prophecy to David:

> "'When you die and join your ancestors, I will make one of your sons the next king, and I will set up his kingdom. He will build a house for me, and I will let his kingdom rule always. I will be his father, and he will be my son. When he sins, I will use other people to punish him. They will be my whips. I took away my love from Saul, whom I removed before you, but I will never stop loving your son. But your family and your kingdom will continue always before me. Your throne

---

*Another image of Jesus being both king and shepherd, can be found in Zechariah chapters 9-11, which give a messianic collage of the Messiah being both the coming king and the rejected shepherd.

will last forever.'" (12-16)

But what if, this prophecy has been misunderstood? What if instead of talking about Solomon, that God was referring to Jesus? For Jesus did establish a Kingdom that will last forever, unlike Solomon, and he even refers to himself as the Temple in John 2:19-22:

> Jesus answered them, "Destroy this temple, and in three days I will raise it up." The Jews then said, "It has taken forty-six years to build this temple, and will you raise it up in three days?" But he was speaking about the temple of his body. When therefore he was raised from the dead, his disciples remembered that he had said this, and they believed the Scripture and the word that Jesus had spoken.

However, the biggest problem with explaining this theory, is that Jesus never sinned; therefore, God didn't have to 'use other people to punish him,' as He states in the 2 Samuel account (though this line is absent from the one found in 1 Chronicles). So it's possible that this a duel prophecy concerning both Solomon and Jesus. For the Lord does allow the Temple to be built later by Solomon (even though this was perhaps not what He wanted, but allowed Israel to have, just as He had allowed them to have a king years before), but not David. For He had told the king, that, "'You have shed much blood and have waged great wars. You shall not build a house to my name, because you have shed so much blood before me on the earth" (1 Chronicles 22:8).

***

SHEEP NEED A *shepherd*, the words echoed in my head. We need something to follow. If it's not the Good Shepherd, then it will be the Bad Shepherd, Satan. A tyrant who promises demonic love through alcohol, drugs, sex, money, instead of the comforts of green pastures and still waters. If we don't choose to graze from His fields, we graze from the wastelands of the Devil.

I snapped my attention back to Kyler, as he made an invitation to join the flock of the Lord in baptism, before we stood and sang. I don't remember what song . . . I'm just going to say it was, "The Lord is My Shepherd." Sounds like a great book end, and it would be a hymn which we would sing. For Jesus is indeed the Good Shepherd, who cares for each of us. Who gives us direction, searches for the lost, protects us from the evil one, and maketh us lie down in green pastures, and leadeth us beside the still waters.

NOTES

1. Fig. 1: Simoni, Michelangelo di Lodovico Buonarroti. *David*. 1501-1504. Galleria dell'Accademia: Florence.
2. Barker, Kenneth L. *Zondervan NIV Study Bible*. Grand Rapids, MI: Zondervan, 1984. Print.
3. Fig. 2: Blake, William. *Goliath Cursing David*. 1803-1805. Museum of Fine Arts: Boston.
4. Fig. 3: A display in the Linda Byrd Smith Museum of Biblical Archaeology at Harding University. A modern sling alongside stones collected from the Brook of Elah.
5. Fig. 4: A lead sling bullet on display in the Linda Byrd Smith Museum of Biblical Archaeology at Harding University.
6. Fig. 5: Cordier, Nicolas. *Statue of King David. Photograph.* 1590-1612. Basilica di Santa Maria Maggiore: Rome.
7. Fig. 6: Blake, William. *Songs of Innocence: The Shepherd*, copy B. 1789. Lessing J. Rosenwald Collection, The Library of Congress: Washington, D.C.

Psalm 23*

The L<small>ORD</small> is *my* shepherd; I shall not be in want.

He makes me lie down in green pastures.

He leads me beside waters of rest.

He restores my soul.

He leads me in right paths

for His name's sake.

Even though I walk through the valley of

deep darkness,

I will fear no evil,

for YOU ARE WITH ME;

Your rod and Your staff,

they comfort me.

You prepare a table before me

in the presence of my enemies;

You anoint my head with oil;

my cup is overly and abundantly filled.

Only goodness and mercy shall chase me

all the days of my life,

and I shall return to dwell in the house of the L<small>ORD</small>

Forever.

---

*Near the beginning of this chapter, I included a more traditional version of the 23rd Psalm. Here, is another slightly different version of it, arranged from footnotes found in the *ESV*, notes from a Psalms class, and carefully placed emphasis. My hope, is that it may be more connective with you. And a tool you can use for your own personal meditation.

CHAPTER 9

*ELIJAH & ELISHA:

DON'T MAKE FUN OF BALD PEOPLE

Would you like to know a secret?

It's an important one. One which may save your life some-
day. It's *that* important. Such as *don't* play dead if you come into contact with a black bear, important. One which you should know if you
hope to make something of yourself. It will also keep you out of fights.
And-and who knows? It may inspire someone to find a cure for cancer or to create world peace.

So would you like to hear it then? I mean if you don't, I could just
dive into the next lesson. But if I did that, you would be missing out
on an important revelation of life. Insight which dwarfs the insight of
Gandhi, Einstein, and Yoda.

Are you sure you would like to hear it? For once I write it, it will no
longer be a secret. I'm hoping at least 10,000 people are going to buy
this book. . . . Okay, at least ten. But we all know ten people *cannot*
keep a secret. Two people have trouble keeping secrets. Why else do
we know about the super soldier program Russia had during the Cold
War, or about the aliens kept in the basement of Area 51, or about the
emails deleted from Hillary Clinton's laptop?

And once a secret is known, it cannot be unknown.

Okay, sorry, just trying to see if you really want to know this secret. If you're actually willing to suffer through this anticipation, or if you're one of *those* people who are going to cheat and skip down to read it.

The secret is . . . if you would still like to know. That men . . . and I do mean men. I guess this may affect some women too, but it's more of a man ego thing.

That men don't like . . . Drum roll, please—

That men don't like it when you insult their fire starting techniques.

There, it's out.

I'm super *serious* when I say this, too. There were a few times that summer when I was insulted by how long it took me to start a fire. Mostly because I was starting a fire with wet wood, which made the feat even more incredible. It's funny to start singing, "Light the Fire" when someone else has trouble getting the flames burning. Or laughing at a friend who breaks out the gasoline and almost catches his leg on fire (DON'T TRY THIS AT HOME!!! Be smart and use diesel or lighter fluid, *not* gasoline—it's *explosive* and leads the fire straight to you. Like I tell both teens, friends, and pretty much anybody I know, don't be dumb. God did give you a gray thing between your ears for a reason.) But when it happens to you, when people make fun of *your* fire skills, oh, it's on like Donkey Kong! It just . . . just . . . torches your ego.

With a team of four young men and a Frisbee, we achieved the near impossible. We created fire! Yes, it took some effort and time, but we persevered and created the flames to cook our bacon, that's what's important. I don't know if you know this or not, but wet wood does *not* like to burn. And we all just can't call down fire from the sky. . . . Or can we? (We do worship the same God . . . Hmmm . . .)

***

THE PROPHET ELIJAH called down fire from the heavens. He had this competition with the prophets of Ba'al on top of Mount Caramel, in the game show, Whose God is Real? And of course, the prophet of Yahweh won. Not to say the prophets of Ba'al didn't give a valiant effort; they tried their hardest. They jumped and danced around, they cut themselves until "the blood gushed out" (1 Kings 18:28), they even cried out with loud voices in case Ba'al couldn't hear them because he was asleep or on the toilet; nevertheless, nothing they did could convince the imaginary god to give them fire. For there is *only* one God. This was a mountaintop experience that Elijah got to live through. Before going into the valley of depression, when he began to fear for his life from Queen Jezebel who was *ticked* that Elijah had killed all of her prophets, and so wanted his life in exchange.

Jesus himself went through his own mountaintop experience, which Elijah, was actually a part of:

And after six days Jesus took with him Peter and James, and John his brother, and led them up a high mountain by themselves. And he was transfigured before them, and his face shone like the sun, and his clothes became white as light. And behold, there appeared to them Moses and Elijah, talking with him. And Peter said to Jesus, "Lord, it is good that we are here. If you wish, I will make three tents here, one for you and one for Moses and one for Elijah."* He was still speaking when, behold, a bright cloud overshadowed them, and a voice from the cloud said, "This is my beloved Son, with whom I am well pleased; listen to him." When the disciples heard this, they fell on their faces and were terrified. But Jesus came and touched them, saying, "Rise, and have no fear." And when they lifted up their eyes, they saw no one but Jesus only.

And as they were coming down the mountain, Jesus commanded

---

*I've always wondered, how did the disciples recognize that they were seeing Elijah and Moses? Did they know at the time by some act of God? Or did Jesus reveal this fact to them later?

them, "Tell no one the vision, until the Son of Man is raised from the dead." And the disciples asked him, "Then why do the scribes say that first Elijah must come?" He answered, "Elijah does come, and he will restore all things. But I tell you that Elijah has already come, and they did not recognize him, but did to him whatever they pleased. So also the Son of Man* will certainly suffer at their hands." Then the disciples understood that he was speaking to them of John the Baptist. (Matthew 17:1-13)

Like the Hebrews on top of Mount Carmel, the disciples witnessed an *amazing* sight on top of a mountain. In fact, it was so amazing, they thought they should stay on top of that mountain, to create tabernacles and dwell there. But no one, can stay on a mountaintop experience

---

*Jesus referring to himself as "Son of Man," is a quiet witness to his humility. This phrase is used 100 times in the Old Testament, with 93 of those found in Ezekiel. But each time God calls His prophet, "son of man," He is not elevating but reminding His prophet that *He* is God, and Ezekiel is but a man.[2] This is another example of Jesus embracing us in our humanity.

forever. This is the truth whenever we hit a spiritual high, that there is a time when we have to come down into the valley—which isn't necessarily bad. Yes, a valley may be a place of war and trials, but it could also be a place of fertility and strengthening. Just as there are different mountains, so too are there different valleys within our lives.

ELIJAH AND JESUS have more in common than mountains, though. They do share some similarities, which is one reason why some believed Jesus may have been Elijah, who had returned to earth since he had never died: "Now when Jesus came into the district of Caesarea Philippi, he asked his disciples, 'Who do people say that the Son of Man is?' And they said, 'Some say John the Baptist, others say Elijah, and others Jeremiah or one of the prophets.'" (Matthew 16:13-14). Similarities between Elijah and Jesus include, but are not limited to:

- HAVING POWER OVER H2O. Such as Elijah prophesying the ceasing and coming of the rain in Israel, and Jesus calming the storm of the Sea of Galilee (1 Kings 17:1, 1 Kings 18:41; Matthew 8:23-27, Mark 4:35-41).
- HAVING POWER OVER FOOD. Elijah multiplying the widow at Zarephath's flour and oil during a famine, for she could bake bread for both him and her family, and Jesus multiplying fish and bread to feed the crowds of over 5,000 and 4,000 (1 Kings 17:8-16; Matthew 14:13-21, 15:32-38).
- RESURRECTING A WIDOW'S SON.* Both performed this miracle, though Jesus just had to touch the man for him to be healed, while

---

*Fun Fact: According to an ancient and unverifiable Hebrew tradition, mentioned by Saint Jerome, the widow's son whom Elijah raised, later grew up to be the prophet Jonah.

Elijah performed the strange ritual of laying stretched out on the boy three times to resuscitate him (1 Kings 17:17-24; Luke 7:11-17).

- REBUKING THE RELIGIOUS LEADERS. Elijah chastising Ahab for worshipping Ba'al, who by being king influenced the people of Israel to worship the god too, and Jesus rebuking the religious leaders for also misguiding the people of Israel (1 Kings 18:18-21; Matthew 23).

- FASTING FOR FORTY DAYS IN THE WILDERNESS (1 Kings 19:4-8; Matthew 4:2).

- PROMISING THEIR FOLLOWERS THAT THEY WILL DO GREATER DEEDS THAN THEY. Elisha is also promised that he shall have a double portion of Elijah's spirit, and the disciples are given the promise of the Holy Spirit (2 Kings 2:9-14; John 14:12-14, Acts 1:4-5).

- ASCENDING INTO HEAVEN. Elijah riding in a fiery chariot, and Jesus ascending into the clouds (2 Kings 2:1-14; Luke 24:50-52, Acts 1:6-11).

However, though Elijah and Jesus have some similarities, Elijah is more associated with Jesus' predecessor, John the Baptist, the voice 'crying out in the wilderness:' "and he will go before him in the spirit and power of Elijah, to turn the hearts of the fathers to the children, and the disobedient to the wisdom of the just, to make ready for the Lord a people prepared" (Luke 1:17). Jesus, on the other hand, shares many more similarities with Elijah's successor—Elisha:*

---

*Some of these similarities I do admit are a little of a stretch; however, they do share some common elements. Also, there are some homologous miracles which Elisha shares with his master.

- GIFT OF THE SPIRIT. Elisha receives a double portion of Elijah's spirit at the Jordan after his rabbi ascends, as Jesus receives the Holy Spirt at the Jordan when he's baptized (2 Kings 2:1-14; Matthew 3, Luke 3:22 John 1:32).

- POWER OF PLENTY. Elisha produces an abundance of oil to fill many vessels for a widow to sell and to pay off her debt, while Jesus transforms six jars (thirty gallons) of water into an abundance of wine for a wedding at Cana (2 Kings 4:1-7, John 2:1-11).*

- POWER OVER DEATH. Elisha raises the Shunammite woman's son from the dead by laying stretched out on top of him twice, while Jesus resurrects Jairus' daughter, Lazarus, and himself (2 Kings 4:18-37; Mark 5:35-43, John 11, John 2:19-22, Luke 24:1-12).

- POWER OVER FOOD. Elisha uses 20 loaves and some grain to feed at least 100 men with food being leftover, while Jesus fed crowds by breaking bread and fish with 12 and 7 baskets being left over.† (2 Kings 4:38-41; Matthew 14:13-21, Mark 8:1-10).

- POWER OVER THE BODY. Naaman, a Syrian general, approached Elisha for healing of his leprosy, just as a Roman centurion approached Jesus to heal his servant. Elisha also heals Naaman's leprosy, just as Jesus healed both a leper on one occasion, and ten lepers on another (2 Kings 5:1-14; Matthew 8:5-13, Matthew 8:1-4, Mark 1:40-45, Luke 17:11-19).

- A FALLEN DISCIPLE. They both had a disciple fall away and give into his greed, Gehazi for two talents of silver and two changes of

---

*Did Jesus use a magic wand when performing his miracles? The answer is yes—that is, if you believe some of the earliest depictions of Jesus. From the 3rd century to the 5th century, are pieces of art illustrating Christ changing water into wine, multiplying the bread and the fish, and raising Lazarus from the dead by utilizing a wizard's tool of choice.

†Jesus possessing this power over food, is perhaps why he was tempted by Satan to transmute stones into bread before breaking his forty day fast in the wilderness. Satan knowing that Jesus *could* do it.

clothes, and Judas for thirty pieces of silver (2 Kings 5:15-27, Matthew 26:14-16).

- POWER OVER WATER. Elisha made an iron ax head float on the water, while Jesus had the power for both him and Peter to walk on the Sea of Galilee (2 Kings 6:1-7, Matthew 14:22-33).

- LED A HOST OF CAPTIVES. (2 Kings 6:18-20, Ephesians 4:1-8).

- POWER OVER SIGHT. Elisha caused the blindness of the Syrian soldiers who were sent to seize him, while Jesus caused the blindness of Saul when he was on the road to Damascus to seize Christians. Both the soldiers' and Saul's lives were spared, and their sight regained. For Elisha and Jesus also both gave sight to the blind (this being the *only* time blindness was healed in the Old Testament. For the time of Christ, was the time of sight). (2 Kings 6:18-20; Acts 9:1-19, Mark 8:22-25, Luke 18: 35-43, John 9).

- DINED WITH SINNERS. (2 Kings 6:20-23; Luke 5:27-32, Mark 2:13-17).

- BROUGHT LIFE THROUGH DEATH. Elisha's bones brought life to a dead man,* just as Jesus' death awakened many from their graves† and gave us eternal life (Matthew 27:50-53, John 3:16).

All these similarities point to two things. The first, giving a glimpse of what kind of man Jesus would be. Before Jesus, the prophets acted as God's avatars upon the world. Delivering His messages, and both

---

*"So Elisha died, and they buried him. Now bands of Moabites used to invade the land in the spring of the year. And as a man was being buried, behold, a marauding band was seen and the man was thrown into the grave of Elisha, and as soon as the man touched the bones of Elisha, he revived and stood on his feet" (2 Kings 13:20-21).

†*Not* zombies. They were not undead, but fully resurrected, for God doesn't bake half-cooked miracles. This detail, found in Matthew, shows that death had finally been defeated at the cross! That Sheol, that the grave, could no longer hold us forever, for Jesus is greater! It spat up these bodies, as it would his three days later. Though it makes you wonder, what happened to these saints? For never again are they mentioned. (This passage also brings Ezekiel 37 to mind, for these dry bones did indeed live again.)

feeding and healing His people. They were the glimpses, the trailers of Who God is and who Jesus would be. At the same time, the miracles which Jesus performed solidified his identity, by pointing back to the prophets. Though he was more powerful, the types of miracles which he worked were not only to bring aid to the people whom he loved, but were signs that he *was* the Son of God. That he had been sent by God and was performing miracles with the power of the Holy Spirit, not by some other deity, demonic or otherwise. Many of the miracles which Jesus performed had been in some way done before, giving him credibility that he was who he said he was, as he lived out the motif of a prophet.

Despite these similarities; however, there is one interesting comparison between Elisha and Jesus, which can be observed in 2 Kings 2:23-25:

> He went up from there to Bethel, and while he was going up on the way, some small boys came out of the city and *jeered* at him, saying, "Go up, you baldhead! Go up, you baldhead!" And he turned around, and when he saw them, he cursed them in the name of the LORD. And two she-bears came out of the woods and tore forty-two of the boys. From there he went on to Mount Carmel, and from there he returned to Samaria.

Wait, did that just happen?!

Yes, this is another passage that makes you scratch your head and wonder what you're getting yourself into when studying the Bible. Especially when compared to Jesus, who was a silent lamb led to slaughter before his accusers, who cried out to God, "Father, forgive them, for they know not what they do" (Luke 23:34), upon the cross.

So why did Elisha call down a curse upon a group of boys who were making fun of his bald head?

Well first off, who were they making fun of? And not just making fun of, but קָלַס (qalas) him, *mocked* him. Elisha, correct? And who was Elisha?

He was the prophet of Yahweh. Meaning that Elisha was both the voice and the face of God. Which translates as the boys were not merely making fun of the prophet, but were directly making fun of God Himself. Therefore in this instance, Elisha demonstrates an act of judgement (which came from God), while Jesus during his trial and crucifixion demonstrates an act of mercy (which came from God, though he does demonstrate judgement when he flips tables and weaves a whip when he angrily cleanses the Temple). And notice, that the text says the she-bears "tore" the boys. The root for this word, בָּקַע (baqa) can be translated as "tear," meaning the boys may have only been mauled and not killed by the ursas. ... Baqa can also mean 'split open,' meaning the boys may have indeed suffered the ultimate

And he went up from thence unto Beth-el: and as he was going up by the way, there came forth little children out of the city, and mocked him, and said unto him, Go up, thou bald head; go up, thou bald head. And he turned back, and looked on them, and cursed them in the name of the Lord. And there came forth two she bears out of the wood, and tare forty and two children of them.—2 Kings ii. 23. 24.

price for mocking the Lord to His face, and His servant as well. This is but one reason why we should respect our Lord, and be careful not to carelessly use His name in vain. . . . And on the safe side, *don't* make fun of bald people.

***

I DID *NOT* call out for she-bears to take my revenge for the mocking of my fire skills (though I may have considered it if I had remembered is was an option—only considered. I'm pretty sure I would have had to confront some angry parents if I had acted on it. . . . Maybe I could have gotten away with asking for the help of some she-squirrels to maul the young men, teaching a lesson without the death penalty).

Nevertheless, the fires were built, allowing us to enjoy some bacon, s'mores, bacon, eggs, and some bacon.

NOTES

1. Fig. 1: Blake, William. *The Transfiguration*. 1757-1827. Victoria and Albert Museum: London.
2. Moore, Mark E. *How to Dodge a Dragon: A Devotional Reading of Revelation*. Joplin, MO: College Press Publishing Company, 1998. Print. p. 11.
3. Fig. 2: Heston, Watson. *Old Testament Stories Comically Illustrated*. New York: The Truth Seeker Co., 1892.

CHAPTER 10

JONAH: "I THOUGHT IT SMELLED BAD, ON THE OUTSIDE."

That Saturday, was amazing! Seeing a group of almost a dozen teens volunteering for the Community Partnership Resale Shop. A flea market that raises money for the non-profit organization, to aid kids and families in several cool ways. Such as assisting those who are physically challenged, mentoring, and helping in pursuing a post-secondary education. It is definitely an awesome local program. And I'm thankful I happened to have stumbled upon their website, while looking for a community service project for the youth group.

The teens worked hard unloading a truck, sorting, organizing, and shining their lights. The ladies at the Partnership were pleased by their hard work ethic, and were impressed in how they never once heard a complaint, complimenting several times how awesome the teens were and how *appreciative* they were for the help.

That Saturday was *amazing*! Seeing the youth group answer the call which Jesus commissioned us in Matthew 25:34-40, to be the sheep who feed those who are hungry, to give drink to those who are thirsty, to welcome those who are a stranger, to clothe those who are naked, and to visit those who are sick or in prison.

The teens answered this call on that day. Unlike a prophet, who had tried to run away from the call that the Lord had given to him.

***

JONAH WAS A prophet. Surprisingly, his story does not actually begin in the book of Jonah, but beforehand in 2 Kings 14:23-27:

> In the fifteenth year of Amaziah the son of Joash, king of Judah, Jeroboam the son of Joash, king of Israel, began to reign in Samaria, and he reigned forty-one years. And he did what was evil in the sight of the LORD. He did not depart from all the sins of Jeroboam the son of Nebat, which he made Israel to sin. He restored the border of Israel from Lebo-hamath as far as the Sea of the Arabah, according to the word of the LORD, the God of Israel, which he spoke by his servant Jonah the son of Amittai, the prophet, who was from Gath-hepher. For the LORD saw that the affliction of Israel was very bitter, for there was none left, bond or free, and there was none to help Israel. But the LORD had not said that he would blot out the name of Israel from under heaven, so he saved them by the hand of Jeroboam the son of Joash.

This, is our first introduction to the prophet Jonah. He was a contemporary of King Jeroboam, who was an evil king of Israel. Normally, if a king was evil, he would not reign for long and was removed from the throne by the Lord. However, Jeroboam was an exception, reigning for *forty-one years*. It appears that Yahweh through His prophet Jonah had delivered a message of mercy to the king and to Israel. Instead of punishing them for their idolatry, He allowed for them to prosper. This message through Jonah, both I and the Professor believe, was given to soften the heart of Jonah for his next message.* God wanted to extend His mercy to Israel, before He would

---

Many of my thoughts concerning Jonah, come from and have been shaped by the Professor's commentary that he has published, *Jonah: God's Scandalous Mercy*. I highly encourage you to read it for yourself. For there's so much good information from the Professor's research, which I'm just unable able to fit within this single chapter.[1]

soon extend the same mercy to the Gentiles. And *not* just any Gentiles, the Ninevites.

"They were more evil than slapping others with fishes," I began to explain to the class. Two sisters smiled with excitement from my *VeggieTales* reference. But it was true, the Ninevites were a *cruel, sinful* people. The Assyrians were known as one of the *cruelest* people in Jewish history. They were bloodthirsty neighbors who constantly raided Israel. Their armies would descend upon a city like a plague of locusts. It would be common for them to kill the men and the children, piling their decapitated heads outside the city walls and to rape the women.

They were also known to take prisoners and to impale them on poles, burn them alive, or to bury them up to their necks in the desert's sand and to leave them to go mad by the sun before they died. A temple in the city of Nimrud holds a record of what King Ashurnasirpal II did to rebels in the city of Suru. Describing a pillar he had built, which was covered with the skins of the men that he had flayed while they were still alive, serving as a warning for others to not resist the power of Assyria. And in another city conquest, after slaying 3,000 men and hanging their heads from trees, he captured many others alive and had their arms, hands, noses, ears, and lips cut off, and their eyes gouged out. True, Ashurnasirpal was king about a century after Jonah; however, he still serves as a perfect example of

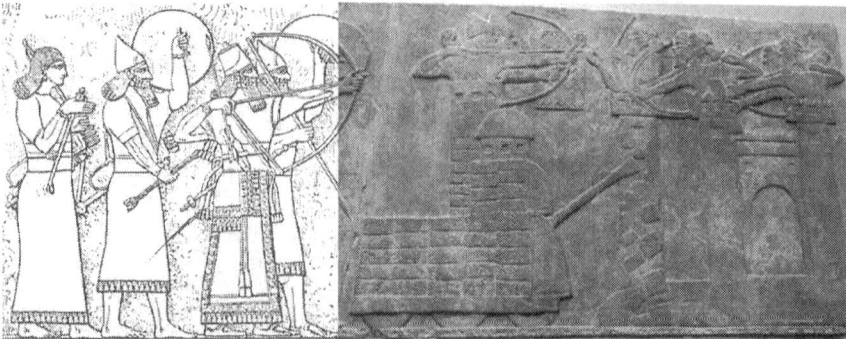

the cruelty of the Assyrians, who glorified their practices of violence. And he also carried out barbaric acts which were common by the Assyrians even in Jonah's time. The Assyrians were the enemies of Israel and were *hated* by them. *These* were the people who God commanded Jonah to go to, when He said, "Arise, go to Nineveh, that great city, and call out against it, for their evil has come up before me" (1:2).

The book of Jonah has a very Genesis flavor to it, for God calls Jonah to go east, to Nineveh. In Genesis, east is used as a literary device to reveal when someone was moving away from God: Adam and Eve were driven out east of the garden after the Fall, Cain traveled east after murdering Abel, the peoples of the earth migrated from the east when they settled to build the Tower of Babel, Lot went east when he separated from Abraham toward Sodom, and Abraham came from the east, from Ur, and traveled west to the Land of Promise, to Canaan. God even instructed for the Tabernacle and the Temple to face east, causing His people to travel west when they came to worship and to sacrifice to Him, and to travel east when they would leave the dwellings of His glory. Jonah was told to travel east, to Nineveh. Yet he goes as *far* west as was known to the Israelites at that time, to Tarshish, which is thought to be somewhere either in southern Spain or somewhere in Africa.

When God told Jonah to קוּם (qūm [arise]) he instead goes יָרַד (yarad [down]). He goes down to Joppa, goes down to the belly of the ship, before he will finally goes down to the belly of the fish. This constant descent is perhaps a detailed expression of Jonah's spiritual journey as he defies Yahweh's plan.

Jonah goes down to Joppa and boards a ship. In Jewish tradition, Jonah is a rich man, for it sounds like he rents the entire ship in his haste, as he attempts to run from God and His plan. God could have, if He wished, to have stricken down His prophet for disobeying Him. Yet, he extends the same mercy which He will offer to Nineveh, to Jonah. Not to say God isn't angry at Jonah, for like a javelin, He hurls a storm at the ship. Like the disciples in Mark 4, the sailors were *afraid* by the storm. The sight of the crashing waves, the thunderous roar of thunder, the flashes of lightning all around them, and the scream of the winds must have been terrifying. So they cried out to their gods and hurled cargo overboard to lighten the load, but nothing was working.

And where was Jonah during this fright? Down in the belly of the ship, asleep. Similarly in how Jesus was asleep in the stern on a cushion, before his disciples awakened him and he calmed the storm. The captain finds Jonah and wakes him up saying, "What do you mean, you sleeper? Arise, call out to your god! Perhaps the god will give a thought to us, that we may not perish" (1:6) The captain tells Jonah to *arise*, to break out of his stupor and pray to his God. The sailors are praying to theirs, yet nowhere are we told that Jonah calls out to his until chapter 2. For even during the storm, it appears that Jonah remains silent.

After doing everything they can think of, the sailors decide to cast lots to see who's responsible for the storm, just as the Roman soldiers casted lots for Jesus' clothes. Yes, this was a common practice back in the day, yet it is still a small similarity between the narratives of Jonah and Jesus.

They cast lots, and the lots fall on Jonah. The sailors waste no time in interrogating the prophet, fearing for their lives: "Tell us on whose account this evil has come upon us. What is your occupation? And where do you come from? What is your country? And of what people are you?" Jonah then answers them, "'I am a Hebrew, and I fear the LORD, the God of heaven, who made the sea and the dry land.' Then the men were exceedingly afraid and said to him, 'What is this that you have done!' For the men knew that he was fleeing from the presence of the LORD, because he had told them" (1:8-10) Even these sailors, these Gentiles recognize the folly of Jonah, the prophet who had tried to run from his God.

They then ask Jonah what they should do to calm the storm, so Jonah tells them: "Pick me up and hurl me into the sea; then the sea will quiet down for you, for I know it is because of me that this great tempest has come upon you" (1:11).

Hold on, how did Jonah know this? How did he know that they were supposed to throw him into the sea?

Good question, for the Bible does not specifically mention that God spoke these instructions to him. The Lord could have, just as He had given the interpretation of the dream to Daniel which he relayed to King Nebuchadnezzar; however, there is a stark contrast between the two prophets. For Daniel always gave credit to God, while we do not see that here. In fact, the only credit we see is what Jonah gives to himself, "I am the reason for this storm." Like I said, God could have whispered these instructions to His prophet, yet they were just not recorded, or, these were Jonah's own words. He knew beyond a shadow of a doubt this storm had been caused by him. He knew God had conjured nature against him in a form of judgement. Therefore, what if Jonah was prepared to face God's judgement, rather than to preach His mercy? Jonah, telling the sailors to throw him into the sea in hope he would be killed, and his given mission failed. For why didn't the prophet just jump off the ship? If he knew he was the cause, why didn't he just end it himself?

If he had done so, he would have been responsible of taking his own life, rather than giving it into the hands of these sailors, if they so chose to hurl him overboard.

But the sailors were *not* ready to take the life of another man, especially a prophet. And so they tried to row to safety to no avail, similar to the disciples' attempts to do so on the Sea of Galilea. Only, after all other options were exhausted, did they finally agree to hurl the prophet overboard like the cargo. However, not before praying to *Yahweh*: "O LORD, let us not perish for this man's life, and lay not on us innocent blood, for you, O LORD, have done as it pleased you" (1:14). These *Gentiles* cry out to God before His prophet does. We're even told that these sailors, "feared the LORD with a great fear and they sacrificed sacrifices to the LORD, and they vowed vows" (1:16), after the storm had ceased. Now, it is unclear if these sailors became full-blown converts to the Lord, or if they only added Him as another god to their pantheon of deities; however, what is clear, is that they were ironically more faithful than the Jewish prophet.

The sailors hurl Jonah into the sea and the storm ceases. The Lord halts the judgement which Jonah was prepared to face, and instead extends mercy to him. Appointing a great fish to act out the role of savior by gobbling Jonah up and harboring him from the sea. Similar in how Jesus extended his hand and saved one of his disciples in the midst of another storm:

> Immediately he made the disciples get into the boat and go before him to the other side, while he dismissed the crowds. And after he had dismissed the crowds, he went up on the mountain by himself to pray. When evening came, he was there alone, but the boat by this time was a long way from the land, beaten by the waves, for the wind

was against them. And in the fourth watch of the night he came to them, walking on the sea.* But when the disciples saw him walking on the sea, they were terrified, and said, "It is a ghost!" and they cried out in fear. But immediately Jesus spoke to them, saying, "Take heart; it is I. Do not be afraid."

And Peter answered him, "Lord, if it is you, command me to come to you on the water." He said, "Come." So Peter got out of the boat and walked on the water and came to Jesus. But when he saw the wind, he was afraid, and beginning to sink he cried out, "Lord, save me." Jesus immediately reached out his hand and took hold of him, saying to him, "O you of little faith, why did you doubt?" And when they got into the boat, the wind ceased. And those in the boat worshiped him, saying, "Truly you are the Son of God." (Matthew 14:22-33)

Most of the time, Peter gets a lot a flack from us when reading this story. But notice, he stepped out of the boat. He stepped onto a sea during a raging storm. How many of us would have the faith to do such a thing? I mean, it took me once five minutes to jump off a 40 ft. cliff into calm waters, after a friend had done it in seconds. Yet Peter, stepped onto the waters during a storm, and he walked on those waters. And when he began to sink, was it because he had lost faith in Jesus, or in himself?

All of us encounter storms in life, whether that be grief, depression, persecution. And it is during these storms, that Jesus calls us to come out of the boat, and to walk on the waters towards him. We must have faith in both him and in ourselves. Yet, if we lose that faith along the way, he is there with an extended hand of mercy to lift us up and to save us from drowning. All we have to do, is grab his hand.

---

*Basilisks (lizards in the genus *Basiliscus*) are also known as "The Jesus Christ lizard," because of their ability to run *on* water, at a velocity of 4.9 feet per second, for approximately *15 feet*, before sinking into the liquid and then swimming.

... "Fear not, for I have redeemed you;

  I have called you by name, you are mine.

When you pass through the waters, I will be with you;

  and through the rivers, they shall not overwhelm you; ...

For I am the LORD your God,

  the Holy One of Israel, your Savior. . . . (Isaiah 43:1-3)

WHALE OR FISH?

In the book of Jonah, the fish is first referred to as דָּאג (dag), which translates as 'fish' in the Hebrew. It is not תַּנִּין (tannin), which can be translated as 'whale,' 'sea monster,' or 'serpent' (or crocodile/ alligator in modern Hebrew). However, in Matthew 12:40, when Jesus promises to the Pharisees the sign of Jonah, the great fish is known as κῆτους (kétous). Kétous, on the contrary, can be translated as 'big fish,' or as 'sea monster,' or 'whale' in the Greek. Greek does also have its own word for 'fish,' ἰχθύς (ichthus), which is used when Jesus calls Peter and Andrew to be his disciples, or when he feeds the 5,000— but that word is not used in Matthew 12. Does this mean the New Testament brings a new revelation to what type of animal made Jonah its lunch? Or is it merely a difference in translation? I personally believe it was some type of fish which swallowed Jonah; however, it looks like the New Testament keeps this debate open and unable to be filed away as fact.[*]

_____

*So, you ready for a complete nonsense explanation for this mystery? I kid you not, this is what a textbook said in a dream I had one night, as an answer why it had to be a whale which swallowed Jonah. Apparently, this is the kind of thing which my subconscious really wants to figure out.

So, back in the day, whales had bigger esophagi (even a blue whale today would be unable to swallow a human, having a narrow throat less than 1 ft. wide. Whale sharks (yes, I know they're fish—big fish) also have too small of throats, and would more in likely spit a human out if it had accidently swallowed one, just as they did to grains of rice in a 2010 experiment led by Dr. Phillip J. Motta.[4] However, in theory, a sperm whale could inhale a man, but they have four stomachs full of digestive en-

Many simply mark off the story of Jonah and the fish as an allegory, to do away with the scientific explanations of this miracle. Though Jesus using this specific event as physical evidence for his resurrection complicates this 'simple' explanation. (There is also debate, if an extinct fish could have swallowed Jonah, such as a *Dunkleosteus*. Additionally, don't rule out the fact that God could have engineered a special fish just for Jonah. He could have used a natural species in an unnatural way, or, He may have taken this chance to express His creativity. The same can be said about the plant and the worm which the Lord later uses against Jonah, both of which also ignite discussion of their genus.)

Nevertheless, what is interesting, is that in Jonah 1:17 the fish is known as "dag," which is the masculine form of 'fish' in Hebrew. But in 2:1 "fish" is "dagah," which is 'fish's' feminine form. This distinction is not seen in the English translation; regardless, it brings up the question, "Why this change?" According to the Professor's commentary, the rabbis explained this peculiarity by teaching that a male fish was the first to swallow Jonah, which then spat Jonah out while it was still in the sea, and he was then swallowed up again by a pregnant

---

zymes like a cow, and the only gas within them is methane; therefore, except in the case of a miracle, it is physically impossible for a whale to swallow a man and he remain alive for three days), but to keep them from swallowing too large of prey, they had longer teeth, which kept them from accidently swallowing things like sharks. However, Jonah was able to get pass the teeth, and down the whale's throat. But as the whale evolved, its throat got smaller, and so did the length of its teeth.

In dream logic, this made complete sense. It even came with a picture:

female fish. This may sound silly, but it was a true dilemma to the Hebrews, just as many passages are still troubling to us today which we attempt to explain.

With that said, the Professor proposes another theory, which I am in favor of. We do not believe the fish was a transgender, or pulled a *Jurassic Park* and changed its sex between the end of chapter 1 and the beginning of chapter 2. For what if Jonah was indeed swallowed by a male fish, and therefore resided in its belly to be kept safe. But what if in chapter 2, the fish is referred to as female, to bring to the reader's mind the imagery of Jonah being within a womb? Yes, literally he was in the belly of the fish, but symbolically, what if the writer of Jonah wanted us to think of the prophet being in a place of new life, with hopes that Jonah will repent of his stubbornness, and will later emerge as a faithful prophet to the Lord?

JONAH HAS FINALLY gone down as far as he can go. In his prayer, he says he cries out from "the belly of Sheol" (2:2), from the underworld. It has taken Jonah literally reaching rock-bottom before he cries out to Yahweh. I've never been in the belly of a fish, but being as stubborn as I am, I've had to reach several bellies throughout my own life before I've cried out to our God. Sometimes it takes the very worst to spark our best, igniting our very best to offer to Him.

Can you even imagine what it must have been like within the belly of that fish? Ew! The smell, the slime, the joy of evading stomach acid, and who knows what else the fish had eaten? . . . Maybe even a blue tang or a clown fish, or something far more frightening? Not to mention the darkness. And who knows how much room Jonah had within the scaly critter, if he was cramped or in a cavernous environment. Perhaps his experience was something similar to that of Pinocchio's:

When he recovered his senses the Marionette could not remember where he was. Around him all was darkness, a darkness so deep and so black that for a moment he thought he had put his head into an inkwell. He listened for a few moments and heard nothing. Once in a while a cold wind blew on his face. At first he could not understand where that wind was coming from, but after a while he understood that it came from the lungs of the monster. I forgot to tell you that the Shark* was suffering from asthma, so that whenever he breathed a storm seemed to blow.[5]

Yet, it was in this atmosphere where Jonah finally breaks his silence and prays to the Lord. He acknowledges God's mercy, recognizing he was still alive because God had rescued him from the sea. However, in the end of his prayer, he places too much emphasis on his own piety:

---

*Yes, before Disney's animated film in 1940, Pinocchio was eaten by a fish, not a whale. The Terribile Pescecane (the Terrible Dogfish) to be precise, though translated as a 'Shark' by some.

When my life was fainting away,
  I remembered the LORD,
and my prayer came to you,
  into your holy temple.
Those who pay regard to vain idols
  forsake their hope of steadfast love.
But I with the voice of thanksgiving
  will sacrifice to you;
what I have vowed I will pay.
  Salvation belongs to the LORD!" (Jonah 2:7-9)

Did Jonah remember Yahweh? Or did Yahweh remember Jonah?

Kudos to the prophet for finally crying out to God and giving Him thanksgiving; however, something's a little fishy with his prayer (pun intended). He presents himself as a faithful servant to the Lord, more faithful than those who worship idols. Though we already know that the idol worshipping sailors had "sacrificed sacrifices" at the end of chapter 1, and it was these same sailors who had called out to Yahweh before Jonah ever did, which brings doubt to the sincerity of Jonah's prayer, and perhaps to Jonah's perception as well.

FOR THREE DAYS and three nights, Jonah was in the belly of the fish, the length that was believed for a person to descend to the underworld and return from it, which can be seen in the Sumerian poem, "The Descent of Inanna," a chronicle of the goddess' journey to and from the land of the dead:

From the great heaven she set her mind on the great below. From the great heaven the goddess set her mind on the great below. From the great heaven Inanna set her mind on the great below. My mistress abandoned heaven, abandoned earth, and descended to the under-

world. Inanna abandoned heaven, abandoned earth, and descended to the underworld.

This is one reason why Jesus himself was in the belly of the grave for three days. Now, Jonah makes a *strange* figure to compare with the Son of God. After all, God had given Jonah a mission and he turned his back on it, attempting to run as *far* away as he could from what God had called him to do. This, in contrast to Jesus, who fully accepted his mission. Yes, he cried out for another way within Gethsemane; however, he still did not run away from his mission and fully embraced the cross willingly. Yet, Jesus himself draws this very connection between him and Jonah in Matthew 12:38-42:

> Then some of the scribes and Pharisees answered him, saying, "Teacher, we wish to see a sign from you." But he answered them, "An evil and adulterous generation seeks for a sign, but no sign will be given to it except the sign of the prophet Jonah. For just as Jonah was three days and three nights in the belly of the great fish, so will the Son of Man be three days and three nights in the heart of the earth. The men of Nineveh will rise up at the judgment with this generation and condemn it, for they repented at the preaching of Jonah, and behold, something greater than Jonah is here. The queen of the South will rise up at the judgment with this generation and condemn it, for she came from the ends of the earth to hear the wisdom of Solomon, and behold, something greater than Solomon is here."

175

The religious leaders, the ministers and pastors of the time, came before Jesus and asked him for a sign, so they would know he was truly sent from God. Surely many of them had already heard of Jesus' miracles and had already witnessed some of his healings for themselves. However, perhaps they were demanding something more miraculous, such as parting the Sea of Galilea or calling down fire from the skies? But Jesus is not a magician who performs tricks for the sake of an applause. He did not perform for Satan and he would not perform for them. He even appears to be angered by their demand, declaring to them he will not perform a sign for their entertainment. But, he still alludes to his most amazing trick, his grand finale, which not even Houdini himself would be able to pull off. To be dead three days before resurrecting himself. A feat which makes cutting a woman in half look like child's play.

As if this isn't enough, Jesus is again confronted for another sign in Matthew 16:1-4:[*]

IMMANIS IONAM TRIDVANVM HIC EVOMIT ALVI E LATERIS PISTRIX.POSTQVAM MANDATA RECOXIT.

---

[*]Mark 8:11-13

And the Pharisees and Sadducees came, and to test him they asked him to show them a sign from heaven. He answered them, "When it is evening, you say, 'It will be fair weather, for the sky is red.' And in the morning, 'It will be stormy today, for the sky is red and threatening.' You know how to interpret the appearance of the sky, but you cannot interpret the signs of the times. An evil and adulterous generation seeks for a sign, but no sign will be given to it except the sign of Jonah." So he left them and departed.

Jesus had just recently performed the miracle of feeding the crowd of over 4,000 with seven loaves of bread and some fish, and this was still not enough for the Pharisees, who demanded more signs from the Son of God. They were denied, and Jesus again promises the sign of Jonah.

GOD IS THE God of second chances. After three days and three nights, Jonah is vomited onto dry land. This mode of ejection is perhaps to humiliate/humble the prophet, before he finally begins his mission. The Lord again tells Jonah to "Arise, go to Nineveh, the great city, and call out against it the message that I tell you" (3:2). This time, Jonah "arose" and went to Nineveh; however, just as quickly as we gain faith in the prophet's conversion, it rapidly fades.

Jonah enters the future Assyrian capital, which is described of being so big, that it would take *three* days to travel through it. Yet the Bible says Jonah only travelled one. Additionally, he delivers the shortest sermon, yet it had the greatest conviction, "Yet forty days, and Nineveh shall be overthrown" (3:4).

"Does anyone see anything wrong with Jonah's message?" I asked the class. Several hands shot up.

177

First off, unless this is just a portion of Jonah's message, which I don't believe it is, it doesn't mention repentance, which was Yahweh's intent in sending His prophet. There's not even a mention that wrath is coming from Yahweh. Just, "Yet forty days, and Nineveh shall be overthrown." It appears Jonah once again is resisting his calling. He does *not* want Nineveh to be saved. He wants justice and destruction, and so he delivers a half-baked devo. Yet, God still works, and the hearts of the people cry out to Him.

We are told, that, "the people of Nineveh believed God. They called for a fast and put on sackcloth, from the greatest of them to the least of them" (3:5). Another red flag here, is that the people begin to fast *before* the news reaches the king of Nineveh. Jonah did not go to the king of the city who would have been the head religious leader, but instead appears to have just wandered around preaching his dooms-day proclamation. Yet even the king is convicted when he hears Jo-nah's words and is struck to the heart:

> The word reached the king of Nineveh, and he arose from his throne, removed his robe, covered himself with sackcloth, and sat in ashes. And he issued a proclamation and published through Nineveh, "By the decree of the king and his nobles: Let neither man nor beast, herd nor flock, taste anything. Let them not feed or drink water, but let man and beast* be covered with sackcloth, and let them call out mightily to God. Let everyone turn from his evil way and from the violence that is in his hands. Who knows? God may turn and relent and turn from his fierce anger, so that we may not perish." (Jonah 3:6-9)

Even the king of this *wicked*, sinful people repents. He gets up from his throne and humbles himself. He even makes a decree for the en-

---

*בְּהֵמָה (behemah)

178

tire city to fast, so that God may have mercy on them. Even the animals are commanded to fast, which would be a feat in itself, involving restraining and constant supervision. For it would be a *task* to keep these beasts from obeying one of their most basic survival instincts, to eat. Yet Nineveh, the *bloody* city with men impaled on its walls, with piles of hands and feet, and with heads shish kabobed on spears, this Nineveh repented to the God of Mercy.

Nahum would later prophecy of the fall of Nineveh, of the Lord's judgment upon the city, yet in Jonah, God showered this city with His mercy and relented of His wrath. Jonah, of course, was *not* a happy camper to say the least; he was *angry*. And he makes sure that God knows it:

> "O LORD, is not this what I said when I was yet in my country? That is why I made haste to flee to Tarshish; for I knew that you are a gracious God and merciful, slow to anger and abounding in steadfast love, and relenting from disaster. Therefore now, O LORD, please take my life from me, for it is better for me to die than to live." (Jonah 4:2-3)

Jonah had fled to Tarshish, because he knew that the God of the Old Testament, the one Who had flooded the earth, Who had opened up the earth to swallow rebellious men, Who had poured out fire from the sky, this God, was a "*gracious* God and *merciful, slow to anger* and *abounding in steadfast love*, and *relenting of disaster.*" Too often, we think of Jesus as the loving Savior, and the Father as the wrathful God of the Old Testament; however, there were times Jesus poured out his own wrath, and there are so many occasions when the Father's mercy is seen throughout the Old Testament, which is why Jonah did not want to go to Nineveh in the first place. He did *not* want

God's mercy to bless them. It was okay for God to show His mercy to Israel and to himself, but not to these heathens.

Jonah is so mad, that he offers an ultimatum in the form of a corrupt reversal of what Moses had done for Israel. For when God had threatened to wipe out the Israelites in Exodus 32, Moses had pleaded for God to take his life instead and to spare the people. Jonah does just the opposite, asking God to take his life in hopes that the Lord will either enact His divine judgement on him at last, or to wipe out Nineveh and to spare his prophet. God does neither.

Again, His mercy is seen as He spares the life of his stubborn prophet. And Jonah, still hoping for God's judgement, goes out of the city and finds a place to the east of it to make camp. He sets up a booth for himself and waits for the fireworks. Yet, just as Adam and Eve's fig thongs were inadequate to clothe themselves, it appears that Jonah's booth was not the best for shade. And so, just as God had clothed Adam and Eve, He grows a plant for Jonah to give him shade from the desert's sun. This comfort gave to Jonah joy. Nevertheless, what the Lord gives, the Lord can take away.

Just as Jesus had the power over nature to curse the fig tree and make it wither, so too does his Father hold that power, "God appointed a worm that attacked the plant, so that it withered" (4:7). The sun rises, bringing heat down upon the prophet, and God only adds to his discomfort by appointing a hot, scorching wind. The joy Jonah had the day before is gone. He is so discomforted, that he again asks the Lord to take his life:

> But God said to Jonah, "Do you do well to be angry for the plant?" And he said, "Yes, I do well to be angry, angry enough to die." And the LORD said, "You pity the plant, for which you did not labor, nor did you make it grow, which came into being in a night and perished in a

night. And should not I pity Nineveh, that great city, in which there are more than 120,000 persons who do not know their right hand from their left, and also much cattle?" (Jonah 4:9-11)

God makes one final object lesson for Jonah. Showing how foolish he is to pity a plant he did not even grow—that which had been grown for him as a gift—over the lives of the Ninevites. A people, though they had been *sinful*, a people whom He loved more than any plant. As His prophet, God wanted Jonah to understand His love and mercy. The same love that Jesus will express during his Sermon on the Mount, in Matthew 5:43-48:

"You have heard that it was said, 'You shall love your neighbor and hate your enemy.' But I say to you, Love your enemies and pray for those who persecute you, so that you may be sons of your Father who is in heaven. For he makes his sun rise on the evil and on the good, and sends rain on the just and on the unjust. For if you love those who love you, what reward do you have? Do not even the tax collectors do the same? And if you greet only your brothers, what more are you doing than others? Do not even the Gentiles do the same? You therefore must be perfect, as your heavenly Father is perfect."

Jesus preached this message to the descendants of those who were persecuted by the Assyrians, who were suffering under the Romans—another cruel and bloodthirsty people. To these people Jesus commanded to love their enemies, just as he commands us to love our enemies. To love those who bully and make fun of us, to love serial killers, rapists, Nazis, and ISIS. And to pray for them. If God could love Nineveh, so too can we love our enemies.

THE END. THAT is how the book of Jonah ends, mentioning Nineveh and its cows. I thought it was super strange that cows would be the last thing which this book would mention, until the Professor pointed out that the animals had also been involved in the salvation of the city, they too had fasted and so had been spared from God's wrath, like the animals on Noah's ark. But that is how the book of Jonah ends, on a cliffhanger. We do not know if Jonah finally repented of his ways or remained in his selfish thinking. You could build a convincing case for either one, but we simply do not know what happened to Jonah afterwards. All we know, is that 120,000 persons were saved and much cattle.

"Any questions or comments before we end class?" I asked. A hand popped up. "Yes, Chuck?"

"I was wondering, the Bible says there were '120,000 persons who didn't know their right hand from their left.' Is that number just the children who were in Nineveh? Or what does it mean?"

Chuck had brought up an interesting question, which I had not thought of before. I took a jab at it by answering, "Honestly, I don't know. I've never thought about it before. But my guess, it's not talking about the children, but something to do with ignorance. Sort of like when Jesus said, 'don't let your left hand know what your right hand is doing.' Or perhaps it's some type of Jewish idiom. I could be wrong, but that's my guess. Sorry it's not much help.*

"Are there any other questions? . . . No? Then would one of the young men like to close us out in prayer?"

***

THE TEENS DID an *amazing* job serving the Partnership that Saturday. Doing everything which was asked of them, and going beyond what was expected of them. I cannot brag enough how impressed I was with them.

Four came around, and the night was just beginning. We said our goodbyes to the ladies at the Partnership, and then headed back to the church building to prepare coolers, and to gather other last minute preparations for the photo-scavenger-hunt-pizza-movie-night.

NOTES

1. Youngblood, Kevin J., ed. Daniel I. Block. *Jonah: God's Scandalous Mercy: Hearing*

---

*I had not yet read that far into the Professor's commentary, who addresses this very question within his last chapter: "YHWH employed a phrase that occurs frequently with reference to proper Torah observance in Israel. God often warned Israel not to turn to the right or to the left as they walk the path of obedience (Deut. 5:32; 17:11, 20; 28:14; Josh 1:7; 23:6). These references indicate that this language is associated with Israel's access to special revelation, which distinguished for Israel between the right and the left. Nineveh, however, had no such access to YHWH's special revelation. He took this into account when administering his justice and mercy."

the *Message of Scripture: A Commentary on the Old Testament.* Grand Rapids, MI: Zondervan, 2013. Print.

2. Fig. 1: Drawing of relief from the North-West Palace at Nimrud.

3. Fig. 2: *Assyrian Relief, North-West Palace of Nimrud* (room B, panel 18). 865-860 BCE. British Museum: London. An Assyrian besieges a fortress. What appears to be a tank, is actually a battering ram.

4. Motta, Philip J., et al. "Feeding Anatomy, Filter-Feeding Rate, And Diet Of Whale Sharks *Rhincodon typus* During Surface Ram Filter Feeding Off The Yucatan Peninsula, Mexico." Zoology 113. (2010): 199-212. *ScienceDirect.* Web. 21 Feb. 2017.

5. Collodi, Carlo. *The Adventures of Pinocchio: A Tale of a Puppet.* Pisa: Aonia edizoni, 2012. Print. p. 69.

6. Fig. 4: Mazzanti, Enrico. *The Terrible Dogfish.* 1883.

7. Fig. 5: Cylinder seal depicting The Descent of Inanna. Courtesy of the Oriental Institute of the University of Chicago.

8. Fig. 6: Galle, Philips after Maarten van Heemskerck. *Jonah Cast on Shore by the Whale; A Monstrous Fish Regurgitates Jonah on to Dry Land Overseen by the Lord Above.* 1566.

9. Fig. 7: *The Rescue of Jonah from the Belly of the Fish.* 1647. Tsarskoye Selo Arsenal: Saint Petersburg, Russia.

CHAPTER 11

DANIEL,

SHADRACH, MESHACH, & ABEDNEGO:

WHEN YOUR LIFE BECOMES LIKE GARLIC BREAD

N ot to brag too much, but I make a mean spaghetti. Pasta is my top most favorite food group. I'm constantly resisting the temptation of moving to Italy; otherwise, I would be obese from inhaling all those carbs. Me and pasta go together like peanut butter and jelly, sailors and the sea, warts and toads, and any other good combination that you can think of. I've always loved spaghetti, even before I can remember. My parents on more than one occasion have shared a story of toddler me sitting in a highchair, being covered in orange sauce from head to toe.

But I learned to love pasta even more when I took Italian for a semester and a half, having to drop out for grade reasons/my brain not wanting to learn the language of those who make *good* food. My teacher hosted the class over at her place a couple of times, such as for Columbus Day, giving me the opportunity to experience the taste of homemade noodles and sauces.

Anyways, not only do I love to eat pasta, but I'm a pro at making it. Hey, just because I'm a desirable bachelor, doesn't mean I fall into the stereotype of only knowing how to cook Ramen, PB&J's, and cereal.

Not to brag, but I can cook quite a variety: chili, tacos, cookies, and pretty much anything with instructions on the box. I even know how to do my own laundry . . . and unfortunately, not ignorant in the ways in cleaning the toilet. I know what you're thinking, it's shocking that a guy like this isn't already married. . . . Or not.

Anyways, the sauce was ready, the noodles had just been drained, and the oven was beeping, which meant it was time for the garlic bread to come out. I could already smell their garlicky goodness seeping out of the miniature furnace.

***

I WAS EXCITED to teach that Sunday. I mean, I'm always excited to teach. But this was a different kind, a special kind. For the passages which we were going to be studying (Daniel 2-3), I had actually translated from the Aramaic into English during my super senior year at Harding.

The story of the three Jews and the fiery furnace is indeed told in Daniel chapter 3; however, there's an *important* detail which comes before that in chapter 2. That detail being a dream. In this chapter, King Nebuchadnezzar, or King Neb, has this *disturbing* dream. So

frightening! the Bible says, "his spirit was troubled," or "his spirit was impaled," in the Hebrew, being the idiom for such *deep* distress, "and his sleep left him." Unable to sleep, the king summons to him all his, "magicians, the enchanters, the sorcerers, and the Chaldeans," to interpret to him his dream (2:1-2). (As you'll quickly find out, the author of Daniel loves making list of synonyms. It's as if he took a Hebrew thesaurus and wrote every synonym he came across to craft a list of emphasis.) *All* of the king's necromancers were summoned to him, for King Neb was *starved* for an answer to his dream.

Now, though King Neb makes some *dumb* mistakes in the book of Daniel, for he is portrayed as a very comical foreign figure in this Jewish propaganda, such as making a 90 ft. statue of himself to compensate for his insecurities, or punished to be a naked, grazing beast for his arrogance—for the Lord *hates* pride, "Everyone who is arrogant in heart is an abomination to the LORD; be assured, he will not go unpunished" (Proverbs 16:5). Pride was even the sin, which disallowed Moses from entering into the Promise Land. Because he gave himself and Aaron the credit for miraculously giving to the people water, instead of Yahweh, . . . "Hear now, you rebels: shall *we* bring water for you out of this rock?" (Numbers 20:10).

Though King Neb makes some dumb mistakes, he's not a complete fool. This dream is so impaling, that he wants a genuine answer. He wants truth, not an opportunity for his conjurers to take advantage of him. Therefore, he puts his magicians to a test.

"I had a dream," announced King Neb. No, not a dream that his, "four little children will one day live in a nation where they will not be judged by the color of their skin but by the content of their character," but a dream that he demands his enchanters to not only interpret, but to tell him his dream as well. If they did so correctly, then they would receive, "gifts and rewards, and great honor." However, if they failed to both tell King Neb his dream and its interpretation, then they would be "torn limb from limb" and their houses made into a "dunghill" (2:5-6), not "ruins" as it says in the *ESV*, נְוָלוּ (nevula) being the Aramaic here for 'dunghill' or 'refuse heap.'

The sorcerers are baffled. Sweat probably dotting their foreheads, soaking their turbans and their other forms of headdresses, *nervous* from what King Neb had just asked of them. Like great politicians, they try to buy time by asking, "Let the king tell his servants the dream, and we will show its interpretation" (2:7). King Neb is not fooled by their hesitation, answering:

> "I know with certainty that you are trying to gain time, because you see that the word from me is firm—if you do not make the dream known to me, there is but one sentence for you. You have agreed to speak lying and corrupt words before me till the times change. Therefore tell me the dream, and I shall know that you can show me its interpretation." The Chaldeans answered the king and said, "There is not a man on earth who can meet the king's demand, for no great and powerful king has asked such a thing of any magician or enchanter or Chaldean. The thing that the king asks is difficult, and no one can show it to the king except the gods, whose dwelling is not with flesh." (Daniel 2:8-11)

These same Chaldeans who could 'read' the stars, smoke patterns, animal and people behavior, and sheep entrails could not 'read' nor divulge King Neb's dream. These sages knew that if the king did not tell them his dream, they would die. For they did not know what the king had seen; therefore, they could not invent an interpretation for it. What they answered next is interesting, "There is not a man on earth who can meet the king's demand, for no great and powerful king has asked such a thing of any magician or enchanter or Chaldean. The thing that the king asks is difficult, and no one can show it to the king except the gods, whose dwelling is not with flesh." Did you catch that? No man could possibly know this dream. It would take the power of a god to meet King Neb's demand. 'And the gods do *not* dwell with man.' Notice who says this. Not Jews, but the mages. Even these pagan wise men understood that God could not be with man. These divinators were not alone in their thinking, for it was a common thought throughout the nations that gods could not dwell with humans. The Jews believed this too, and they were right. Because of sin, God could not dwell with humanity. They were right.

Until Jesus came. Until the divine became flesh and dwelt amongst us (John 1:14). Accomplishing like he did so many times, the impossible.

KING NEB WAS *furious*! And so he sent a decree to his soldiers to slaughter all of the magi of Babylon.

The guards were dispatched, and along with the astrologers, they sought out Daniel and his amigos, or 'mere'im' as we say in Hebrew, and were going to kill them too. That was, before Daniel questioned their captain, "What is this about?" He then learned of the king's troubles and requested an audience with King Neb. Permission was granted to him, and the king's dream was revealed to Daniel by the King of Heaven. Straightaway, Daniel asked the captain again to see the king and for the lives of the wizards to be spared.

Just as Joseph had been brought before Pharaoh many years ago to interpret the monarchy's dream because his magicians could not, so does Daniel come before Nebuchadnezzar, divulging both his dream and its interpretation because of the power of Yahweh, "You had a dream."

He described how King Neb had seen a great image. The head of this statue was *gold*, its chest and arms were silver, its middle and thighs bronze, and its legs were iron with its feet partly clay and partly iron. There was then a stone, not cut by human hands, that smashed into the statue and shattered it into pieces.

There's not enough time to dissect the dream in its entirety; however, take note that the head of this image is *gold*.

Daniel does provide the interpretation from the Lord, explaining to King Neb that the statue represents different kingdoms or reigns. Additionally, while he does this, it's interesting that he mentions, "Now *we* will tell the king its interpretation" (2:36). It could mean that Daniel is using the plural in order to give God credit for this interpretation, or maybe he's providing credit also to the warlocks, attempting to convince the king in sparing their lives?

There are a few of different ways to interpret this dream. The first being the more traditional, that the gold is Babylon, the silver is the Medes and the Persians, the bronze is Greece, and the iron is Rome. However, this word מַלְכוּ (malku) can also be translated as 'reigns.' Meaning, King Neb's dream may serve as a table of contents of sorts for the book of Daniel, laying out a succession of human kingdoms: the *gold* head being King Neb (1-4), the silver King Belshazzar (5,7,8), the bronze King Darius (6,9,11-12), and the iron King Cyrus (10). (Note, the book of Daniel is not arranged in chronological order. Also, notice how each chapter (with the exception of 12) begin by mentioning which king Daniel or his mere'im are under.)

The statue could also be a dual prophesy, representing both these kings and the great kingdoms to come, similarly to how Isaiah 7:14

both predicts the birth of a child during the reign of King Ahaz, and of the birth of Christ.

The stone is the Kingdom of Heaven, which plays a pivotal role in the theme of this book—that the kings and kingdoms of man will rise and fall, but the Kingdom of YHWH will last forever. And notice that the kingdoms of man are represented as an image, but not the Lord. He is seen as an imageless stone, for to represent Him as an image would break the second commandment. Did I mention that the head of this statue was gold?

Anyways, after Daniel reveals to King Neb his dream and its interpretation, what happens next is *amazing*. King Nebuchadnezzar, the ruler of the Babylonian Empire, "fell upon his face and paid homage to Daniel, and commanded that an offering and incense be offered up to him" (2:46). King Neb *bows* before Daniel, which means he pays homage to Yahweh. Recall from Elisha, the prophet of the Lord was His avatar, His representative here on earth. Daniel was the image of God, and the cool thing is, so are we. Remember back in Genesis 1:26 when God said, "Let us create man in our *image*"? That word for image, is the very same which is used in Daniel 2 in King Neb's dream, and again in Daniel 3 when the king creates an image of himself, צֶ֫לֶם (tselem). We are the images, the idols of the living God. Wow! That's . . . an honor—both humbling, and *scary*.

The king pays homage to Daniel, before fulfilling his promise, awarding him for providing the answers which he sought, even making him head prefect over the shamans of Babylon. And he also promotes Daniel's three friends, as Daniel had requested, Shadrach, Meshach, and Abednego, putting them over the affairs of Babylon. Or as they're called in *VeggieTales*: Rach, Shach, and Benny.

NOW, YOU DID not forget that the head of the statue in King Neb's dream was *gold* did you? The whole point of looking at Daniel 2, was to provide fundamental information for reading chapter 3. "What metal was the head of the statue?" I asked the class.

"Gold," they answered.

"Awesome! Yes, gold."

ONCE UPON A time, there were three Jews. These three Jews had been kidnapped from their families and had been taken to a kingdom far, far away. This kingdom was ruled by a prideful king with a funny name, at least it's funny to us. No, it was not King Nebula as some would say. Nor was it King Nebgoulash, as others would butcher it. But the name of this king was King Nebuchadnezzar. Now King Nebenezer was a prideful king. So prideful indeed, that he wanted a statue of himself. A tall, tall statue that would be built up, up, up, high, high, high into the sky. A tall statue. Taller than any beanstalk. The tallest statue in all the kingdom. . . .

SORRY, I COULDN'T resist. "The Three Jews and the Fiery Furnace" sounds like it would make the perfect title for a fairytale version of this story. You know, like the "The Three Little Pigs," "The Three Billy Goats Gruff," "The Three Little Jews." Anyways, so King Neb decided to make a statue as big as his ego, 60 cubits high and 6 cubits wide. The metal of this statue, you guessed it, *gold*. Also, the dimensions of this statue are strange. It's extremely tall, but not too wide. It's not like these magnificent statues of a giant man as we're used to seeing in depictions for this story, but more like a tiny idol on top of a really high pole. I also do not think it's a coincidence that both of the dimensions for this project involves a 'six,' for six is the number of man.

Man was created on the sixth day, though Creation was not completed until the Lord rested on the seventh. Therefore, in Jewish literature, six is often associated with 'man' or 'incompleteness,' since man was created on the sixth day, while seven is often associated with 'God' or 'completeness,' since Creation was completed when God rested on the Sabbath.

So King Neb, being the dictionary example of 'narcissistic', in all his arrogance, builds for himself a 90 ft. image of himself. With the foolishness of the builders of the Tower of Babel, he has this golden image built. For he believes that he is so great, he can manipulate the God of the heavens. Notice, not just the head, but the entire image is gold. Perhaps, he truly believes he can assert his eternal reign. Inspired by the image in his dream to create this image to thwart his fate of being overcome by the silver or the stone. But he will soon discover, that Yahweh is not like other gods.

Not only does King Neb have this tselem built, but he gathers all, "the satraps, the prefects, and the governors, the counselors, the treasurers, the justices, the magistrates, and all the officials of the provinces to come to the dedication of the image" (3:2), which he had set up. He then commanded the satraps, the prefects, and the governors, *all* the governmental officials, to bow down and to worship this idol whenever they would hear the sound, "of the horn, pipe, lyre, trigon*, harp, *bagpipe*, and every kind of music" (3:5).

What? Bagpipes? The Babylonians had bagpipes?

I thought this was a strange detail too, and brought it up

---

*An instrument with four strings like a lyre, not a DC demon who fights the Teen Titans.

193

to the Professor in class. He believes that 'bagpipe' is a poor translation in the *ESV*, thinking it was more of a panpipe with a sackbut, possibly made with an animal bladder. Sadly, there were probably not kilt-wearing Babylonians who loved to eat haggis and to drink Scotch.

So the king had made this decree, that when the governmental officials heard these instruments, they would pay homage to the king's image he had erected. But if they did not, they, "shall immediately be cast into a burning fiery furnace" (3:6). No one wants to be thrown into an oven to be cooked like garlic bread. So whenever they heard the sound of ~~the horn, pipe, lyre, trigon,~~ the instruments, they would bow down to this statue.

All of them but *three*, Rack, Shack, and Benny.*

Wait, where's Daniel?

A very good question. One which I've often wondered myself, for are we not reading a book named after him? And surely as faithful as Daniel is throughout his book, he would have not fallen under this negative peer pressure in this chapter; it's uncharacteristic of him.

Most in likely, because of his promotion in the last chapter, Daniel was away on a business trip to another part of the kingdom during this episode. This isn't officially within the Bible, but it's the best hy-

---

*I've always found it interesting, that we remember Shadrach, Meshach, and Abednego by their Chaldean names, but we remember Daniel by his Hebrew. I don't know why this is; it's even written this way in the Bible. What makes this mystery even more bizarre, is that each of these men have a theophoric name, a name which bears the name of a god within it. Daniel means, "God is my judge;" Hananiah, "Yahweh is gracious;" Mishael, "Who is like God?;" and Azariah, "Yahweh has helped." These are their Hebrew names, yet when they're brought into Babylon, their given new names, Babylonian names which are also theophoric: Belteshazzar, "Beltis protects the king;" Shadrach, "Command of Aku;" Meshach, "Who is as Aku is?;" and Abednego, "Servant of Nebo." King Neb attempts to assimilate these four men into Babylon, giving them new names with their gods, trying to assert his dominance and have them forget their God. However, the opposite happens. For these four men do not assimilate into the world, but stand strong and courageous against it. Even when they're given titles of the world, they do not become of the world. Just as C. S. Lewis found truth in Norse Mythology, which helped in leading him to Christ, so too did truth shine through the lives of these men, who bore the names of Babylonian gods.

pothesis I've heard of the whereabouts of this missing Waldo.

The only officials who don't bow before the bunny, I mean statue, are these three mere'im. All of the others obey the king. Either bowing because the king said so, because they don't want to be thrown into the furnace, or because everybody else is doing it. Just like everyone else, Rack, Shack, and Benny knew the consequences for not worshipping this idol, yet they still chose to be strong and courageous. To stand up, even when *everyone* else was worshipping this idol. Even when everyone else is cussing, partying, smoking weed, sleeping around, or believing homosexuality is okay, we need to also be both strong and courageous. Yes, we may be thrown into our own furnaces of insults, isolation, and physical abuse, but if we are to be the people we should, to be the Christians we should be, we need to rise above. To stand firm in our faith and to be the images, the representatives, the visible faces of the invisible God.

And this choice these three Jews make does *not* go unnoticed. "Certain Chaldeans," were aware of the actions of these three mere'im. And what do these sharks do? while probably hoping for a swift demotion for these Jews? Why, they go and tattle to the king:

> "O king, live forever! You, O king, have made a decree, that every man who hears the sound of the horn, pipe, lyre, trigon, harp, bagpipe, and every kind of music, shall fall down and worship the golden image. And whoever does not fall down and worship shall be cast into a burning fiery furnace. There are certain Jews whom you have appointed over the affairs of the province of Babylon: Shadrach, Meshach, and Abednego. These men, O king, pay no attention to you; they do not serve your gods or worship the golden image that you have set up." (Daniel 3:9-11)

195

Firstly, the mystics butter up the king, stroking his pride like a cat in an old lady's lap. They then snakely recall the king's own words of how he had commanded for all the officials to worship his idol, before they go in for the kill, "Certain Jews disobeyed *you*, o greatness. They think they know better than you, your majesty. And these Jews are Rack, Shack, and Benny." Which of course ignites King Neb's pride. *Furious* that there would be men who would disobey *him*, King Neb. The king of kings, the head monarchy, the ruler of the mighty empire of Babylon. Who would *dare* to have the audacity to defy *him*?

The answer of course, is our three mere'im. They who understood that though King Nebuchadnezzar is great, Yahweh God is greater still.

King Neb then summons before him Rack, Shack, and Benny, reacting to this news brought to him by his priests. (Maybe even the same druids whom had their skins saved by Daniel in chapter 2.)

He then asks them, "Is it true, O Rack, Shack, and Benny, that you do not serve my gods or worship the golden image that I have set up? Now if you are ready when you hear the sound of the instruments to fall down and worship the image that I have made, well and good. But if you do not worship, you shall immediately be cast into a burning fiery furnace. And who is the god who will deliver you out of my hands?"

This trio of young men stand before King Neb. *The* king of Babylon. This is not similar if you or I were standing before President Donald Trump. True, the president could get you arrested if he desired, but the king could have you executed just because he didn't like your hair style. I know this is a silly example, but it's to emphasize my point. A king was *the* ultimate power. Political cartoons, poking-fun memes, and negative press which a president of the United States is bombardment with daily, would not fly in an empire such as Babylon, and would be equally met with brute force and bloodshed. No, we do not live in a country with a monarch ruler such as King Neb, which is why I'm trying to stress the predicament that Rack, Shack, and Benny were in. They were before *the* man who could either take or spare their lives with but a single word.

Yet, even knowing this, the three mere'im are *courageous*. They wouldn't need a Sorting Hat to tell them they would be in Gryffindor. Despite being before a king with unlimited power and just as much arrogance, him believing that not even their God could save them, the three men replied:

> "O Nebuchadnezzar, we have no need to answer you in this matter. If this be so, our God whom we serve is able to deliver us from the burning fiery furnace, and he will deliver us out of your hand, O king. But if not, be it known to you, O king, that we will not serve your gods or worship the golden image that you have set up." (Daniel 3:16-18)

These three Jews had such *amazing* faith, that they answer the king, "If God saves us, He is God. And if He doesn't save us, He is God."

But of course, this only infuriates the king even more. As his anger rises, so too he commands for the temperature of the furnace to rise, seven times more than it normally is. The three men are then bounded, "in their cloaks, their tunics, their hats, and their other garments, and they were thrown into the burning fiery furnace" (3:21). And the heat of the oven was so great, that it killed the men who threw Rack, Shack, and Benny into the oven. "Down, down, down. Sorry, I had to do the Hebrew Johnny Cash," I remember the Professor saying, when we had been translating this part.

Like my garlic bread, the three Jews were thrown into the furnace.

Perhaps even serving as a *twisted* inspiration for the brutality at Auschwitz.

Yet, the story does not end there. For when King Neb looks into the furnace, he does not see three men, but four. He even asks his witch doctors if they had thrown three men into the fiery furnace, and they assure the king that they did. Yet King Neb then states, "But I see four men unbound, walking in the midst of the fire, and they are not hurt; and the appearance of the fourth is like a *son of the gods*" (3:25). Now, remember who's speaking; it's King Nebuchadnezzar. The fourth man he is seeing could be an angel, a spiritual being clothed in holiness which would be thought of as a lower god to a Pagan king. King Neb even calls this deity an "angel" in verse 28. Or maybe he did not mean "angel" but "messenger," which מַלְאָךְ (malak) can also be translated as, (just as Greek's ἄγγελος (ángelos) can also be translated as either "angel" or

"messenger").

Or, who he saw could have been the actual Son of God, Jesus:

"Does anyone have a problem with this?" I asked the class. "Are any of you uncomfortable with the idea of Jesus appearing on earth before he came to us as a man?"

I was sweating a little, waiting in anticipation for what the teens would say. For some people don't like this idea—Jesus only came once [as a man]. He would not yet be a man in this instance, which should make his appearance here in Daniel not a problem. Similar in how he had showed himself to Saul after his ascension, and yet it was not the occasion of his 'second' coming.

"I don't have a problem with it," Karrie spoke up.

"How come?" I asked surprised.

"Well for me, I've always thought that the fourth man was Jesus here, which gives me comfort. For it lets me know that Jesus is right beside me in my own trials. Just as he's in the furnace with Shadrach, Meshach, and Abednego."

"Alright, cool!" I replied. "I've never thought of that before. Cool insight, Karrie!"

KING NEB THEN commands the mere'ım to come out of the furnace, *amazed* to see them unharmed. Not only are they themselves not burnt, but neither are their clothes (which the three mar'erim are probably thankful for), nor do they smell like fire. The only things which did burn, were the ropes that had bounded them. They were delivered, not only from the fire, but from their very bounds. For God can rescue us from anything. Even from the wages of sin.

King Neb then praises Yahweh, even making a new decree that anyone who goes against the God of Rack, Shack, and Benny should be torn limb from limb and his house made into a dunghill, "for there is no other god who is able to rescue in this way" (3:29). King Neb then promotes Rack, Shack, and Benny, only adding to the blessings which the Lord had already showered upon them, before the king again praises Yahweh:

"How great are his signs,

how mighty his wonders!

His kingdom is an eternal kingdom;

his dominion endures from generation to generation" (4:3).

This is such an awesome story—more than a little kid story. For it is a tale which expresses the amazing courage of three men, who stood firm in their faith and trusted in their God.

And one day, they'll live happily, ever after.

... "Fear not, for I have redeemed you;

I have called you by name, you are mine.

... when you walk through fire you shall not be burned,

and the flame shall not consume you.

For I am the LORD your God,

the Holy One of Israel, your Savior.... (Isaiah 43:1-3)*

———

THE FIRST SIX chapters of Daniel are court tales, narratives of the

---

*In Daniel 6, Daniel goes through his own faith trial, and, like his friends, remains faithful to God. This story is known famously as "Daniel and the Lions' Den." A tale, that has a few echoes of the story of Christ. Such in how King Darius did *not* wish to punish Daniel and tried to deliver him, similar to how Pilate knew that Jesus was innocent and tried to release him. And how Daniel was sealed in a tomb by a stone, stamped with the king's signet ring, before the stone was rolled away, and Daniel came out of the grave, alive! (No, he wasn't physically resurrected from death, but symbolically, Daniel went into the ground, which was the final resting place to the others who had become lion snacks, he had gone into Sheol, but was brought back because of the power of Yahweh.)

experiences of Daniel and his friends. The rest of Daniel, 7-12, is apocalyptic literature. A series of visions and their interpretations given to Daniel by angels, dominantly by Gabriel.

In chapter 7, Daniel has a vision of four beasts which come up out of the sea: a winged lion which loses its wings, being made to walk like a man and given the mind of a man; a bear with three ribs in its mouth, a leopard with four wings and four heads, and a terrifying beast with ten horns. A beast which sounds awfully similar to the imagery of the first beast in Revelation:

> And I saw a beast rising out of the sea, with ten horns and seven heads, with ten diadems on its horns and blasphemous names on its heads. And the beast that I saw was like a leopard; its feet were like a bear's, and its mouth was like a lion's mouth. And to it the dragon gave his power and his throne and great authority. One of its heads seemed to have a mortal wound, but its mortal wound was healed, and the whole earth marveled as they followed the beast. (Revelation 13:1-3)

As will be apparent throughout this chapter, Revelation has a lot of similar imagery as Daniel [and Ezekiel], which has a lot to do with them both being apocalyptic literature. For like Daniel, Revelation has a lot of symbolism within it, which is a trait of this type of literature. Therefore, Revelation is probably *a lot* different than what we have been led to think, such as by the influence of Tim LaHaye's fictional *Left Behind* series. (Many of my own views of Revelation stem from a commentary by Dr. Edward P. Myers,[4] who, in my opinion, presents a more balanced view of this book than many of the theories which are out there.)

Daniel is later told that these beasts he sees are four kings which are to come (7:17). But, there is another king. After the four beasts, Daniel saw the Ancient of Days on His throne (7:9-10, Revelation 4) who slayed and destroyed the beast. And after His victory, Daniel sees another lord:

"I saw in the night visions,
and behold, with the clouds of heaven
there came one like a son of man,
and he came to the Ancient of Days
and was presented before him.
And to him was given dominion
and glory and a kingdom,
that all peoples, nations, and languages
should serve him;
his dominion is an everlasting dominion,
which shall not pass away,
and his kingdom one
that shall not be destroyed. (Daniel 7:13-14)

The kingdom of men come and go, yet another Kingdom comes. After the reigns of the four beasts comes the Kingdom of the Son of Man who establishes an everlasting Kingdom. The Kingdom established by the blood of Christ.

DANIEL LATER HAS other visions which are interrupted for him, such as the battle between a ram and a goat (Daniel 8). And in chapter 10, he sees a *frightful* being that causes him to faint, a being who then touches him and tells him to, "Fear not." A something or a someone who is very much like the being described in Revelation 1, who makes John fall at his feet. The Son of Man who touches him and tells him to, "Fear not." In Daniel, it sounds like this holy being is an angel. However, there's a theory that Jesus may be seen at the end of Daniel. There's little evidence to support this claim, but it's something to consider. Daniel has been told of the Son of Man who will establish an everlasting Kingdom. So what if he's actually given the chance, after all the other frightening imagery he has seen, after experiencing the reigns of so many earthly kings, actually given the chance to see—the Messiah?

> Then I, Daniel, looked, and behold, two others stood, one on this bank of the stream and one on that bank of the stream. And someone said to the man clothed in linen, who was above the waters of the stream, "How long shall it be till the end of these wonders?" And I heard the man clothed in linen, who was above the waters of the stream; he raised his right hand and his left hand toward heaven and swore by him who lives forever that it would be for a time, times, and half a time, and that when the shattering of the power of the holy people comes to an end all these things would be finished. I heard, but I did not understand. Then I said, "O my lord, what shall be the outcome of these things?" He said, "Go your way, Daniel, for the words are shut up and sealed until the time of the end. Many shall purify themselves and make themselves white and be refined, but the wicked shall act wickedly. And none of the wicked shall understand, but those who are wise shall understand. And from the time that the regular burnt offering is taken away and the abomination that makes desolate is set up, there shall be 1,290 days. Blessed is he who waits and arrives at the 1,335 days. But go your way till the end. And you shall rest and shall stand in your allotted place at the end of the days." (Daniel 12:5-12)

***

As the oven beeped, I carefully removed the bread from it, having learned my lesson about sticking my arm into ovens from the scar on my left arm for reaching into one for a pizza. The scent of garlic in-stantly activated my saliva glands. I had skipped my afternoon nap to cook such a meal before evening service that Wednesday.

I fixed myself a plate of spaghetti and bread and a glass of sweat tea, before sitting at the table. With a watering mouth, I said a silent prayer before picking up my fork. *Buon appetito*, I thought, slurping my first bite.

Mmmm, delizioso, the words echoed within my head, before quick-ly twirling another mouthful upon my fork.

NOTES

1. Fig. 1: Blake, William. *Nebuchadnezzar*. 1795-1805. Tate Britain: London.
2. Fig. 2: *The Image of Gold*. 2016. *SpiritualandTruth.org*. Web. 25 January, 2017.
3. Fig. 3: *Yaroslavl Icon Painting XIII,* Inv. 41418, IR 314. 1981. Yaroslavl Historical, Architectural, and Art Museum Preserve: Yaroslavl, Russia.
4. Myers, Dr. Edward P. *After These Things I Saw: A Commentary on the Book of Reve-lation*. College Press, 1997. Print.

CHAPTER 12

ESTHER: SHOWDOWN IN PERSIA:
HUMILITY VS. PRIDE

O n one fun Wednesday, instead of a group of us going to Dairy Queen for codename 'carrot sticks' after evening service, we went to the home of the Brunners for a *VeggieTales* night. Equipped with scrumdiddlyumptious snacks, we enjoyed the stories of Dr. Jiggle and Mr. Sly, Snoodle Doo, and Sheerluck Holmes.

Somewhere, there's a myth that *VeggieTales* are only for kids, which I believe as false. I am a huge advocate for this ministry from Big Idea. Though I do admit there are elementary elements to it, *VeggieTales* also presents some amazing messages using satire—planting seeds and opening doors for discussion. Not to mention, creating fun opportunities to share laughter and to rock out to silly songs.

***

IN LATE WINTER or early spring, (on the 14th day of Adar to be exact), is one of the most merry and fun festivals on the Jewish calendar—Purim. It is a time of carnival with pageants, plays, costumes, charitable gift baskets, food, wine, even jokes and pranks amongst those who think of it as a Jewish April Fool's Day. The entire book of Esther (also referred to as Megillah, which means 'scroll') is read in the synagogue on both the eve of Purim and during the day of it. As it is read, whenever Haman's name is recited, there is noise made to try and blot it out—booing, hissing, stomping of feet, and twirling of gragers (noisemakers), while cheering springs up by the mention of "Mordecai" or "Esther." Purim, is a humorous holiday, perhaps because of the irony of the humbling of Haman, and the elevation of Esther and Mordecai.

However, in the midst of these fun festivities, is the purpose for this holiday. The remembrance of God's salvation for His people during the time of the Persians. How He had used Esther, to preserve their people.

I HAD BROUGHT up the fun *VeggieTales* memory on the page before this, not only because it was a great one, but because of how it affects the story of Esther [hooray!]. In the *VeggieTales* version of her story, King Xerxes gets rid of his wife because she refuses to make him a sandwich at three o'clock in the morning. A very humorous scene which I still remember today. The real story though, is not as so.

Though it does make an interesting tale to try and explain to kids.

King Xerxes* was in a drunk stupor, since he was drinking more than sweet tea during his seven day banquet. Which was following his six month banquet that had been used to show -off his riches and power (in a display, many scholars

---

*Xerxes I, or, 𒀭𒆠𒀴𒊭 (x-š-y-a-r-š-a) in Old Persian, is believed to be the King Ahasuerus within the Book of Esther.

believe, was used to impress his subjects, installing awe in them, so Xerxes would have their faith in him as they strategized his war against Greece). The king was drunk, when he ordered his eunuchs to bring forth Queen Vashti, so he could display her to his guests. Yet Queen Vashti, surprisingly, refuses the summons of the mighty king, not wanting to be presented like some show-Pomeranian. Her disobedience creating the means of her being removed from the throne,* for the king's magicians who offered him wisdom feared that if the queen refused to listen to her husband—to the *king* of Persia—that so too would their wives refuse to head their voices:

> "For the queen's behavior will be made known to all women, causing them to look at their husbands with contempt, since they will say, 'King Ahasuerus commanded Queen Vashti to be brought before him, and she did not come.' This very day the noble women of Persia and Media who have heard of the queen's behavior will say the same to all the king's officials, and there will be contempt and wrath in plenty." (Esther 1:17-18)

SOMETIME AFTER, BELIEVED to be preceding Xerxes' defeat in his Grecian invasion, such as his humiliating victory at Thermopylae (where he faced the force of 300 Spartans), and his naval failure at Salamis, the king holds a national beauty pageant to both fill his harem and to find his next wife. Beautiful virgins were collected from across the Persian Empire (400 according to Josephus). They were taken into the king's palace in the city of Susa, which today would be in modern day Iran. They were forced to be contestants in *The Bachelor: Persian Edition*. One of these women who was ~~kidnapped~~ taken,

---

*It is unclear what became of Queen Vashti, for the Bible does not say. It is unknown if she was simply banished, or if she was executed for disobeying the summons of King Xerxes.

was the Jew, Esther [hooray!]. She then suffered twelve months of cruel torture. Or maybe not: "after being twelve months under the regulations for the women, since this was the regular period of their beautifying, six months with oil of myrrh and six months with spices and ointments for women" (2:12). After a year of beauty treatment, one by one the women were brought before the king. And when it was Esther's [hooray!] turn, her beauty won the king's heart. "She's hot!" he probably exclaimed, or something more like, "او گرم است" ("aq grm ast!"). Like Joseph* in Egypt and Daniel in Babylon, this Jew was given a place of honor in the empire of a foreign country, as Esther [hooray!] was crowned Miss Persia—as she was crowned as King Xerxes' queen.

Esther [hooray!] was more than a pretty face though, for it appears she was also very humble and loving, "winning favor in the eyes of all who saw her" (2:15). She may have also had some help supporting her. Not a fairy godmother, but God working behind the scenes. This is later implied by this book, for the Bible is cryptic in the Masoretic Text of Esther [hooray!] (the Hebrew text which is the version used in most Protestant churches). For Esther [hooray!] is unique; it is one of only two books in the Bible that do not contain the name of God within them, the other being Song of Solomon. Not once is He ever mentioned by name within Esther [hooray!]—not by "LORD" or even by "God." Perhaps being because it was written in code during the time of the Persian Empire, similarly how Revelation was during the Roman Empire. Or, the author wrote it so, choosing this style to hint that God doesn't always work directly, but sometimes He does behind the scenes. For we don't always see God or His hands in motion within

---

*Speaking of Joseph, one of his brothers who had sold him into slavery, was Judah. The same Judah who is found within both of Jesus' genealogies (Matthew 1:2-3, Luke 3:33). Though Judah sold his brother into slavery, Jesus redeems his family by the cross, and rescues us from our bondage.

the moment.*

ESTHER [HOORAY] IS *more* than a Cinderella story. More than the tale of an orphan who was raised by her, no, not her butler—she wasn't rich, and she wasn't Batman—who was raised by her cousin, before becoming queen. For it doesn't end with her marrying the prince and living happily ever after, or in this case the king. Marriage, being just the beginning of Esther's [hooray!] story.

Chapter three introduces the main antagonist within this book—Haman [boo!]. Haman [boo!] is a vizier to the king, a high official. A pristine man with great power and sway with the Persian monarchy. And this power fills Haman's [boo!] head with pride and arrogance. It is most apparent that he did not listen to the wisdom of ol' Uncle Ben, "With great power comes great responsibility."[2] A man who relishes the worship given to him by others. Yet Haman [boo!] is so puffed up, that he is *angered* by one little Jew, by Mordecai [hooray!] not bowing down to him. For Mordecai [hooray!] does not worship what the world worshipped. He did not fall into the pressure of the culture around him and bow down to something which he should not.

Can we say the same? For we too feel pressure from the culture around us, yet do we stay strong and courageous? or do we bow

---

*In the Greek versions of the text (which remains canonical for the Roman Catholic and the Eastern Orthodox churches), there appears to be six additions which may have been later attached to the book of Esther. These additions appear to have been made, to show that God was, without a doubt, at work within this story. And to give this book a more 'biblical' flavor. But by doing so, it feels, to me, as if they've over compensated for the lack of His name being mentioned, such in Mordecai's beautiful prayer:

"Then Mordecai prayed to the Lord, calling to remembrance all the works of the Lord.
    He said, 'O Lord, Lord, you rule as King over all things, for the universe is in your power and there is no one who can oppose you when it is your will to save Israel, for you have made heaven and earth and every wonderful thing under heaven. You are Lord of all, and there is no one who can resist you, the Lord. . . .'" (Addition C, 13:8-11, *NRSV*)

down to things which we ought not?

So angered is Haman [boo!], that he wants to kill Mordecai [hooray!]. But not only to kill him, but to wipe out the entire Jewish race, to commit genocide. (Did this very thing happen to Hitler? Is that why he used the Jews as an escape goat in order to seize power? Or was it because the Führer was kicked out of art school? . . . Or *bit* by a goat?) Haman's [boo!] plot is much darker than in the *Veggie-Tales* version, in which he makes a plan to banish the Jews to the Island of Perpetual Tickling.

Haman [boo!] then cast lots on which day he should exterminate the Jews, the lots falling on the 13th of Adar. This is where Purim gets its name. For פּוּר ('Pur') (or 'Purim,' being the plural) means 'to cast lots.' With a date assigned, Haman [boo!] then approaches the king and asks for his permission to carry out his scheme. Xerxes doesn't even ask any questions. He just hands over his signet ring to Haman [boo!] and tells him to do what he wants. And so Haman [boo!] issues his decree:

> Then the king's scribes were summoned on the thirteenth day of the first month, and an edict, according to all that Haman [boo!] commanded, was written to the king's satraps and to the governors over all the provinces and to the officials of all the peoples, to every province in its own script and every people in its own language. It was written in the name of King Ahasuerus and sealed with the king's signet ring. Letters were sent by couriers to all the king's provinces with instruction to destroy, to kill, and to annihilate all Jews, young and old, women and children, in one day, the thirteenth day of the twelfth month, which is the month of Adar, and to plunder their goods. A copy of the document was to be issued as a decree in every province by proclamation to all the peoples to be ready for that day. The couriers

went out hurriedly by order of the king, and the decree was issued in Susa the citadel. And the king and Haman [boo!] sat down to drink, but the city of Susa was thrown into confusion. (Esther 3:12-15)

The Jews were endangered by one man's ego. (That, is one BIG ego.) When Mordecai [hooray!] learned of Haman's [boo!] plot, he began to weep. He tore his clothes and put on sackcloth and ashes, as was the Jewish custom of mourning, as well as crying loud and bitterly within the city. For it was a time of great lament, of sorrow, and fear for the Jewish people. They needed help; they needed a savior.

Because of his sackcloth, Mordecai [hooray!] was not allowed to enter into the gates of the king's palace. And so, both he and Esther [hooray!] used eunuchs to communicate between them. Unlike Haman [boo!], Esther [hooray!] did not become a Bridezilla from power, yet remained an incredible women with a loving heart. When she heard what her cousin was wearing, she sent to him clothes for him to wear (I could make a joke here . . .). Yet Mordecai [hooray!] refused the clothes because of his mourning. He then revealed to Esther [hooray!] the fate of their people, pleading for her help, asking her to beg the king on the behalf of her people. But Esther [hooray!] was afraid, for the Persians had a law, that if a person approached the throne of the king without being announced, and if the king did not hold out his golden scepter to them, they would be put to death. Esther [hooray!] reminded her cousin of this rule. Mordecai [hooray!] then responded:

> Then Mordecai [hooray!] told them to reply to Esther [hooray!], "Do not think to yourself that in the king's palace you will escape any more than all the other Jews. For if you keep silent at this time, relief and deliverance will rise for the Jews from another place, but you and your father's house will perish. And who knows whether you have not come to the kingdom for such a time as this?" (Esther 4:13-14)

It appears that Mordecai [hooray!] implies that God's hand is at work. Speculating that perhaps Esther [hooray!] became queen because God knew this very circumstance would arise. Therefore, He had prepared Esther [hooray!] to combat evil and to save His people. However, Esther [hooray!] is like us—she had a choice. A choice to stand up for her people, to be strong and courageous, to approach the king with her neck on the line. Or, to play it safe, and allow this great evil to be carried out against her people. The choice was hers to make; however, Mordecai [hooray!] does also say in his wisdom, that if Esther [hooray!] refused to accept this mission, then help would come from somewhere else. That God's purpose would be fulfilled by another.

Wow! How strongly should this speak to us? For each of us also have been given missions from the Lord, opportunities to share the Gospel, to share His love. However, how many times do we ignore these chances? How many times are our missions given to another agent, because we did not sacrifice our time or did not seize courage in order to fulfill them?

Let us bloom where we have been planted.

Esther [hooray!] then replies to Mordecai [hooray!]:

> "Go, gather all the Jews to be found in Susa, and hold a fast on my behalf, and do not eat or drink for three days, night or day. I and my young women will also fast as you do. Then I will go to the king, though it is against the law, and if I perish, I perish." Mordecai [hooray!] then went away and did everything as Esther [hooray!] had ordered him. (Esther 4:16-17)*

Wow! This woman not only embodies courage and love, but the very truth which Paul expresses in Philippians 1:21, "For to me to live is Christ, and to die is gain." No, Esther [hooray!] did not know Jesus, no she did not know of the hope of Heaven, but she *knew* it would be better to risk her life for her people and to be killed, rather than to live and do nothing—even if by chance she was somehow spared by the upcoming slaughter.

"If I perish, I perish." Do we have the courage to say such a thing? Would we be willing to risk our very lives for the Lord and His plans? Or on a smaller scale, are we willing to risk our friends, our jobs, our Facebook statuses? Are we courageous enough to say, "If I'm unfriended, I'm unfriended?" "If I'm fired, I'm fired?" "If I'm deleted, I'm deleted?" "If I perish, I perish?"

ON THE THIRD day, Esther [hooray!] came before the king. She was

---

*Trivia: Do you know what other biblical queen proclaimed a fast?

Answer: Queen Jezebel, though for an opposite motive. Creating a ruse so she could steal the vineyard and life of Naboth, so that her husband, King Ahab, could have his vineyard (1 Kings 21).

risking *everything*, even willing to forfeit her life to save her people, just as Jesus was willing to offer up his. Esther [hooray!] came before the king knowing that she may die, just as Jesus entered Jerusalem knowing that he would (Matthew 16:21).

Esther [hooray!] had reasons to fear. For if King Xerxes, the king who had gotten rid of his first wife for disobeying him and not displaying herself, did not offer his golden scepter to her, she was dead. She and the king were also no longer newlyweds, being married for about five years by this episode. And she may have had fear of their possible rocky relationship, for Esther [hooray!] had told Mordecai [hooray!] that she had not seen her husband in thirty days (4:11).

On the third day, Esther [hooray!] was *courageous* enough to enter the throne room—

Esther [hooray!] came before the throne of the king on behalf of her people, just as Jesus appears before the throne of the Father on our behalf. Through Jesus, we have no restrictions before the throne of God. We do not have to wait to be summoned or need a golden scepter extended to us, for as it says in Hebrews 4:15-16, "For we do not have a high priest who is unable to sympathize with our weaknesses, but one who in every respect has been tempted as we are, yet without sin. Let us then with confidence draw near to the throne of grace, that we may receive mercy and find grace to help in time of need." However, though we can freely come before the King once saved, we should have the same fear as Isaiah, Ezekiel, Daniel, and John when they were before His throne. For God is holy, and though we are made clean by the blood of Christ we still fall short, we still sin. We are not fully holy, not yet. But as the Professor says, "The fear of the Lord, is the beginning of holiness."

Esther [hooray!] was willing to number herself with her people, like Jesus, as she came before the presence of the king. Can you imagine being in her slippers? The thumping of her rapidly beating heart? Her steps echoing down the hall with all eyes upon her? Her heavy breaths, not knowing which one would be her last?

But:

On the third day Esther put on her royal robes and stood in the inner court of the king's palace, in front of the king's quarters, while the king was sitting on his royal throne inside the throne room opposite the entrance to the palace. And when the king saw Queen Esther standing in the court, she won favor in his sight, and he held out to Esther the golden scepter that was in his hand. Then Esther approached and touched the tip of the scepter. (Esther 5:1-2)

God is good! and Esther [hooray!] is safe! Still loved and in favor with her husband, he extends his scepter to her. Not only does he do this, but he then asks Esther [hooray!], "What's wrong?" And even offers to give to her half of his kingdom. And so, Esther [hooray!] invites both him and Haman [boo!] to a banquet. The king quickly accepts; he collects Haman [boo!], and they go to this party which Esther has prepared.

Feasting plays an important role in the book of Esther [hooray!]. It was with a banquet that King Xerxes displayed his power and wealth, and it was during another when he was disgraced by the disobedience of Vashti. Esther [hooray!] also prepares two banquets, with the second being the one she reveals the danger of her people. Just as feasting plays an important role in Jesus' ministry, especially in the Gospel of Luke:

- Jesus dines with tax collectors and sinners in the house of Levi (5:27-31).

- Jesus eats at a Pharisee's house, where a woman washes his feet with ointment, and he forgives her of her sins (7:36-50).

- Jesus feeds the crowd of over 5,000* (9:10-17).

- Jesus dines in the house of a Pharisee with other Pharisees and lawyers, where he proclaims woes upon them (11:37-52).

- Jesus dines at the table of a Pharisee, where he heals a man on the Sabbath, and tells "The Parable of the Wedding Feast," and "The Parable of the Great Banquet," illustrating the Kingdom (14:1-24).†

- Jesus describes a feast to celebrate the return of the prodigal son within his parable (15:23-24).

- Lastly, Jesus also celebrates the Passover with his disciples, and

---

*"And those who ate were about five thousand men, besides women and children" (Matthew 14:21).

†Jesus also alludes to a feast in Heaven within Matthew's Gospel, "I tell you, many will come from east and west and recline at table with Abraham, Isaac, and Jacob in the kingdom of heaven" (8:11), which is also mentioned by John in Revelation, "And the angel said to me, 'Write this: Blessed are those who are invited to the marriage supper of the Lamb'" (19:9).

institutes the Lord's Supper (22:7-38).*

So, why is food so important within the books of Esther and Luke?

Because of the fellowship which comes from around a table. There is a lot which you can learn, a lot that you can experience, a lot which you can give, by sharing a meal with another. The table, is the ideal location for fellowship.

AFTER DRINKING MORE wine, King Xerxes again asks Esther [hooray!] . . . "Now Esther [hooray!], what do you want to ask for? Ask for anything, I will give it to you. So what is it you want? I will give you anything you want, up to half my kingdom" (5:6). Now whether Esther [hooray!] chickens out or it's a part of her plan, she does not reveal Haman's [boo!] plot in that moment, but instead invites him and the king to another banquet.

Haman [boo!] then leaves the party feeling great about himself. Greater than Frosted Flakes. That is, until he sees Mordecai [hooray!] sitting outside the gate—which just infuriates him. Therefore, he goes home and gets his friends together and his wife and begins to boast to them:

And Haman [boo!] recounted to them the splendor of his riches, the number of his sons, all the promotions with which the king had hon-ored him, and how he had advanced him above the officials and the servants of the king. Then Haman [boo!] said, "Even Queen Esther [hooray!] let no one but me come with the king to the feast she pre-pared. And tomorrow also I am invited by her together with the

---

*Luke even continues this theme of feasting within Acts, such as him describing the church breaking bread with each other (2:42), and by accounting Peter's vision, which gave the Jews freedom to dine with the Gentiles (10:1-33).

king. Yet all this is worth nothing to me, so long as I see Mordecai [hooray!] the Jew sitting at the king's gate." (Esther 5:11-13)

Haman's [boo!] hubris is astounding. He has all these blessings in his life—so many things to be thankful for which he proudly brags about to his wife and his friends. But despite these blessings, he can't see past one little Jew. Warning: Don't let this happen to you. Don't let one little thing in your life overshadow the blessings which God has given to you. Don't be a Haman [boo!].

Haman's [boo!] wife and friends then comes up with a solution for his dilemma:

> Then his wife Zeresh and all his friends said to him, "Let a gallows fifty cubits high be made, and in the morning tell the king to have Mordecai [hooray!] hanged upon it. Then go joyfully with the king to the feast." This idea pleased Haman [boo!], and he had the gallows made. (Esther 5:14)

Haman [boo!] falls in love with his wife's idea of building a 75-foot pole* to execute his rival upon. The *ESV* provides a poor translation here, describing Haman's [boo!] choice of execution to be a gallows, which is odd since the gallows wasn't invented until 1892 by Cheyenne architect James P. Julian. Before then, a gallows had never been used, though other forms of hanging had. Hanging has been a more common method of execution since the medieval times, with the earliest mention of someone being executed by this method being found within Homer's *Odyssey*:

---

*This may have been a literal measurement, a structure higher than the walls of Susa, or maybe even constructed upon the walls; or a hyperbolical expression. Either way, Haman didn't want to just kill Mordecai, he wanted to make a spectacle of him for all to see.

With that, taking a cable used on a dark-prowed ship
he coiled it over the roundhouse, lashed it fast to a tall column,
hoisting it up so high no toes could touch the ground.
Then, as doves or thrushes beating their spread wings
against some snare rigged up in thickets—flying in
for a cozy nest but a grisly bed receives them—
so the women's heads were trapped in a line,
nooses yanking their necks up, one by one
so all might die a pitiful, ghastly death . . .
they kicked up heels for a little—not for long.[5]

Hanging though didn't always mean to kill someone by strangulation or by breaking their neck. Hanging also referred to someone being crucified or impaled since their body would remain "hanging" upon the cross or pole after death. Dying from impalement was a common execution by the Persians and a precursor to crucifixion by the cross.* A large pole would be erected, and the one to be executed would be pushed off above it, being impaled by the pole. Darius makes a threat to do this very thing within Ezra 6:11, as he makes a decree concerning the rebuilding of the Temple: "Also I make a decree that if anyone alters this edict, a beam shall be pulled out of his house, and he shall be impaled on it, and his house shall be made a dunghill." Therefore, Haman [boo!] probably did not have a gallows built to hang Mordecai [hooray!], but a giant pole to have him impaled upon. The Hebrew word תָּלָה (talah), which means "to hang," being used here as a common idiom, to refer to Mordecai's [hooray!] body after death, and not the method of his execution.

*Crucifixion was first invented by the Persians and later 'perfected' by the Romans. Our first historical record of crucifixion comes from the Greek historian Herodotus, who describes Darius I the Great having 3,000 political opponents crucified, who were part of an uprising in Babylon in 519 BCE.

ON THAT VERY night, King Xerxes had trouble sleeping. And so, he gave orders to have the chronicles read to him—not the bedtime story I would have chosen; however, the one which was needed. For as the book is read to Xerxes, it brings up an account of when Mordecai [hooray] had saved the king's life, the event recorded, yet Mordecai [hooray!] had never been honored (Esther 2:19-23). Surprised, the king summons Haman [boo!], who was ironically on his way to ask the king about impaling Mordecai [hooray!]. The king then asks him how he would honor a man. Arrogantly thinking that the king was referring to him, Haman [boo!] unbounds the desires of his pride:

> "Let royal robes be brought, which the king has worn, and the horse that the king has ridden, and on whose head a royal crown is set. And let the robes and the horse be handed over to one of the king's most noble officials. Let them dress the man whom the king delights to honor, and let them lead him on the horse through the square of the city, proclaiming before him: 'Thus shall it be done to the man whom the king delights to honor.'" (Esther 6:8-9)

It appears the king's insomnia was good timing (or God's timing?). King Xerxes is in favor of Haman's [boo!] ideas, and dubs Haman [boo!] as the noble official to lead Mordecai [hooray!] through the city and have others honor him. Haman's [boo!] oysters are cooked as he fulfills the king's commands. *Humiliated*, as soon as the parade is over he, "hurried to his house, mourning and with his head covered" (6:12). He then whines to his wife and friends, before he is summoned to Esther's [hooray!] second banquet.

THIS SCENE UNFOLDS like a Jewish soap opera.

Haman [boo!] was a man who was on top of the world. He had money, power, materials, yet all of that was about to be taken. For at the party, after the king drinks more wine, he again asks Esther [hooray!] as if he's a grateful genie, "What do you wish for?" (7:2). It is then that Esther [hooray!] asks for her life, as she reveals Haman's [boo!] plot against her and her people:

Then Queen Esther [hooray!] answered, "If I have found favor in your sight, O king, and if it please the king, let my life be granted me for my wish, and my people for my request. For we have been sold, I and my people, to be destroyed, to be killed, and to be annihilated. If we had been sold merely as slaves, men and women, I would have been silent, for our affliction is not to be compared with the loss to the king." Then King Ahasuerus said to Queen Esther [hooray!], "Who is he, and where is he, who has dared to do this?" And Esther [hooray!] said, "A foe and enemy! This wicked Haman! [boo!]" Then Haman [boo!] was terrified before the king and the queen. (Esther 7:3-6)

The king is *FURIOUS*. He steps out of the room as Haman [boo!] is humbled, falling (naphal) before Esther [hooray!], begging her for his life. But when the king returns and sees Haman [boo!] on the same couch as his Esther [hooray!], his rage explodes. He immediately has Haman [boo!] executed, impaled on the very pole which he had built for Mordecai [boo!].

Haman [boo!] is defeated, but the Jews are not saved yet. The humble Esther [hooray!] weeps at the king's feet and begs him to rescue her people, for the law was still in effect. A law which not even the king could undo. For under the laws of the Medes and the Persians, once a decree was put into writing, it could never be repealed (Daniel 6:8). The decree had been made; it was too late to stop it. Similarly, in how once Adam and Eve had sinned, sin was now in the world. It could not be magically gotten rid of. Just as the Jews were doomed to die, so were all of mankind.

But, even under the most impossible of circumstances, God found a way to save us from the wages of sin—through Jesus, providing mercy while still upholding law. Just as through Xerxes, God saved the Jews from the same fate as the dinosaurs, extinction. Xerxes could not erase the law which Haman [boo!] had made, but he allows Mordecai [hooray!] to proclaim another decree to protect the Jews, giving them permission to fight back. The fate of the Jews had appeared to be irreversible doom—but *nothing's* impossible with God on your side.

When the thirteenth of Adar came, the Jews fought back. But not only did the Jews fight back, but they also had allies, "All the officials of the provinces and the satraps and the governors and the royal agents also helped the Jews, for the fear of Mordecai [hooray!] had fallen on them" (Esther 9:3). 500 plus the 10 sons of Haman [boo!] were killed in Susa; 75,000 enemies of the Jews were killed throughout the Persian Empire. The Jews were saved!

Purim was then established as a national holiday for the Jews. A festival to celebrate the foiled plot of Haman [boo!], and the salvation which came from the Lord. And from the courage of an amazing woman—Queen Esther [hooray!].

"But what if Haman had succeeded?" asked a Neoshian teen, during one of my youth minister's lessons.

"I think we must be careful when asking questions like that," he answered. "Especially since it didn't happen."

*"But if it had, some Jews would have survived, right? They all would-
n't have been wiped out."*

*"... True, we know at least two Jews would have somehow survived,
so that God's promise could be fulfilled. So that Jesus would have been
born. But wouldn't their genetics be weird by the time of Jesus' birth?"
Another teen mumbled something. "What was that?"*

"They would have had flippers!" he repeated.

My youth minister laughed. "And gills in their earlobes!"

EVEN IN A book where God is not specifically mentioned, the power
of His hand is seen. And even in a book where God is not directly
mentioned, Jesus too is seen. Jesus had two natures, both human and
divine, just as he was both king and servant. To a lesser degree, Esther [hooray!] too exhibited this duel nature. She was both a queen
and a Jew, which made her the perfect intercessor for her people, just
as Jesus was our perfect intercessor, the great high priest who can
empathize with us (Hebrews 4:15). Esther herself sympathized with
her people, "For how can I bear to see the calamity that is coming to
my people? Or how can I bear to see the destruction of my kindred?" (8:6).

Esther [hooray!] was a queen who saved her people. Rescuing the
Jews from foreign powers by risking her life for them. Jesus was the
king who saved his people. Rescuing the Church from foreign powers,
from sin, by sacrificing his life for us. Providing the gifts of mercy,
grace, and salvation. And just as Haman [boo!] suffered the punishment which he had constructed with his own hands, so too will Satan
suffer the punishment which he has constructed by his own hands,
for Hell was not originally prepared for man, but for the Devil and his
angels (Revelation 20:10, Matthew 25:41).

***

SADLY, THE TWO-FILM marathon came to an end. The TV was turned off, the remains of popcorn were picked up, cups and bowls were dumped into the sink, as we said our goodbyes to each other. And to Bob the Tomato, and to Larry the Cucumber . . . for now.

NOTES

1. Fig. 1: Cyron, Marcus. *Xerxes Enthroned*. National Archaeological Museum: Tehran, Iran.
2. Raimi, Sam, director. *Spider-Man 2*. Columbia Pictures, 2004.
3. Fig. 2, 4, 5, 6: *The Hague*, KB, 78 D 38 II. 1430. Koninklijke Bibliotheek (National Library of the Netherlands).
4. Fig. 3: Blake, William. *Mary Magdalene Washing Christ's Feet*. 1803-1805. Philadelphia Museum of Art.
5. Homer and Robert Fagles. *The Odyssey*. London: Penguin , 2006. Print. Book 22, Lines 491-498.

EPILOGUE UNO

J esus, has been promised. He has acted. He has been prophesied. He has participated. He has been cried out for, alluded to,
begged for. Yet, though we have seen him in the Old Testament, he
has not yet come to earth as the promised Messiah. *Long* has Israel
been waiting, as the wicked prosper. Longer than Abraham had for
Isaac, for God to send the One, who will save them:

Behold, my servant shall act wisely;
  he shall be high and lifted up,
  and shall be exalted.
As many were astonished at you—
  his appearance was so marred, beyond human semblance,
  and his form beyond that of the children of mankind—
so shall he sprinkle many nations.
  Kings shall shut their mouths because of him,
for that which has not been told them they see,
  and that which they have not heard they understand.
Who has believed what he has heard from us?
  And to whom has the arm of the LORD been revealed?
For he grew up before him like a young plant,
  and like a root out of dry ground;
he had no form or majesty that we should look at him,
  and no beauty that we should desire him.

He was despised and rejected by men,
    a man of sorrows and acquainted with grief;
and as one from whom men hide their faces
    he was despised, and we esteemed him not.
Surely he has borne our griefs
    and carried our sorrows;
yet we esteemed him stricken,
    smitten by God, and afflicted.
But he was pierced for our transgressions;
    he was crushed for our iniquities;
upon him was the chastisement that brought us peace,
    and with his wounds we are healed.
All we like sheep have gone astray;
    we have turned—every one—to his own way;
and the Lord has laid on him
    the iniquity of us all.
He was oppressed, and he was afflicted,
    yet he opened not his mouth;
like a lamb that is led to the slaughter,
    and like a sheep that before its shearers is silent,
    so he opened not his mouth.
By oppression and judgment he was taken away;
    and as for his generation, who considered
that he was cut off out of the land of the living,
    stricken for the transgression of my people?
And they made his grave with the wicked
    and with a rich man in his death,
although he had done no violence,
    and there was no deceit in his mouth.
Yet it was the will of the Lord to crush him;
    he has put him to grief;
when his soul makes an offering for guilt,

he shall see his offspring; he shall prolong his days;

the will of the LORD shall prosper in his hand.

Out of the anguish of his soul he shall see and be satisfied;

by his knowledge shall the righteous one, my servant,

  make many to be accounted righteous,

  and he shall bear their iniquities.

Therefore I will divide him a portion with the many,

  and he shall divide the spoil with the strong,

because he poured out his soul to death

  and was numbered with the transgressors;

yet he bore the sin of many,

  and makes intercession for the transgressors. (Isaiah 52:13-53:12)

JESUS:

IN THE NEW TESTAMENT

CHAPTER 13

JESUS WAS HUMAN, PART 1:

A CUTE, BURPING, POOPING, BABY

Oh Boy! I thought to myself. I was more nervous on my first Wednesday night, than what I had been on my first Sunday morning. This was because not only was I teaching a class of teens, but many of their parents as well. It's one thing teaching those who are younger than you. It's another matter entirely teaching those who are old enough to be your parents.

I knew there were things which I could teach them, and I also knew there were things that they could teach me and share with the class. (Which many of them did. Having some pretty cool insights that I'm glad they were willing to share with us, making me very thankful that they were there.)

You don't know everything, I reminded myself. One of the hardest things about being a teacher, is also remembering that you never stop being a student. Either younger or older, everyone has something which they can teach you.

"Who remembers what the theme is for this summer?" I asked.

"Jesus," answered one of the teens after a moment of hesitation.

"Yes, Jesus. On Sunday, we began by talking about how Jesus is in the Old Testament, or how the Old Testament points to Jesus. We noticed this in Genesis 3:15, from the prophecy that Jesus will crush the head of the serpent. And we also compared how Eve was tempted by the snake to how Jesus was tempted by the Devil in the wilderness.

"Tonight, we're going to begin our discussion of Jesus in the New Testament. Beginning with what we know as 'the Christmas story.' The birth of Christ."

I paused, just for a bit to think how to word my next thoughts, before I again opened my mouth:

"I wish his birth wasn't known as 'the Christmas story.' Don't get me wrong, I *love* Christmas. It's my favorite holiday, and I love the atmosphere of Christmas. The merriment, the joy, and the attitude of giving which it brings. And eggnog! I love me some eggnog." A few chuckles came from the crowd (or there probably would have been, if I had remembered to confess my love for eggnog).

"I do appreciate that we have at least one day a year which we think about his birth. However, in my opinion, we should think of it more often. Just as we shouldn't think about the Crucifixion and the Resurrection just on Easter or on Sundays. In my opinion, Jesus' birth is just as important as his death. For if he had not been born like you and me, the cross and the tomb would have meant nothing, for he would have just died as a god. He wouldn't have been fully human if he had just magically appeared, or if the stork had just dropped him off at Mary's and Joseph's doorstep. That's not how we get babies.

"Like us, Jesus was born as a helpless baby. Who would grow into a boy, who would grow into the man who would become our Savior. With that said, let's begin with Matthew 1." I tried to hide my grin, as I heard pages flipping to the entry of a list of names, some which can be quite 'fun' when trying to pronounce on the spot, like Jechoniah, Shealtiel, and Zerubbabel.

When almost everyone had reached Matthew, I revealed, "I'm joking. Though we could talk about Jesus' genealogy and the importance which it holds, for the sake of time, we're not going to tonight. Please instead turn with me to Luke 1, and keep a finger in Matthew, for we'll return to it later. Luke 1," I repeated, turning there myself.

***

LUKE BEGINS HIS Gospel with an introduction to Jesus' cousin, John the Baptist. He intertwines John's story with Jesus', whose begins in verse 26:

In the sixth month the angel Gabriel was sent from God to a city of Galilee named Nazareth, to a virgin betrothed to a man whose name was Joseph, of the house of David. And the virgin's name was Mary. And he came to her and said, "Greetings, O favored one, the Lord is with you!" But she was greatly troubled at the saying, and tried to discern what sort of greeting this might be. And the angel said to her, "Do not be afraid, Mary, for you have found favor with God. And behold, you will conceive in your womb and bear a son, and you shall call his name Jesus. He will be great and will be called the Son of the Most High. And the Lord God will give to him the throne of his father David, and he will reign over the house of Jacob forever, and of his kingdom there will be no end."

And Mary said to the angel, "How will this be, since I am a virgin?"

And the angel answered her, "The Holy Spirit will come upon

you, and the power of the Most High will overshadow you; therefore the child to be born will be called holy—the Son of God. And behold, your relative Elizabeth in her old age has also conceived a son, and this is the sixth month with her who was called barren. For nothing will be impossible with God." And Mary said, "Behold, I am the servant of the Lord; let it be to me according to your word." And the angel departed from her. (Luke 1:26-38)

Mary is believed to have been between the ages of 12-15, when Gabriel had came to her and announced that she would be the mother of the Messiah. Maybe 16, but probably not too much older then that. (Their culture then was different than ours today. Older men who had already established themselves in financial stability, would marry younger women as soon as they were able to conceive children, since child bearing and raising was a dangerous business, many more children [and mothers] dying compared to those who became adults.)

You can't help but imagine what kind of woman Mary must have been. Yes, she was just as human as you or me, she wasn't some mysterious, heavenly thing, being a sinner who was also in need of a Savior for redemption. On one hand, this can be easily forgotten, and too much praise can be given to Mary since she was the 'chosen one' to be the mother of Jesus. But on the other hand, she must have been an amazing woman of character, special for the Lord to have chosen her to conceive His son. This too can be overshadowed within the Protestant church, in fear that honoring Mary is one step too close to Catholicism. Like many, many things within religion, there needs to be a balance. To recognize that Mary was human, but that she was pretty special as well.

As angels almost always say when they appeared before men (for it is a humbling experience to be before such a holy being), Gabriel tells Mary, "Do not be afraid" ("Μὴ φοβοῦ," ["Me phobou,"]), before he delivers to her the news of her being the mother of Immanuel. Angels, when they're not disguised, are *scary* things. They are *not* like the pictures we see of cute like cherubs with their butt cracks showing or Precious Moments dolls. They're holy, surrounded in bright light, faces like lightning, with flaming eyes (Daniel 10:5-6). They are *not* something which you would want to bump into in a dark alley.

But Mary is confused at Gabriel's news, for she had not had sex with a man, being still a virgin. How then could she be pregnant with the Messiah? Gabriel then reveals to Mary that her baby would be conceived by the Holy Spirit. (No, this does *not* mean that Mary had intercourse with the Spirit/with God, which would not be an oddity in other religions, such as Greek mythology: Epaphus, Helen, Hercules, Perseus, Pollux, and Tityos all being children from relations between Zeus and mortal women. However, by some other mysterious means, which can only be explained as a miracle, the Spirit provided the other half of genetic material needed to conceive a baby. For Mary was still a virgin when she gave birth to Jesus. A child of the gods is not a new concept, demigods being many of the famed heroes in Greek mythology. But Jesus was not a demigod; he was simultaneously man and God, which is something that was/is believed to be impossible.) In great submission, Mary accepts the angel's words.

Overjoyed, Mary could not keep this news a secret, and so she traveled to a town in the hill country of Judea to tell her cousin, Elizabeth, the 'good news.' Elizabeth too is excited for Mary, "and she exclaimed with a loud cry, 'Blessed are you among women, and blessed is the fruit of your womb!'" (1:42). And so is fetus John, who leaps in Elizabeth's womb with joy (1:44). It was truly a time of celebration!

At last, the Messiah was coming!

IT APPEARS THAT during her visit, or sometime during this period, Mary sung the only Christmas song we're not afraid to sing in the Church of Christ all year long, "The Magnificat."* I have many fond memories of singing this song. . . . Perhaps one of my favorites which stick out, is when a group of us sang it in the sanctuary of the Little Rock Cathedral of St. Andrew during our visit. It was . . . such a powerful, and beautiful moment.

Mary's song is *powerful*. A tune that it countercultural, for it gives glory to the Lord who uplifts the humble and brings down rulers from their thrones. Lyrics that go against the song that the world sings, which takes pride in self and sin. The song of Lamech:

Lamech said to his wives:
"Adah and Zillah, hear my voice;
   you wives of Lamech, listen to what I say:
I have killed a man for wounding me,
   a young man for striking me.
If Cain's revenge is sevenfold,
   then Lamech's is seventy-sevenfold." (Genesis 4:23-24)

---

*Luke's Gospel is unique, in that it is the only one which features the Four Songs within in the tale of Jesus' birth: Mary's Song, "The Magnificat" (1:46-55); Zechariah's Song, "The Benedictus" (1:67-79); the Angels' Song, "Gloria Dei" (2:13-14); and Simeon's song, "Nunc Dimittis" (2:28-32).

Mary's Song

¹And Mary said,
"My soul magnifies the Lord,
  and my spirit rejoices in God my
Savior,
 for he has looked on the humble estate
of his servant.
  For behold, from now on all generations will call me blessed;
 for he who is mighty has done great
things for me,
  ²and holy is his name.
And his mercy is for those who fear him
  from generation to generation.
He has shown strength with his arm;
  ³he has scattered the proud in the
thoughts of their hearts;
  ⁴he has brought down the mighty
from their thrones
  ⁵and exalted those of humble estate;
⁶he has filled the hungry with good
things,
  ⁷and the rich he has sent away empty.
 He has helped his servant Israel,
  in remembrance of his mercy,
 as he spoke to our fathers,
  to Abraham and to his offspring forever."
(Luke 1:46-55)

Hannah's Prayer

¹And Hannah prayed and said,
"My heart exults in the LORD;
  my horn is exalted in the LORD.
My mouth derides my enemies,
  because I rejoice in your salvation.
²"There is none holy like the LORD:
  for there is none besides you;
  there is no rock like our God.
³Talk no more so very proudly,
  let not arrogance come from your
mouth;
 for the LORD is a God of knowledge,
  and by him actions are weighed.
⁴The bows of the mighty are broken,
  but the feeble bind on strength.
 Those who were full have hired themselves out for bread,
  ⁶but those who were hungry have
ceased to hunger.
 The barren has borne seven,
  but she who has many children is for-
lorn.
 The LORD kills and brings to life;
  he brings down to Sheol and raises up.
⁷The LORD makes poor and makes
rich;
  he brings low and he exalts.
⁵He raises up the poor from the dust;
  he lifts the needy from the ash heap
 to make them sit with princes
  and inherit a seat of honor.
 For the pillars of the earth are the LORD's,
  and on them he has set the world.
 "He will guard the feet of his faithful ones,
 but the wicked shall be cut off in darkness,
  for not by might shall a man prevail.
 The adversaries of the LORD shall be broken to pieces;
  against them he will thunder in heaven.
 The LORD will judge the ends of the earth;
  he will give strength to his king.

and exalt the horn of his anointed."
(1 Samuel 2:1-10)

Lamech sings how he will take down any who challenge him. That he will meet any conflict with even more conflict to get what he wants. A catchy anthem that is chanted by those who worship their own strength and desires.[3]

Yet Mary sings another song that is not of the world and is a liberation from it. There's a reason why it was banned to be recited in India when the British occupied it, or in Guatemala in the 1980s, or in Argentina during the Dirty War. It is revolutionary, as noted by Dietrich Bonhoeffer in his 1933 Advent sermon, before he was executed by the Nazis:

"The song of Mary is the oldest Advent hymn. It is at once the most passionate, the wildest, one might even say the most revolutionary Advent hymn ever sung. This is not the gentle, tender, dreamy Mary whom we sometimes see in paintings; this is the passionate, surrendered, proud, enthusiastic Mary who speaks out here. This song has none of the sweet, nostalgic, or even playful tones of some of our Christmas carols. It is instead a hard, strong, inexorable song about the power of God and the powerlessness of humankind."

Mary's song of praise for her child is also interesting, in that it echoes Hannah's prayer when she praised the Lord for her son, for Samuel. Aspects of Jesus' life mirrors the lives of the prophets, such as Samuel, Moses, and Elijah, perhaps providing evidence that he too was a prophet. In the first two chapters of Luke, there are several similarities between both Jesus and John to Samuel: Eli and Zechariah both being priests, and both loosing one of their senses, Eli his sight and Zechariah his speech (though temporarily); both Hannah and

Elizabeth being barren, the prophetess at the temple being named "Anna," which is the Greek equivalent to the Hebrew "Hannah;" and the similarity of how John and Jesus "grew," just like Samuel (1 Samuel 3:19, Luke 1:80, 2:40, 52).

Additionally, not only does this typology provide a foil between Jesus and John with the prophet, but perhaps Luke also draws attention that Jesus' birth was a time of change. For Samuel too was a pivotal character in an era of transformation, for he was the last of the judges, and he was the one who anointed the first two kings of Israel.

After spending some time with Elizabeth, Mary returned to Nazareth.

MARY, WAS NOT a queen. Not only was she not a perfect saint, but she did not stick out as an important figure during her time. She did not live in a palace nor a mansion, but was instead a simple peasant girl who was engaged to a carpenter. Now, it is unclear if she told her fiancé, Joseph, before or after she had told Elizabeth the news of her pregnancy. However, what is clear, is that Joseph was *shocked* when he heard the news:

> Now the birth of Jesus Christ took place in this way. When his mother Mary had been betrothed to Joseph, before they came together she was found to be with child from the Holy Spirit. And her husband Joseph, being a just man and unwilling to put her to shame, resolved to divorce her quietly. (Matthew 1:18-19)

Even back then, people knew where babies came from. And when Mary told Joseph that she was pregnant, his heart was probably shattered. For babies are only conceived through sex—*never* had a virgin given birth to a child before, never. Even though some of us would like to claim that we have. Therefore, it had to be impossible. Mary must have slept with another guy and had concocted this elaborate story of an angel in order to protect the other man and to justify her actions/mistake.

Now, Joseph could be thought of here as harsh. Here Mary is given a child from the Lord and he decides to divorce her; however, just as I have already mentioned, never before had a virgin given birth. It's just not a common thing that happens; that's not how things naturally work. What else should Joseph have thought? Yet he was the man, who decided to divorce her quietly. Not even to make it a show to shame her, an honorable man. And not only that, but under the legality of the Law, Joseph had the right to have Mary stoned (Leviticus 20:10). But he decided instead to show mercy to the woman he believed had caused him wrong, rather than to demand judgement.

The *only* thing which would be enough evidence for any man that Mary was not impregnated by another dude, would be by Divine Intervention. And that's exactly what it took to reveal to Joseph the truth:

But as he considered these things, behold, an angel of the Lord appeared to him in a dream, saying, "Joseph, son of David, do not fear to take Mary as your wife, for that which is conceived in her is from the Holy Spirit. She will bear a son, and you shall call his name Jesus, for he will save his people from their sins." All this took place to fulfill what the Lord had spoken by the prophet:

"Behold, the virgin shall conceive and bear a son,
　and they shall call his name Immanuel [Isaiah 7:14]"
(which means, God with us). When Joseph woke from sleep, he did as the angel of the Lord commanded him: he took his wife, but knew her

not until she had given birth to a son. And he called his name Jesus. (Matthew 1:18-25)

Not only does Joseph take Mary back and marries her, but he also does not have sex with her until after Jesus is born. Like I said before, Joseph was an honorable guy. And though we know little about him, it sounds like he was a great man of character like Jonathan Kent or Ben Parker, a great teacher to guide and to teach his adopted son what it means to be a man of God.

In those days a decree went out from Caesar Augustus that all the world should be registered. This was the first registration when Quirinius was governor of Syria. And all went to be registered, each to his own town. And Joseph also went up from Galilee, from the town of Nazareth, to Judea, to the city of David, which is called Bethlehem, because he was of the house and lineage of David, to be registered with Mary, his betrothed, who was with child. And while they were there, the time came for her to give birth. And she gave birth to her firstborn son and wrapped him in swaddling cloths and laid him in a manger, because there was no place for them in the inn. (Luke 2:1-7)

There is a lot to unpack from these seven verses. First off, where's the donkey? Usually featured in plays or movies of the Christmas story, is a donkey. We see Joseph leading it, with prego Mary riding on top of it, but where in the Bible is it? Matthew doesn't mention it, and if you look in Mark or John you won't find it there either; they don't even mention the Birth Narrative. And if *Shrek* has taught us anything, it's that donkeys are loud creatures that can't go unnoticed. So where in the Bible is the donkey?

The tradition of the donkey is actually not rooted within the Bible, but comes from another source, *The Protevangelium of James*. This is a fanciful tale written to glorify Mary, with the author adding things to the story that are not supported within the Bible. Such as Mary being miraculously born to elderly parents, who take her to be raised at the temple when she is three. And that Jesus miraculously appeared beside Mary instead of being born, so that her birth canal was not used and she remained a virgin. Though it is inaccurate, it is still the source of some honored views of Jesus' birth, such as Joseph taking Mary to Bethlehem on a donkey and Jesus being born in a cave. This is one example why it's important to dig into the Bible and see what it says, not being afraid to question tradition and wonder why we believe or do things the way we believe or do things. Now, Mary and Joseph may have had a donkey, but solely focusing on the evidence in the Bible, we don't know that for sure. There is one in Numbers 22 though—a talking donkey! And Jesus later rides one into Jerusalem, but that's not until Palm Sunday.*Samson also uses a donkey's jaw-

---

*If you get a chance, look at a donkey, or Google one. If you do, you'll notice that there is a natural cross pattern upon its back. Though there are many theories why this is, one legend, is because it was a blessing from Jesus riding the back of one in his Triumphal Entry. Others argue, that crosses didn't just appear on don-

bone to slaughter a thousand Philistines (Judges 15:15-17), and "and threescore and one thousand asses" (Numbers 31:34 *KJV*) were taken as a portion of spoils from Midian. Truthfully, I can't help but to smile and chuckle to myself whenever I read this verse in Numbers, for it reminds me of an incident at Neosho High:

We were watching a documentary in Biology, with some British voice actor describing an arid habitat. I might have been dozing off a little, when all of a sudden, a herd of wild donkeys come racing onto the screen, with the British dude saying, "Look at the majestic asses." Being an immature sophomore, I couldn't help but laugh along with my entire class.

Though today, donkeys are many times the bottoms of jokes, Charbonneau-Lassay makes known in his bestiary, that they were honored by many ancient cultures. True, they did develop some negative connotations, such as being stubborn beasts, or sometimes foolish (like Bottom in "A Midsummer Nights Dream"), or even red donkeys representing Evil Spirits;[8] however, they were also valuable animals associated with carrying, plowing, being symbols of wealth, and even

keys' backs one day, but that they have always had them, because God knew, even from the beginning when He had created them, that Jesus would ride one into Jerusalem:

Rejoice greatly, O daughter of Zion!
  Shout aloud, O daughter of Jerusalem!
Behold, your king is coming to you;
  righteous and having salvation is he,
humble and mounted on a donkey,
  on a colt, the foal of a donkey. (Zechariah 9:9)

Additionally, because of the donkey's role in the Triumphal Entry, some countries even dub this animal the title, "Christophore," "Christ-Bearer."[5]

Did you know: That during Mediaeval times, Europeans would use hairs from the crosses on donkeys' backs as remedies to cure some sicknesses? such as measles or whooping cough in children?[6] Additionally, around 1400 AD, there was a physician who listed 'riding a donkey backwards' as a cure for scorpion stings, "If a man who is riding a donkey is bitten by a scorpion, turns around and faces the donkey's tail, the pain will leave him and go to the donkey."[7]

being beasts who could be redeemed by the blood of a lamb: "The firstborn of a donkey you shall redeem with a lamb, or if you will not redeem it you shall break its neck. All the firstborn of your sons you shall redeem. And none shall appear before me empty-handed." (Exodus 34:20).

Donkeys do have important roles in the Bible, just not in the Birth Narratives. There being *much*, much more to them, then merely being symbols for a political party.

ANOTHER QUESTION WHICH arises, is, "How prego was Mary?" Again, looking at normal depictions of this story, Mary is usually bloated, ready to burst by the time she and Joseph reach Bethlehem. But the Bible only says, "while they were there," she gave birth; it doesn't state how long they stayed in the city. True, it would be hard depicting a pregnant woman without a large belly, and with only an hour or so to tell the story, time needs to be condensed in order to present a mystery play. However, we don't know how pregnant Mary was when she and Joseph left for Bethlehem. It was a mandatory mi-gration, but being a dangerous road, it would have been even more so if Mary was in the last stages of her pregnancy. She may have been, but we also do not know how long she and Joseph were in the House of Bread before she gave birth to Jesus. It could have been days, weeks, or even months.

Additionally, where did Mary give birth? A stable, a cave, or else-where? We're accustomed to seeing an innkeeper turn Mary and Jo-seph away because there was no room for them, but where is the inn-keeper in this passage? The Greek word for 'inn' used here, is κατάλυμα (kataluma), which is also used in Luke 22:12, when Jesus asks his disciples to go to a "large upper room" to prepare the Passover. (The *ESV* does mark in a footnote that 'kataluma' can be translated as 'guest room.') Ancient Israel did have commercial inns, which are more like what we normally think of when we hear this word. Luke mentions one later in his Gospel, using the Greek word for it in 10:34 within Jesus' parable of "The Good Samaritan," πανδοχεῖον (pandocheion); however, he does not use that noun in this passage.

HUMANS ASSUME THEIR own cultural norms are normal. I was surprised one night, when I was reading a chapter from *Grasping God's Word* for an assignment for my hermeneutics class. Chapter 7 begins with an anecdote of a missionary family who had spent years in Ethiopia. During their time there, they witnessed a Christmas pageant,

which was somewhat different than plays we see here in the States. Not only was it performed in a church building with dirt floors, surrounded not by snow but warm weather and banana trees, but Mary and Joseph were accompanied by many women from Mary's family, "who were chatting and giggling merrily about babies and 'motherly' things,'" on their way to Bethlehem. Mary then gives birth to Jesus in a sheep pen, and all the

women cried out a high, piercing note when Jesus was born, which is the typical joy cry of Ethiopians to announce the birth of a baby.

Like us, the Ethiopians filled in the gaps of the Christmas story with elements of their own culture. To them, it wouldn't make sense for Mary to be alone in the last weeks of her pregnancy, she would have had her family there with her to provide support. It is also normal for babies to be born in homes not hospitals, with women family members and midwives there to assist in the birthing process, since men are not allowed to be involved. At first, the missionaries were shocked, for this was not the story which they had grown up with. But then they realized that sometimes, we get too comfortable with how we see the world. Sometimes, we mistakenly think the way we see it, is the 'right' way to see things. Sometimes, we don't think, that there may be other ways in which to see it too.[10]

With that said, we read this story of Jesus' birth with much different lenses than that of the ancient Mediterraneans. This is because of the images passed down to us from our Western traditions.

BECAUSE OF THE census, Joseph was returning to his ancestral home, meaning he probably had family there in Bethlehem. So when Luke states, "because there was no place for them in the inn," he might have meant that the guest room was already taken. The Jews gave those who were older the higher honor, meaning that Grandma and Grandpa probably got the comfortable guest room upstairs, which would also be normal in most of our homes, while Mary and Joseph got the stable area. Or maybe, they were given these less desirable accommodations, because of the thought-illegitimacy of Mary's pregnancy?

Also, similarly in how we have cats or dogs that live in the house with us today, so too did the Jews have their animals live indoors with them—which would be safer than keeping them outside in town where they could be stolen. Even in some countries today, it's not uncommon to have chickens, goats, pigs, or other animals of the sorts under the same roof of the family, though it may sound foreign to us who think of these as farm animals, or have plenty of land to keep them separate. I remember going to H.U.T.* for a weekend years back, a missionary training ground. There, they had houses built like those around the world, such as an African mud hut, a Haiti shack, and a Chinese stilt house—which had goats and chickens penned under the house, that could be heard and smelled from the cracks of the bamboo floor.

One average home-type in first-century Palestine, would have had a stable area in the house, so that folks could keep their unattended animals from roaming off. However, this stable area may have been cleaned out for Mary and Joseph for their stay, and the animals tied up somewhere else, if the family was able to. For Luke doesn't mention if there were animals around Mary and Joseph when Christ was born, as we usually assume so, only that he was placed in a manger.

AND SO, MARY gave birth to Jesus, probably with the assistance of the women of Joseph's extended family (men were not allowed to help with such things). She then wrapped him in swaddling clothes and laid him in a manger.

Jesus was born, which means he had a belly button just like you or me. Our first scar and proof that we were born into this world. Which brings up one of the greatest Biblical mysteries for me. There's no way to prove it either way, but it makes you think—did Adam and Eve have belly buttons? I know it sounds a little silly, but think about

---

*Harding University Tahokdah

it. They were not born. But did God create them with one? If not, can you imagine the look on Adam's face when he first sees Cain? "God, what is that?! Is he broken?!"

Jesus was born. He did not pop out of the womb as a man, but as a helpless baby who needed to be fed, burped, and changed. In order to become like us, Jesus humbled himself to become an infant, which means he was probably *not* a talking baby ministering and spouting out prophecies, but a baby who threw up, pooped, and sadly, contrary to what is sang in one of my favorite Christmas songs, "Away in the Manger," even cried.

Now, I'm not pointing out these differences in an attempt to say, "Christmas is corrupt, it needs to be done away with." That's the last thing that I want. Nor am I saying that it's necessarily bad how we've translated and filled in the gaps of this story. What point I do want to

make though, is that the way we interrupt this story, is not the only way. Nor may it be culturally correct; however, it has been adapted in such a way, that each year it touches the hearts of many Americans, showing us the truth how Jesus came into this world.

AND THIS *AMAZING* event, did not go unnoticed. Nor was it kept just between the Mary and Joseph family. But heavenly heralds were sent out to announce that the King of the Jews had been born!

And in the same region there were shepherds out in the field, keeping watch over their flock by night. And an angel of the Lord appeared to them, and the glory of the Lord shone around them, and they were filled with great fear. And the angel said to them, "Fear not, for behold, I bring you good news of great joy that will be for all the peo-

250

ple. For unto you is born this day in the city of David a Savior, who is Christ the Lord. And this will be a sign for you: you will find a baby wrapped in swaddling cloths and lying in a manger." And suddenly there was with the angel a multitude of the heavenly host praising God and saying,

"Glory to God in the highest,

and on earth peace among those with whom he is pleased!"

When the angels went away from them into heaven, the shepherds said to one another, "Let us go over to Bethlehem and see this thing that has happened, which the Lord has made known to us." And they went with haste and found Mary and Joseph, and the baby lying in a manger. And when they saw it, they made known the saying that had been told them concerning this child. And all who heard it wondered at what the shepherds told them. But Mary treasured up all these things, pondering them in her heart. And the shepherds returned, glorifying and praising God for all they had heard and seen, as it had been told them. (Luke 2:8-21)

Notice to whom the angels appear to. Not to royalty, or priests, nor the rich, but to simple shepherds attending their flocks. Shepherds were not the most wealthy of people. In fact, they were at the bottom of the totem pole with tax collectors and dung sweepers. They were a labor class who by Jesus' day were looked down on. Some believe this to be the case, because Israel was becoming more developed, forgetting their rural roots (which can be seen in America today). And arguably because of the possible prejudices that the Egyptians had for shepherds, which may have seeped into the Israelite culture during their enslavement.

Now, there is much speculation if the Egyptians looked down upon shepherds or not. Some claim they do, because of the negativity in their historical records, their dislike for their Arab neighbors who were shepherds, and because of the oppression of the Hyksos who conquered Lower Egypt in the 15th century. ("Hyksos" is translated by Josephus as "king-shepherds" or "captive shepherds.") There is also a reference of this taboo in Genesis 46:34:

> "You shall say, 'Your servants have been keepers of livestock from our youth even until now, both we and our fathers,' in order that you may dwell in the land of Goshen, for every shepherd is an abomination to the Egyptians."

Now, it is unclear within this passage, if Joseph means as he's talking to his brothers, that the Egyptians thought of 'shepherds' as abominations, or if 'foreign shepherds' were. For the Egyptians did have their own flocks and shepherds to provide pastures for, which can be hard to find in an arid landscape under a seven-year famine. Also note, it was not socially acceptable for Egyptians to eat at the same table with the Hebrews (which may apply to all types of foreigners), described as an "abomination" (Genesis 43:32). Interestingly though, one of the Egyptians main deities, Osiris, the god of the underworld, is often depicted holding a shepherd's crook.

Another verse which is brought up in this discussion, is Exodus 8:25-26:

> Then Pharaoh called Moses and Aaron and said, "Go, sacrifice to your God within the land." But Moses said, "It would not be right to do so, for the offerings we shall sacrifice to the Lord our God are an abomination to the Egyptians. If we sacrifice offerings abominable to the Egyptians before their eyes, will they not stone us?"

The Egyptians had *many* gods; therefore, they had many sacred animals associated with these gods, such as frogs (Heqet), cats (Baset), crocodiles (Sobek), scarab beetles (Ra), etc. Some of these animals the Egyptians would *not* kill under pain of death, such as frogs (which is one reason why the second plague was so devastating. Sorry, no frog legs in ancient Egypt), since killing that sacred animal would offend the gods. These animals also had proper rituals which surrounded them, such as any dead cat, even one found in an alley, would be mummified and given a proper funeral. However, though like many ancient cultures in which vegetables were eaten more than meat (meat being more expensive than leafy greens), it is believed that there were certain sacred animals which the Egyptians could eat, like pigs (which were associated with Set), unlike sacred animals within India—but with some restrictions. Such as sheep (though not in Thebes; rams were associated with Amun and Khnum), goats (though not in Mendes), and cows by the upper class (though not white cows, or a bull with a sacred mark. Cows were associated with

Isis and bulls with Apis. The Apis bull would also not be killed (unless it reached age 28). A bull that would be chosen from the herd if it had certain markings,* which would then be brought to the temple, given a harem of cows, and lavished until it died by natural causes. There would then be mourning in all of Egypt for the beast, and an elaborate funeral given, such as removing the bull's internal organs and mummifying it, just like a pharaoh).

All that to say, animals were *important* to the Egyptians. Therefore, Moses may have been afraid that the Israelites would have offended the Egyptians if they performed sacrifices to Yahweh within Egypt. Yahweh Himself not even being an Egyptian deity.

As far as I have been able to find (or the lack of finding) in my research, the Egyptians themselves did not practice animal sacrifices. I could be wrong, but I have been unable to find any evidence of it, though they did for a time practice human retainer sacrifices, killing and burying the pharaoh's servants with him, so they would be able to serve him in the afterlife. (The pharaohs were also buried along with their pets, as well as mounds of dead fish, accompanied with grains and other foods which would serve as nutrition.)

The angels appeared to lowly shepherds. Not to kings or priests, but to the lower class. Divine reversal is a major theme within Luke's Gospel. God may have also decided to send His messengers to the shepherds, as perhaps a reminiscent of David being a shepherd boy before he was crowned as king. However, the shepherds who were "out in the field, keeping watch over their flock by night," spark another controversy: "Was Jesus born on December 25th?"

The answer is, I don't know.

Though we can't know for sure since the Bible does not specifical-

---

*A black bull with double the hair on its tail, a white image of an eagle on its back, a white diamond on its forehead, and a scarab-beetle mark under its tongue.

ly say, I can make an educated guess and say probably not—but not for the reasons which are normally argued. Many point out that if it was December, it would have been too cold for the shepherds to spend the night outside with their flock; however, that is comparing Israel with the winters we know in America. December in Israel is during the rainy season. True, it is colder; however, it is normally around 47-60 degrees F, which would be like living in Lake City, Florida. Mild weather would be the commonality during this time, with only a few freezing, frosty nights. However, Jesus was probably not born in December for another reason other than temperature. From what little I know of shepherding from reading W. Phillip Keller, if it was winter in Israel, the sheep would be locked up in their pens on their home ranches for safety from the rains. Therefore, since the shepherds were outside of town with their sheep, it was most likely summer or fall during this occasion.

Then why do we celebrate Christmas* on the 25th?

This is because December 25th, under the adoption of the Julian calendar, had become the climax of the Roman seven-day festival, Saturnalia, which celebrated the god Saturn during the time of the winter solstice, before it was Christianized by Emperor Constantine in 336 A.D. (*Dies Natalis Solis Invicti*, "Birthday of the Unconquerable Sun," was another Roman holiday celebrated during this time. Though not as ancient as Saturnalia, it was established by the teen emperor Elagabalus at the beginning of the 3rd century, to worship his favored sun god, Sol Invictus.)

---

*Did you know, you can't take "Christ" out of Christmas? First off, 'Xmas', long ago, became a common abbreviation for 'Christmas.' 'X' not only representing the Greek letter chi, but also Χριστος (Christos), which is the Greek word for 'Christ.' Secondly, even if you wish someone a, "Happy Holiday!" which encompasses Christmas, Hanukah, and Cuanza, 'holiday' originates from the Old English word, 'hāligdæg' which means 'holy day'—a day of rest, or shabbaṭ. Christmas in its very nature, is Christ/God focused!

Though we do not know the exact day of Jesus' birth, I am still thankful there is at least one day each year dedicated in celebrating it!

I promise I am not trying to be a Grinch or a Scrooge by bringing up all these controversies and possible fallacies about the Christmas story. Like I said, I love Christmas; it's my favorite holiday. However, it is important to study and to think of what the Bible says vs. what we know, or what we think we know from practicing our traditions. Or, "Tradition, tradition! Tradition!" Tevye would have sung.

"Traditions, traditions. Without our traditions, our lives would be as shaky as, as . . . As a fiddler on the roof."[14]

***

"THE SHEPHERDS WERE overjoyed by the angels' tidings!" I exclaimed. "They went into Bethlehem to see the Messiah for themselves with their own two eyes. And after seeing him, they just couldn't keep this news to themselves, proclaiming to others what they had seen. They were excited about the coming of Jesus. The greatest Christmas gift we could ever ask for.

They were *excited*. Just as excited as we should be about Jesus. Let us keep reading," I said.

NOTES

1. Fig. 1: Hongnian, Lu. *The Annunciation to Mary*. 1948. The Ricci Institute for Chinese-Western Cultural History: San Francisco.[1]
2. Fig. 2: Delgado, Carlos. *Cathédrale Notre-Dame de Paris*. 2012.
3. Storment, Jonathan. *How to Start a Riot*. Abilene, TX: Leafwood Publishers, 2014. Print. p. 19-22.
4. Fig. 3: Blake, William. *The Nativity*. 1799-1800. Philadelphia Museum of Art.
5. Charbonneau-Lassay, p. 109.
6. Oliver, Harry. *Black Cats & Four-Leaf Clovers: The Origins of Old Wives' Tales and Superstitions in Our Everyday Lives*. New York: Penguin Group, 2010. Print.
7. "Hundreds of Odd Remedies Found in Old Book." *Popular Mechanics*, October 1923, p. 556.
8. Charbonneau-Lassay, p. 110.
9. Fig. 4: Shiyun, Lü. *The Birth of Jesus 2, The Nativity*. 1948. The Ricci Institute for

Chinese-Western Cultural History: San Francisco.

10. Duvall, J. Scott, J. Daniel Hays. *Grasping God's Word: A Hands-On Approach to Reading, Interpreting, and Applying the Bible: Third Edition*. Grand Rapids, MI: Zondervan, 2012. Print. p. 137-139.

11. Fig. 5: Blake, William. *The Descent of Peace*. 1809. Whitworth Art Gallery: Manchester, England.

12. Fig. 6: Blake, William. *The Annunciation to the Shepherds*. 1809. Whitworth Art Gallery: Manchester, England.

13. Fig. 7: Xiaoxian, Hua. 1948. *The Angel Spreads the Good News to the Shepherds*. The Ricci Institute for Chinese-Western Cultural History: San Francisco.

14. *Fiddler on the Roof*. Dir. Norman Jewison. United Artists, 1971. DVD.

15. Garcia, Cathy Rose A. "Paintings Depict Jesus Christ in Korea." 9 July 2008. Web. 2 Feb.

---

[1]Concerning these wonderful, Oriental pieces of art. When I asked for permission to use them within this book, Mark Mir, the archivist at The Ricci Institute, included this within his emailed response: "I should point out that the paintings you mention were done at the Furen University Art Dept. in Beijing in the late 1940's. Historically, localized or "inculturated" Christian art was encouraged and developed several times with varying degrees of success. They existed alongside traditional (i.e. "European") motifs and styles, just as they do today." Please, do not think of these masterpieces as blasphemy. Remember, Jesus was not a white man; he was a Middle Eastern Jew. Europeans and Americans are not the only ones who have imagined him in our image. Both Jesus and the Gospel have been adapted to ethnicities around the world.

[Surprisingly, and unknown to many, some Chinese ideographs are silent witnesses that their ancestors knew, or where inspired by, events found within Genesis. (Or maybe, this was part of the package that came from the event of the Tower of Babel?) For the majority of their characters are composed of a combination of other characters. Here are but a *few* examples of this:

告 (talk) [土 (dust) + 丿 (alive) + 口 (mouth)] + 辶 (walk) = 造 (create)

土 (dust) + 丿 (alive) + 儿 (person) = 先 (first)

土 (dust) + 口 (mouth) + 仆 (two persons) + 口 (enclosure) = 園 (garden)

一 (one) + 口 (mouth, man) + 田 (garden) + 礻 (God) = 福 (happiness)

木 (tree) + 木 (tree) + 示 (God [abbreviated form]) = 禁 (forbidden)

木木 (two trees) + 女 (woman) = 婪 (to covet, desire)

舟 (vessel) + 八 (eight) + 口 (mouths, people) = 船 (ship)

羊 (lamb) + 我 [above] (me) [(手 (hand) + 戈 (weapon)] = 義 (righteousness)

(This truth also seems to suggest, that the Chinese own language could be used as an effective tool in sharing the Gospel within their country.)]

Another artist who also shared Jesus to his country through art, is the Korean, Woonbo Kim Ki-chang. "'I was praying for the quick end of the Korean War and a unified peace, and soothed my painful mind with a paintbrush,' Kim said. 'I tried to make Koreans experience Jesus through the paintings. . . . I think I portrayed the noble sacrifices and the spirit of love of Christianity successfully.'"[15] Within Kim's thirty paintings, Jesus and his followers are depicted as if they are in Korea, such as the beautiful landscapes surrounding them, and their clothing. Jesus often wearing a gat, a traditional Korean hat worn by governmental officials and scholars.

CHAPTER 14

JESUS WAS HUMAN, PART 2:

WHERE ARE THE WISE MEN?

In actuality, we only spent one night upon the subject of Jesus' birth, though it does take up two chapters within this book. There's just so much to consider and to explore concerning this popular story, and a book provides much more freedom to do so. A story that became the dominant focus for the Roman Empire on December 25th, long before there was Cindy Lou Who, Frosty the Snowman, Rudolph the Red-Nosed Reindeer, or even, St. Nicholas—a man who became immortalized by his story, evolving into the loving Santa Claus, who is now fat because of Coca-Cola.

***

AFTER JESUS HAD been born, he was taken to the Temple. Just as any good Jewish parent would, they brought him there to be purified, circumcised, and presented before the Lord:

> And when the time came for their purification according to the Law of Moses, they brought him up to Jerusalem to present him to the Lord (as it is written in the Law of the Lord, "Every male who first opens the womb shall be called holy to the Lord") and to offer a sacrifice according to what is said in the Law of the Lord, "a pair of turtledoves, or two young pigeons." Now there was a man in Jerusalem, whose name was Simeon, and this man was righteous and devout,

waiting for the consolation of Israel, and the Holy Spirit was upon him. And it had been revealed to him by the Holy Spirit that he would not see death before he had seen the Lord's Christ. And he came in the Spirit into the temple, and when the parents brought in the child Jesus, to do for him according to the custom of the Law, he took him up in his arms and blessed God and said,

"Lord, now you are letting your servant
depart in peace,
  according to your word;
for my eyes have seen your salvation
  that you have prepared in the presence of all peoples,
a light for revelation to the Gentiles,
  and for glory to your people Israel." (Luke 2:22-32)

There are some pretty cool things within this passage. Not only do we have a man with the Holy Spirit living within him before the day of Pentecost (whom others, such as David and Elijah, may have housed too), or Simeon revealing that the Messiah had come for both the Jews and the Gentiles—for all peoples, but we also have God re-

turning to the Temple through Jesus. Remember, the Spirit of the Lord departed from the first temple, from Solomon's Temple, some-time during the events of the Captivity, which is described in Ezekiel 10:18-19:

> Then the glory of the LORD went out from the threshold of the house, and stood over the cherubim. And the cherubim lifted up their wings and mounted up from the earth before my eyes as they went out, with the wheels beside them. And they stood at the entrance of the east gate of the house of the LORD, and the glory of the God of Israel was over them.

The Spirit of God, or His Shekinah Glory, left the Temple because of the unfaithfulness of Judah; it was a *sad* day. The Temple was even destroyed and plundered by the Babylonians, with the Ark of the Cov-enant possibly hidden, destroyed, or taken too. Another temple was later constructed, Herod's Temple, which is where Jesus was brought to, though it did not possess the glory of the former, nor did the Spirit of God fill it as It had the first. But . . . through Jesus, He entered the second temple—many times. Yahweh had finally returned to His Temple. Not wrapped in a cloud, but a diaper.

No, God is not restricted to one location. But for a Jew, this is an awesome revelation. That after the Captivity, after Solomon's Temple had been destroyed, that He again would enter His holy place.

Secondly, the wishes of an old man were granted. He was *happy*. Simeon had been promised before he died, that he with his own two eyes would see the Messiah! Who knows how long he had waited for this moment. If he had to wait as long as Abraham had for Isaac, be-fore this promise was fulfilled. But in that moment, the Promise Keep-er kept His word. After seeing such a sight, Simeon sang out a beautiful hymn unto the Lord.

ON A SIDE note, I just want to point out that God is a genius. The time of the Roman Empire was the perfect time for Jesus to come into this world. True, the Romans were *not* the best role models; however, they had shaped a world that was ripe for Jesus. They had conquered a large empire, which thanks to the Hellenization of Alexander the Great, had one common language that almost everyone could speak, Greek. The Romans had also invented roads, which provided safer and faster routes for travel. Jesus also came during a time in which the Jews (thanks to the book of Daniel), were seeking a Messiah—searching for redemption. True, God could have sent Jesus during the time of the Tower of Babel before He had mixed up our languages, but I believe that would have been too early. Look at how much He reveals of Himself between Babel and Malachi. He also could have waited until today, with tools such as computers, the internet, and Google Translate to help Jesus reach large amounts of people. However, I believe that it would have been too late. Can you imagine the ancients waiting 2,000 years longer for their Savior? The Roman Empire was *not* perfect, *not* the ideal society—being like the U.S. and having some severe moral issues; nevertheless, it was the Goldilocks of times for the birth of Christ.

LIKE THE BEGINNING of the *Lego Movie*, everything is awesome. The start of Luke's Gospel begins with the announcement of the Messiah, Jesus being born into the world, the shepherds witnessing his birth with Mary treasuring their words in her heart, and with Simeon finally seeing the long promised Savior and singing out to Yahweh. Everything is awesome. Until Simeon kills the mood—

And his father and his mother marveled at what was said about him. And Simeon blessed them and said to Mary his mother, "Behold, this child is appointed for the fall and rising of many in Israel, and for a sign that is opposed (and a sword will pierce through your own soul also), so that thoughts from many hearts may be revealed." (Luke 2:33-35)

Talk about being a downer. "Congratulations on your baby boy, Mary! He's only eight days old, but know he is destined for great things. Oh, and by the way, a sword will pierce through your own soul." Thanks Simeon.

Nevertheless, his words were true. Yes, Jesus was only eight days old when this prophecy was announced, but his very purpose of coming to earth was the cross. And there is perhaps no other than Jesus who suffered more than he at his crucifixion, than his mother. . . . Mothers . . . can you even imagine what it would be like? To see your baby boy beaten, whipped, and executed before you and the whole town? Hanging upon a cross before your very eyes? Naked, and in pain? Dying a slow death, and-and you can't do anything to save him? . . .

Simeon was also not the only prophet present at the Temple, for the Bible also mentions another:

And there was a prophetess, Anna, the daughter of Phanuel, of the tribe of Asher. She was advanced in years, having lived with her husband seven years from when she was a virgin, and then as a widow until she was eighty-four. She did not depart from the temple, worshiping with fasting and prayer night and day. And coming up at that very hour she began to give thanks to God and to speak of him to all who were waiting for the redemption of Jerusalem.

And when they had performed everything according

to the Law of the Lord, they returned into Galilee, to their own town of Nazareth. And the child grew and became strong, filled with wisdom. And the favor of God was upon him. (Luke 2:36-40)

———

IN THE PREVIOUS chapter, the nativity scene was mentioned, but what was missing from it? What was missing which we normally see positioned around the manger with Marry and Joseph from our nativity models?

"The wise men," answered a teen.

"Correct. The wise men are not in this scene, for they come, we think, about two years after Jesus' birth":

Now after Jesus was born in Bethlehem of Judea in the days of Herod the king, behold, wise men from the east came to Jerusalem, saying, "Where is he who has been born king of the Jews? For we saw his star when it rose and have come to worship him." When Herod the king heard this, he was troubled, and all Jerusalem with him; and assembling all the chief priests and scribes of the people, he inquired of them where the Christ was to be born. They told him, "In Bethlehem of Judea, for so it is written by the prophet:

"'And you, O Bethlehem, in the land of Judah,
   are by no means least among the rulers of Judah;
for from you shall come a ruler
   who will shepherd my people Israel.'" [Micah 5:2]

Then Herod summoned the wise men secretly and ascertained from them what time the star had appeared. And he sent them to Bethlehem, saying, "Go and search diligently for the child, and when

263

you have found him, bring me word, that I too may come and worship him." After listening to the king, they went on their way. And behold, the star that they had seen when it rose went before them until it came to rest over the place where the child was. When they saw the star, they rejoiced exceedingly with great joy. And going into the house, they saw the child with Mary his mother, and they fell down and worshiped him. Then, opening their treasures, they offered him gifts, gold and frankincense and myrrh. (Matthew 2:1-11)

Magi in the East, saw a star in the sky, and read it as an announcement of the birth of a king. And so, they followed the star of David from the *east*, west to the City of David. Notice, that they entered a "house," the οἰκίαν (oikian), which can be translated as "house," "household," or "home." Is it perhaps Joseph's family's home, where Jesus could have been born in Luke 2? Or, had Mary and Joseph bought their own house by this time, no longer living in the stable? Ironically, the magi found the King of the Jews by gathering information from a pseudo-king. Herod the Great was not of the lineage of David. Though he had converted to Judaism, his father was an Edom-

ite. Herod had been appointed king of Judea by Rome and was used more as a figurehead, serving under Caesar rather than being a true king of Israel himself, being just another king of man. He was like Jadis, the White Witch in *The Lion, the Witch, and the Wardrobe*, a declared king, with not a drop of royal blood.

The Herods are also main antagonists in the story of Jesus: Herod the Great being a textbook example of a tyrant afraid of losing his power, attempting to kill Jesus when he was only a *baby*. While his son, Herod Antipas, executed John the Baptist, and was involved in one of Jesus' trials before his crucifixion.

The magi come before Jesus and offer to him praise, while also blessing his family with kingly gifts (which were perhaps used to fund their escape?). Notice how Luke focused upon the poor, Jewish shepherds, while Matthew's focus is on these richer, Gentile magi. For just as Simeon had sung, the Messiah had not only come for the Jews, but for both Jew and Gentile. This is why I don't believe we should disassemble our nativities. For though they may not be historically accurate, they paint a beautiful picture of both Jews and Gentiles uniting around the manger of the Savior.

Getting to see these Gentiles having access to the King of kings, brings amazing comfort for a goyim like me! Men who would be restricted to the outer courts of the Temple, getting to interact with the Holy of holies.

"How many wise men were there?" I asked the class. An eager teen raised his hand. "Primo?"

"We don't know," he answered.

"Why do you say that?"

"Because the Bible doesn't say. We know there are three gifts, but we don't know how many wise men there were."

"Exactly!" I praised. We don't know how many there were. We do know there were at least two, for they're referred to as wise *men*. There could have been three, or maybe even more.* Travelling such a far distance, coming to Bethlehem in a large caravan would have been a lot safer than three men trekking cross country by themselves.

The wise men are then warned that Herod's words of wanting to worship the Messiah too were not genuine, but a trap so that he could kill the babe:

And being warned in a dream not to return to Herod, they departed to their own country by another way.

Now when they had departed, behold, an angel of the Lord appeared to Joseph in a dream and said, "Rise, take the child and his mother, and flee to Egypt, and remain there until I tell you, for Herod is about to search for the child, to destroy him." And he rose and took the child and his mother by night and departed to Egypt and remained there until the death of Herod. This was to fulfill what the Lord had spoken by the prophet, "Out of Egypt I called my son [Hosea 11:1]."

Then Herod, when he saw that he had been tricked by the wise men, became furious, and

---

*Maybe 12?

he sent and killed all the male children in Bethlehem and in all that region who were two years old or under, according to the time that he had ascertained from the wise men. Then was fulfilled what was spoken by the prophet Jeremiah:

"A voice was heard in Ramah,

weeping and loud lamentation,

Rachel weeping for her children;

she refused to be comforted, because they are no more [Jeremiah 31:15]." (Matthew 2:12-18)

Just like how the Joseph, way back in Genesis, had saved his family by bringing them to Egypt so they could have food during the famine, so too does Joseph, Mary's husband, save his family by fleeing to Egypt. (Isn't it also interesting how God talks to Joseph through dreams, just as He had done for his ancestor, Joseph?) In order to save Mary and his son, Joseph leaves everything else behind, his home, his family, becoming a refugee, leaving to a foreign country, just like his forefather Abraham.

Sadly, there is also another Old Testament similarity here. For when Herod discovered that the magi were not returning to him, he became enraged. Not wanting to take the chance of another stealing his throne (even just a baby), he orders for all the two-year-olds in Bethlehem and the surrounding areas to be slaughtered, just as Pharaoh had done in Exodus 1:22, "Then Pharaoh commanded all his people, 'Every son that is born to the Hebrews you shall cast into the Nile, but you shall let every daughter live.'" However, like Moses, Jesus' life was spared because of the faithfulness of Joseph.

Just as God aided Joseph and Mary, I believe the Devil was also at work, whispering into the ear of Herod. For if the Enemy could have killed our Savior when he was only a baby, then there would have been no hope for mankind. But because of both the actions of God and the faith of man, Jesus' life was spared, and he was allowed to carry out his mission.

And God is an avenger. It is believed that it was the Lord Who struck Herod with a terrible and excruciating disease some time later, sometimes referred to "Herod's Evil." Jan Hirschmann, a physician at the University of Washington School of Medicine in Seattle, has diagnosed Herod as having chronic kidney disease, complicated by Fournier's gangrene from the descriptions Josephus has documented:

> But now Herod's distemper greatly increased upon him after a severe manner, and this by God's judgment upon him for his sins; for a fire glowed in him slowly, which did not so much appear to the touch outwardly, as it augmented his pains inwardly; for it brought upon him a vehement appetite to eating, which he could not avoid to supply with one sort of food or other. His entrails were also exulcerated, and the chief violence of his pain lay on his colon; an aqueous and transparent liquor also had settled itself about his feet, and a like matter afflicted him at the bottom of his belly. Nay, further, his privy-member was putrefied, and produced worms; and when he sat upright, he had a difficulty of breathing, which was very loathsome, on account of the stench of his breath, and the quickness of its returns; he had also convulsions in all parts of his body, which increased his strength to an insufferable degree. It was said by those who pretended to divine, and who were endued with wisdom to foretell such things, that God inflicted this punishment on the king on account of his great impiety;
> (*Antiquities of the Jews* 17.6.5)

I think, only two words can accurately describe what Herod must have been going through: 'ouch!' and 'ew!'

But when Herod died, behold, an angel of the Lord appeared in a dream to Joseph in Egypt, saying, "Rise, take the child and his mother and go to the land of Israel, for those who sought the child's life are dead." And he rose and took the child and his mother and went to the land of Israel. But when he heard that Archelaus was reigning over Judea in place of his father Herod, he was afraid to go there, and being warned in a dream he withdrew to the district of Galilee. And he went and lived in a city called Nazareth, so that what was spoken by the prophets might be fulfilled, that he would be called a Nazarene. (Matthew 2:19-23).

After the threat of Herod had passed, Joseph and his family had their own little exodus, as they left Egypt, and returned to the Promise Land.

IN LUKE'S ACCOUNT, after the narrative of Jesus' birth, he tells of a brief instance of Jesus' childhood twelve years later. Interestingly, this being the *only* story of Jesus as a boy recorded within the Bible:

Now his parents went to Jerusalem every year at the Feast of the Passover. And when he was twelve years old, they went up according to custom. And when the feast was ended, as they were returning, the boy Jesus stayed behind in Jerusalem. His parents did not know it, but supposing him to be in the group they went a day's journey, but then they began to search for him among their relatives and acquaintances, and when they did not find him, they returned to Jerusalem, searching for him. After three days they found him in the temple, sitting among the teachers, listening to them and asking them questions. And all who heard him were amazed at his understanding and his answers. And when his parents saw him, they were astonished. And his mother said to him, "Son, why have you treated us so?

269

Behold, your father and I have been searching for you in great distress." And he said to them, "Why were you looking for me? Did you not know that I must be in my Father's house?" And they did not understand the saying that he spoke to them. And he went down with them and came to Nazareth and was submissive to them. And his mother treasured up all these things in her heart.

And Jesus increased in wisdom and in stature and in favor with God and man. (Luke 2:41-52)

That's it. This strange episode is the only glimpse we get into what Jesus was like growing up. We won't see him again until he is around thirty-years-old, waiting until he is a full-grown man before he begins his short, three-year ministry. Though the whole Bible is about Jesus, it's interesting how we're given just a small portion of his life here on earth.

When you approach this story, you have to wonder what Mary and Joseph were thinking when they were wondering, "Where is our son?!" Not only was he their son, but he was also the Son of God. It's one thing to leave your own kid at the park, or the Temple in this case, it's another to leave the Son of the Universe. I can imagine hysterically, though it wasn't at the time, Mary and Joseph frantically searching their family caravan for their child:

MARY: "Did you check all the camels?"

JOSEPH: "Yes, honey."

MARY: "What about the sheep? You know he likes to pet the lambs."

JOSEPH: "Yes, dear. I've already checked. He's not here."

MARY: "Then we gotta turn this donkey around!"

JOSEPH: "Yes, dear."

So they turn the donkey around, and find Jesus just sitting in the

Temple, hanging with the rabbis. He's then probably embraced by his worried mother, followed by a scolding, before he respectfully replies, "Mom, why were you looking for me? Did you not know I would be in my Father's house?" He then returns home with his parents, and even though he did no wrong, Jesus still submitted himself to his guardians, following the Lord's command, to, "Honour thy father and thy mother" (Exodus 20:12).

There's also an interesting comparison within this passage. In verse 47, Luke describes the teachers being amazed at Jesus' answers. Some translate this passage as twelve-year-old Jesus teaching these older men, which he probably does some; however, they also assume it's because of his omniscience, since he was God. Yet, I don't believe that's what's happening here. For Luke also says in verse 52 that Jesus, "increased in wisdom." How could he have increased in wisdom,

if he already knew everything? Also notice, that it is Jesus, not the teachers, who is listening and *asking* questions.

But Logan, was not Jesus both man and God? Therefore, if he was truly God in the flesh, wouldn't he know everything?

That's a very good question, and one to struggle with. The truth is, we don't know how much he knew while he was here. Such as he did speak prophecies about the future, like his death, that Peter would deny him three times, and that Judas would betray him. And he also knew things about individuals, such as the personal relationships of the woman at the well. However, if he was truly human, I don't believe he knew everything. He could have (except for the date of his second coming (Mark 13:32)). I may be wrong, but the best passage which helps me to personally understand Jesus' balance of both man and God, is in Philippians:

> Have this mind among yourselves, which is yours in Christ Jesus, who, though he was in the form of God, did not count equality with God a thing to be grasped, but emptied himself, by taking the form of a servant, being born in the likeness of men. And being found in human form, he humbled himself by becoming obedient to the point of death, even death on a cross. Therefore God has highly exalted him and bestowed on him the name that is above every name, so that at the name of Jesus every knee should bow, in heaven and on earth and under the earth, and every tongue confess that Jesus Christ is Lord, to the glory of God the Father. (2:5-11)

Paul describes that in order for Jesus to become a man, he had to 'empty himself.' This is commonly known as 'kenosis,' ἐκένωσεν (ekenosen) being the form of the verb κενόω (kenoó) that is used within this passage. Jesus was both fully human and fully God when he was here on earth. But in order to become fully man, he had to give up or suppress certain aspects of his God-self, kind of like dormant genes. Thinking of this concept in a super simplified metaphor, there were some God-genes which were still a part of Jesus' DNA, still a part of him; however, they were suppressed, in hibernation like an inactive cancer gene.

Yet, is kenosis (self-limitation) not an aspect of God's very nature? Did He not limit Himself when He created the cosmos? For before the universe was only God—*everywhere*. Therefore, did He not need to carve out a space within Himself, so that we could exist? Or to whom did He give dominion over the earth?

This concept could also be thought of as a man who gives up his freedom to marry, to have sex and kids, in order for him to become a monk. The man has the freedom to choose to marry a woman, has the tools to have intercourse with her, to create life, but he chooses to give up these pleasures, in order to become a monk. It's not enough for him to wear the right clothes or to chant the right hymns, the man has to give up his choice of choosing a wife and to take a vow of celibacy, in order to truly be a monk. He also does not have to be a monk, having the same freedom to be a teacher or even a doctor, yet he still *chooses* to become one.

Another aspect of this mystery, is that it's easy to imagine man being anti-God, both being polar opposites from one another; however, I do not believe that is the case. For were we not created in His image? Therefore, I believe being man, is being more Godlike than what we normally think. Yes, currently, humankind are sinners; however, we weren't created so, were we?

Another way to look at Jesus' duel nature, is a metaphor one of my professors used in one of his classes: What if one day, Dr. McLarty, decided to give up his title as president of Harding University. He gave up his diplomas, sold his house, his suits and ties, gave up everything he owned, to move to a ghetto in New York, so that he could serve others at a soup kitchen. Though he gave up all these things, would not Dr. McLarty still be Dr. McLarty?

And though we do not know exactly what it means for Jesus to be both fully God and fully man in the same moment, we do know one characteristic of his Godhood that separates him from us. For every man has the opportunity to live eternally after death; however, every man has had a beginning. Yet Jesus is eternal in both ways, by never having an end nor a beginning:

In the beginning was the Word, and the Word was with God, and the Word was God. He was in the beginning with God. All things were made through him, and without him was not any thing made that was made. In him was life, and the life was the light of men. The light shines in the darkness, and the darkness has not overcome it. (John 1:1-5)

One last way to think of this concept, is a metaphor Young uses in *The Shack*. That when Jesus became human, he accepted the limitations which came with that, such as a bird, let's say a blue jay, accepting to only be grounded. It was created to fly, and it still has wings, it still has the ability too; however, it chooses not to, to only walk. Yet, though the blue jay chooses to only walk, it's still a bird, born with the nature to fly. But it limits itself in acceptance to fully embrace walking. (However, as a mentor of mine has pointed out, this analogy would not work if Jesus came as a bird because we were birds. For though Jesus is like God, he was also like us. Therefore, if we couldn't fly though we had wings because ours were clipped, Jesus' wings too would have been clipped. Every metaphor has it's limits and breaks down somewhere.[5] Another way to think of this concept, is that if you saw a slug and that slug needed a savior, you could somehow become a slug, yet at the same, still remain human.)

With that said, no one can fully explain this biblical mystery, just as we can't fully explain baptism or God Himself. But I think Paul's words help. That in order for Jesus to become man, he had to humble himself, make himself less, so that he could make us more. As it says in Hebrews 2:9-11:

> But we see him who for a little while was made lower than the angels, namely Jesus, crowned with glory and honor because of the suffering of death, so that by the grace of God he might taste death for everyone.
>
> For it was fitting that he, for whom and by whom all things exist, in bringing many sons to glory, should make the founder of their salvation perfect through suffering. For he who sanctifies and those who are sanctified all have one source. That is why he is not ashamed to call them brothers.

AS I MENTIONED before, we don't know much about Jesus' childhood. His birth and the incident of him being twelve at the Temple are the only records we have of him in the Bible. True, there are some extra-biblical material with stories of Jesus' boyhood; however, there's reasons why they're not part of the canon:

> After that again he went through the village, and a child ran and dashed against his shoulder. And Jesus was provoked and said unto him: Thou shalt not finish thy course (lit. go all thy way). And immediately he fell down and died. But certain when they saw what was done said: Whence was this young child born, for that every word of

his is an accomplished work? And the parents of him that was dead came unto Joseph, and blamed him, saying: Thou that hast such a child canst not dwell with us in the village: or do thou teach him to bless and not to curse: for he slayeth our children. (The *Infancy Gospel of Thomas*, Greek Text A)

Hopefully, you see why this story isn't in the Bible; it doesn't sound like the character of the Jesus who we know. Also, would we think of Jesus as being truly one of us, if he could do these things as a child? Additionally, according to John, Jesus' first sign was him turning water into wine (2:11). This is also not the strangest literature revolving around Jesus either, such as in the Gospel of Thomas, Jesus teaches that women must become men in order to be saved, and in the Gospel of Peter, the cross comes walking and talking from out of the tomb.

Though we may not like it, which is why some of these other accounts were written to fill in the gaps, we cannot help the fact that there is so much vagueness about Jesus' life, such as what happened to Joseph? After Luke 2, he just disappears. Did he run away, divorce Mary, or if he died, why didn't Jesus save him? You think after how awesome Joseph is at the beginning of Jesus' story, that the Gospels would at least mention what happened to him. Yet strangely, we get nada.

We do know some small details about his family, such as the fact that Jesus wasn't an only child, having four brothers and at least two sisters: "'Is not this the carpenter, the son of Mary and brother of James and Joses and Judas and Simon? And are not his sisters here with us?' And they took offense at him" (Mark 6:3), meaning, that the Virgin Mary did not stay a virgin, sexual relations being a part of a healthy marriage.

And can you imagine what it would have been like being the brother of Jesus?

MARY: "James! Quit picking fights with Simon. Why can't you be more like Jesus?"

Ouch! No pressure there.

Also, we can speculate, and assume that Mary may have been treated as a harlot. Given this stigma and living her life branded with a scarlet letter for the price of being faithful to God. In small towns, people talk. Even back then, it took nine months to form a baby. Meaning her neighbors may have done the math and figured out that she was pregnant before her wedding day. Adultery being one of the greatest sins in the Jewish culture, punishable by death. (Is this, maybe, one reason why Jesus spared the woman caught in adultery? Not only because he loved her, but because she reminded him of his mother?)

BEFORE CONCLUDING, I have a question for you, "What makes Jesus' story so unique?" There were other gods who made themselves appear as men many times, such as Zeus. Or other gods who were born as men, such as the Hindu deity, Krishna. He even grew up as one of us:

When Krishna was five years old he took the cattle out into the woods to graze; that day Kans sent a demon in the shape of a crane, and he came to Brindāban and sat on the river-bank like a mountain. All the herd-boys were frightened; but Krishna went up to the crane and allowed it to take him up in its huge beak. Then Krishna made himself so hot that the crane was glad to put him out, and then he held open the crane's jaws and tore them apart; and collecting the calves, the herd-boys all went home with Krishna, laughing and playing.

Another time Kans sent a dragon named Aghāsur; he came and hid himself in the woods with his mouth open. The herd-boys thought this open hole was a mountain cave, and they all went near and looked in. Just then the dragon drew in his breath, and all the gopas and calves were swept into his mouth and felt the poisonous hot vapour, and cried out in distress. Krishna heard that and jumped into the dragon's mouth too, and then the mouth was shut. But Krishna made himself bigger and bigger till the dragon's stomach burst, and all the herd-boys and calves fell out unhurt.[6]

These narratives, are amongst a collection of Hindu stories found, in *Myths of the Hindus and Buddhists*. These are but two stories from Krishna's childhood, which involved many more miraculous feats. Such as him killing the rākshasī Putana as an infant. A demon who tried to assassinate Krishna by poisoning her breasts, but instead had her life taken because of Krishna's harsh suckling, powerful enough to suck her life-air from out of her. Of him killing Trinavarta, another demon, at five-months old, who had come in the form of a whirlwind and had picked Krishna up. Krishna then made himself as heavy as a mountain, clinging to the demon's neck. Its eyes popping out of their sockets before falling to the ground and dying. (This story comparable in how Hercules had killed two, giant, venomous snakes sent by Hera at eight-months-old). Or of Krishna's mother seeing the entire universe within his opened mouth, of him making the herd-boys look like the gods just because he could, and of him killing the naga Kālīya as a boy by assuming "the weight of the whole universe," and dancing on the naga's head.

Though the stories of little Krishna are miraculous, they are not too outlandish when compared to the stories of the *Infancy Gospel of Thomas*, such as five-year-old Jesus playing in the mud and creating sparrows from it on the Sabbath. Perhaps providing even more evidence, that these stories don't belong within the Christian canon. Still—

***

"So, what makes Jesus becoming a baby different than these other gods?" I asked. "What makes Jesus different than Zeus or Krishna?"

There was quietness in the room for a moment . . . before a brave teen spoke up, "Because both Zeus and Krishna only appeared as human. But they weren't really humans. Such as if Jesus didn't have Mary and Joseph, Herod would have killed him. He wouldn't have been able to defend himself like Krishna, because Jesus was only a baby."*

"Exactly! Though there are stories of other gods becoming man, they don't fully become human. They are only gods which look like men. Jesus was still God, but he emptied himself of some of his godly attributes in order to also become a man. Does this make sense? . . . Sort of?" (For it is a concept I believe we can't fully understand while living in this life. . . . But one day, we will [maybe]. And isn't that a most comforting thought?)

NOTES

1. Fig. 1: Blake, William. *The Presentation in the Temple: "Simeon Was Not to See Death Before He Had Seen the Christ."* 1803-1805. Fogg Art Museum: Cambridge, MA.
2. Fig. 2: Blake, William. *Adoration of the Kings.* 1799. Brighton and Hove Museums & Art Galleries, Brighton, England. The Athenaeum.
3. Fig. 3: Xiaoxia, Hua. *The Adoration of the Magi, The Three Kings.* 1948. The Ricci Institute for Chinese-Western Cultural History: San Francisco.
4. Fig. 4: *Christ in the Temple of Jerusalem (The Conversation of Christ with the Scribes, Preliminaries).* 15th-16th Century.
5. Young, p. 101.
6. Coomaraswamy, Ananda K. and Sister Nivedita. *Myths of the Hindus and Buddhists.* NY: Dover Publications Inc., 1967. Print. p. 217-228.
7. Fig. 5: Maler, Indischer. *Bhagavata Purana manuscript, scene: Krishna Defeats the Serpent Kaliya.* 1640.

---

*Another comparison between Jesus versus Zeus and Krishna, is unlike these other gods who made moral mistakes, Jesus did not. To some religions, such as Christianity, Judaism, and Islam, this is a significant fact, because we believe *only* a god can be perfect. Perfection being a mandatory characteristic of being a god. However, for others, such as the Greeks, this trait does not define a god, for they were as flawed and made the same mistakes as their human worshippers.

CHAPTER 15

JESUS IS LORD:

SORRY CAESAR, BUT CHRIST IS #1

S weat was dribbling down my neck, as I continued to skate around and around the rink. A blister was forming under my right foot; nevertheless, though I knew there would be later pain, I tried to focus upon the moment. A nearly impossible task for a future-minded person as myself.

Several of us were enjoying Christian song night at The Zone, adults, teens, and kids. I was blessed in seeing their smiles and laughs. Blessed in witnessing Mason win the limbo challenge and Leo's pretty impressive skate-moves, playing a game of tag or two, and eating pizza. It was then for a moment, that a nasty thought crept into my brain: *This is all because of ME.*

Though I hate to admit it, I do acknowledge that for a brief second I bathed in this thought and said, *Yes, yes it is.* Righteous reasoning then entered the conversation, and with blushed cheeks I admitted, *No, no it isn't. It's all because of Him.*

Ministry can be a difficult job, in the fact that it offers many opportunities to indulge oneself with personal pride. Though tempting, these very same opportunities also offer reminders that nothing can happen without Him. That He is truly a living God at work, providing us time and time again reminders of this truth. And to thank Him for all that He has done, and all that He continues to do.

Thank you, I thought, as I kept skating around and around.

***

JUST AS THE theme of Hebrews is 'Jesus is Greater,' and the theme of Revelation is 'Jesus Wins,' the theme for Mark's Gospel, is 'Jesus is Lord.' Both in chapters 13 and 14 of this book, we focused on the humanity of Jesus. However, within this chapter, we'll focus on the opposite, on Jesus' deity.

Mark makes known his theme in the very introduction of his Gospel:

As it is written in Isaiah the prophet,

"Behold, I send my messenger before your face,

who will prepare your way [Malachi 3:1],

the voice of one crying in the wilderness:

'Prepare the way of the Lord,

make his paths straight [Isaiah 40:3],'" (Mark 1:2-3)

Unlike Matthew and Luke, Mark does not begin his Gospel from the beginning of Jesus' time as a human, but at the start of his ministry. A trait that is also seen in the Gospel of John as he too focuses on Jesus' divinity, elaborating upon how Jesus was the Lógos before the beginning. Therefore, neither Mark nor John include a birth narrative. This difference in theme providing a perfect example, that if we just had one Gospel within our Bibles, we would know everything needed for salvation, but we would be seriously lacking in our understanding of Christ, for he is indeed very complex.

Mark also begins, like John, with John the Baptist. Giving us the background of this prophet who had come to prepare the way for the Lord. John himself not being the Christ, being lesser than he who would later come to baptize with the Holy Spirit.

However, this idea of Jesus being Lord would have been a foreign concept for both the Jews and to the Gentiles, the Romans especially. You see, in our English translations of the Old Testament, there is both 'Lord' and 'LORD.' Have you ever wondered why there is this difference? And why 'LORD' is not seen in the New Testament? This is because 'Lord' in the Old Testament, comes from the Hebrew word אָדוֹן (Adon). Adon can be used for either the Lord (God), or a lord, either royalty or the 'lord of the home.' בַּעַל (Ba'al) is a synonym of adon. Ba'al being a Hebrew word whose meaning is also 'lord' or 'master;' however, Ba'al is *never* ever, never, ever, NEVER EVER associated with God, never ever, because of its affiliation with the Canaanite deity. The Jewish man of the house, or the master of the house, could be called Ba'al, being perfectly okay. But *never* would God be called Ba'al.

'LORD' on the other hand is the Tetragrammaton, or YHWH in Hebrew. Now, don't let 'Tetragrammaton' scare you; it's just the fancy, scholarly word which means 'four letters' in Greek, being associated with the tradition that surrounds the name YHWH. You see, YHWH is God's personal name, His Divine Name. Some would argue His most holy name, even. Because of this, the Jews held it with the *highest* of respect. They wouldn't even say it, in fear of breaking the Fourth Commandment, using the Lord's name in vain. Also know, that originally when Hebrew was written, only the consonants would be scribed. This being okay since every Jew spoke Hebrew, which at the time was more of an oral language. However, because of the Captivity, Aramaic began to become the native tongue of the Jews, who were then forgetting their Hebrew. Similar in how many Native American tribes have lost their native tongues to English. Therefore, in order to preserve the texts, the Masoretes dotted the Hebrew manuscripts with vowel points. They did not change the sacred texts, but added markers so that readers would know how to pronounce them.

However, 'YHWH' is a special word. In order to keep their tradition of not pronouncing this name, without deleting it from the text, but at the same time discouraging the oral use of it, the Masoretes dotted it with the vowels of adonai (the plural form of 'adon'). Forming a word that would confuse the eye, for it was supposed to be un-pronounceable, creating a reminder that when a Jew saw 'YHWH,' he was not supposed to say 'YHWH,' but 'Adonai' instead* This would be sort of like taking the name 'Justin,' but replacing the vowels with the vowels from 'Billy.' So that each time you saw 'Jistyn' you wouldn't say 'Jistyn,' but instead be prompted to say 'Billy.' (Before this tradition of the Tetragrammaton was known by non-Jews, a 16th century German translator mistakenly kept the Masoretic vowels along with the yod-he-vav-he, and came up with a mispronunciation of the Divine Name, though it has become a common name for God today—Jehovah.)

---

*Because of the Masoretic method of using the vowel points for Adonai in YHWH, we do not know 100% how this name for God is supposed to be pronounced. Commonly, many pronounce His name as 'Yahweh.' However, it could very well be 'Yehowah' or 'Yahuwah' as well.

One theory that is out there, and it is very . . . *cool* to think about; is that these aspirate consonants of the Divine Name when spoken, are the sound of breathing, the in and out of the air which fills up our lungs and keep us alive. A concept that is explored by Jason Gray, who beautifully expresses this thought in his song, "The Sound of Our Breathing."

What if, this is because with each breath, we witness? What if with each breath, we preach God's name? With His breath, He gave to us life (Genesis 2:7). And with ours, we worship Him in return. Saying His name again and again. On average, 26,000 times a day!

Rob Bell raises the question in his Nooma video, *Breathe*, "Wh-When a baby is born . . . what's the first thing it must do, or this baby isn't going to make it? Does this baby have to take a breath? Or . . . say the name, of God? And-and what's the last thing you do, and-and then you die? The last thing we do, we take our last breath? Or is it that when we can no longer say the name of God . . . we die?"[1] . . . What if this is further evidence, that the Sustainer is the One who keeps us living? The One Who's name we praise with each and every breath? "Yod. Hey. Vav. Hey."

Only God is Yahweh. To call anyone else 'Yahweh' would be *blasphemy* of the worst kind, being a foe of the Ten Commandments. In the New Testament, the word 'YHWH' is not directly seen in itself, the Greek texts using the word κύριος (kurios) instead. For this was the Greek word used for 'YHWH' within the Septuagint portions of the Old Testament, though it was also used for 'adon' as well. Therefore, Jesus calling himself, "Lord," was him associating himself with YHWH. Which if he was not the Son of God, he would have been either stupidly brave/foolish, a liar, or a lunatic to proclaim his own death sentence.

However, making such a claim would not only have offended the Jews, but the Romans as well. For Caesar was Lord. No, not the salad, the emperor. For to make such a claim would be putting oneself at the same level or higher than the Roman emperor, this too being an act that would have been punishable by death. Some even believing the emperors to be divine beings. Yet, Jesus was Lord. Yes, he was a man, but He was also God. A theme Mark makes well known within his

Gospel:

• JESUS IS LORD OF OUR BODIES: This theme is first seen in 1:29-45, as Jesus heals Peter's mother-in-law, many who are sick and possessed by demons, and a leper. There are two interesting facts to point out here. The first, is that Mark mentions Jesus, "would not permit the demons to speak, because they knew him" (34). Perhaps because Jesus wanted his people from their own lips and revelation to proclaim him as Lord, instead of from these demonic characters. The second being that Jesus heals the leper by touching him. A good Jew would *not* touch a leper, for he would not want to become unclean (Leviticus 5:3). But with Jesus, he changed the direction of the defilement. Instead of him becoming unclean, the leper became clean. For the Lord Jesus is the Purifier who came to restore all things.

This theme is then carried throughout Mark's Gospel, as he heals many, many others from various ailments throughout his ministry. Not one disease or disfigurement proving too challenging for the Lord of our bodies.

- JESUS IS LORD OF SIN: Not only is Jesus Lord of physical ailments, but also spiritual ones as well. In 2:1-17, a paralytic man is brought to Jesus by four friends. But when Jesus sees him, his first words are not, "Rise, pick up your bed and go home," but instead, "Son, your sins are forgiven." This comment stirs up the scribes who are amongst the crowd. In their hearts they are questioning, stating to themselves that Jesus saying such words are blasphemous, for only God can forgive sins. Yet Jesus reads their thoughts and tells them, "The Son of Man has authority to forgive sins," before he gives to the lame man the ability to walk. Jesus is the Purifier of both the physical and the spiritual, for he is the Lord of sin.

- JESUS IS LORD OF FASTING: In 2:18-22, there is an occasion in which the Pharisees and John's disciples are fasting, but Jesus' disciples are not. Jesus is confronted about this, and he asks them, "How can they fast while the bridegroom is here?" For it was a time of celebration. However, there would be another time in which to fast again, after the bridegroom had been taken away.

For Jesus is the Lord of fasting.

- JESUS IS LORD OF THE SABBATH: Jesus and his disciples are walking through a field in 2:23-28, picking heads of grain as they did so. The Pharisees see this and confront Jesus about it, asking why he would encourage work on the Sabbath. As a part of his answer he replies, "The Sabbath was made for man, not man for the Sabbath. So the Son of Man is lord even of the Sabbath." No, Jesus is not defying God and denouncing the Sabbath. For the Father had declared: "Six days shall work be done, but on the seventh day is a Sabbath of solemn rest, a holy convocation. You shall do no work. It is a Sabbath to the LORD in all your dwelling places" (Leviticus 23:3). Jesus obeys the laws of the Sabbath which his Father had laid out (Exodus 23:10-19); however, he does go against the laws which man, that the Pharisees had placed around God's law.

  Jesus also casts out an unclean spirit on a Sabbath in 1:21-28. Additionally, in 3:1-6, Jesus asks the Pharisees before he heals a man with a withered hand on another Sabbath, "Is it lawful on the Sabbath to do good or to do harm, to save life or to kill?" (And in John 5:8-9, Jesus heals a man who had been lame for *thirty-eight* years on a Sabbath. Healing on the Sabbath, seeming to indicate that Jesus was greater than it.) For Jesus is Lord of the Sabbath.

- JESUS IS LORD OF THE WEATHER/STORMS/NATURE: The disciples are amazed when Jesus calms a storm while they are out on the sea, even questioning: "Who then is this, that even the wind and the sea obey him?"(4:35-41). In 6:45-52, Jesus *walks* on water (during a storm—during large waves and harsh, howling winds), and the disciples are again amazed when the winds cease because of Jesus when he enters the boat. And in 11:20-26, Jesus curses a fig tree and it dies, because Jesus is the Lord of the weather/ storms/nature.

- JESUS IS LORD OF FOOD: Jesus fed a crowd of over 5,000 people with five loaves of bread and two fish (6:30-44), he declared all foods clean (7:19) (which is later seen fulfilled in Acts 10), he declaring that, "There is nothing outside a person that by going into him can defile him, but the things that come out of a person are what defile him" (7:15); he fed the 4,000 with seven loaves of bread and some fish (8:1-10), and he instituted the Lord's Supper (14:22-25). True, Caesar too provided bread in Rome so that his citizens would call him, "Lord;" yet, that is not what Jesus does. He does provide bread to fill stomachs, but in John he makes it very clear he did not do so for the sake of followers. He is not Caesar who wants numbers to follow him, but quality, disciples who tru-

JESUS IS LORD: SORRY CAESAR, BUT CHRIST IS #1

ly believe his lordship. Fulfilling a physical need because of his compassion, and showing that he is Lord.

However, this method angered the crowd and he lost many followers. He even asked the Twelve if they too would leave. Yet Peter responded, "Lord, to whom shall we go? You have the words of eternal life, and we have believed, and have come to know, that you are the Holy One of God" (John 6:68-69).

Yes, this topic does have some overlap with fasting, though also being the opposite. Nevertheless, just as Jesus is the Lord of fasting, so too is he the Lord of food.

• JESUS IS LORD OF THE DEMONS : This may sound weird to say, but it is also true:[*] "You believe that God is one; you do well. Even the demons believe—and shudder!" (James 2:19). In 5:1-20, a possessed man comes and falls at Jesus' feet in fear, before Jesus exorcises the demon within him:

And crying out with a loud voice, he said, "What have you to do with me, Jesus, Son of the Most High God? I adjure you by God, do not torment me." For he was saying to him, "Come out of the man, you unclean spirit!" And Jesus asked him, "What is your name?" He replied, "My name is Legion, for we are many." And he begged him earnestly not to send them out of the country. Now a great herd of pigs was feeding there on the hillside, and they begged him, saying, "Send us to the pigs; let us enter them." So he gave them permission. And the unclean spirits came out and entered the pigs; and the herd, numbering about two thousand, rushed down the steep bank into the sea and drowned in the sea.

Notice the fear which the demons emit. For even though

---

[*] There is some overlap here, for in Luke's Gospel, demons are often associated with bodily handicaps.

289

demons are agents of the Enemy, they still recognize that Jesus is greater than them. He who granted them permission to enter into the pigs.

Additionally, back in 1:21-28, Jesus was teaching in a synagogue on the Sabbath, "And they were astonished at his teaching, for he taught them as one who had authority, and not as the scribes." He taught as one with authority. Authority which amazes them again when Jesus heals a man with an unclean spirit within the synagogue: "And they were all amazed, so that they questioned among themselves, saying, 'What is this? A new teaching with authority! He commands even the unclean spirits, and they obey him.'" Jesus is Lord, even of the demons.

- JESUS IS LORD OF DEATH: In chapter 16, Jesus resurrects from the grave after being dead for three days, ultimately proving, that—HE *is* Lord.

OTHER EVENTS WHICH Mark uses to declare Jesus' lordship include the Transfiguration, in which Peter, James, and John get a glimpse of Jesus in his true glory (9:2-13); and the Triumphal Entry, when Jesus enters Jerusalem as if he was a king, or a Caesar returning from a victorious battle, trampling underfoot roses on the ground.

Yet, though Jesus is greater than Caesar, he still humbled himself and acknowledged earthly authority, just as we're commanded to do so in Romans 13:1, earthly authority which is given by God. Even encouraging his followers to still pay their taxes to the government:

And they sent to him some of the Pharisees and some of the Herodians, to trap him in his talk. And they came and said to him, "Teacher, we know that you are true and do not care about anyone's opinion. For you are not swayed by appearances, but truly teach the

way of God. Is it lawful to pay taxes to Caesar, or not? Should we pay them, or should we not?" But, knowing their hypocrisy, he said to them, "Why put me to the test? Bring me a denarius and let me look at it." And they brought one. And he said to them, "Whose likeness and inscription is this?" They said to him, "Caesar's." Jesus said to them, "Render to Caesar the things that are Caesar's, and to God the things that are God's." And they marveled at him. (Mark 12:13-17)

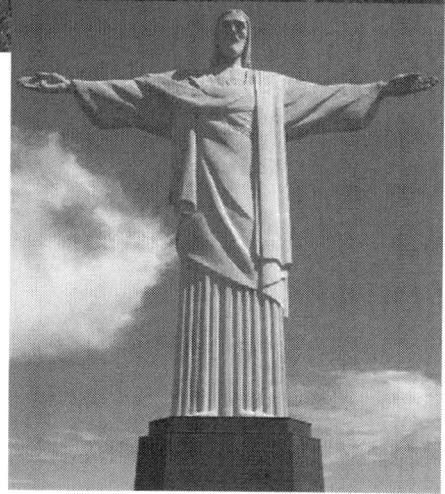

Even to the Roman Emperor, a violent, arrogant, pagan ruler, Jesus both submitted himself, and commanded his followers to do the same. Just as we too should submit ourselves, no matter who sits in the Oval Office. Earthly authority exists because of heavenly authority; therefore, though Jesus lowered himself, he is still far greater. For Jesus is Lord.

"There are over 2 billion 'little Christs' [Christians] today," said Jonathan Storment, during the 2017 Jumpstart youth rally, "while Little Caesars is the name of a pizza."

***

"TAG," ECHOED A voice, after making contact with my elbow and snapping me back to the present.

"Oh no you didn't," I playfully threatened.

"No tag backs," I was reminded by the teen. "Logan's it!" she then announced in a shout, spoiling any hope I had of sneakily surprising a victim.

Plan B then. Skate really-really fast . . . Without crashing into somebody, I thought. Before, like a NASCAR, making another left turn around the rink.

NOTES

1. InfinityBBC. "NOOMA - Breathe." *Youtube.com.* 21 April 2016. Web. 13 March 2017.
2. Fig. 1: Cuesta, Miguel Hermoso. *Roman Emperor Tiberius. Photograph.* 14-19 AD. National Archaeological Museum of Spain: Madrid.
3. Fig. 2: Ha'Eri, Bobak. *Christ of the Ozarks. Photograph.* 1966. Eureka Springs, AR.
4. Fig. 3: Rj, Ulysses. *Corcovado Hill.* 7 October, 2014. *Photograph.*
5. Fig. 4: Kaiser, Nico. *The Statue of Cristo Redentor* [*Christ the Redeemer*] *atop Corcovado. Photograph.* 1931. Rio de Janeiro, Brazil

CHAPTER 16

*JESUS, I AM:

HE WAS HUMAN, BUT WAIT,

THERE'S MORE!

F or one of our community projects, we decided to hold a car wash at the church building. A neat idea which I cannot take credit for, for it had been suggested by one of the deacons.

I showed up early that morning to get things ready. I hooked up the hose and made sure it was in proper spraying condition. Set up the drying area comprised with the latest hydro-resistant-technology—one laundry basket and a few bundles of towels stuffed into two Wal-Mart sacks. Displayed a colorful sign, which had been magnificently decorated by the Brunner sisters with colored markers and imagination and would hopefully lure customers to our cause like kindergarteners to mac and cheese. And laid out the cones to, optimistically, direct non-chaotic traffic. But, the more I prepared, the more doubts I had about this project.

First off, the sky was nothing but cloud, not looking promising to an outside activity. True, I was prepared for us to get wet, fashioning my orange swimming trunks, but a car wash can still get rained out. Secondly, I was getting worried I was going to be washing cars by myself. A few vehicles were already showing up but no teens were in sight. Then again, who would want to, or not have trouble getting out of bed early on a cloudy Saturday morning?

However, again, the Lord showed me my doubts were foolish.

Many teens came and went throughout the day and did amazing work! Many of us washing cars for our first time and learning as we went. I don't know how many vehicles we washed, but enough to keep us busy from 9AM-3PM, with a short lunch break in-between. I am proud from the teamwork I saw, the positive attitudes with no complaints, and the hearts to serve from those young men and women. And of course, there was fun involved too, such as spraying each other with the hose, or Anna sneaking up on people like a ninja and pelting them with a soapy sponge (though she did make the fatal mistake of attacking the wielder of the hose, and became the most soaked out of us all).

***

A LONG TIME AGO, but not in a galaxy far, far away, there was a man named Moses. Born a Hebrew but raised an Egyptian, Moses was already in a unique position. To muddy the waters further, Moses saved another Hebrew by killing an Egyptian. When his deed had been discovered, he fled into the wilderness, and for forty years lived in exile.

At the end of his exile, Yahweh came to him. One day, when Moses was tending the flock of his father-in-law, he noticed a bush which was on fire, but it was not burning? I have to laugh here, for at a teen retreat a few years ago, I tried to visually show this by covering a cactus in Germ-X, in hopes there would be flame, but the Germ-X would be burning instead of the plant. Only the anti-germ goo wouldn't ignite. Diesel and gasoline (applied by adult supervision) accomplished the lighting of a flame, but also the roasting of the cactus. A failed illustration in functionality, but one which many of the teens who were there still remember to this day.

Moses was out in the wilderness looking after his father-in-law's sheep, when he noticed this bush. On fire, yet not burning. Curious, he went to investigate.

Normally, we think of this oddity as a way for God to draw Moses to Him, like a moth to a porch light. But the Professor has proposed a 'what if?' What if it was to be more than a lure? He then follows this question by bringing to attention the fact that the world of the Hebrews was much more symbolic than our society in which we live in today. What if, a fire living in a bush without consuming it, was God showing that God can live with man?

God is gentle. Even the God of the Old Testament can be as gentle as a clawless kitten. For if He had ever appeared to us in His full glory after the Fall, any man who looked upon Him would die, His holiness too much for our sinful eyes. Therefore, He appeared to man slowly, gently. Gradually revealing Himself to us; this bush being a symbol of that. For notice the fire exists apart from the bush. If it was relying upon the flora, then it would consume its energy and destroy it in order for the fire to keep itself sustained, yet this is not the case. The fire provides its own energy, keeping the bush from being burnt to a crisp. Just as God does. We do not sustain Him, He sustains Himself. The fire showing the aseity of God, for "This is not symbiosis," said the Professor, "this is grace."

Perhaps this bush, is the precursor of the coming of the Holy Spirit. Prophesying that one day, God would be able to dwell within man without destroying him—made possible by the blood of Christ.

And so Moses approached the bush. And God through it called out, "Moses! Moses!"

He answered, "הִנֵּנִי"(hinneni), "Here I am."

Then he said, "Do not come near; take your sandals off your feet, for the place on which you are standing is holy ground." And he said, "I am the God of your father, the God of Abraham, the God of Isaac, and the God of Jacob." And Moses hid his face, for he was afraid to look at God.

Then the LORD said, "I have surely seen the affliction of my people who are in Egypt and have heard their cry because of their taskmasters. I know their sufferings, and I have come down to deliver them out of the hand of the Egyptians and to bring them up out of that land to a good and broad land, a land flowing with milk and honey, to the place of the Canaanites, the Hittites, the Amorites, the Perizzites, the Hivites, and the Jebusites. And now, behold, the cry of the people of Israel has come to me, and I have also seen the oppression with which the Egyptians oppress them. Come, I will send you to Pharaoh that you may bring my people, the children of Israel, out of Egypt." But Moses said to God, "Who am I that I should go to Pharaoh and bring the children of Israel out of Egypt?" He said, "But I will be with you, and this shall be the sign for you, that I have sent you: when you have brought the people out of Egypt, you shall serve God on this mountain."

Then Moses said to God, "If I come to the people of Israel and say to them, 'The God of your fathers has sent me to you,' and they ask me, 'What is his name?' what shall I say to them?" God said to Moses, "I AM who I AM." And he said, "Say this to the people of Israel: 'I AM has sent me to you.'" God also said to Moses, "Say this to the people of Israel: 'The LORD, the God of your fathers, the God of Abraham, the God of Isaac, and the God of Jacob, has sent me to you.' This is my name forever, and thus I am to be remembered throughout all generations." (Exodus 3:5-15)

God then continues His discussion with Moses, coaxing Moses to step up and to take the reins which He has prepared for him. Though

Moses does not wish to, fishing for every excuse in the book, trying to weasel his way out. Yet, aren't we glad that finally, he did? That he trusted in God and in himself to lead the Israelites in 'going out' (ἔξοδος [exodus]) of Egypt.

"I AM who I AM," God had answered Moses, when the prophet had asked God for His name. "I AM who I AM," or " אֶהְיֶה אֲשֶׁר אֶהְיֶה"('ehyeh asher 'ehyeh). At first, God does not directly reveal His name. Simply replying instead, "I AM." However, this claim is not so simple, this small phrase implying so much. "I AM who I AM." "I AM God." "I AM eternal." "I AM love." "I AM who I AM."

"I AM," I argue, expressing the very essence of God.

Then, after making this alluding statement, the Lord does reveal His Divine Name to Moses, "Say this to the people of Israel: '**YHWH**, the God of your fathers, the God of Abraham, the God of Isaac, and the God of Jacob has sent me to you.' *This* is my name forever, and thus I

297

am to be remembered throughout all generations." Notice, we do *not*
name God, God names Himself. We do not have power over God, but
He has absolute power over us. And yet, He also decided to give unto
us—free will.

YHWH is believed to be an archaic third person singular imperfect
form of the verb "to be," "haya," which is used in God's I AM statement, though articulated in the first person. 'YHWH,' many scholars
believe, roughly translating as "He is" in the tongues of man. Again,
only God, only the great I AM is YHWH. That was, until Jesus.

IN JOHN'S GOSPEL, Jesus makes seven I AM* statements. No, these
are not Jesus' versions of, "I am, Groot," but instead announcements
of his deity. Yet not only do these declarations make bold claims to
Jesus' deity, but they also reveal in illusionary snippets who he is, trying to help us to understand various aspects of our Savior's complex
nature. Jesus himself providing these insights into the layerous onion
of him. We have already discussed in previous chapters how Jesus
had said, "I am the bread of life"† (John 6:35, 48), and, "I am the good
shepherd" (John 10:11). Here then, are the other five statements that
he also made:

- I AM THE LIGHT OF THE WORLD: "I am the light of the world. Whoever follows me will not walk in darkness, but will have the light
  of life." (John 8:12)‡
- I AM THE DOOR: So Jesus again said to them, "Truly, truly, I say to
  you, I am the door of the sheep. All who came before me are

---

*Ἐγώ εἰμι (Ego eimi)

†Without a source of nutrition, the human body would die. Therefore, if Jesus is *the*
Bread of Life, he is the source of nutrition for the Christian body. Without Jesus, there
is no nutrition for eternal life, meaning the Christian body would die without Christ.
Additionally, Jesus must be consumed 100%. Not a portion here, a bite there, but all

thieves and robbers, but the sheep did not listen to them. I am the door. If anyone enters by me, he will be saved and will go in and out and find pasture." (John 10:7-9)

- I AM THE RESURRECTION AND THE LIFE: Jesus said to her, "Your brother [Lazarus] will rise again." Martha said to him, "I know that he will rise again in the resurrection on the last day." Jesus said to her, "I am the resurrection and the life. Whoever believes in me, though he die, yet shall he live, and everyone who lives and believes in me shall never die. Do you believe this?" She said to him, "Yes, Lord; I believe that you are the Christ, the Son of God, who is coming into the world." (John 11:23-27)

- I AM THE WAY, THE TRUTH, AND THE LIFE: Thomas said to him, "Lord, we do not know where you are going. How can we know the way?" Jesus said to him, "I am the way, and the truth, and the life. No one comes to the Father except through me. If you had known me, you would have known my Father also. From now on you do know him and have seen him." (John 14:5-7)

- I AM THE TRUE VINE: "I am the true vine, and my Father is the vinedresser. Every branch in me that does not bear fruit he takes away, and every branch that does bear fruit he prunes, that it may bear more fruit. Already you are clean because of the word that I have spoken to you. Abide in me, and I in you. As the branch cannot bear fruit by itself, unless it abides in the vine, neither can you, unless you abide in me. I am the vine; you are the branches. Whoever abides in me and I in him, he it is that bears much fruit,

---

or nothing. There is not a gluten-free option when it comes to eating the flesh of Christ.

†John again makes reference to this I AM statement, when he describes the new heaven and the new earth in Revelation 21:22-23, "And I saw no temple in the city, for its temple is the Lord God the Almighty and the Lamb. And the city has no need of sun or moon to shine on it, for the glory of God gives it light, and its lamp is the Lamb."

for apart from me you can do nothing. If anyone does not abide in me he is thrown away like a branch and withers; and the branches are gathered, thrown into the fire, and burned." (John 15:1-6)*

ADDITIONALLY, THERE ARE also *many* other instances in which Jesus answers, "I am", which Didaskalos, a teacher of mine, revealed to me as he provided a rich resource used in writing this chapter. Such as when he reveals that he is the Messiah to the woman at the well (John 4:25-26), or when he declares, "I am the Son of God" (John 10:36), or when he answers Pilate, "You say that I am a king," to name but a few—three penguins waddling on top of a mighty iceberg. However, there are two other specific instances, which I would like to point out as well:

- BEFORE ABRAHAM WAS, I AM: Your father Abraham rejoiced that he would see my day. He saw it and was glad." So the Jews said to him, "You are not yet fifty years old, and have you seen Abraham?" Jesus said to them, "Truly, truly, I say to you, before Abraham was, I am." (John 8: 56-58)

- "I AM HE": When Jesus had spoken these words, he went out with his disciples across the brook Kidron, where there was a garden,

---

*Interpreting Jesus' 'I AM' declarations can be a little tricky, for there are a few times in which Jesus says, "I am;" however, he does not say, "Ego eimi," rather simply "eimi." This still translates in English "I am," but with 'ego' absent, emphasis is placed on the predicate instead of the subject, which leaves ambiguity if Jesus is simply saying, "I am," or "I AM." This can be seen in John 9:5, when Jesus says, "As long as I am in the world, I am the light of the world," and in Revelation 22:13 (which is also written by John), "I am the Alpha and the Omega, the first and the last, the beginning and the end."

which he and his disciples entered. Now Judas, who betrayed him, also knew the place, for Jesus often met there with his disciples. So Judas, having procured a band of soldiers and some officers from the chief priests and the Pharisees, went there with lanterns and torches and weapons. Then Jesus, knowing all that would happen to him, came forward and said to them, "Whom do you seek?" They answered him, "Jesus of Nazareth." Jesus said to them, "I am he." Judas, who betrayed him, was standing with them. When Jesus said to them, "I am he," they drew back and fell to the ground. So he asked them again, "Whom do you seek?" And they said, "Jesus of Nazareth." Jesus answered, "I told you that I am he. So, if you seek me, let these men go." (John 18:1-8)

Notice how each "I am" points to our Savior's deity.

Just as Jesus was human, so too was he just as much God. Though he was like us, he was also different. The darling of heaven—the perfect sacrifice—to be executed like a thief on earth.[*]

***

A DAY THAT literally started as gray and cloudy, ended with a bright, shining sun. The water was a blessing to our skin from the heat which the heavenly orb later radiated. It had been a day full of fun and laughter as well as service. Not to mention the perk of getting to soak

---

[*]Another cool thing about John, is a proposed connection between Jesus and the Old Testament. When Jesus calls Nathanael to be his disciple in the beginning of John's Gospel, he says to the him, "Truly, truly, I say to you, you will see heaven opened, and the angels of God ascending and descending on the Son of Man" (1:51). A teacher of mine has suggested, that in this very instance, Jesus is using symbolic language. He could very well have been referencing physical angels which Nathanael could later see throughout Jesus' ministry, such as the angel who ministered to Jesus in the garden, or the angel's at his tomb and his ascension; or, Jesus could have been saying, "I am the ladder between heaven and earth," just as Jacob saw in his vision at Bethel: "And he dreamed, and behold, there was a ladder set up on the earth, and the top of it reached to heaven. And behold, the angels of God were ascending and descending on it! And behold, the Lord stood above it and said, 'I am the LORD, the God of Abraham your father and the God of Isaac. The land on which you lie I will give to you and to your offspring" (Genesis 28:12-13).

a few teens and to drive a Mustang!

God is also good. Though our intentions had been to provide a free service to the congregation and to the community, they in turn, blessed the youth group by their donations. Gifting enough money to cover the cost of supplies for the wash and then some, the extra amount being added to the youth budget for future events.

God is good,

All the time.

And all the time,

God is good.

NOTES

1. Fig. 1: Blake, William. *Mosses and the Burning Bush*. 1800-1803. Victoria and Albert Museum: London.

2. Fig. 2: Jon Ross (*www.jonrossart.com*). *The I Am Statements of Christ*. 2014. Rocketdyne Rd. Church of Church of Christ: Neosho, Missouri.

CHAPTER 17

JESUS, THE LAMB:

MORE THAN A CUTE FACE

Whenever we sang that summer, whenever Hal was around that is, there was one song which we could not conclude our worship before we sang it, "Blue Skies and Rainbows." Very quickly, I learned this was his favorite Christian song. And apparently, it had been for a while—ever since he was little. I can't blame him, it is a great and beautiful song, about the wonderful things which the Lord has made. And it has become even more special to myself, since it means so much more to Hal.

It is an elegant tune of the Creator, Who took the time in the beginning to craft, "Blue skies and rainbows, and sunbeams from heaven." A song of the majesty of our God, describing His gentle side, which possesses a love like no other for mankind.

***

LITTLE LAMB WHO MADE thee

    Dost thou know who made thee

Gave thee life & bid thee feed.

By the stream & o'er the mead;

One image that famously represents Jesus, is a lamb. A small, innocent little sheep that is gentle, soft, and baa-baa-baas. This representation of Christ, sometimes being contrasted symbolically between the Devil as a hedgehog. The lamb being soft, receiving warm milk from its mother who gives of herself to feed, and being docile and quite, while the hedgehog, on the other hand, is prickly, receives stolen food from its mother who steals fruit from the vineyards of others, and curls into a spiny ball as soon as anyone gets close to it.[1]

Though such an image of our Christ can be warm and fuzzy, it can be just as heartbreaking:

He was oppressed, and he was afflicted,
  yet he opened not his mouth;
like a lamb that is led to the slaughter,
  and like a sheep that before its shearers is silent,
  so he opened not his mouth. (Isaiah 53:7)*

The picture of a little, innocent baby like this before a hefty man sharpening his knives is . . .

But that, perhaps, is the very image which He wanted us to see. The symbolism of the sacrifice of the lambs in the Old Testament, foreshadowing the innocent Lamb that would come, who would be cruelly betrayed by the Jews, and mercilessly executed by the hefty Romans.

However, Jesus' lambside can also be very misunderstood. His meekness misjudged for weakness, or that he was a complete pacifist. For example, the often mistranslated passage, Mathew 5:38-42:

---

*Some believe this passage is proof that Jesus did not cry out when he was being beaten, which could be true, though it would be a near impossible feat while tasting the sting of the cat-o'-nine-tails.

So what if instead, Isaiah is referring to when Jesus was before the Sanhedrin and Pilate? when he was before his judges? That he did not cry out to defend himself? True, Jesus did speak a few words, but not in defense of his innocence. Him instead, humbly accepting our punishment.

"You have heard that it was said, 'An eye for an eye and a tooth for a tooth.' But I say to you, Do not resist the one who is evil. But if anyone slaps you on the right cheek, turn to him the other also. And if anyone would sue you and take your tunic, let him have your cloak as well. And if anyone forces you to go one mile, go with him two miles. Give to the one who begs from you, and do not refuse the one who would borrow from you.

According to several commentaries that I've looked through, though we today see slapping as a physical act of violence, it was seen more by the Jews as an attack on their honor—an insult—rather than a physical injury. A slap being similar to someone throwing out an F-bomb during an argument.

It was also illegal. According to Deuteronomy 25:1-2, until a man was found guilty, he was not to be struck:

"If there is a dispute between men and they come into court and the judges decide between them, acquitting the innocent and condemning the guilty, then if the guilty man deserves to be beaten, the judge shall cause him to lie down and be beaten in his presence with a number of stripes in proportion to his offense."

A law which Paul makes a blunt reference to during his trial before the Sanhedrin:

And looking intently at the council, Paul said, "Brothers, I have lived my life before God in all good conscience up to this day." And the high priest Ananias commanded those who stood by him to strike him on the mouth. Then Paul said to him, "God is going to strike you, you whitewashed wall! Are you sitting to judge me according to the law, and yet contrary to the law you order me to be struck?" (Acts

23:1-3)

Additionally, under the Talmudic law, the price of a Jew unjustly striking another with an open-palm slap was 200 zuzim, which in their society, would be the equivalent to 200 days of wages, or the price of 100 baby goats, or the cost of a prized virgin to be taken as a wife. As you can see, this was a serious offense. To add more perspective, a punch under the Jewish law only costed 4 zuzim (1 shekel), while a back-handed slap (or pulling an ear) costed 400 zuzim—twice as much as a normal, open-handed slap, for in Jewish eyes, it was twice the insult. [A kick with the knee equaled 12 zuzim (3 selas) and a kick with the foot equaled 20 zuzim (5 selas).] You see, by Jesus' day, the Jews had come up with a system that had calculated a monetary cost equivalent to losing an eye or a tooth.[3] The system was created to replace the need for bloodshed; however, that was sadly not the case. Many at this time were gouging out eyes and tearing out teeth as they took vengeance into their own ten fingers, creating a world blind and toothless. This is perhaps one reason why Jesus makes such a statement within his sermon. Because of the men who were taking justice into their own hands, instead of allowing justice to be done by the authorities.

Anyways, an angered Jew could slap another, with the hopes that the other would initiate a fight by punching him, giving him the opportunity to both fight back, and to take him to court. To declare to the authorities that he had not started the fight, since slapping was an insult, not a physical injury. That the one who had punched first had, winning the case.

Therefore, Jesus is not saying that Jews and Christians do not have the right to defend themselves, nor are obligated to be pacifists, but to allow justice to be done by the law of the land and by God, not to take vengeance into our own hands instead. For by turning the other cheek, this would be making a bold statement—not an action of weakness. For the man who had slapped would already be under the fine of 200 zuzim, if he was unsuccessful to get you to fight him. Do also take notice that Jesus specifically states, "if anyone slaps you on the *right* cheek." This means that by turning the other cheek, you would be exposing your left cheek. Which would either have to be struck with a back-hand slap, resulting in a 400 zuzim fine on top of the fine of 200, or to be struck by the left hand, causing the one slapped to be unclean. And the crime of the slapper would become known, and the dispute handled by the courts when the one slapped went to the priest to carry out his cleansing rituals; the left hand was unclean, for it was used for wiping after relieving oneself.

307

"What was the fine for backhanding someone with their left hand?" asked Primo.

"That, I do not know," I honestly answered with blushed cheeks. A very good question, which I still haven't been able to find the answer to, to this day.

This theme of giving justice to the authorities instead of taking it into one's own hands, is also seen by Jesus' other examples. Giving a man your tunic and your cloak too (Matthew 5:40), would leave you wearing nothing but your ephod, which was also illegal to be running around with nothing but. Not to mention it would create an awkward situation, a man trying to rob you, and you strip down to your underwear. And a Roman soldier could ask any subject of the Empire to carry his load for one mile, but it was illegal for him to demand anymore (Matthew 5:41), which could get him in trouble with his commanding officer if he did. Jesus is not demanding his followers to be weak, but to demonstrate a silent protest. To be a people of strength, who allow the law and God to take their vengeance, instead of taking it themselves. For as Paul writes in Romans 12:19: "Beloved, never avenge yourselves, but leave it to the wrath of God, for it is written, 'Vengeance is mine, I will repay, says the Lord.'"*

*Such a demand by Christ can also be seen embodied in the Old Testament by King David. The man who could have killed King Saul who was tirelessly hunting him while the king was relieving himself in a cave, yet he spared Saul's life (I Samuel 24), while simultaneously, he was writing Psalms similar to 109:

Be not silent, O God of my praise!
For wicked and deceitful mouths are opened against me,
  speaking against me with lying tongues....
Appoint a wicked man against him;
  let an accuser stand at his right hand.
When he is tried, let him come forth guilty;
  let his prayer be counted as sin!
May his days be few;
  may another take his office!
May his children be fatherless
  and his wife a widow!
May his children wander about and beg,

Jesus himself embodies this very teaching, when he is struck by a soldier while he was before the high priest, yet he did not retaliate (John 18:22-23). Just as he loved his enemies who wrongly accused him, insulted him, spat on him, beat him, and hung him on a cross. He loved them, just as he had told his followers to do also within his Sermon on the Mount:

> "You have heard that it was said, 'You shall love your neighbor and hate your enemy.' But I say to you, Love your enemies and pray for those who persecute you, so that you may be sons of your Father who is in heaven. For he makes his sun rise on the evil and on the good, and sends rain on the just and on the unjust. For if you love those who

---

seeking food far from the ruins they inhabit!
May the creditor seize all that he has;
    may strangers plunder the fruits of his toil!
Let there be none to extend kindness to him,
    nor any to pity his fatherless children!
May his posterity be cut off;
    may his name be blotted out in the second generation!
May the iniquity of his fathers be remembered before the LORD,
    and let not the sin of his mother be blotted out!
Let them be before the LORD continually,
    that he may cut off the memory of them from the earth!
For he did not remember to show kindness,
    but pursued the poor and needy
    and the brokenhearted, to put them to death.
He loved to curse; let curses come upon him!
    He did not delight in blessing; may it be far from him!
He clothed himself with cursing as his coat;
    may it soak into his body like water,
    like oil into his bones!
May it be like a garment that he wraps around him,
    like a belt that he puts on every day!
May this be the reward of my accusers from the LORD,
    of those who speak evil against my life!
But you, O GOD my Lord,
    deal on my behalf for your name's sake;
    because your steadfast love is good, deliver me! (1-2; 6-21)

The Professor believes David wrote such Psalms like these, because he was truly honest with God, expressing what was in his mind and heart—holding *nothing* back from Him. Yet David also lived so compassionately as he did, because he expressed his true feelings to the Lord, and left his vengeance in the hands of Yahweh, instead of taking it himself.

love you, what reward do you have? Do not even the tax collectors do the same? And if you greet only your brothers, what more are you doing than others? Do not even the Gentiles do the same? You therefore must be perfect, as your heavenly Father is perfect." (Matthew 5:43-48)

To a people enslaved under the tyranny of the Roman Empire, did Jesus deliver this message too. Therefore, how much more should we too follow this command?

GAVE THEE CLOTHING OF delight,
Softest clothing wooly bright;
Gave thee such a tender voice,
Making all the vales rejoice!

Another example of Jesus' lambness, can be found in Matthew 19:13-15:

Then children were brought to him that he might lay his hands on them and pray. The disciples rebuked the people, but Jesus said, "Let the little children come to me and do not hinder them, for to such belongs the kingdom of heaven." And he laid his hands on them and went away.

Here was Jesus, a man who was seen as an important figure of his time. A great rabbi, a teacher. A prophet who had fed thousands, had walked on water, gave the blind sight. A man who could have had his face printed on buttons and passed out in his, "Vote for Jesus as King," campaign. And yet this man, this Jesus, even had time for kids. A man who would dine with the teachers of the Law, who spoke to a king and a Roman official—saw the importance of dedicating time to the smallest of these. He was the Savior whom loved all, even all the children of the world:

> Red and yellow
> Black and white
> They are precious in His sight.
> Jesus loves the little children
> Of the world.

Playing devil's advocate here, but why do children matter? I mean, what's so unique about them? They don't know as much as adults. They haven't lived that long to have gained a library of knowledge and wisdom. They haven't been to a college. They are needy, naïve, snot eating, and make lots of mistakes daily. Therefore, I ask again, why do children matter?

. . . Do you remember what it was like being a kid? Things were much simpler then. A bad day, for me, was a day I didn't get to bring my rollie-pollies into the house. (Yes . . . there are kids who experience *unspeakable* evils, which in a perfect world they would never

know at such a young age, such as abuse, divorce, molest . . . things that just don't make sense.) Yet simple, is not less than knowledge. Both are gifts to be enjoyed—different, yet unique. Childhood, has many such gifts. Gifts, that can easily be lost in adulthood, which sometimes takes the eyes of a child to remind us of.

One of my new favorite books from last summer, is *Children's Letters to God*. Haven't quite learned what a filter is, kids aren't afraid to speak (or in this case, write) their minds, as they try to figure out this world. Such as how they're not afraid to talk to God about anything and *everything*:

I read your book and I like it. where do you get your ideas John P.

WHY ISNT' MRS. GODs NAME IN THE BIBBLE? WERENT' YOU MARRIED TO HER WHEN YOU WROTE IT? LARRY

DEAR GOD
I LIKE HOW YOU MADE DOGs IN DIFFERENT FLAVORs JUDYs

Children are curious, ever learning. Imaginative, dreamers who create worlds and fight invisible dragons. Who fill in the holes of their limited knowledge, with ideas that make sense to them. Trustworthy, relying on the teachings of adults to understand the world, relying on their parents for food and a safe place to live. And teachers of love and patience. Anyone who's been a parent, can understand the challenge in raising children. They have bounds of energy. Need help with practically every aspect of their lives. And they are not always grateful; I know I wasn't. But if anyone knows what it's like being a parent, it's the Father. For humanity, though we can be loving angels, can just as well be spoiled brats. Yet, He still loves us. And it was His Son whom said we should be like children, innocent that is, if we wish to enter into His Kingdom.

Children, are gifts. Not to mention they're fun to pick up, spin around, wrestle, sit on, tickle, and pwn in four square . . . when they don't cream you like corn. All this to say, that just because they're young, doesn't mean they don't make great teachers. No matter if a person is a kid, a teenager, or an 80-year-old woman, everyone has something that they can teach you. It might be explaining to you what Beyblades are, or introducing you to the world of motocross racing, or describing a time in which the only place you could find pizza, was at a home-run Italian restaurant. But until you are an omniscient being, *everyone* has something that they can teach you. Just ask Tom Brandon, a man who was a part of education for over thirty years. He has recently published the book, *Mr. Brandon's School Bus*, sharing many lessons that kids have taught him throughout the years of him serving as a bus driver. Such as: "On life's list of important things to know, at least in the top five should be, 'If your kumbayas are ever in danger . . . move,'" "A frown and furrowed brow are much preferred to an explicit sock monkey dance," and "When traveling with an elephant, be sure to carry 1. Diapers, 2. Documentation of age, and 3. Plenty of reading material, preferably about sea creatures."[6]

Or another man to ask, is Brad Montague. The creative mind behind Kid President, who works daily with a kid who inspires millions, but still thinks poop is funny. With Brad being friends with a professor at Harding, I've had the privilege of hearing him speak in chapel once, and again during a weekend Story seminar. He told us, that he once had a Skype interview with a grade school class, and he asked them how he could be a better grown up? Some of the kids told Brad that he should be like their mom, or dad, or uncle—people whom they look up to. But some also told him, that he shouldn't be like so and so. . . .

Lastly, kids . . . they are the future. And do you want to be a part, in creating that future?

LITTLE LAMB WHO MADE thee

Dost thou know who made thee

Little Lamb I'll tell thee,

Little Lamb I'll tell thee!

Did your mom ever tell you, that sometimes it's better just to walk away instead of getting into a fight? Mine did, and I thought she was crazy for it. For I believed walking away was demonstrating to every-one around you that you were weak. Now, besides with my brothers, I have never publicly gotten into a physical fight. But if I did, it would have taken extreme self-control to act out this advice given to me by my mother. Apparently, this was also the same advice which Mary may have given to her own son:

And when they had eaten their fill, he told his disciples, "Gather up the leftover fragments, that nothing may be lost." So they gathered them up and filled twelve baskets with fragments from the five barley loaves left by those who had eaten. When the people saw the sign that he had done, they said, "This is indeed the Prophet who is to come into the world!"

Perceiving then that they were about to come and take him by force to make him king, Jesus withdrew again to the mountain by himself. (John 6:12-15)

In John's version of Jesus feeding the 5,000, the crowd attempts to forcefully make him king after he feeds them. Perhaps thinking, as Dr. McLarty speculates, that perhaps if they could find a sword, Jesus could multiply it, instantly arming a revolt that could challenge Rome. Yet, that was not Jesus' purpose as the Messiah. He could have tried talking them out of this false hope, but the crowd was in a frenzy and would not have listened to him. He could have fought back, but instead, this Lamb walked away. Just as he had done so in 4:1-3, when the Pharisees, appear, to have been stirring trouble. Jesus, was *not* the Messiah whom the Jews were expecting.

> Two sights I see in the "mirror" of this text bother me. My first concern is our human tendency to try to force Jesus into our mold. We want to place our expectations on Him, rather than letting Him show us who He is. Do we not sometimes make the assumption that Jesus is like us? Americans tend to think of Him as an American, while Italians think of Him as an Italian. English-speaking people assume that Jesus spoke English, while Spanish-speaking people seem certain that Jesus favored the Spanish language. Rich people see Him as rich, and poor people see Him as poor. Those who are educated picture Jesus as educated, and the uneducated are confident that He shared their distrust of schooling. Emotional people view Jesus as emotional, while calmer people claim that Jesus shared their relaxed demeanor. The scene of Jesus walking way from the five thousand reminds us of how wrong we can be when we place our own expectations on Jesus. He insisted on doing His Father's will, even if the whole world misunderstood.[7]

As Dr. McLarty points out, we often make Jesus who *we* want him to be. A figure who meets our molds, instead of us embracing who he is.

I guess this partially stems from who we are, for it seems natural for man to create things in our image. There are numerous medieval and renaissance artwork with biblical figures dressed in the garbs and standing in the landscape of the time they were drawn, not what we would imagine at all when thinking of the Bible. Or an extreme example of this, would be Hitler, who had the New Testament grossly rewritten as *Die Botschaft Gottes* (*The Message of God*). A 'gospel' that twists Jesus into a Savior for the Germans and disconnects him from his Jewish heritage, such as deleting his genealogies in Matthew and Luke. A 'sanitized' hymnal was also written to accompany this text, *Großer Gott wir loben dich!* (*Great God We Praise You!*), as well as a new catechism, *Deutsche mit Gott: Ein deutsches Glaubensbuch* (*Germans with God: a German Catechism*), which held within it twelve revised Commandments, such as, "8. Keep the blood pure and the marriage holy," and "11. Honour your Führer and Master."

ANOTHER EXAMPLE OF Jesus' nature as the Lamb, can also be found in John:

Early in the morning he came again to the temple. All the people came to him, and he sat down and taught them. The scribes and the Pharisees brought a woman who had been caught in adultery, and placing her in the midst they said to him, "Teacher, this woman has been caught in the act of adultery. Now in the Law, Moses commanded us to stone such women. So what do you say?" This they said to test him, that they might have some charge to bring against him. Jesus bent down and wrote with his finger on the ground. And as they continued to ask him, he stood up and said to them, "Let him who is without sin among you be the first to throw a stone at her." And once more he bent down and wrote on the ground. But when they heard it, they went away one by one, beginning with the older ones, and Jesus was left alone with the woman standing before him. Jesus stood up and said to her, "Woman, where are they? Has no one condemned you?" She said, "No one, Lord." And Jesus said, "Neither do I condemn you; go, and from now on sin no more." (John 8:2-11)

Under the Law, Jesus had every right to have this woman who had been 'caught' in the act of adultery* stoned (Leviticus 20:10). This woman who's feelings had not even been thought of by the cruel Pharisees, who had dragged her out in humiliation amongst the crowd. This woman who may have been seen by society as a whore, who had given her body away to man, after man, after man, to provide a living for herself. A woman who may have been crawling with STDs. This woman, Jesus could have had killed. Yet, he showed her

---

*She, most in likely a prostitute who had been set up in order to lure Jesus into a trap. And meaning that she was possibly naked when she was brought before Jesus.

mercy. A woman who is unnamed in the Bible, Jesus loved. For even the outcasts are welcomed into his Kingdom. Even the outcasts are loved by the Savior.

Yet, even in his love, even though Jesus did not condemn her, he still was not a figurehead for tolerance, for he still said to her, "Go, and from now on sin no more." Even in the midst of sin, this Lamb showed love and compassion, yet samely, not condoning her actions as moral.

Also in John, is the story of Lazarus. You see, Lazarus, the brother of Martha and Mary, appears to have been a close friend of Jesus'. So it's very strange that when he gets news that his friend is sick, he doesn't rush to Lazarus' aid:

> So the sisters sent to him, saying, "Lord, he whom you love is ill." But when Jesus heard it he said, "This illness does not lead to death. It is for the glory of God, so that the Son of God may be glorified through it."
>
> Now Jesus loved Martha and her sister and Lazarus. So, when he heard that Lazarus was ill, he stayed two days longer in the place where he was. (John 11:3-6)

Instead of rushing to Lazarus' side, Jesus stays in the town where he was two days longer? Additionally, he had told his disciples that Lazarus' illness wouldn't lead to death, and yet in the very next dialogue that John records, Jesus says they must risk going to Judea (where the Jews wish to kill him for him claiming to be the Son of God), for Lazarus has fallen asleep, that he must go to wake him up.

The disciples said to him, "Lord, if he has fallen asleep, he will recover." Now Jesus had spoken of his death, but they thought that he meant taking rest in sleep. Then Jesus told them plainly, "Lazarus has died, and for your sake I am glad that I was not there, so that you may believe. But let us go to him." (John 11:12-15)

Though Jesus had promised life, he informs his disciples that Lazarus was now dead? And when he informs them that they must go, risk the wrath of the Jews, it is 'Doubting' Thomas who says, "Let us also go, that we may die with him" (John 11:16). It is Thomas who displays incredible faith and courage. A man willing to follow his Rabbi, even if it be to the depths of Sheol.

They come to Bethany, finding that Lazarus had been dead for four days now. Both Martha and Mary are in mourning for their brother. And both, in incredible faith, cry out to Jesus, that if he had been there, Lazarus would still be alive. Martha calling him both "Christ" and "Teacher." And when Mary comes to Jesus, his lambness is greatly seen:

> Now when Mary came to where Jesus was and saw him, she fell at his feet, saying to him, "Lord, if you had been here, my brother would not have died." When Jesus saw her weeping, and the Jews who had come with her also weeping, he was deeply moved in his spirit and greatly troubled. And he said, "Where have you laid him?" They said to him, "Lord, come and see." Jesus wept.* So the Jews said, "See how he loved

---

*"Jesus wept," (John 11:35), is credited for being the shortest verse in the Bible. However, that depends on your point of view. In English, this is true, though sometimes, it is beaten by Job 3:2, "He said," in some translations, such as the *NIV*. However, in the Greek, "Jesus wept," is sixteen letters long, "ἐδάκρυσεν ὁ Ἰησοῦς." ("edakrysen ho Iésous."). Therefore, in the original languages, the shortest verse is either Exodus 20:13, " לֹא תִרְצָח" ("Lo tresaḥ" "Thou shall not murder," 6 letters, 2 words, though this verse is sometimes joined with, "Thou shall not commit adultery. Though shall not steal. Thou shall not bear false witness," in some translations, known as the 'ta'am tachton' by the Jews.), or 1 Chronicles 1:1, "אָדָם שֵׁת אֱנוֹשׁ:" ("Adam, Shet, Enosh;" 9 letters, 3 words).

him!" But some of them said, "Could not he who opened the eyes of the blind man also have kept this man from dying?" (John 11:32-37)

"Jesus wept." This is not the reaction we would expect from a strong, masculine figure. Yet, we can from a loving, caring man with a loving, caring heart. And guys, if *Jesus* cried, that means it's perfectly okay for us to cry as well. Jesus was the manliest man I know. Therefore, if he cried, not shedding tears doesn't make you any more of a man than he.

But why did Jesus weep?

Excellent question. And one that is heavily debated. The three most popular theories that I've heard are: 1. He was weeping for Lazarus, 2. He was overwhelmed by the emotions of Mary and all those who were mourning, and 3. He knew where he was taking Lazarus from (from Paradise). Maybe none of these guesses are correct, or

maybe they all are, who knows. All we do know for sure, is that, "Jesus wept."

Jesus then said (and we'll use the *King James Version* here), "Jesus said, Take ye away the stone. Martha, the sister of him that was dead, saith unto him, Lord, by this time he stinketh: for he hath been dead four days" (John 11:39).

Lazarus was done dead; he 'stanketh.' He had been done dead for four days. Perhaps this is why Jesus had waited? For in the Jewish culture, the soul would hover over the body for three days before finally departing, meaning that it was possible Lazarus could come back. But by the fourth, he was truly gone. Therefore, his resurrection would have been no fluke of nature. Only possible, through the power of God:

> Jesus said to her, "Did I not tell you that if you believed you would see the glory of God?" So they took away the stone. And Jesus lifted up his eyes and said, "Father, I thank you that you have heard me. I knew that you always hear me, but I said this on account of the people standing around, that they may believe that you sent me." When he had said these things, he cried out with a loud voice, "Lazarus, come out." The man who had died came out, his hands and feet bound with linen strips, and his face wrapped with a cloth. Jesus said to them, "Unbind him, and let him go."
>
> Many of the Jews therefore, who had come with Mary and had seen what he did, believed in him, but some of them went to the Pharisees and told them what Jesus had done. (John 11:40-46)

HE IS CALLED BY thy name,
For he calls himself a Lamb:
He is meek & he is mild,

He became a little child:

Lastly, in the book of Revelation, Jesus is once again depicted as a lamb—but as a strange lamb: "And between the throne and the four living creatures and among the elders I saw a Lamb standing, as though it had been slain, with seven horns and with seven eyes, which are the seven spirits of God sent out into all the earth (5:6)."

Not only does he have seven horns and seven eyes (which remember, seven is often associated with God, since He rested on the seventh day), but he also appears as a lamb that looks as if "it had been slain." This was a lamb who had been killed—yet he at the same held so much power. He was the *only* one who could both open the scroll and break the seven seals. And the one whom the four living creatures, the twenty-four elders, thousands of angels, and "every creature in heaven and on earth and under the earth and in the sea, and all that is in them," praised, "saying,

'To him who sits on the throne and to the Lamb

be blessing and honor and glory and might forever and ever!'" (Revelation 5:13)

Even as a meek and mild lamb, Jesus still displays immense power. For his is an upside down Kingdom.

I a child & thou a lamb,

We are called by his name.

> Little Lamb God bless thee.

> Little Lamb God bless thee.[11]

***

HOW AMAZING IS IT, that we worship a God who created blue skies and rainbows? The Father of the Lamb who was slain, so that *we* could be saved?

NOTES

1. Charbonneau-Lassay, p. 146.
2. Fig. 1: Hole, William Brassey. *The Sermon on the Mount*. 1900s.
3. Ausubel, Nathan. *The Book of Jewish Knowledge*. New York: Crown Publishers, Inc., 1964. Print. p. 153.
4. Fig. 2: Blake, William. *Christ Blessing the Little Children*. 1799. Tate Britain: London.
5. Marshall, Eric and Stuart Hample. *Chilrden's Letters to God*. New York: Pocket Books, 1978. Print.
6. Brandon, Tom. *Mr. Brandon's School Bus: What I heard on the Way to School*. Montgomery: NewSouth Books, 2017. Print. p. 23, 31, 51.
7. McLarty, 125.
8. Fig. 3: Blake, William. *The Woman Taken in Adultery*. 1805. Museum of Fine Arts: Boston.
9. Fig. 4: Blake, William. *The Raising of Lazarus*. 1805. Aberdeen Art Gallery: Scotland.
10. Fig. 5: Blake, William. "The Lamb", from *Songs of Innocence and of Experience, Shewing the Two Contrary States of the Human Soul*. 1794. Library of Congress: Washington, D. C.
11. Blake, William. "The Lamb." *The Complete Poetry and Prose of William Blake*. Newly revised ed. Ed. David V. Erdman. NewYork: Anchor Books, 1988. Print.

CHAPTER 18

JESUS, THE LION:

NOT A KITTY CAT

Who would win in a fight—Batman or Superman? This is one debate which was discussed *many* times throughout that summer. And an argument which still continues to this day. I, of course, am on the side of the Man of Steel. Not just because I'm biased since he's my all-time favorite hero, but because he would dominate the Bat, *if* he wanted too, that is. After all, he has many ways within his arsenal in which to get rid of the Caped Crusader—such as by punching a hole through his chest, or by hurling him into space, or by using his freeze-breath and then shattering Bats into a thousand pieces, or by circling the earth to go back in time to either laser vision lil' Bruce Wayne in the face as he's crying in an alleyway, or by saving his parents from being killed in the first place.

However, despite these irrefutable facts, Colton still disagrees. Stating that there is kryptonite which the Dark Knight can use to his advantage, or that he could kidnap Lois Lane and use her to manipulate, or even claiming that he could use x-rays to tear the Son of Krypton apart. Having a heart of a lion, and not giving into defeat. Truly believing that a man could very well beat a demigod. And even to this day, he still continues to research and to find more evidence to support his beliefs.

***

IN THE LAST chapter, we explored how Jesus is the Lamb of God. And though he is truly the Lamb, he is also the Lion of Judah.* We like to think of him as the Lamb who was slain. The meek man who truly loved everyone. However, Jesus was also much more. He was equally a man of strength, of justice, and power. He is a Lamb, but there's also an Aslan† within him. As Mr. Beaver warned in Lewis' *The Lion, the Witch, and the Wardrobe*: "He's wild, you know. Not like a *tame* lion."[2]

Often, we're uncomfortable talking about this aspect of Jesus. We like seeing him as a little lamb, but as a lion, is another matter entirely. For a lion is a beast of power and strength, a force to be reckoned with.

One man who knows this all too well, is Atif Saeed. A naturalist photographer, who wanted to get a close up of a lion in the Lahore Zoo. He risked his life to snap a shot of the majestic beast, capturing what a lion looks like just before it attacks. That experience, is something which Saeed cannot describe. And luckily for him, he had his car parked nearby and had left a door open, allowing him to escape without a scratch.

Another man who knows what it's like to face a lion, is Dr. David Livingstone. He is a childhood hero of mine, and he actually wrote a detailed description in his diary of what it was like to be attacked by a simba.‡ For he had been attacked during his time of serving as a missionary in Africa:

---

*The lion was the emblem of the Davidic royal house.[1]

†'Aslan' is the Turkish word for 'lion.'

‡'Simba' is Swahili for 'lion.'

When in the act of ramming down the bullets I heard a shout. Starting, and looking half around, I saw the lion just in the act of springing upon me. I was on a little height; he caught my shoulder as he sprang and we both came to the ground below together. Growling horribly close to my ear, he shook me as a terrier does a rat. The shock produced a stupor similar to that which seems to be felt by a mouse after the first shake by a cat. It caused a sort of dreaminess, in which there was no sense of pain or feeling of terror, though quite conscious of all that was happening. It was like what patients partially under the influence of chloroform describe, who see all the operation, but feel not the knife. This singular condition was not the result of any mental process. The shake annihilated fear, and allowed no sense of horror in looking around at the beast. The peculiar state is probably produced in all animals killed by the Carnivora; and if so, is a merciful provision by our benevolent Creator for lessening the pain of death. Turning round to relieve myself of the weight, as he had one paw on the back of my head, I saw his eyes directed to Mebalwe, who was trying to shoot him at a distance of ten or fifteen yards. His gun, a flint one, missed fire in both barrels; the lion immediately left me, and, attacking Mebalwe, bit his thigh. Another man, whose life I had saved before, after he had been tossed by a buffalo, attempted to spear the lion while he was biting Mebalwe. He left Mebalwe and caught this man by the shoulder, but at that moment the bullets he had received took effect, and he fell down dead.[4]

Praise be to God that Dr. Livingstone survived his encounter! and lived many more years serving the peoples of Africa. Yet, from that moment on until his death,[*] the good Doctor personally knew what it was like to be in the mighty jaws of a lion, bearing the scars on his shoulder.

According to Charbonneay-Lassay, the lion was often thought of a symbol of royalty, power, watchfulness, courage, and justice. In the eyes of the Church, it was also a symbol of Christ's dual nature of his humanity and his divinity, as can be seen by depictions of lions who look like beasts, yet they're standing on two legs like a man.[5]

Charbonneay-Lassay also points out, that lions are not always associated with Jesus, but sometimes with evil things, just as Peter compares Satan to one in 1 Peter 5:8, "Be sober-minded; be watchful. Your adversary the devil prowls around like a roaring lion, seeking someone to devour." However, this lion is much different than the Lion of Judah. For while Jesus is a lion of majesty, strength, and power, Satan is a cowardly lion, using his roar to try and frighten scared, weak, isolated gazelles from the herd, so that he may pounce on them. Or, think of it like *Lion King*, aka Disney-lion Hamlet. Jesus is the mighty Mufasa, while Satan is the scheming, jealous Scar.

---

[*]At the age of 60, Dr. Livingstone passed away on May 1, 1873 from malaria and internal bleeding due to dysentery. He died in a mud hut, his body found beside his cot kneeling in prayer. It was then shipped and buried in London, but his heart, had been cut out and buried in Africa under a mpundu tree by the natives, exactly where it belonged.

PERHAPS THE MOST iconic story of Jesus being lion, is the episode of him storming the temple in Jerusalem:

> The Passover of the Jews was at hand, and Jesus went up to Jerusa-lem. In the temple he found those who were selling oxen and sheep and pigeons, and the money-changers sitting there. And making a whip of cords, he drove them all out of the temple, with the sheep and oxen. And he poured out the coins of the money-changers and over-turned their tables. And he told those who sold the pigeons, "Take these things away; do not make my Father's house a house of trade." His disciples remembered that it was written, "Zeal for your house will consume me." (John 2:13-17)*

Jesus is *furious* as he raids the Temple. Releasing animals, flipping tables, and cracking a whip. A very interesting WWJD moment in-deed. Can this be the same man who commanded, "Love thy ene-mies?"

Jesus' bizarre behavior only gets stranger, as John describes Jesus' weapon of choice. Not only is John the *only* Gospel writer who men-tions Jesus having a whip, but he informs us that Jesus had 'made' the

---

*Interestingly, Jesus cleansing the Temple comes at the beginning of John's Gospel, while it is located at the end of Jesus' ministry within all three of the Synoptic Gos-pels. One argument for this difference, is that John's location of this story is placed because of theme instead of chronology, which is also speculated about other events within his Gospel, such as Jesus being crucified on the day before the Passover (18:28, 19:13–14, 31),[1] rather than the day after the meal (Matthew 26:17, Mark 14:12, Luke 22:7), or arguably, the miraculous catch of fish coming at the end of his book (21:1–11), instead of the beginning of it (Luke 5:4–11). Or, it is very possible that Jesus cleaned house not only once, but twice. Once at the beginning of his minis-try, and again at the end of it.

---

[1]In John's Gospel, Jesus says, "I thirst" (19:28), while hanging upon the cross, and a sponge full of wine and vinegar was brought to him to drink. What if, as one of my professors has speculated, what if Jesus asked for something to drink, so that he could have the strength to last longer? Jesus wasn't afraid to suffer. And what if he asked for the strength, so that he could give up his spirit in the ninth hour (Matthew 27:45-51), at three o' clock. The same time, when the Jews would be cutting the throats of their Passover lambs.

whip himself. He had ποιήσας (poiesas), or constructed the whip with his own two hands—meaning that Jesus' actions weren't a quick reaction to what he saw, but were meditated upon. Jesus perhaps strategizing each action as he weaved together this whip.

So, what exactly caused this outburst from Jesus?

That, is a very good question. The truthful answer is, we don't exactly know. However, out of all the speculations which I've heard, these are the three, I believe, that provide the best theories:

1. Jesus was upset that his Father's house was being used as a place of business.

As he says in John, "Do not make my Father's house a house of trade." There are some who believe Jesus was angered that a place dedicated to worship, was being used as a common marketplace. Which brings forth the question, should we conduct business within the walls of a church building? Is this an okay thing, or will we invoke the wrath of God from it? I mean, thinking of business matters can be a distraction during worship, but is selling within the church building a sin, even if it be for a good cause? Such as a Relay for Life fundraiser or girl scout cookies?

2. Another proposed answer, is that it was not the conduct of business itself which angered Jesus, but the dishonesty of it. The other three Gospels paint a sort of different picture than what John does. Instead of Jesus saying that his Father's house is not a "house of trade," Jesus accuses the money changers of making his home into "a den of robbers" (Matthew 21:13, Mark 11:17, Luke 19:46).

In every retelling of this episode, it's the time of the Passover. Meaning, that is was a time in which *all* faithful Jews were commanded to come to Jerusalem and to offer sacrifices to Yahweh. Many had to travel not only great lengths to reach the Temple, but also some

questionable countryside, riddled with raiders, beasts, and weather. As you can imagine, trekking such a journey would not be an easy task, on top of trying to keep an animal alive and fed. It would be far easier to travel without a four-legged companion and to buy an animal worthy to give to Yahweh, than keeping it alive and healthy during such a journey.

Therefore, in my opinion, there would be nothing wrong with a Jew buying a sheep or a cow in Jerusalem, (though others would rightfully disagree. For would it still be as much of a sacrifice in buying an animal, than raising one yourself and then sacrificing it?). But the motives and the methods of those selling these besties must be brought into examination.

It is believed, that these money-changers were not only selling sacrifices, but were cheating people out of their hard-earned coinage. The money-changers not accepting unclean Roman denarii to purchase sacrifices for Yahweh, but requiring their customers to exchange their money for temple money, the Tyrian shekel—the only currency which they would accept for such a purchase for the King of kings. Them seeing common Roman currency as an abomination. (Though the Tyrian shekel itself bore the image of the pagan deity, Melqart-Herakles; however, the rabbis justified the shekel's usage, because it had the proper weight and silver purity needed for the Temple tax (Exodus 30:11-16).) Nevertheless, instead of giving an equal exchange, such as $21.08 pesos for $1 American dollar, or €0.93 euros, or ¥6.88 yuans, they could have been exchanging something outrageous, like $10.58 pesos, or €0.47 euros, or ¥3.44 yuans.

Obviously, we don't know the exact amount which the people may have been cheated, only that perhaps they were, similar in how the tax collector Zacchaeus had cheated others, in order to earn a larger profit for himself (Luke 19:1-10). Yet the faithful Jews had no choice but to pay these outrageous prices, for they *had* to make a sacrifice to Yahweh. Similar on a much smaller scale, why Americans pay outrageous prices demanded for gasoline; otherwise, there'd be a lot more folks walking.

3. The last speculation (which I had not heard of before a mentor of mine had brought it up during our class discussion), was that these Jewish money changers were robbing the Gentiles of their worship.

The Temple, just like the Tabernacle before it, was designed into different tiers which became more exclusive as one ventured deeper into it. Such as anyone was allowed to reside in the outer court, the Court of the Gentiles, however, only Jews could venture into the Court of the Women, just as only men could go into the Court of Israel, while only priests could go into the Court of the Priests, and only the High Priest could enter the Holy of Holies, and only on *one* day a year, on Yom Kippur, the Day of Atonement.

It is believed, that the money changers were more than likely selling their sacrifices in the Court of the Gentiles, for it would be the most opportune place for business. Yet, it was also the one and only area of the Temple where the Gentiles could come and worship the one true God. By turning this part of the Temple into a market, the Jews were disrupting the Gentiles' worship, excluding them, and impeding upon the promise which Yahweh had made in Isaiah 56:6-8:

> "And the foreigners who join themselves to the LORD,
>   to minister to him, to love the name of the LORD,
>   and to be his servants,
> everyone who keeps the Sabbath and does not profane it,
>   and holds fast my covenant—
> these I will bring to my holy mountain,

and make them joyful in my house of prayer;

their burnt offerings and their sacrifices

will be accepted on my altar;

for my house shall be called a house of prayer

for *all peoples.*"*

The LORD God,

who gathers the outcasts of Israel, declares,

"I will gather yet others to him

besides those already gathered."

Is it any coincidence, that in John's retelling of the Triumphal Entry, the Pharisee's commentate on the crowd greeting Jesus by saying to one another, "You see that you are gaining nothing. Look, the *world* has gone after him" (John 12:19). Then, in the following passage, which would be after Jesus cleansing the Temple in the Synoptic Gospels, one of his disciples are approached by Greeks who wish to see him:

"Now among those who went up to worship at the feast were some Greeks. So these came to Philip, who was from Bethsaida in Galilee, and asked him, 'Sir, we wish to see Jesus.' Philip went and told Andrew; Andrew and Philip went and told Jesus" (John 12:20-22).†

---

*Or "nations" in the *NIV*.

What's awesome about this passage, is that in Hebrew, the Jews had two words for 'people.' גּוֹיִם (goyim), which is mainly used for nations outside of Israel, and עַם (am), which is exclusive in referring to Israel herself. However, within this verse, the word used is הָעַמִּים (ha-'ammim), the plural of am. Yahweh, in the Old Testament, sends an invite for even the Gentiles to join His people. He makes a promise in Isaiah, that even the Gentiles [through Jesus] may one day, be one with Israel!

†There's also another theory concerning this event, which I once overheard the Professor discussing with another teacher. I promise I wasn't droppin' no eaves; nevertheless, to paraphrase what I overheard the Professor ask: what if, Jesus clearing the Temple, was a sort of reversal? a metaphor? For the Promise Land was cleared for the Israelites to move in. So what if, Jesus cleared the Temple, so that the Gentiles

Interior Design of Jerusalem's Temple

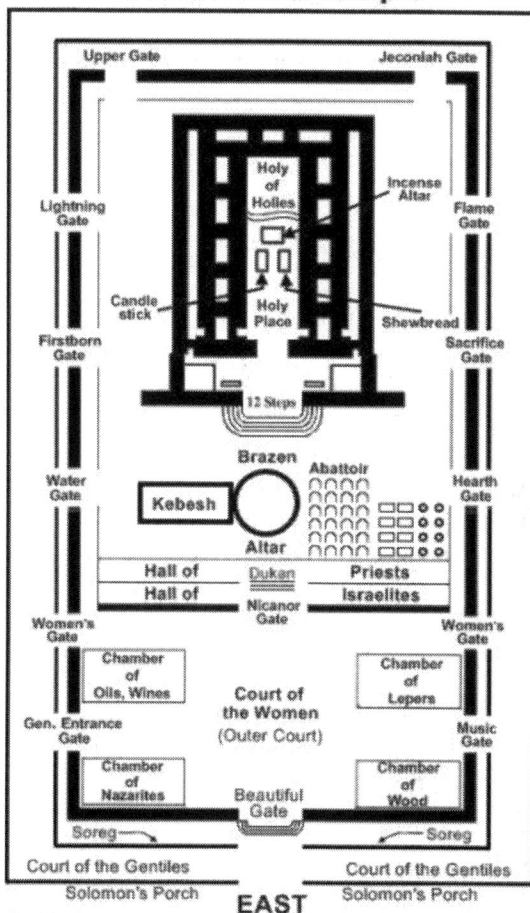

Like I stated beforehand, we don't know exactly why Jesus was so angry. One of these answers could very well fit the bill, or maybe tis a combination of all three? We can try to psychoanalyze Jesus till we're blue in the face, and we will be as 100% satisfied with an answer, as a horse-leech is drinking blood.[‡]

---

could move in? For according to Mark 11:17, Jesus said, "Is it not written, 'My house shall be called a house of prayer for *all the nations*'? But you have made it a den of robbers."

[‡]The leech has two daughters:
  Give and Give.
Three things are never satisfied;
  four never say, "Enough":

Yet, what we do know, was that out of a righteous anger, Jesus had overturned tables and had chased people with a whip out of his Father's house. That is was an anger for justice, not vengeance nor self. That the fires of a lion were burning within him.

THE NEXT INSTANCE we shall look at of Jesus being the Lion of Judah, actually comes from a story that we've already discussed while studying his lambness. However, under the light of another Gospel, we can also see his león as well:

> And they were bringing children to him that he might touch them, and the disciples rebuked them. But when Jesus saw it, he was indignant and said to them, "Let the children come to me; do not hinder them, for to such belongs the kingdom of God. Truly, I say to you, whoever does not receive the kingdom of God like a child shall not enter it." And he took them in his arms and blessed them, laying his hands

Sheol, the barren womb,
  the land never satisfied with water,
  and the fire that never says, "Enough." (Proverbs 30:15-16)

on them. (Mark 10:13-16)

Angered by his disciples attempting to keep the children away from him, Mark tells us that Jesus was "indignant," that he was ἠγανάκτησεν (eganaktesen). Jesus was angered by his disciples' actions, so he "rebuked" them:

"Peter! James! John! What do you think you're doing, Maṭim? Are these yaladim not my followers too? Let the yaladim come to me. Let the children come to me. And do not hinder them, for to such belongs the kingdom of God."

Just like in the Temple, Jesus' anger was ignited by justice. Our Lord making a stand for the lesser, standing up to defend those who are weaker, smaller, and have a desire for their Savior.

This is also not the only time in which Jesus is angered by his disciples either, as can be seen in Matthew 16:

Now when Jesus came into the district of Caesarea Philippi, he asked his disciples, "Who do people say that the Son of Man is?" And they said, "Some say John the Baptist, others say Elijah, and others Jeremiah or one of the prophets." He said to them, "But who do you say that I am?" Simon Peter replied, "You are the Christ, the Son of the living God." And Jesus answered him, "Blessed are you, Simon Bar-Jonah! For flesh and blood has not revealed this to you, but my Father who is in heaven. And I tell you, you are Peter, and on this rock I will build my church, and the gates of hell shall not prevail against it. I will give you the keys of the kingdom of heaven, and whatever you bind on earth shall be bound in heaven, and whatever you loose on earth shall be loosed in heaven." Then he strictly charged the disciples to tell no one that he was the Christ. (13-20)

Simon faithfully answers Jesus' question, declaring that he is the

Messiah, and the Son of God. Jesus then praises Simon for his declaration, and even renames him Petros [in Greek] or Cephas [Aramaic], which means 'rock.' For Jesus then announces that upon the rock of Peter's confession,* shall he build his church. Yet, it's amazing how quickly pride can transform into anger. For look what Matthew writes next:

> From that time Jesus began to show his disciples that he must go to Jerusalem and suffer many things from the elders and chief priests and scribes, and be killed, and on the third day be raised. And Peter took him aside and began to rebuke him, saying, "Far be it from you, Lord! This shall never happen to you." But he turned and said to Peter, "Get behind me, Satan! You are a hindrance to me. For you are not setting your mind on the things of God, but on the things of man." (21-23)

Jesus then tells his disciples that he must go to Jerusalem ... to die. And rash Peter, like he does on so many occasions, puts his foot into his mouth. For he is a zealous man, and he cannot imagine harm coming upon his rabbi. And so he tells Jesus, "Far be it from you, Lord! This shall never happen to you."

Though Peter had good intentions, some believe that he had overstepped his bounds. That this disciple was trying to hold power over his teacher, similarly like a child telling his mom, "No, you will clean the house." If so, this explains why Jesus quickly answers, "Get behind me, Satan!"

Whoa! Wasn't that harsh? Why would Jesus call one of his most

---

*This verse must be translated with caution, as a mentor of mine once pointed out to me. For if translated that Jesus shall build his church upon Peter, not upon his faith/ confession, the argument that Peter was the first Pope can be made. (Though, there is still the complication that Peter was already married by this time, since Jesus healing his mother-in-law was one of his first known miracles (Matthew 8:14-15).)

loyal disciples "Satan?"

First off, if Peter was talking down to Jesus, this comment would have quickly humbled him—reminding him that he was not merely talking to another man, but to the Son of God.

Second, what does Jesus mean when he calls Peter "Satan"? Is Jesus truly comparing Peter to the Devil? Or, perhaps he was calling Peter, "enemy" or "adversary," which remember is the meaning of 'satan' in Hebrew. And if so, I believe this would have cut Peter to the quick. Can you imagine what it would feel like, to have your best friend call you his enemy? . . . I mean . . . it would *hurt*. But it shows how serious Jesus was to go to Jerusalem. . . . How committed he was to hang upon that cross. And no one, not even a man whom he loved and had spent the last three years with, was going to stop him from his mission.

NOT ONLY DOES Jesus rebuke those whom follow him, but he also calls out those whom would think of him as an enemy. Within Matthew 23, Jesus gives a sermon against the leaders of the Law, calling out the hypocrisy of these religious leaders—challenging them to step up and to be better. Both for their sake, and for the sake of the people:

> Then Jesus said to the crowds and to his disciples, "The scribes and the Pharisees sit on Moses' seat, so do and observe whatever they tell you, but not the works they do. For they preach, but do not practice. They tie up heavy burdens, hard to bear, and lay them on people's shoulders, but they themselves are not willing to move them with their finger. They do all their deeds to be seen by others. For they make their phylacteries broad and their fringes long, and they love the place of honor at feasts and the best seats in the syna-

gogues and greetings in the marketplaces and being called rabbi by others. But you are not to be called rabbi, for you have one teacher, and you are all brothers. And call no man your father on earth, for you have one Father, who is in heaven. Neither be called instructors, for you have one instructor, the Christ. The greatest among you shall be your servant. Whoever exalts himself will be humbled, and whoever humbles himself will be exalted.

"But woe to you, scribes and Pharisees, hypocrites! For you shut the kingdom of heaven in people's faces. For you neither enter yourselves nor allow those who would enter to go in. Woe to you, scribes and Pharisees, hypocrites! For you travel across sea and land to make a single proselyte, and when he becomes a proselyte, you make him twice as much a child of hell as yourselves.

"Woe to you, blind guides, who say, 'If anyone swears by the temple, it is nothing, but if anyone swears by the gold of the temple, he is bound by his oath.' You blind fools! For which is greater, the gold or the temple that has made the gold sacred? And you say, 'If anyone swears by the altar, it is nothing, but if anyone swears by the gift that is on the altar, he is bound by his oath.' You blind men! For which is greater, the gift or the altar that makes the gift sacred? So whoever swears by the altar swears by it and by everything on it. And whoever swears by the temple swears by it and by him who dwells in it. And whoever swears by heaven swears by the throne of God and by him who sits upon it.

"Woe to you, scribes and Pharisees, hypocrites! For you tithe mint and dill and cumin, and have neglected the weightier matters of the law: justice and mercy and faithfulness. These you ought to have done, without neglecting the others. You blind guides, straining out a gnat and swallowing a camel!

"Woe to you, scribes and Pharisees, hypocrites! For you clean the outside of the cup and the plate, but inside they are full of greed and self-indulgence. You blind Pharisee! First clean the inside of the cup and the plate, that the outside also may be clean.

"Woe to you, scribes and Pharisees, hypocrites! For you are like whitewashed tombs, which outwardly appear beautiful, but within are full of dead people's bones and all uncleanness. So you also outwardly appear righteous to others, but within you are full of hypocrisy and lawlessness.

"Woe to you, scribes and Pharisees, hypocrites! For you build the tombs of the prophets and decorate the monuments of the righteous, saying, 'If we had lived in the days of our fathers, we would not have taken part with them in shedding the blood of the prophets.' Thus you witness against yourselves that you are sons of those who murdered the prophets. Fill up, then, the measure of your fathers. You serpents, you brood of vipers, how are you to escape being sentenced to hell? Therefore I send you prophets and wise men and scribes, some of whom you will kill and crucify, and some you will flog in your synagogues and persecute from town to town, so that on you may come all the righteous blood shed on earth, from the blood of righteous Abel to the blood of Zechariah the son of Barachiah, whom you murdered between the sanctuary and the altar. Truly, I say to you, all these things will come upon this generation." (1-36)

Wow! Did Jesus really say these things? Did these words really leave his lips?

Yes, yes they did. And if you're still not convinced, open a Bible with red letters in it and see for yourself. For you see, Jesus was not always meek and gentle, there were times in which Jesus could be quite ferocious, yet bluntly truthful. Jesus was not politically correct, he was not always nice, but he was good. *Everything* he did or spoke, was out of love—even in the midst of his wrath.

There is a difference between niceness and goodness. It might not be 'nice' to call someone a, "Hypocrite! A whitewashed tomb!"; nevertheless, it is good to stand up against hypocrisy, which is what Jesus totally does as he calls out the Pharisees and says to them seven woes. And as Christians, we too should not always be nice, but should always be good. Such as it may not be 'nice' to call a brother out on his porn addiction [in love], but, if done right, it can be very good. Referring back to the words of Lewis: "'Then he isn't safe?' said Lucy.

'Safe?' said Mr. Beaver; 'don't you hear what Mrs. Beaver tells you? Who said anything about safe? 'Course he isn't safe. But he's good. He's the King, I tell you.'"9

Jesus was no stranger to controversy. In fact, he seems to stir it up by his very nature. Not just in *heated* debates today, but even then. For either because of their jealousy, hurt of pride, fear of the wrath of the Roman Empire, or because they truly believed Jesus to be a blasphemer, or some combination of all four of these motives, the teachers of the Law were Jesus' opponents throughout the Gospels. Jesus was both loved and hated, which is the nature of Christ. You can either believe he is the Son of God or you don't; there is no middle ground when it comes to Christ.

DAVID MURROW, THE author of the Christian bestseller, *Why Men Hate Going to Church*, was the man besides my youth minister who bluntly pointed out this lion-side of Christ. He writes in another book of his, *The Map: The Way of all Great Men*, that:

> "The Christ revealed in chapters 8-25 of Matthew's gospel bears little resemblance to the helpless babe we met in the hay. The man who declared, 'Blessed are the meek,' is now anything but. He who taught, 'Love your enemies,' suddenly finds himself surrounded by them. And how does he show his enemies love? By plunking them with rebukes, curses, and put-downs."10

Murrow's book also helped me to realize, that Jesus' lion-self is often overlooked. In a society that favors tolerance, it's easy to over focus on Jesus' love and grace, yet neglect his anger and judgement.

Just like us, Jesus hated religious hypocrisy. Unfortunately, hypocritical ministers are just as much of a stereotype as lying lawyers or sleazy politicians, (and every stereotype, sadly, has some truth to it). With that said, there are men who have followed in Jesus' footsteps, who have not been afraid to call out religious leaders. Men such as Geoffrey Chaucer, who does so in his prose, *The Canterbury Tales*:

> Since riding and the hunting of the hare
> Were all his love, for no cost would he spare.
> I saw his sleeves were decorated at the hand
> With fur of grey, the finest in the land;
> Also, to fasten hood beneath his chin,
> He had of good wrought gold a curious pin:
> A love-knot in the larger end there was.
> His head was bald and shone like any glass
> And smooth as one anointed was his face.
> Fat was this lord, he stood in goodly case.
> His bulging eyes he rolled about, and hot
> They gleamed and red, like fire beneath a pot;
> His boots were soft; his horse of great estate.
> Now certainly he was a fine prelate:
> He was not pale as some tormented ghost.
> A fat swan he loved best of any roast.[12]

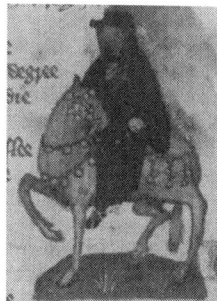

In a satirical manner, Chaucer pokes fun at two religious characters. Such as the monk who is described above. He who lives for himself, indulging in worldly passions, wearing only the best of clothes and eating only the best of foods, instead of dedicating himself in living a more simple life entuned to God. And also a pardoner, who speaks out against greed, while simultaneously selling pardons in hope to collect more and more profit.

No one is perfect; however, *terrible* things have been done in the name of God, of Jesus, and the Church. And terrible scandals have happened by many who are supposed to be 'God-fearing' men. Mistakes happen, and there is always grace and forgiveness for them, but both the Church as well as her ministers, need to guard their hearts, and work at being faithful to our Lord. Again, no one is perfect, yet there is a difference in committing a sin, and living a lifestyle of sin. Furthermore, *every* Christian, not just religious leaders, need to work at not being hypocrites. Of dedicating ourselves to God, and living in a manner pleasing to Him.

Let us work at making who we are, who we are. Not being two-faced, living one way on Sunday and another Monday—Saturday, but being genuine through and through.

AS WE KNOW, Jesus performed many miracles while he was here on earth. Though each have their own abnormalities, the one in John 5 is very interesting:

Now there is in Jerusalem by the Sheep Gate a pool, in Aramaic called

Bethesda, which has five roofed colonnades. In these lay a multitude of invalids—blind, lame, and paralyzed. One man was there who had been an invalid for thirty-eight years. When Jesus saw him lying there and knew that he had already been there a long time, he said to him, "Do you want to be healed?" The sick man answered him, "Sir, I have no one to put me into the pool when the water is stirred up, and while I am going another steps down before me." Jesus said to him, "Get up, take up your bed, and walk." And at once the man was healed, and he took up his bed and walked. Now that day was the Sabbath. (John 5:2-9)

Jesus comes to the pool at Bethesda, where he encounters a man with a disability. He asks the man if he wants to be healed, and instead of answering, "Yes!", he gives Jesus an excuse of why he hasn't been healed already. Jesus doesn't appear to be impressed by the faith of this man, as he had the official in the chapter before, or the Roman centurion with a sick servant (Matthew 8:5-13). And what does this man do after Jesus heals him? He tattles on Jesus to the Jews:

So the Jews said to the man who had been healed, "It is the Sabbath, and it is not lawful for you to take up your bed." But he answered them, "The man who healed me, that man said to me, 'Take up your bed, and walk.'" They asked him, "Who is the man who said to you, 'Take up your bed and walk'?" Now the man who had been healed did not know who it was, for Jesus had withdrawn, as there was a crowd in the place. Afterward Jesus found him in the temple and said to him, "See, you are well! Sin no more, that nothing worse may happen to you." The man went away and told the Jews that it was Jesus who had healed him. And this was why the Jews were persecuting Jesus, because he was doing these things on the Sabbath. But Jesus answered them, "My Father is working until now, and I am work-ing." (John 5:10-17)

Here, we see a more stern than merciful Jesus, "See, you are well! Sin no more, that nothing worse may happen to you." Jesus delivers a pretty fearful warning here. For what could be worse than being par-alyzed for thirty-eight years?

And what sin was Jesus speaking of? Truthfully, there's no telling. But one theory, was that the man was absorbed in himself, that he may not have wanted to give up his victim status. Remember, he nev-er truthfully answered Jesus if he wanted to be healed, and he doesn't even thank him (similar to nine of the ten lepers in Luke 17:11-19).

Perhaps this case proves, that faith is more than seeing miracles to believe. That a person, has to want transformation, in order to be changed. That someone can experience Jesus, yet still have the choice to choose to remain the same.

PERHAPS THE STRANGEST example of Jesus' wrath, comes from the story of him cursing the fig tree:

In the morning, as he was returning to the city, he became hun-gry. And seeing a fig tree by the wayside, he went to it and found nothing on it but only leaves. And he said to it, "May no fruit ever come from you again!" And the fig tree withered at once.

When the disciples saw it, they marveled, saying, "How did the fig tree wither at once?" And Jesus answered them, "Truly, I say to you, if you have faith and do not doubt, you will not only do what has been done to the fig tree, but even if you say to this mountain, 'Be taken up and thrown into the sea,' it will happen. And whatever you ask in prayer, you will receive, if you have faith." (Matthew 21:18-22)

This story is told in both Matthew's and in Mark's Gospels (Mark 11:12-14, 20-25); however, it's told slightly different in both. In Matthew's, this episode takes place the day after he clears the Temple, and the tree withers immediately. While in Mark's, he curses the tree before he clears the Temple, and then he and his disciples find the tree withered on the next day when they're returning to the city. Yet, despite these differences, the premise is basically the same. Jesus sees a fig tree that has no fruit, so he curses it, it dies, and all tree huggers begin to question their faith.

So what's with Jesus killing this poor, unsuspecting fig tree? I mean it's just sitting there photosynthesizing, enjoying its day?

Well, perhaps this tree isn't as innocent as it first appears to be. You see, in the first place, it wasn't the right season for figs. Which, Jesus would have known this, making it strange that he would get mad enough to curse this tree to wither. But, the tree was being deceptive, for sometimes fruit is ready early within a season. The fig tree had leaves, which normally meant it also had fruit, for in actuality, the fig's fruit usually appeared before its leaves did. So when Jesus had spotted it from a distance, he may have thought it truly had fruit, only to find it had none when he had made the venture to it.

But, doesn't Jesus know everything? Wouldn't he have known it didn't have fruit before he reached it?

Did Jesus know everything while he was here? We know he did have foreknowledge of some things, or that the Father had revealed certain things to His Son. Such as knowing that Nathanael was under a fig tree before he had called him to be his disciple (John 1:48), that the Samaritan woman at the well had five husbands and was currently living with a man who she was not married to (John 4:18), that he would be killed in Jerusalem (Luke 18:31-34), that Judas would betray him (John 13:18-30), and that Peter would deny him three times before the rooster crowed (Matthew 26:34). However, we do not know the extent of Jesus' knowledge, nor when he knew these things; I don't believe he did at his conception. But, we do know Jesus had some ignorance, perhaps by choice, or perhaps not, for he does reveal one thing that he does not know, the day of his Second Coming:

"From the fig tree learn its lesson: as soon as its branch becomes tender and puts out its leaves, you know that summer is near. So also, when you see these things taking place, you know that he is near, at the very gates. Truly, I say to you, this generation will not pass away until all these things take place. Heaven and earth will pass away, but my words will not pass away.

"But concerning that day or that hour, no one knows, not even the angels in heaven, nor the Son, but only the Father. Be on guard, keep awake. For you do not know when the time will come. It is like a man going on a journey, when he leaves home and puts his servants in charge, each with his work, and commands the doorkeeper to stay awake. Therefore stay awake—for you do not know when the master of the house will come, in the evening, or at midnight, or when the rooster crows, or in the morning—lest he come suddenly and find you asleep. And what I say to you I say to all: Stay awake." (Mark 13:28-

36)

Just because Jesus is God, doesn't mean he knows everything. Furthermore, let's open up this can of worms, does the Father know everything? Yes, He has the ability to, God is God after all. However, saying that He does know everything at this very moment is putting God into a box. And saying that He doesn't, is also putting Him into a box. We must be very careful when stating things about God, not trying to describe who He is with labels.

Like Jesus, there are definite things which the Scriptures reveal that He does know, such as how we discussed that way back in Genesis 3:15, He prophesied the victory of Christ. He promised Abraham a son from his own body, and it happened. He also prophesied to Abraham that his people would be enslaved by a foreign nation for a time before He would free them (Genesis 15:13-14), and He did. He used Jeremiah to warn the peoples of Judah that Babylon was coming. He revealed to Daniel the rise and falls of future kingdoms. And throughout the Old Testament, He delivered promise after promise of the coming Messiah.

However, there are also some verses which use strange language as if God doesn't know every single little detail. Such as before the Flood, He "regretted" that He had ever formed mankind (Genesis 6:6). How could God have regretted this decision, if He had already known they were going to become so corrupt? Or why does Abraham attempt to bargain with God to save Sodom, if God had already declared He would destroy it (Genesis 18:22-33)? Or how did Moses change God's mind as he interceded for Israel and convinced God not to utterly wipe them out (Numbers 14)? Or why did God almost kill Moses, after telling him as the burning bush that he would lead His people

347

out of Egypt (Exodus 4:24-26)? And why does He try to kill Balaam but then doesn't (Numbers 22:21-39)? Or why did He tell King Hezekiah that he shall die from his illness and then heals him (2 Kings 20:1-11)?

There's plenty of other examples too, just as there's other verses which could be used to defend predestination, but the point is, are all these phenomenons tests from an all-knowing God? He whom a good Calvinist believes has already destined who shall eternally live in heaven or hell? Or is God a liar? which we know can't be, for then He wouldn't be God.

Some suggest, that God has the capability to know everything, but He chooses not to. Another view, presented by Boyd in his book, *God of the Possible: A Biblical Introduction to the Open View of God*, is the theology that God chooses to live in the moment of linear time with us. And just as He had given us dominion over His creation in Genesis, He allows man a degree of dominion over time. That together, God and man forge the future. Which if true, explains how the Bible can support the views of both free will and predestination.

Interesting, I've never thought of that before. But I'm still curious, why did Jesus curse the fig tree?

Well, remember what week it was. It was the beginning of the Passion Week. Jesus knew what was coming for him. So perhaps his disappointment, mixed with anger, and stress of what was coming, were enough emotions within Jesus to excite him in releasing them in this act.

Maybe . . . but would that be an abuse of his power?

. . . Truthfully, I don't know. His action may have been caused by personal strife, but Jesus does not use this moment for himself, but as an opportunity to teach others—to teach his disciples about faith. Therefore, it wasn't just a selfish act.

But perhaps another explanation, is the symbolic importance of the fig tree. Remember, Israel was a much more symbolic society than ours today, and the fig tree was a symbol of spirituality. After all, Nathanael believed in Jesus, and decided to follow him when Jesus had told him that he had been under a fig tree (perhaps in meditation) with his foreknowledge (John 1:43-51), and the prophet Amos makes known to King Jeroboam, that he had not been born a prophet, that he had first been "a herdsman and a dresser of sycamore figs" before Yahweh had called him (Amos 7:14).

Perhaps this fig tree, was a symbol of Israel's spirituality. That they appeared to be alive and growing, that they had leaves, that they had shouted, "Hosanna! Hosanna in the highest!", but they were truly dead inside. That they weren't growing any fruit. That in less than a week, the same crowd [maybe] would be crying out, "Crucify! Crucify him!" Therefore, if this fig tree symbolized Israel, perhaps it wasn't the tree who Jesus was upset with?

Maybe, Jesus was making another statement against hypocrisy. Reinforcing his actions at the Temple with this demonstration. That if a tree appears alive, but it doesn't produce any fruit, then it's good for nothing then to be cut down, just as he had said in a parable within Luke's Gospel (13:6-9). For what does Jesus discuss with his disciples after the fig tree dies?

Faith.

He discusses faith with his disciples. Telling them if they have genuine, living faith, they can tell a mountain to toss itself in the sea and it will do so. But was he talking about physical mountains, or metaphorical ones?

And if a Christian is truly living for the Lord, what kind of fruit does he produce? (Matthew 13: 8-9, 23; Galatians 5:22-23)

THIS FIFTH EXAMPLE of Jesus' leo, actually comes outside of his earthly ministry, being found after his resurrection and even after his ascension, on the road to Damascus:

> But Saul, still breathing threats and murder against the disciples of the Lord, went to the high priest and asked him for letters to the synagogues at Damascus, so that if he found any belonging to the Way, men or women, he might bring them bound to Jerusalem. Now as he went on his way, he approached Damascus, and suddenly a light from heaven shone around him. And falling to the ground, he heard a voice saying to him, "Saul, Saul, why are you persecuting me?" And he said, "Who are you, Lord?" And he said, "I am Jesus, whom you are persecuting. But rise and enter the city, and you will be told what you are to do." The men who were traveling with him stood speechless, hearing the voice but seeing no one. Saul rose from the ground, and although his eyes were opened, he saw nothing. So they led him by the hand and brought him into Damascus. And for three days he was without sight, and neither ate nor drank. (Acts 9:1-9)

True, during this instance the Bible does not specifically mention that 'Jesus was angry.' But, even if he wasn't, he was no cuddly lamb in this moment either. For Saul was *afraid* of him; he fell to the ground, which was a common reaction for anyone in the presence of a heavenly being. He was surrounded by a light brighter than the noonday sun (Acts 26:13). And he was in the presence of the Messiah, who's people he had been persecuting. This Jesus encounter had to have been anything but friendly, and yet, it was this very encounter, which changed Saul's life forever. He became an apostle who boldly proclaimed the Gospel, who suffered for it, and even died for it.

Sometimes, an encounter with Jesus can be painful. As can be seen by the life of Paul. Or even by the examples Lewis illustrates for us. Such as in *The Horse and His Boy*, when Aslan attacks the girl Aravis, tearing her back with his claws. So that she would know the pain, the stripes she had caused her step-mother's slave to receive, for drugging the maid to sleep in her escape. And again in his *Voyage of the Dawn Treader*, when the boy Eustace needed Aslan's help to transform him into a boy again, after his own greed had changed him into a dragon. This was only done, however, by Aslan shredding off his scaly hide with his claws. Sometimes, an encounter with Jesus is *painful*, but he's always transformational.

OUR LAST EXPLORATION into Jesus' nature of lion, can be found in the book of Revelation. In the last chapter, we saw Jesus as the Lamb that had been slain, but there is also a much scarier depiction of Jesus in this book as well.

Before we even see the Lamb, the elders said to John when he was in despair when he thought there was no one who could open the scroll, to, "Weep no more; behold, the Lion of the tribe of Judah, the Root of David, has conquered, so that he can open the scroll and its seven seals" (5:5). The Messiah is first described as a conquering Lion, before we see him seated on the throne as the Lamb.

And as the Lamb opens the scroll and its seals, some *strange* things begin to take place. After each of the first four seals are opened, John sees a horseman. The first being a rider on a white horse, and a conquer: "And I looked, and behold, a white horse! And its rider had a bow, and a crown was given to him, and he came out conquering, and to conquer" (6:2).

The second rider was seated upon a red horse holding a sword, and he took away peace so that people would kill each other [let's call him Aries]. The third rider sat on a black horse holding a scale and calling out measurements. And the last rider, the fourth horseman, Death, was on the back of a pale horse, who slayed using sword, famine, and pestilence.

Many arguments have been given of who these four horsemen could be, for they're not your typical racetrack jockeys. Some believing they're actual, spiritual beings who will come when the seals are broken during the Apocalypse. I admit they could be right, but I personally believe that John's vision is much more symbolic. That these riders together symbolize war. For in war, peoples are conquered, peace is taken, blood is spilt, the days of men and goods are measured, and death takes many by sword, famine, and pestilence. What if these four horsemen together, represent war?

But who is the horseman on the white horse?

Good question. This rider could very well be a separate being associated with these other horseman. Or, the rider on the white horse could be the victorious Christ, for we see him also seated on a white horse in a later chapter within Revelation:

> Then I saw heaven opened, and behold, a white horse! The one sitting on it is called Faithful and True, and in righteousness he judges and makes war. His eyes are like a flame of fire, and on his head are many diadems, and he has a name written that no one knows but himself. He is clothed in a robe dipped in blood, and the name by which he is called is The Word of God. And the armies of heaven, arrayed in fine linen, white and pure, were following him on white horses. From his mouth comes a sharp sword with which to strike down the nations, and he will rule them with a rod of iron. He will tread the winepress of the fury of the wrath of God the Almighty. On his robe and on his thigh he has a name written, King of kings and Lord of lords.
>
> Then I saw an angel standing in the sun, and with a loud voice he called to all the birds that fly directly overhead, "Come, gather for the great supper of God, to eat the flesh of kings, the flesh of captains, the flesh of mighty men, the flesh of horses and their riders, and the flesh of all men, both free and slave, both small and great." And I saw the beast and the kings of the earth with their armies gathered to make war against him who was sitting on the horse and against his army. And the beast was captured, and with it the false prophet who in its presence had done the signs by which he deceived those who had received the mark of the beast and those who worshiped its image. These two were thrown alive into the lake of fire that burns with sul-

fur. And the rest were slain by the sword that came from the mouth of him who was sitting on the horse, and all the birds were gorged with their flesh. (19:11-21)

Wow! This rider isn't Jesus, is he? After all, verse twelve states, "he has a name written that no one knows but himself."

True, but look at the other names which are also associated with him. He is called, "Faithful and True," "The Word of God, (just as John calls him the "Lógos" in John 1), and the "King of kings and Lord of lords" (1 Timothy 6:15, Revelation 17:14).

No, this is *not* the Jesus whom we are accustomed too; however, when Jesus came the first time, ". . . God did not send his Son into the world to condemn the world, but in order that the world might be saved through him" (John 3:17). Jesus' first mission was one of mercy, but his second will be in judgement. That is the drastic difference between the Lamb who was slain on the cross, and the conquering King who shall refine his creation. The Savior who is to come to reclaim all that was taken when the fruit was eaten in Eden. And that is no easy feat. For when he does, all creation will be finally sanctified . . . but there will be no more chances for repentance. On that day, judgement will come, and all mankind will either be saved or damned. In Revelation, we see Jesus as a *frightful* being, who we can only ask, "In what distant deeps or skies.

Burnt the fire of thine eyes?"[16]

Furthermore, how Jesus is described in this chapter, is very similar in how John describes him in the beginning of Revelation:

Then I turned to see the voice that was speaking to me, and on turning I saw seven golden lampstands, and in the midst of the lampstands one like a son of man, clothed with a long robe and with a golden sash around his chest. The hairs of his head were white, like white wool, like snow. His eyes were like a flame of fire, his feet were like burnished bronze, refined in a furnace, and his voice was like the roar of many waters. In his right hand he held seven stars, from his mouth came a sharp two-edged sword, and his face was like the sun shining in full strength.

When I saw him, I fell at his feet as though dead. But he laid his right hand on me, saying, "Fear not, I am the first and the last, and the living one. I died, and behold I am alive forevermore, and I have the keys of Death and Hades. Write therefore the things that you have seen, those that are and those that are to take place after this. (1:12-19)

The Jesus whom John sees, is very different than the one whom he had last observe ascend into the sky. A Jesus who John is *afraid* of, though he is the same Jesus who he had walked with—had lived with. The same Jesus whom John affectionally said loved him. Yet, though he is the same Jesus, John no longer sees him as the humbled Lamb who became man to live amongst us, but the Lion with his full mane, with glory and power surrounding him. Yet, this may not be the first time in which John had seen this side of the powerful and triumphant Christ. For maybe, he had seen Jesus like this, on the Mount of Transfiguration?

Jesus *is* the Lion of Judah.[*]

***

WHO WOULD WIN in a fight? Batman or Superman? Perhaps a question which has no true answer, depending on circumstance and per-

---

[*]There are also times in the Old Testament, in which Yahweh is compared to a lion: Job 10:16, Isaiah 38:13, Jeremiah 25:38, 49:19, 50:44; Lamentations 3:10-12, Hosea 5:14, 11:10, 13:7-8.

haps personal bias. . . . But what is known, is that in the ultimate battle between God and sin, there is no contest. Jesus wins!

Jesus won the battle upon his cross. No, there are many days it doesn't feel like it, surviving in the world that we live in. But one day, the conquering king will return to judge this world, and to reclaim his people! For he left to prepare a place for us! If it were not so, he would not have told us (John 14:1-3).

NOTES

1. Ausubel, p. 262.

2. Lewis, C. S. *The Chronicles of Narnia: The Lion, the Witch, and the Wardrobe.* New York: HarperCollins, 1994. Print. p. 182.

3. Fig. 1: Saeed, Atif. *Angry Lion.* 2012.

4. Livingstone, David. *Missionary Travels and Researches in South Africa.* London: John Murray, 1857. Print.

5. Charbonneay-Lassay, p. 6-14.

6. Fig. 2: A denarius on display in the Linda Byrd Smith Museum of Biblical Archaeology at Harding University. The face of Tiberius Caesar is printed on the coin.

7. Fig. 3: A Tyrian half shekel on display in the Linda Byrd Smith Museum of Biblical Archaeology at Harding University.

8. Fig. 5: Blake, William. "The Little Black Boy", from *Songs of Innocence and of Experience, Shewing the Two Contrary States of the Human Soul,* copy Y. 1825. Metropolitan Museum of Art: New York City.

9. Lewis, p. 80.

10. Murrow, David. *The Map: The Way of all Great Men.* Nashville: Thomas Nelson, 2010. Print. p. 139.

11. Fig. 6: The Monk in the Ellesmere Chaucer of the *Canterbury Tales.* 15th Century. Huntington Library: San Marino, California.

12. Chaucer, Geoffrey, and J. U. Nicolson. *Canterbury Tales.* Cheswold, DE: Prestwick House, 2004. Print. p. 22.

13. Fig. 7: Blake, William. Chaucer's Canterbury Pilgrims. 1810. The Morgan Library and Museum: New York City.

14. Fig. 8: Rahib, Ilyas Basim Khuri Bazzi. *Jesus Curses the Fig Tree.* 1684. Walters Art Museum: Baltimore.

15. Fig. 9: Blake, William. *Death on a Pale Horse*. 1800. Fitzwilliam Museum: Cambridge, England.

16. Blake, William. . "The Tyger." *The Complete Poetry and Prose of William Blake.* Newly revised ed. Ed. David V.

CHAPTER 19

*JESUS, THE STORYTELLER:

NOT THE BEST BEDTIME STORIES

O ne of the greatest perks working in ministry, is getting to be around people. As an extreme extrovert, I can confidently say this, for it is the truth about 80% of the time. There are moments in which I like to be by myself, such as sleeping snuggly in my bed at 3 A.M. But 80% of the time, it's great to be around people.

One thing that I especially love, is getting to know them. Getting to discover who they are. Such as what they like or what they're good at, such as motocross racing or bowling. Or what they dislike or afraid of, such as spiders or sasquatch. Or what is their story, or their stories within their story. Not only does talking to people satisfy my archeologist-detective curiosity, but talking also appeases my author-self, which is almost always thirsty to hear another story. That is why I love talking to people, as well as why I'm easily addicted to reading books or watching movies.

I was privileged in getting to meet many new people that summer, and experienced the joy of getting to hear *many* new stories. One such person who was always a blessing getting to talk to, was Mamma Brunner.

Many of our most memorable conversations, revolved around "nasty" squirrels. I found it quite amusing hearing how her dislike had evolved for these furry creatures, the menaces that terrorized her birds to steal free food from her feeders. The bucktooth scavengers that found enjoyment throwing her feeders on the ground.

At first, she tried to be merciful. Capturing the critters in traps and releasing them away from her home, having painted their tails pink so she would know if they ever returned. Yet the nut-collectors never learned their lesson, always returning for the feed. Their stubbornness transforming Mamma Brunner's dislike for them, into a heated rivalry.

I understand her frustration, having personally witnessed my youth minister struggle to keep his garden alive from the burrowing forces of bloodthirsty rabbits, and the thieves from the trees, the acrobatic squirrels with the stomachs of black holes. Yet, it's still fun to tease her about such things. . . . Just as I have friends who get a kick out my enmity for Disney.

I guess we all have our own little quirks, which gives each of us our own snowflake uniquenesses.

***

JESUS WAS A physician (Luke 5:31), the Great Physician even. Able to give sight to the blind, walk to the lame, hearing to the deaf—able to perform *miraculous* healings without the need of a scalpel or operating table.

Jesus was also a rabbi. A teacher who taught the Law of God, not the rules of man. A skilled orator, who hung crowds with every word. A talented instructor, who incorporated his signs, as visual examples of what he was teaching. A keen opportunist, who used everyday life to unveil a hint of the Kingdom. And he was a gifted storyteller.

Jesus utilized multiple means to deliver his messages to us. Knowing that we each learn differently, and that knowing something in more than one way, helps it be less forgetful. One such method he used, was storytelling.

Yes, Jesus gave some magnificent sermons, such as his Sermon on the Mount. But he also appealed to one of man's most basic candies, stories.

Honestly, when do you usually perk up and listen during the Sunday sermon? Isn't it usually the part, when the minister starts telling a story? Or what films usually pull our heartstrings more than any other? Aren't they the ones with compelling stories? Or why do we love to share with our friends our personal experiences? Changing our voices and using hand motions to describe what happened, even by those who claim they can't act? Isn't it because

we like sharing our stories? and listening to the stories of others?

In his book, *A Million Miles in a Thousand Years: How I Learned to Live a Better Story*, Donald Miller makes a great case of what makes a great story. That, "A story is a character who wants something and overcomes conflict to get it," and greater the conflict, better the story.[2]

Jesus, being both human and God, tapped into this natural desire, sharing stories in order to reveal how to live a better, God-fearing life. Sadly, I believe we've become desensitized to many of his parables, not feeling the same significance as his Jewish audience would have felt. Not saying that Jesus' illustrations are not still meaningful for us today, but being separated by the barriers of time and culture, I believe, have deluded them for us Americans living in the 21st century. Not that this is necessarily true for all of Jesus' parables, but for example, why does Jesus tell the story of the good Samaritan? Today, a 'Good Samaritan' is a coined term for a man or woman who does something unexpected for the benefit of another. But in Jesus' day, to the Jews, there were no Good Samaritans. They were no better than dogs or swine, making Jesus' parable *very* controversial.

To us, many of Jesus' metaphors are foreign, while planting seed by hand, catching fish with nets, or molding pots were things of everyday life to the Jews living 2,000 years ago. These things were just a part of their culture.

With that said, I have taken three of Jesus' parables, and have rewritten them with a modern twist. Know I do not believe these stories are better than Christ's, nor hold the same weight as his words. But my hope, is that by seeing these same stories with modern eyes, may hopefully change your perspective. Hopefully, exciting similar emotions, shock, and questioning, which were brought up by the words of Jesus.

One last note. Back in the day, Jesus' parables did not have the fancy titles which we see posted above his tales within our Biblias. Therefore, in order to hopefully not spoil these modern parables, I will put the title for each story at the end of them, as well as the reference for which biblical anecdote I drew from. I ask you to please, not to hunt these titles down. Please, read these modern parables with an open mind, and attempt to read them as if you have no prior knowledge of the Bible beforehand. Please try to read them as if you're reading a story for the first time, and not trying to play detective of which parable is being retold. Read in this way, and I believe they will be much more meaningful to you.

TWO MEN TOOK a seat at a table of a local coffee shop. One was dressed in a suit and tie with a Café Mocha at his fingertips. He had walked over from the courthouse after many hours of defending his business client, who was being sued from a customer who had fallen and broken a hip at his establishment from a wet floor, with a wet floor sign absent from the scene.

The other man was dressed more casual, jeans, T-shirt, and sipping from a Caramel Frappuccino. He was a teacher, who had spent the day substituting a College Algebra class at a private Christian School, mind-blowing their worlds with the quadratic formula.

"So Chris," the lawyer said to the teacher, wanting to test him and to prove his superiority, "I have a question for you."

"Shoot," the teacher replied.

"How can I get into Heaven?"

"What does the Bible say?" asked the teacher. "How do you read it?"

"Well, the Greatest Command is to love the Lord your God with all your heart, soul, strength, and mind, and to love your neighbor as yourself," the lawyer replied with a grin.

"True," replied the teacher, "and that is your answer. Do this, and you will live for eternity." He took another sip of his caffeine.

But the lawyer, hoping to justify himself, asked, "And who is my neighbor?"

Chris took another sip, before he placed his cup on top of the table. He then looked at his friend and replied, "A man was walking down the shoulder of the highway, when a car pulled over and parked in front of him. The driver and his gang jumped out of the car and attacked the man. They stripped him naked, taking everything that the man had; beat him up, and left him half dead on the highway as they sped away.

"Now, it so happened that a pastor was driving down the same road on his way to a church building, and he saw the bloodied man lying there. He looked at his watch and saw that he was already running late for an elders' meeting. He had already been severely late the month before, there was surely no way that he could stop and help the man now. Praying that God would forgive him, he crossed over to the left lane so there was no chance that he would hit the man, while also trying to alleviate his guilt, and passed him by.

"A few minutes later, a youth minister was driving down the

highway, and he was almost blinded by the sun reflecting off the man's white body. He was on his way to the airport, to meet a group of teens who he was taking on a mission trip to Honduras. He looked at his watch. If he stopped to help the man now, they might miss their plane. . . . The youth minister couldn't disappoint the teens, or their to-be angry parents who had sacrificed their time and money for their kids to spend a week sharing Christ. So the youth minister prayed that God would forgive him, as he crossed over to the left lane so there was no chance that he would hit the man, while also trying to alleviate his guilt, and passed him by.

"Now, a Muslim was driving down the highway and he saw the man, who was now glowing red from the burning of the sun. His heart ached from seeing the man who was lying on the shoulder; therefore, he pulled over. He took out a first aid kit and a blanket from his trunk and aided the man, wiping away the blood, disinfecting and Band-Aiding his cuts, and wrapping his naked body in the blanket. The Muslim then carried the man to his car and laid him in the passenger's seat. Future blood stains were leaking onto his seat and floorboard as the Muslim took the man to a hospital. The Muslim then helped the man to be admitted and stayed in his room that night as a companion.

"In the morning, the Muslim asked the man's nurse to take good care of him as he healed, before he paid the hospital for the man's stay and told them if there were any extra fees, that he would pay them when he came back.

"Which of these three, do you think, proved to be a neighbor to the man who had been beaten up?"

The lawyer replied, "The one who showed him mercy."

And Chris said to him, "You go, and do likewise."

(Luke 10:25-37)

The Good Muslim[*]

ONE SUNDAY AFTER service, a minister decided to order the #1 on the Wendy's menu, with a Frosty added of course, before taking a seat at a nearby table. It wasn't long, before a group of men who were cussing and speaking profane things, with the stench of beer still on their breaths from the night before, joined the minister at his table. Turning a table of one into a table of many.

At another table close by, some folks who had listened to the minister's sermon earlier that morning, began to grumble amongst themselves, saying, "This man receives sinners and eats with them." Of course, being at a table nearby, and the churchgoers not being the most quiet of gossipers, the minister heard their words.

He then calmly dipped another fry into his Frosty and munched on it, before speaking in a mild voice, yet loud enough for the other

---

[*]The parable of the Good Samaritan, is sadly, also comparable to a youth minister, who was running late to his brother's rehearsal dinner after getting stuck behind traffic. He saw two men on the shoulder of the highway—one carrying a tire, and the other a pack of water. He thought about helping them when he zoomed past, before seeing a van pulled over on the opposite highway. *Good, they don't have that far*, he thought. Only to see a jacked car missing a tire a mile or two away. . . . *Lord, I'm sorry*, I thought.

365

table to hear:

"There was a father, who lived on a Kansan farm with his two sons. One day, his youngest came home from school, and just as soon as he had slung his backpack on to the couch, he said to his father, 'Dad, I want my college fund, now. And everything that I'm supposed to get in your will.'

"His father then divided his savings between his two sons, as well as giving to his youngest the keys to his truck, and the deed to the house to his oldest. Saturday came around, and the youngest son threw all of his belongings into the back of his new truck and took off to Las Vegas. There, he squandered his money. Gambling it away, getting wasted every night, hosting outrageous parties, and hiring hookers for 'good times.' Needless to say, it wasn't long before he had spent every penny that had been given to him. The son had even sold his truck, to settle a debt from a poor hand.

"The fun was gone, the son no longer having money to gamble away, to buy drinks, to host parties, or to mess around with girls. After sleeping a few nights on park benches and under newspapers in alleys, the son was *desperate*. He tried looking for work, but the only place which was willing to hire him, was a strip club. The son becoming an underpaid waiter, who lost half his tips each night to the club's owner.

"The son was so hungry, that he would dig through the dumpster outside of the club, to munch on any food that had been thrown out.

"But one night, the son broke down to his knees in tears. It took reaching rock bottom, before he finally came to himself. And he said in-between his sobs, 'How many of my father's hired help have more than enough food to eat, while I starve here! . . . I will leave here and go back home, and I will say to him, 'Father, I have sinned against heaven and before you. I am no longer worthy to be called your son. Treat me as one of your hired men.'

"So the son, got up from his knees, and managed to hitchhike across country, back to his Kansan home. And when he was walking up the dirt road to his house, his father saw him through the bathroom window, right before he was about to jump into the shower. Seeing his son, the father felt love bursting in his heart, and in a towel, he dashed out of the house, running up the road, embracing his son in his arms and kissing him.

"When his father had finally released him, his son said to him, 'Father, I have sinned against heaven and before you. I am no longer worthy to be called your son.'

But the father said to his hired men, 'Quickly, go to my room and grab my Sunday suit and give it to my son to wear. And put my prized college ring, the one on the bookshelf, on his hand. And get some shoes and put them on his feet. And-and go get the fattest steer we have kept and kill it, and let us eat and celebrate! For this is my son. He was dead, and is alive again! He was lost, and is found!' And so, all that the father had asked was done, and they began to celebrate.

"Now his oldest son had still been working out in the field. And as he was coming toward the house, he heard music booming from speakers and saw many dancing through the window of the house. He approached one of his father's hired men and asked him, 'What's going on?'

And the hired man said to him, 'Your brother has come home.

And your father has killed the fattest steer, and called for this party, because he has received your brother back safe and sound.'

Hearing these words, the oldest son was angry and refused to go into the house. His father saw him standing out in the darkness through the living room window, so he came out and entreated him, but the son answered his father, 'Look, these many years I have served you, and I never disobeyed your command, yet you never gave me a hen, that I might celebrate with my friends. But when this son of yours came, who has devoured your property with whores, you killed the fattest calf for him!'

And the father said to him, 'Son, you are always with me, and all that is mine is yours. It was fitting to celebrate and be glad, for this your brother was dead, and is alive. He was lost, and is found.'"

The churchgoers heard all these things, and they ridiculed the minister for them, as they picked up their trays and left. But the minister, took another fry and dipped it into his Frosty, as he continued to fellowship with the men who were cussing and speaking profane things, with the stench of beer still on their breaths from the night before.

(Luke 15:11-32)

The Modern-Day Prodigal Son

TWO TEENS WERE volunteering their Saturday, working at an animal shelter. They had spent many hours pampering puppies, bathing kittens, and cleaning up mounds of poop and pee. Being worn out and sweaty, one of the teens wiped the perspiration from his brow, before he said to the other teen, "You know what, today reminds me of when Jesus will come again."

"What do you mean?" the other teen asked.

"Well, for instance, look at this room." The other teen did, seeing where they were standing was a hall with cages filled with barking and meowing critters on either side of them. "Now imagine, if the cages on the right were filled only with dogs. And the cages on the left, were only filled with cats."

"Okay," said the other teen.

"Well, when Jesus comes back in his glory, and all the angels will be with him, he will then sit in his glorious throne. Before him will be gathered all the nations of the earth. Not just Israel and Rome, but America, Russia, China, everyone will be there. And he will separate people one from another as an animal shelter volunteer separates the dogs from the cats. And he will place the dogs on his right, but the cats on the left. Then the King will say to those on his right, 'Come, you who are blessed by my Father, inherit the kingdom prepared for you from the foundation of the world. For I was hungry and you gave me food, a feast fit for a king. I was thirsty and you gave me drink. I was a stranger and you welcomed me, opening your home as if I was family. I was naked and you clothed me, wrapping me with the shirt from your own back. I was sick and you visited me, bringing me some of the best chicken noodle soup that I have ever had. I was in prison and you came to me.'

"Then the righteous will answer him, saying, 'Lord, when did we see you hungry and feed you, or thirsty and give you drink? And when did we see you a stranger and welcome you, or naked and clothe you? And when did we see you sick or in prison and visit you?'

"And the King will answer them, 'Truly, I say to you, as you did it to one of the least of these my brothers, you did it to me.'

"Then he will say to those on his left, 'Depart from me, you cursed, into the eternal fire prepared for the Devil and his angels. For I was hungry and you gave me no food, not even a scrap from your table. I was thirsty and you gave me no drink, no soda or even a bottle of water. I was a stranger and you did not welcome me. Naked and you did not clothe me, not even with underwear to hide my shame. Sick and in prison and you did not visit me.' Then they also will answer, saying, 'Lord, when did we see you hungry or thirsty or a stranger or naked or sick or in prison, and did not minister to you?'

"Then he will answer them, saying, 'Truly, I say to you, as you did not do it to one of the least of these, you did not do it to me.' And these will go away into eternal punishment, but the righteous into eternal life."

"I get it," said the other teen, "but I think you need to work on another analogy."

"How come?"

"I don't like the thought that cats go to Hell."

"Only speaking the truth. We know all dogs go to heaven. And if cats have nine lives and still die, they really don't deserve an afterlife, do they?" The other teen punched him in the arm. "Ow!"

"Oh, whatever, baby. I didn't even punch you that hard," said the other teen. "Wanna grab that bucket before we're caught slacking off."

"Yes, ma'am," replied the teen, grabbing the bucket after rubbing his arm. ... *But like it or not, it still holds truth*, he thought to himself, before following his friend outside to dump the feces.

(Matthew 25:31-46)

The Dogs and the Cats

***

PLEASE, DON'T UNDERESTIMATE the human need for stories. I believe they are a need of humanity, just as much as the hunger for food or the desire for sex. Therefore, I would like to challenge you, to both live a great story, and to take the time to listen to the stories of others. Who knows what kind of things you'll experience, or what kind of details you'll learn, from utilizing the power of story.

NOTES

1. Fig. 1: Tissot, James. *Jésus enseigne le peuple près de la mer* (*Jesus Teaches the People by the Sea*). 1886-1894. Brooklyn Museum: New York.
2. Miller, Donald. *A Million Miles in a Thousand Years: How I Learned to Live a Better Story.* Nashville: Thomas Nelson, 2009. Print. p. 48, 156.
3. Fig. 2: Blake, William. *Young's Night Thoughts*, Page 37, "Love, and love only, is the loan for love." 1797. Yale Center for British Art: New Haven, Connecticut.
4. Fig. 3: Blake, William. "The Little Vagabond", from *Songs of Innocence and of Experience, Shewing the Two Contrary States of the Human Soul*, copy L. 1795. Yale Center for British Art: New Haven, Connecticut.

CHAPTER 20

JESUS, THE SAVIOR, PART 1:

THE CRUCIFIXION:

HE DIED ON A TREE, FOR YOU AND ME

his chapter, will be much different than the others. Just as
this lesson, was much different than the others. To the best
of my abilities, I have pieced together a chronological account of
Christ's crucifixion, using no other words than the four Gospels. I then
took this story and read it to the teens.

I ask you, just as a suggestion, to go ahead and skim the chapter,
look at the footnotes. And then go back, and just read this story, of
Christ.

***

NOW BEFORE THE Feast of the Passover, when Jesus knew that his
hour had come to depart out of this world to the Father, having
loved his own who were in the world, he loved them to the end.

When it was evening, he reclined at table* with the twelve. And he
said to them, "I have earnestly desired to eat this Passover with you

---

*Unlike what is portrayed in Leonardo da Vinci's beautiful and renowned painting,
The Last Supper, Jesus and his disciples were probably not seated around a grand
table. Most in likely, they were guests of a lower income host, meaning the table that
they were seated at, was probably much smaller. And it's very possible, there may
have been more than one table which he and his disciples occupied. Sort of like a
dinner at a family reunion or a church potluck.

before I suffer. For I tell you I will not eat it until it is fulfilled in the kingdom of God."

During supper, when the devil had already put it into the heart of Judas Iscariot, Simon's son, to betray him, Jesus, knowing that the Father had given all things into his hands, and that he had come from God and was going back to God, rose from supper. He laid aside his outer garments, and taking a towel, tied it around his waist. Then he poured water into a basin and began to wash the disciples' feet* and to wipe them with the towel that was wrapped around him. He came to Simon Peter, who said to him, "Lord, do you wash my feet?"

---

*Since the most common shoe fashion in Jesus' day were sandals, feet would be pretty nasty from traveling. Therefore, it was a Jewish custom for the host to provide a basin of water for his guests when they entered his home, so they could wash their own feet. The Jews would also wash their feet before a meal, similar in how we wash our hands. Additionally, if the master of the home was rich, then he would have servants who would wash the feet of his guests. (Also notice, that even though Jesus knew Judas had betrayed him, he still loved him; he still served him by washing his feet.)

Submit, submit, submit, is a huge theme within this story. Not only does Jesus teach about serving others, he lives it out himself. He chose to wash the stinky feet of twelve men. He could have called down 10,000 angels to save himself, yet he chose to be taken,[1] he chose to be condemned though he was innocent. He allowed us to break his flesh and to spill his blood, and allowed us to kill him in one of the most *painful* and *humiliating* ways possible. Jesus was *not* obligated to do any of these things. Yet, he chose to, so that we could be free from our sins. So that we can one day, live with him. For freedom always comes with a price.

---

[1]He could have escaped; he had before: John 4:28-30, 6:15, 7:30, 8:59, 10:39.

Jesus answered him, "What I am doing you do not understand now, but afterward you will understand." Peter said to him, "You shall never wash my feet." Jesus answered him, "If I do not wash you, you have no share with me." Simon Peter said to him, "Lord, not my feet only but also my hands and my head!" Jesus said to him, "The one who has bathed does not need to wash, except for his feet, but is completely clean. And you are clean, but not every one of you." For he knew who was to betray him; that was why he said, "Not all of you are clean."

When he had washed their feet and put on his outer garments and resumed his place, he said to them, "Do you understand what I have done to you? You call me Teacher and Lord, and you are right, for so I am. If I then, your Lord and Teacher, have washed your feet, you also ought to wash one another's feet. For I have given you an example, that you also should do just as I have done to you. Truly, truly, I say to you, a servant is not greater than his master, nor is a messenger greater than the one who sent him. If you know these things, blessed are you if you do them. I am not speaking of all of you; I know whom I have chosen. But the Scripture will be fulfilled, 'He who ate my bread has lifted his heel against me.' I am telling you this now, before it takes place, that when it does take place you may believe that I am he. Truly, truly, I say to you, whoever receives the one I send receives me, and whoever receives me receives the one who sent me."

And he took a cup,* and when he had given thanks he said, "Take this, and divide it among yourselves. For I tell you that from now on I

---

*There are many mythical elements which surround the story of Jesus' crucifixion, just as the cup at the Last Supper becoming the Holy Grail, and the spear that pierced his side being known as the Spear of Destiny. However, though Jesus transformed many people, there's no biblical evidence that he transformed the properties of any objects. Though he was *extraordinary*, he was also pretty ordinary.

Also, there are some additions to this story which are told, though they themselves

will not drink of the fruit of the vine until the kingdom of God comes."
And he took bread, and when he had given thanks, he broke it and
gave it to them, saying, "This is my body, which is given for you. Do
this in remembrance of me." And likewise the cup after they had eat-
en, saying, "This cup that is poured out for you is the new covenant in
my blood. But behold, the hand of him who betrays me is with me on
the table. For the Son of Man goes as it has been determined, but woe
to that man by whom he is betrayed!"†

are not found within Scripture, such as five scenes from the Stations of the Cross:
Jesus falling while carrying his cross three times, Jesus meeting his mother while
carrying his cross, Veronica wiping Jesus' bloody face with her veil, and Mary holding
Jesus' body, as he's taken down from the cross.

†Yes, there were multiple cups taken during the Lord's Supper, as pointed out to me
by a mentor. For better understanding, here is a *brief* summary of the fourteen parts
of a Passover meal:
1. *Kaddesh* (Sanctification): A blessing is given over the wine, which is then drunk,
    and a second cup is poured (Luke 22:17).
2. *Urechatz* (Washing): Hands are washed, with no blessing, in preparation for
    eating the vegetables (John 13).
3. *Karpas* (Vegetable): The Jews' lowly origins and tears from their slavery, are
    symbolized by a vegetable, usually parsley, being dipped into salt water and
    then eaten.
4. *Yachatz* (Breaking): One of the three matzahs (unleavened bread) is broken,
    with a part being returned to the pile and another part being set aside for the
    end of the meal.
5. *Maggid* (the Story): The story of the first Passover and the Exodus is told, which
    begins by the youngest person asking four questions. The story ends with a
    blessing given over the second cup of wine, which is then drunk.
6. *Rachtzah* (Washing): Hands are washed again, with a blessing, in preparation for
    eating the unleavened bread.
7. *Motzi Matzah* (Blessings): A blessing for the bread is given, and a bit of the mat-
    zah is eaten.
8. *Maror* (Bitter Herbs): A blessing is given over the bitter herbs that are then eat-
    en (which symbolize the Hebrew's slavery) with a mixture of apples, nuts, cinna-
    mon, and wine (which symbolize the mortar that they used to build).
9. *Korech* (Sandwich): In honor of Rabbi Hillel, bitter herbs are eaten as a sandwich
    between the unleavened bread. (There is no paschal (a Passover lamb) offering,
    since there are no longer animal sacrifices.)
10. *Shulchan Orech* (Dinner): A feast of unleavened foods is eaten.
11. *Tzafun* (Dessert): The unleavened bread that was set aside is then eaten as the
    "dessert"—the last food of the meal (Luke 22:20).
12. *Barech* (Grace): The third cup of wine is poured, and grace after the meal is giv-
    en. After which, the wine is drunk and the fourth cup is poured, with one set
    aside for Elijah, who is expected to one day come before the Messiah (Luke
    22:20)
13. *Hallel* (Praise): Several psalms are recited, before a blessing is given over the

And they were very sorrowful and began to say to him one after another, "Is it I, Lord?" He answered, "He who has dipped his hand in the dish with me will betray me. The Son of Man goes as it is written of him, but woe to that man by whom the Son of Man is betrayed! It would have been better for that man if he had not been born."

One of his disciples, whom Jesus loved, was reclining at table at Jesus' side, so Simon Peter motioned to him to ask Jesus of whom he was speaking. So that disciple, leaning back against Jesus, said to him, "Lord, who is it?" Jesus answered, "It is he to whom I will give this morsel of bread when I have dipped it." So when he had dipped the morsel, he gave it to Judas, the son of Simon Iscariot. Judas, who would betray him, answered, "Is it I, Rabbi?" He said to him, "You have said so." Then after he had taken the morsel, Satan entered into him. Jesus said to him, "What you are going to do, do quickly." Now no one at the table knew why he said this to him. Some thought that, because Judas had the moneybag, Jesus was telling him, "Buy what we need for the feast," or that he should give something to the poor. So, after receiving the morsel of bread, he immediately went out. And it was night.

When he had gone out, Jesus said, "Now is the Son of Man glorified, and God is glorified in him. If God is glorified in him, God will also glorify him in himself, and glorify him at once. Little children, yet a little while I am with you. You will seek me, and just as I said to the Jews, so now I also say to you, 'Where I am going you cannot come.' A new commandment I give to you, that you love one another: just as I have

fourth cup which is then drunk.
14. *Nirtzah* (Closing): A wish is given, that hopefully the next Passover may be celebrated in Jerusalem and that the Messiah will come within the year, followed by other songs and stories.[2]

Additionally, the cup holds even more significance. For the cup, has often been used as a symbol of God's wrath and judgement (Psalm 60:3, 75:8; Isaiah 51:17, 22; Jeremiah 25:15, Obadiah 16, Revelation 14:10). Yet Jesus, drunk that cup for us.

loved you, you also are to love one another. By this all people will know that you are my disciples, if you have love for one another.

"Let not your hearts be troubled. Believe in God; believe also in me. In my Father's house are many rooms.* If it were not so, would I have told you that I go to prepare a place for you?† And if I go and prepare a place for you, I will come again and will take you to myself, that where I am you may be also. And you know the way to where I am going." Thomas said to him, "Lord, we do not know where you are going. How can we know the way?" Jesus said to him, "I am the way, and the truth, and the life. No one comes to the Father except through me. If you had known me, you would have known my Father also. From now on you do know him and have seen him."

Philip said to him, "Lord, show us the Father, and it is enough for us." Jesus said to him, "Have I been with you so long, and you still do not know me, Philip? Whoever has seen me has seen the Father. How can you say, 'Show us the Father'? Do you not believe that I am in the Father and the Father is in me? The words that I say to you I do not speak on my own authority, but the Father who dwells in me does his works. Believe me that I am in the Father and the Father is in me, or

---

*Notice that Jesus says, there are many, "rooms" μοναὶ (monai). He does *not* promise a 'mansion' as some translations translate. For they believe that 'mansion' better describes than room. "Mansion" portraying an extravagant detached building that makes up the new Jerusalem (Revelation 21:1-4), whereas "room" portrays a modest dwelling within a home. One reason for this debate, is because of the unknowing if the "Father's house" is referring to a single building or the new city. However, just a room in heaven, made by the hands of our Savior, will be far greater than any mansion constructed by man on earth. And is heaven truly about all the gifts that we're getting? I mean, that's what Christmas is all about, right? And besides, Jesus makes only the best (John 2:10).

(This is the reason I personally don't like to sing the hymn, "Mansion, Robe and Crown." I mean, I can't sing it, without feeling super selfish.)

†It was a Jewish custom for the groom to return to his father's house, and to prepare a place (a honeymoon chamber) for his bride, *before* he would be able to take her to be his wife. It was *not* a task which could be completed in haste either, like trying to write a ten page essay assigned at the beginning of a semester in one night. For only the best would be appropriate for his bride.

377

else believe on account of the works themselves.

"Truly, truly, I say to you, whoever believes in me will also do the works that I do; and greater works than these will he do, because I am going to the Father. Whatever you ask in my name, this I will do, that the Father may be glorified in the Son. If you ask me anything in my name, I will do it.

"If you love me, you will keep my commandments. And I will ask the Father, and he will give you another Helper, to be with you forever, even the Spirit of truth, whom the world cannot receive, because it neither sees him nor knows him. You know him, for he dwells with you and will be in you.

"I will not leave you as orphans; I will come to you. Yet a little while and the world will see me no more, but you will see me. Because I live, you also will live. In that day you will know that I am in my Father, and you in me, and I in you. Whoever has my commandments and keeps them, he it is who loves me. And he who loves me will be loved by my Father, and I will love him and manifest myself to him." Judas (not Iscariot) said to him, "Lord, how is it that you will manifest yourself to us, and not to the world?" Jesus answered him, "If anyone loves me, he will keep my word, and my Father will love him, and we will come to him and make our home with him. Whoever does not love me does not keep my words. And the word that you hear is not mine but the Father's who sent me.

"These things I have spoken to you while I am still with you. But the Helper, the Holy Spirit, whom the Father will send in my name, he will teach you all things and bring to your remembrance all that I have said to you. Peace I leave with you; my peace I give to you. Not as the world gives do I give to you. Let not your hearts be troubled, neither let them be afraid. You heard me say to you, 'I am going away, and I will come to you.' If you loved me, you would have rejoiced, because I am going to the Father, for the Father is greater than I. And now I have told you before it takes place, so that when it does take place you may believe. I will no longer talk much with you, for the ruler of this world is coming. He has no claim on me, but I do as the Father has commanded me, so that the world may know that I love the Father. Rise, let us go from here.

"I am the true vine, and my Father is the vinedresser. Every branch in me that does not bear fruit he takes away, and every branch that does bear fruit he prunes, that it may bear more fruit. Already you are clean because of the word that I have spoken to you. Abide in me, and I in you. As the branch cannot bear fruit by itself, unless it abides in the vine, neither can you, unless you abide in me. I am the vine; you are the branches. Whoever abides in me and I in him, he it is that bears much fruit, for apart from me you can do nothing. If anyone does not abide in me he is thrown away like a branch and withers; and the branches are gathered, thrown into the fire, and burned. If you abide in me, and my words abide in you, ask whatever you wish, and it will be done for you. By this my Father is glorified, that you bear much fruit and so prove to be my disciples. As the Father has loved me, so have I loved you. Abide in my love. If you keep my commandments, you will abide in my love, just as I have kept my Father's commandments and abide in his love. These things I have spoken to you, that my joy may be in you, and that your joy may be full.

"This is my commandment, that you love one another as I have loved you. Greater love has no one than this, that someone lay down his life for his friends. You are my friends if you do what I command you. No longer do I call you servants, for the servant does not know what his master is doing; but I have called you friends, for all that I have heard from my Father I have made known to you. You did not choose me, but I chose you and appointed you that you should go and bear fruit and that your fruit should abide, so that whatever you ask the Father in my name, he may give it to you. These things I command you, so that you will love one another.

"If the world hates you, know that it has hated me before it hated you. If you were of the world, the world would love you as its own; but because you are not of the world, but I chose you out of the world, therefore the world hates you. Remember the word that I said to you: 'A servant is not greater than his master.' If they persecuted me, they will also persecute you. If they kept my word, they will also keep yours. But all these things they will do to you on account of my name, because they do not know him who sent me. If I had not come and spoken to them, they would not have been guilty of sin, but now they have no excuse for their sin. Whoever hates me hates my Father also. If I had not done among them the works that no one else did, they would not be guilty of sin, but now they have seen and hated both me and my Father. But the word that is written in their Law must be fulfilled: 'They hated me without a cause.'

"But when the Helper comes, whom I will send to you from the Father, the Spirit of truth, who proceeds from the Father, he will bear witness about me. And you also will bear witness, because you have been with me from the beginning.

"I have said all these things to you to keep you from falling away. They will put you out of the synagogues. Indeed, the hour is coming when whoever kills you will think he is offering service to God. And they will do these things because they have not known the Father, nor me. But I have said these things to you, that when their hour comes you may remember that I told them to you.

"I did not say these things to you from the beginning, because I was with you. But now I am going to him who sent me, and none of you asks me, 'Where are you going?' But because I have said these things to you, sorrow has filled your heart. Nevertheless, I tell you the truth: it is to your advantage that I go away, for if I do not go away, the Helper will not come to you. But if I go, I will send him to you. And when he comes, he will convict the world concerning sin and righteousness and judgment: concerning sin, because they do not believe in me; concerning righteousness, because I go to the Father, and you will see me no longer, concerning judgment, because the ruler of this world is judged.

"I still have many things to say to you, but you cannot bear them now. When the Spirit of truth comes, he will guide you into all the truth, for he will not speak on his own authority, but whatever he hears he will speak, and he will declare to you the things that are to come. He will glorify me, for he will take what is mine and declare it to you. All that the Father has is mine; therefore I said that he will take what is mine and declare it to you.

"A little while, and you will see me no longer; and again a little while, and you will see me." So some of his disciples said to one another, "What is this that he says to us, 'A little while, and you will not see me, and again a little while, and you will see me'; and, 'because I am going to the Father'?" So they were saying, "What does he mean by 'a little while'? We do not know what he is talking about." Jesus knew that they wanted to ask him, so he said to them, "Is this what you are asking yourselves, what I meant by saying, 'A little while and you will not see me, and again a little while and you will see me'? Truly, truly, I say to you, you will weep and lament, but the world will rejoice. You will be sorrowful, but your sorrow will turn into joy. When a woman is giving birth, she has sorrow because her hour has come, but when she has delivered the baby, she no longer remembers the anguish, for joy that a human being has been born into the world. So also you have sorrow now, but I will see you again, and your hearts will rejoice, and no one will take your joy from you. In that day you will ask nothing of me. Truly, truly, I say to you, whatever you ask of the Father in my name, he will give it to you. Until now you have asked nothing in my name. Ask, and you will receive, that your joy may be full.

"I have said these things to you in figures of speech. The hour is coming when I will no longer speak to you in figures of speech but will tell you plainly about the Father. In that day you will ask in my name, and I do not say to you that I will ask the Father on your behalf; for the Father himself loves you, because you have loved me and have believed that I came from God. I came from the Father and have come into the world, and now I am leaving the world and going to the Father."

His disciples said, "Ah, now you are speaking plainly and not using figurative speech! Now we know that you know all things and do not need anyone to question you; this is why we believe that you came from God." Jesus answered them, "Do you now believe? Behold, the hour is coming, indeed it has come, when you will be scattered, each to his own home, and will leave me alone. Yet I am not alone, for the Father is with me. I have said these things to you, that in me you may have peace. In the world you will have tribulation. But take heart; I have overcome the world."

When Jesus had spoken these words, he lifted up his eyes to heaven, and said, "Father, the hour has come; glorify your Son that the Son may glorify you, since you have given him authority over all flesh, to give eternal life to all whom you have given him. And this is eternal life, that they know you, the only true God, and Jesus Christ whom you have sent. I glorified you on earth, having accomplished the work that you gave me to do. And now, Father, glorify me in your own presence with the glory that I had with you before the world existed.

"I have manifested your name to the people whom you gave me out of the world. Yours they were, and you gave them to me, and they have kept your word. Now they know that everything that you have given me is from you. For I have given them the words that you gave me, and they have received them and have come to know in truth that I came from you; and they have believed that you sent me. I am praying for them. I am not praying for the world but for those whom you have given me, for they are yours. All mine are yours, and yours are mine, and I am glorified in them. And I am no longer in the world, but they are in the world, and I am coming to you. Holy Father, keep them in your name, which you have given me, that they may be one, even as we are one. While I was with them, I kept them in your name, which you have given me. I have guarded them, and not one of them has been lost except the son of destruction, that the Scripture might be fulfilled. But now I am coming to you, and these things I speak in the world, that they may have my joy fulfilled in themselves. I have given them your word, and the world has hated them because they are not of the world, just as I am not of the world. I do not ask that you take them out of the world, but that you keep them from the evil one. They are not of the world, just as I am not of the world. Sanctify them in the truth; your word is truth. As you sent me into the world, so I have sent them into the world. And for their sake I consecrate myself, that they also may be sanctified in truth.

"*I do not ask for these only, but also for those* [for you] *who will believe in me through their word*, that they may all be one, just as you, Father, are in me, and I in you, that they also may be in us, so that the world may believe that you have sent me. The glory that you have given me I have given to them, that they may be one even as we are one, I in them and you in me, that they may become perfectly one, so that the world may know that you sent me and loved them even as you loved me. Father, I desire that they also, whom you have given me, may be with me where I am, to see my glory that you have given me because you loved me before the foundation of the world. O righteous Father, even though the world does not know you, I know you, and these know that you have sent me. I made known to them your name, and I will continue to make it known, that the love with which you have loved me may be in them, and I in them."

AND WHEN THEY had sung a hymn, they went out to the Mount of Olives. Then Jesus said to them, "You will all fall away because of me this night. For it is written, 'I will strike the shepherd, and the sheep of the flock will be scattered.' But after I am raised up, I will go before you to Galilee." Peter answered him, "Though they all fall away because of you, I will never fall away." Jesus said to him, "Simon, Simon, behold, Satan demanded to have you, that he might sift you like wheat, but I have prayed for you that your faith may not fail. And when you have turned again, strengthen your brothers." Peter said to him, "Lord, I am ready to go with you both to prison and to death." Jesus said, "I tell you, Peter, the rooster will not crow this day, until you deny three times that you know me." Peter said to him, "Even if I must die with you, I will not deny you!" And all the disciples said the same.

And he said to them, "When I sent you out with no moneybag or knapsack or sandals, did you lack anything?" They said, "Nothing." He said to them, "But now let the one who has a moneybag take it, and likewise a knapsack. And let the one who has no sword sell his cloak and buy one. For I tell you that this Scripture must be fulfilled in me: 'And he was numbered with the transgressors.' For what is written about me has its fulfillment." And they said, "Look, Lord, here are two swords." And he said to them, "It is enough."

Then Jesus went with them to a place called Gethsemane, as was his custom, and he said to his disciples, "Sit here, while I go over there and pray that you may not enter into temptation." And taking with him Peter and the two sons of Zebedee, he began to be sorrowful and troubled. Then he said to them, "My soul is very sorrowful, even to death;* remain here, and watch

*Jesus did *not* want to go to the cross. He knew what was about to happen. . . . Yet, he chose to continue with the Father's plan. For you, and for me.

with me." And he withdrew from them about a stone's throw, and knelt down and prayed, "Abba,* Father, all things are possible for you. Remove this cup from me. Yet not what I will, but what you will." And he came to the disciples and found them sleeping. And he said to Peter, "So, could you not watch with me one hour? Watch and pray that you may not enter into temptation. The spirit indeed is willing, but the flesh is weak." Again, for the second time, he went away and prayed, "My Father, if this cannot pass unless I drink it, your will be done." And again he came and found them sleeping, for their eyes were heavy. So, leaving them again, he went away and prayed for the third time, saying the same words again.† And there appeared to him an angel from heaven, strengthening him. And being in agony he prayed more earnestly; and his sweat became like great drops of blood‡ falling down to the ground. And when he rose from prayer, he

*Abba' means 'Father' in Aramaic; however, it can also be used as a term of tender endearment. Such as a child crying out, "Daddy," or "Papa."

†There is no biblical evidence; however, I personally believe that the Devil was also in the Garden. Like in *The Passion of the Christ*, I believe he was there, tempting Jesus to not go through with the Father's plan. For this would have been Satan's *last* chance to damn man forever; without Jesus, there would have been *no* hope, no salvation, for us.

came the third time and said to them, "Are you still sleeping and taking your rest? It is enough; the hour has come. The Son of Man is betrayed into the hands of sinners. Rise, let us be going; see, my betrayer is at hand."

Now Judas, who betrayed him, also knew the place, for Jesus often met there with his disciples. So Judas, having procured a band of soldiers and some officers from the chief priests and the Pharisees, went there with lanterns and torches and swords and clubs. Then Jesus, knowing all that would happen to him, came forward and said to them, "Whom do you seek?" They answered him, "Jesus of Nazareth." Jesus said to them, "I am he." Judas, who betrayed him, was standing with them. When Jesus said to them, "I am he," they drew back and fell to the ground. So he asked them again, "Whom do you seek?" And they said, "Jesus of Nazareth." Jesus answered, "I told you that I am he. So, if you seek me, let these men go." This was to fulfill the word that he had spoken: "Of those whom you gave me I have lost not one." Now the betrayer had given them a sign, saying, "The one I will kiss is the man; seize him." And he came up to Jesus at once and said,

---

Hematohidrosis, a very rare condition in which the blood vessels that feed the glands rupture due to extreme physical or emotional stress, resulting in blood bleeding into the glands, and the sweat which is excreted being tinged with blood. Jesus *knew* what was about to happen; he was under *severe* psychological stress. And while the extent of blood loss generally is minimal, hematohidrosis also results in the skin becoming extremely tender and fragile. Meaning Jesus' skin was very, very sensitive the next day, while he was being tortured by the Roman soldiers.[6]

Luke is the only Gospel which mentions both Jesus sweating blood (22:44) and him being strengthened by an angel (22:43).

The Greek word for 'band' used here, σπεῖραν (speiran), is used only seven times in the New Testament. And each time that it is, it is always associated with Roman soldiers. (The Antonia Fortress, the Roman barracks within Jerusalem (Acts 21:37), housed 600 troops, and had been constructed in the northwest corner of the Temple Mount. Herod had even constructed a secret tunnel from the fortress to the Temple.) But why was Judas, a *Jew*, guiding an army of *Roman* soldiers?

A professor of mine has speculated, it is because the Sanhedrin had already spoken to Pilate. Both securing troops to arrest Jesus (so he would *not* escape again), and so all Pilate had to do, was to declare this man whom the Sanhedrin had warned him about, "Guilty!" when they brought him before the governor.

"Greetings, Rabbi!" And he kissed him.* Jesus said to him, "Judas, would you betray the Son of Man with a kiss?† Friend, do what you came to do." Then they came up and laid hands on Jesus and seized

---

*No, as far as we know, Judas was not a homosexual. For the Jews, a kiss was a cultural and affectionate greeting, similar in how Italians still greet with a kiss today, or like greeting a friend with a hug or handshake in the U.S. However, that which was supposed to be a greeting, was instead like a bite from a venomous snake.

†Don Richardson, together with his wife Carol, and their seven-month-boy, traveled to Dutch New Guinea to work among the Sawi tribe. At first, it was *very* difficult for them. Not only in learning the language, but the Sawi were cannibals and head hunters who favored deceit and betrayal within their culture. Therefore, when Don shared this story with them, they saw Judas as the hero, instead of the laughable Jesus who had been duped. However, when Don was just about ready to call it quits, he discovered a cultural ritual which allowed him to share the good news with the Sawi, allowing the Spirit to change the tribe forever.

The Sawi were constantly in battle with two other tribes; however, in order to bring peace, the three tribes each exchanged a young child with one another in a ceremony. For if their hated enemy could be trusted to raise one of their own, then they could be trusted to have peace with. Following this event, Don explained to the Sawi that Jesus was the 'Peace Child' sent from God, in order for Him to make peace with us.[8]

him. And when those who were around him saw what would follow, they said, "Lord, shall we strike with the sword?" Then Simon Peter, having a sword, drew it and struck the high priest's servant and cut off his right ear.* (The servant's name was Malchus.) But Jesus said, "No more of this!" So Jesus said to Peter, "Put your sword into its sheath; shall I not drink the cup that the Father has given me? For all who take the sword will perish by the sword. Do you think that I cannot appeal to my Father, and he will at once send me more than twelve legions of angels? And he touched his ear and healed him. But how then should the Scriptures be fulfilled, that it must be so?" At that hour Jesus said to the crowds, "Have you come out as against a robber, with swords and clubs to capture me? Day after day I sat in the temple teaching, and you did not seize me. But all this has taken place that the Scriptures of the prophets might be fulfilled. But this is your hour, and the power of darkness." Then all the disciples left him and fled.

And a young man followed him, with nothing but a linen cloth about his body. And they seized him, but he left the linen cloth and ran away naked.†

SO THE BAND of soldiers and their captain and the officers of the Jews arrested Jesus and bound him. First they led him to Annas, for he was the father-in-law of Caiaphas, who was high priest that year. It

---

*Peter was probably not aiming at the servant's ear, but his neck—Malchus barely dodging his blow. Also, some scholars believe, that Peter may have been left-handed, since he swung and cut off the servant's 'right' ear.

†Just because there's a streaker in the Bible, does not mean that it's okay. I mean, adultery is also in the Bible.

- Garden, snake, nudity, sounds a lot like the Garden of Eden to me.
- This "young man" is only mentioned in Mark, and may even be John Mark himself. It's also speculated, that the Last Supper took place in the upper room of Mark's house, which explains why he followed them, I believe, in curiosity.

was Caiaphas who had advised the Jews that it would be expedient that one man should die for the people.

———

Simon Peter followed Jesus, and so did another disciple. Since that disciple was known to the high priest, he entered with Jesus into the courtyard of the high priest, but Peter stood outside at the door. So the other disciple, who was known to the high priest, went out and spoke to the servant girl who kept watch at the door, and brought Peter in. The servant girl at the door said to Peter, "You also are not one of this man's disciples, are you?" But he denied it, saying, "Woman, I do not know him." Now the servants and officers had made a charcoal fire, because it was cold, and they were standing and warming themselves. Peter also was with them, standing and warming himself.

———

The high priest then questioned Jesus about his disciples and his teaching. Jesus answered him, "I have spoken openly to the world. I have always taught in synagogues and in the temple, where all Jews come together. I have said nothing in secret. Why do you ask me? Ask those who have heard me what I said to them; they know what I said." When he had said these things, one of the officers standing by struck Jesus with his hand, saying, "Is that how you answer the high priest?" Jesus answered him, "If what I said is wrong, bear witness about the wrong; but if what I said is right, why do you strike me?" Annas then sent him bound to Caiaphas the high priest.

Now the chief priests and the whole council were seeking false testimony against Jesus that they might put him to death, but they found none, though many false witnesses came forward. For many bore false witness against him, but their testimony did not agree. At last two came forward and said, "This man said, 'I am able to destroy the temple of God, and to rebuild it in three days.'" And the high priest stood up and said, "Have you no answer to make? What is it that these men testify against you?" But Jesus remained silent and made no answer. And the high priest said to him, "I adjure you by the living God, tell us if you are the Christ, the Son of God." Jesus said to him, "You have said so. But I tell you, from now on you will see the Son of Man seated at the right hand of Power and coming on the clouds of heaven."* Then the high priest tore his robes and said, "He has uttered blasphemy. What further witnesses do we need? You have now heard his blasphemy. What is your judgment?" They answered, "He deserves death."† Then they spit in his face and struck him. And some slapped him, saying, "Prophesy to us, you Christ! Who is it that struck you?"‡

———

Now Simon Peter was standing and warming himself. So they said to him, "You also are not one of his disciples, are you?" And again he denied it with an oath: "I do not know the man." After a little while the bystanders came up and said to Peter, "Certainly you too are one of them, for your accent betrays you." One of the servants of the high priest, a relative of the man whose car Peter had cut off, asked, "Did I

---

*Jesus was so innocent, he had to condemn himself. For not even lies were enough to convict him.

†For a Jew, blasphemy was the *greatest* sin one could commit. For there is only *one* God. Only *one* Yahweh. Just as for the Romans, there was only *one* Caesar (at a time).

‡Paul was also struck when he stood before the high priest Ananias, innocent, yet on trial (Acts 23:2). Additionally, there's an interesting comparison between Paul's four trials in Acts, and Jesus' four trials in Luke:

Paul		Jesus	
1.	Sanhedrin (22:30-23:10)	1.	Sanhedrin (22:66-71)
2.	Judean governor, Felix (24:1-23)	2.	Judean governor, Pilate (23:1-7)
3.	Judean governor, Felix (25:1-12)	3.	Herod Antipas (23:7-12)
4.	Herod Agrippa II (25:23-26:32)	4.	Judean governor, Pilate (23:13-25)

not see you in the garden with him?" Then he began to invoke a curse on himself and to swear, "I do not know the man." And immediately, while he was still speaking, the rooster crowed. And the Lord turned and looked at Peter. And Peter remembered the saying of the Lord, how he had said to him, "Before the rooster crows today, you will deny me three times."* And he went out and wept bitterly.†

WHEN MORNING CAME, all the chief priests and the elders of the people took counsel against Jesus to put him to death. And they bound him and led Jesus from the house of Caiaphas to the governor's headquarters. It was early morning. They themselves did not enter the governor's headquarters, so that they would not be defiled, but could eat the Passover. So Pilate‡ went outside to them and said,

---

*According to Mark, Peter denied Jesus three times before the rooster crowed *twice* (Mark 14:30, 68, 72).

†"The student thought again that if Vasilisa had shed tears, and her daughter had been troubled, it was evident that what he had just been telling them about, which had happened nineteen centuries ago, had a relation to the present—to both women, to the desolate village, to himself, to all people. The old woman had wept, not because he could tell the story touchingly, but because Peter was near to her, because her whole being was interested in what was passing in Peter's soul.

And joy suddenly stirred in his soul, and he even stopped for a minute to take breath. 'The past,' he thought, 'is linked with the present by an unbroken chain of events flowing one out of another.' And it seemed to him that he had just seen both ends of that chain; that when he touched one end the other quivered."

Excerpt from, "The Student" by Anton Chekhov.[10]

‡Normally, Pilate would reside in the seaport city of Caesarea, which culturally, was very Roman. However, he would travel throughout his district—especially to Jerusa-

"What accusation do you bring against this man?" They answered him, "If this man were not doing evil, we would not have delivered him over to you." Pilate said to them, "Take him yourselves and judge him by your own law." The Jews said to him, "It is not lawful for us to put anyone to death." This was to fulfill the word that Jesus had spoken to show by what kind of death he was going to die.

And they began to accuse him, saying, "We found this man misleading our nation and forbidding us to give tribute to Caesar, and saying that he himself is Christ, a king." And Pilate asked him, "Are you the King of the Jews?" And he answered him, "You have said so." And the chief priests accused him of many things. And Pilate again asked him, "Have you no answer to make? See how many charges they bring against you." But Jesus made no further answer, so that Pilate was amazed.

Then when Judas, his betrayer, saw that Jesus was condemned, he changed his mind and brought back the thirty pieces of silver to the chief priests and the elders, saying, "I have sinned by betraying innocent blood." They said, "What is that to us? See to it yourself." And throwing down the pieces of silver into the temple, he departed, and he went and hanged himself. But the chief priests, taking the pieces of silver, said, "It is not lawful to put them into the treasury, since it is blood money." So they took counsel and bought with them the pot-

lem during the time of the Passover, staying at the praetorium, so that his political and military presence would be felt. The Passover was a celebration *disliked* by the Romans. Not only was it a religious holiday, but it was rooted in nationalism, like U.S.' Independence Day, for it was the celebration of the Hebrews being freed from another foreign nation—Egypt. Therefore, tensions were very high. And the people, at this time, were starving for a Messiah to save them from Rome. It would then by Pilate's duty to keep order, quelling any revolution from bursting out of Jerusalem.

Additionally, notice that Pilate comes outside his own house to meet the chief priests, since the Jews were not supposed to enter into the house of a Gentile (before Peter's vision in Acts 10:9-11:18), less they would become unclean (Deuteronomy 7:3, Acts 10:28). Though these hypocrites had no problem scheming how to murder a man on the Sabbath (Matthew 12:9-14) nor during the time of the Passover.

ter's field as a burial place for strangers. Therefore that field has been called the Field of Blood to this day. Then was fulfilled what had been spoken by the prophet Jeremiah, saying, "And they took the thirty pieces of silver, the price of him on whom a price had been set by some of the sons of Israel, and they gave them for the potter's field, as the Lord directed me."*

———

So Pilate entered his headquarters again and called Jesus and said to him, "Are you the King of the Jews?" Jesus answered, "Do you say this of your own accord, or did others say it to you about me?" Pilate answered, "Am I a Jew? Your own nation and the chief priests have delivered you over to me. What have you done?" Jesus answered, "My kingdom is not of this world. If my kingdom were of this world, my servants would have been fighting, that I might not be delivered over to the Jews. But my kingdom is not from the world." Then Pilate said to him, "So you are a king?" Jesus answered, "You say that I am a king. For this purpose I was born and for this purpose I have come into the world—to bear witness to the truth. Everyone who is of the truth listens to my voice." Pilate said to him, "What is truth?"

After he had said this, he went back outside to the Jews and told them, "I find no guilt in this man." But they were urgent, saying, "He stirs up the people, teaching throughout all Judea, from Galilee even to this place."

When Pilate heard this, he asked whether the man was a Galilean. And when he learned that he belonged to Herod's jurisdiction, he sent

---

*In Matthew, there is a foil between Peter and Judas. Peter had denied Christ, while Judas had betrayed him. Both were in a similar boat, yet came out with totally different outcomes. Peter felt shame and wept bitterly, yet he later became an apostle, sharing the Gospel to the ends of the world. While Judas felt shame and hung himself for it. Even for our greatest mistakes, there is forgiveness. Yet, we must choose to either accept it, or to deny it. To be a Peter, or a Judas.

him over to Herod,* who was himself in Jerusalem at that time. When Herod saw Jesus, he was very glad, for he had long desired to see him, because he had heard about him, and he was hoping to see some sign done by him. So he questioned him at some length, but he made no answer. The chief priests and the scribes stood by, vehemently accusing him. And Herod with his soldiers treated him with contempt and mocked him. Then, arraying him in splendid clothing, he sent him back to Pilate. And Herod and Pilate became friends with each other that very day, for before this they had been at enmity with each other.

Pilate then called together the chief priests and the rulers and the people, and said to them, "You brought me this man as one who was misleading the people. And after examining him before you, behold, I did not find this man guilty of any of your charges against him. Neither did Herod, for he sent him back to us. Look, nothing deserving death has been done by him. I will therefore punish and release him."

Now at the feast the governor was accustomed to release for the crowd any one prisoner whom they wanted. And they had then a notorious prisoner called Barabbas.† So when they had gathered, Pilate said to them, "Whom do you want me to release for you: Barabbas, or Jesus who is called Christ?" For he perceived that it was out of envy that the chief priests had delivered him up. Besides, while he was sitting on the judgment seat, his wife sent word to him, "Have nothing to do with that righteous man, for I have suffered much because of him today in a dream." But the chief priests stirred up the crowd to

---

*Herod was *not* a true king of Israel, being more of a figurehead under the Emperor. His father had been appointed by Rome as the "King of the Jews," after they had retaken Jerusalem from the Maccabees.

†A man who had murdered another, during a political rebellion (Luke 23:19, Acts 3:14).

'Barabbas' comes from the Hebrew words 'bar'—'son,' and 'abba'—'father.' The Son of the Father, took the places of 'Daddy's-son,' just as he took the place for you and for me.

have him release for them Barabbas instead and destroy Jesus. The governor again said to them, "Which of the two do you want me to release for you?" And they said, "Barabbas"—a man who had been thrown into prison for an insurrection started in the city and for murder. Pilate addressed them once more, desiring to release Jesus, but they kept shouting, "Crucify, crucify him!" A third time he said to them, "Why? What evil has he done? I have found in him no guilt deserving death. I will therefore punish and release him."

Then Pilate took Jesus and flogged him.* And the soldiers of the governor took Jesus into the governor's headquarters, and they gathered the whole battalion before him. And they stripped him and put a scarlet robe on him, and twisting together a crown of thorns, they put it on his head and put

---

*Roman floggings were *brutal*, for Roman soldiers were skilled tortures, knowing how to dish out the fullest amount of pain without killing their victims. A common weapon of choice (which is believed to have been used against Christ), was the cat-o'-nine-tails. It was a multi-tail whip with the end of each tail intertwined with something sharp, such as bone, broken pottery, or metal. It was common for the victim to receive thirty nine lashes, each strike . . . tearing and exposing the very inward parts of the body. The back would be so shredded, that ribs and the spine were sometimes exposed. Deep lacerations would cover the victim's shoulder's down to the back of his legs. According to Alexander Metherell, M.D., PH.D., signs of Jesus being in hypovolemic shock can be seen as a result from this beating/experiencing severe blood loss. Such as him saying, "I thirst" on the cross.[12]

Jesus, felt the sting of the whip on his back, just as his ancestors had in Egypt many years ago. . . . It's *terrible* how much he suffered. But in a way, he had to. Yes, any story of a man giving up his life for another is amazing. . . . But would Jesus' have been as rememberable, if he had simply had his throat cut or his head chopped off?

Also, *if* Isaiah 50:6 is a prophecy about Christ, then he would of also have had his beard plucked during his beating. A detail that's not included within any of the Gospels: "I gave my back to those who strike, and my cheeks to those who pull out the beard; I hid not my face from disgrace and spitting."

a reed in his right hand. And kneeling before him, they mocked him, saying, "Hail, King of the Jews!" And they spit on him and took the reed and struck him on the head.

Pilate went out again and said to them, "See, I am bringing him out to you that you may know that I find no guilt in him." So Jesus came out, wearing the crown of thorns and the purple robe. Pilate said to them, "Behold the man!" When the chief priests and the officers saw him, they cried out, "Crucify him, crucify him!" Pilate said to them, "Take him yourselves and crucify him, for I find no guilt in him." The Jews answered him, "We have a law, and according to that law he ought to die because he has made himself the Son of God." When Pilate heard this statement, he was even more afraid. He entered his headquarters again and said to Jesus, "Where are you from?" But Jesus gave him no answer. So Pilate said to him, "You will not speak to me? Do you not know that I have authority to release you and authority to crucify you?" Jesus answered him, "You would have no authority over me at all unless it had been given you from above.* Therefore he who delivered me over to you has the greater sin."

From then on Pilate sought to release him, but the Jews cried out, "If you release this man, you are not Caesar's friend. Everyone who makes himself a king opposes Caesar." So when Pilate heard these words, he brought Jesus out and sat down on the judgment seat at a place called The Stone Pavement, and in Aramaic Gabbatha. Now it was the day of Preparation of the Passover. It was about the sixth hour. He said to the Jews, "Behold your King!" They cried out, "Away with him, away with him, crucify him!" Pilate said to them, "Shall I crucify your King?" The chief priests answered, "We have no king but Caesar." So when Pilate saw that he was gaining nothing, but rather

---

*Romans 13:1-7

that a riot* was beginning, he took water and washed his hands before the crowd, saying, "I am innocent of this man's blood; see to it yourselves." And all the people answered, "His blood be on us and on our children!" Then he released for them Barabbas, the man who had been thrown into prison for insurrection and murder, for whom they asked, but he delivered Jesus over to their will. And when they had mocked him, they stripped him of the robe and put his own clothes on him and led him away to crucify him.†

SO THEY TOOK Jesus, and he went out, bearing his own cross.‡ And

---

*Pilate knew Jesus was innocent, and did not want to be responsible for taking this man's life. However, not only was he fighting a severe case of peer pressure/mob mentality, but he was already into the fire with both the Jews and Caesar, as is recorded by both Philo and Josephus:

1. Unlike his predecessor, Pilate had allowed his soldiers to bring into Jerusalem ensigns of Caesar, which caused an uproar by the Jews, and resulted in Pilate surrounding the demonstrators with his soldiers and threatening them with death. The Jews were more than willing to sacrifice themselves in defense of the Mosaic Law, causing Pilate to finally get rid of these images instead of slaughtering them all.
2. Pilate had angered the Jews by setting up gold-coated shields in Herod's Palace in honor of Caesar, though the Jews believed it was more to annoy them, than to venerate Emperor Tiberius. They protested, and when Pilate did nothing, they wrote to Caesar, who chastised Pilate and had him remove the shields.
3. Pilate had used money from the Temple to build an aqueduct. He then positioned disguised soldiers within the crowd when he addressed them, giving a signal for his troops to randomly attack and kill members of the crowd to try and silence their protests. (There's also another incident not recorded by Josephus or any other historian, of Pilate massacring a group of Galilean worshippers (Luke 13:1)).

Pilate was already at three strikes. Therefore he knew, if he released Jesus, it would most definitely be the end of his career in Jerusalem. (That final straw would later come, when he attacked a group of Samaritans making their way to Mount Gerizim, to see rumored artifacts (supposedly buried by Moses), that had been found.)

†As Dr. McLarty points out, at first, Pilate wanted nothing to do with Jesus, attempting to both ignore this problem and to pawn it off onto someone else. However, ultimately, Pilate had to make a choice. Either to release Jesus and face persecution, or to hand him over to the Jews. Pilate took the easy way out. And Pilate's dilemma serves as an example, that we also cannot ignore Jesus, that we have to make a choice. Either to follow him, or to not.[13]

‡Jesus would have been carrying the horizontal beam of his cross—a 125-pound chunk of wood, that would have been placed upon his open wounds from the flog-

as they led him away, they seized one Simon of Cyrene, who was coming in from the country, and laid on him the cross, to carry it behind Jesus. And there followed him a great multitude of the people and of women who were mourning and lamenting for him. But turning to them Jesus said, "Daughters of Jerusalem, do not weep for me, but weep for yourselves and for your children. For behold, the days are coming when they will say, 'Blessed are the barren and the wombs that never bore and the breasts that never nursed!' Then they will begin to say to the mountains, 'Fall on us,' and to the hills, 'Cover us.' For if they do these things when the wood is green, what will happen when it is dry?"

Two others, who were criminals, were led away to be put to death with him. And when they came to a place called Golgotha (which means Place of a Skull), they offered him wine to drink, mixed with gall, but when he tasted it, he would not drink it. And they crucified him.⎮ Pilate also wrote an inscription and put it on the cross. It

ging. . . . Perhaps even on some exposed vertebrae.[14]

⎮How do we know that Jesus was nailed to the cross? This is a detail which we assume from our upbringing, but did you know, that not one of the Gospel writers specifically mention the soldiers driving nails into Jesus' hands? All of them say only that

Jesus was 'crucified,' each using a form of the verb σταυρόω (stauroó). Therefore, how do we know that he was nailed upon the cross, and wasn't just tied up on one?

We can know so, by looking at other passages. In John 20:24-31, Thomas says he will not believe in Jesus' resurrection, unless he puts his fingers into the scars in his hands and feet, which Jesus shows to him the same scars that he also shows off in Luke 24:39. Additionally, this detail was prophesied in Isaiah 53:5, that he would be 'pierced' for our transgressions (though this also could be an allusion to the spear that pierced his side), as well as later mentioned by both Peter (Acts 2:23) and by Paul (Colossians 2:14).

Was Jesus nailed upon the cross? The answer, yes. However, this question should serve as another example, that we should know what the Bible does say, versus what we assume/believe it says.

The Romans would have dislocated both of Jesus shoulders in order to properly stretch him out on the cross. They would have also used 5 to 7 in. spikes to securely fasten Jesus to the cross—*not* like the nails you can buy at Lowes or Home Depot. Furthermore, they would have nailed them through the wrists, providing a solid position, unlike if they nailed them through his palms, which under his weight, would tear and drop Jesus from the cross. (And in Jewish eyes, the wrist was seen as part of the hand.)

Nailing through the wrists would have also been *extremely* painful, because the metal would be puncturing the median nerve, which so happens to be the largest nerve in the hand. It would be a similar feeling to hitting your funny bone, while using pliers to *squeeze* and twist that nerve. In fact, the pain was so unbearable, that a new word was invented just to describe it: *excruciare* in Latin or 'excruciating,' which means, "out of the cross."

The cross was *not* designed like executions today, giving a quick lethal injection or jolt of electricity, for a victim could hang for *days* on a cross in agonizing pain. He wouldn't die from blood loss, but from asphyxiation as a result of pure exhaustion. The cross was designed, so that the stresses on the muscles and diaphragm put the chest into the inhaled position, forcing the victim to push up with his feet to relieve

read, "Jesus of Nazareth, the King of the Jews." Many of the Jews read this inscription, for the place where Jesus was crucified was near the city, and it was written in Aramaic, in Latin, and in Greek. So the chief priests of the Jews said to Pilate, "Do not write, 'The King of the Jews,' but rather, 'This man said, I am King of the Jews.'" Pilate answered, "What I have written I have written." Then two robbers° were crucified with him, one on the right and one on the left. And Jesus said, "Father, forgive them, for they know not what they do."

When the soldiers had crucified Jesus, they took his garments and

---

tension on the muscle, scrapping against splinters with his bare back. And he couldn't just will himself to stop breathing either, for his body would naturally push up to gasp, fighting to keep itself alive. For every single breath, the criminal would push himself up, then ease back down, until his legs no longer had any strength to push up for air and gave out.[17]

°Crucifixion was a *criminal's* death, capital punishment used to execute rebellious slaves, pirates, and enemies of the state, as well as foreigners. *Not* a death for a Roman citizen.
    . . . The cross was a symbol of humiliation, suffering, and death. It was *not* some-

divided them into four parts, one part for each soldier; also his tunic. But the tunic was seamless,* woven in one piece from top to bottom, so they said to one another, "Let us not tear it, but cast lots for it to see whose it shall be." This was to fulfill the Scripture which says,

"They divided my garments among them,

and for my clothing they cast lots."

So the soldiers did these things, but standing by the cross of Jesus were his mother and his mother's sister, Mary the wife of Clopas, and Mary Magdalene. When Jesus saw his mother and the disciple whom he loved standing nearby, he said to his mother, "Woman, behold,

---

thing cute to be hung on a wall or to be made into jewelry.

*Seamless?

Also, if the Roman soldiers were gambling for his clothes, that would mean Jesus might have been hanging on the cross naked. Not only was he in *pain*, but he was also shamed. Hung exposed for all to see....

your son!" Then he said to the disciple, "Behold, your mother!" And from that hour the disciple took her to his own home.*

And those who passed by derided him, wagging their heads and saying, "You who would destroy the temple and rebuild it in three days, save yourself! If you are the Son of God, come down from the cross." So also the chief priests, with the scribes and elders, mocked him, saying, "He saved others; he cannot save himself. He is the King of Israel; let him come down now from the cross, and we will believe in him. He trusts in God; let God deliver him now, if he desires him. For he said, 'I am the Son of God.'"†

One of the criminals who were hanged railed at him, saying, "Are you not the Christ? Save yourself and us!" But the other rebuked him, saying, "Do you not fear God, since you are under the same sentence of condemnation? And we indeed justly, for we are receiving the due reward of our deeds; but this man has done nothing wrong." And he said, "Jesus, remember me when you come into your kingdom." And he said to him, "Truly, I say to you, today you will be with me in paradise."‡

Now from the sixth hour there was darkness over all the land until the ninth hour. And about the ninth hour Jesus cried out with a loud voice, saying, "Eli, Eli, lema sabachthani?"¦ that is, "My God, my God,

*Being a good son, Jesus makes sure that his mother is taken care of after his death, making sure she had someone to care after her, and to take care of her in a very patriarchal society. Though it's strange, that he gives this responsibility to John, instead unto one of his little brothers? (Perhaps because they weren't believers? Therefore, Jesus created a new family at the cross? Redefining family/relationship of the Kingdom.)

†It wasn't the nails that held Jesus to the cross, it was his love for me and for *you*. He could have came down whenever he *chose* to. Yet, he chose to remain and to suffer, so that we may be saved.

‡Jesus came to set us free from our crimes/our sins, like the criminal on the cross.

¦This is what Jesus says, according to Matthew, while Mark records that he said, "Eloi, Eloi, lema sabachthani?" This, however, isn't necessarily a contradiction. Both

why have you forsaken me?" And some of the bystanders, hearing it, said, "This man is calling Elijah." After this, Jesus, knowing that all was now finished, said (to fulfill the Scripture), "I thirst." And one of them at once ran and took a sponge, filled it with sour wine, and put it on a reed and gave it to him to drink. But the others said, "Wait, let us see whether Elijah will come to save him." Then Jesus, calling out with a loud voice, said, "Father, into your hands I commit my spirit! It is finished," and he bowed his head. And having said this he breathed his last and gave up§ his spirit. And behold, the curtain of the temple was torn in two, from top to bottom.▫ And the earth shook, and the rocks were split. The tombs also were opened. And many bodies of the saints who had fallen asleep were raised, and coming out of the tombs after his resurrection they went into the holy city and appeared to many. When the centurion and those who were with him, keeping watch over Jesus, saw the earthquake and what took place, they were filled with awe and said, "Truly this was the Son of God!"· And all the crowds that had assembled for this spectacle, when

---

'Eli' and 'Eloi' are the same word, yet one is Hebrew and the other Aramaic. There are many theories for this difference, such as Matthew recorded what Jesus may have actually said, while Mark changed it to 'Eli' as a literary technique, to emphasize why the bystanders might have mistakenly thought he was calling for Elijah. Also, Jesus quoting this Psalm in Aramaic, may be proof that he was quoting from the Targum.

§Notice, that Jesus "gave up" his spirit. He ἀφῆκεν (apheken [Matthew 27:50]) or παρέδωκεν (paradoken [John 19:30]), both being verbs for 'yielding.' Yes, eventually he would have died upon that cross because of man, because of both the Jews who handed him over and the Romans who beat and hung him—because of both Jew and Gentile, but he didn't. Even Pilate is surprised that Jesus was dead as soon as he was when he receives the news. Not even man could kill our Jesus. He gave up his spirt, he yielded his life for us, so that we could be saved. . . . His life was *his* to give (John 10:17-18). . . .

▫Though the Holy of Holies no longer housed the lost Ark of the Covenant, the curtains being torn symbolized that man was no longer separated from God! No longer did only the High Priest have access to Yahweh one day a year, but now *all* had access to Him!

·The world goes CRAZY! at Jesus' death. At the death of God. The curtain tears, creation cries, and Sheol vomits. . . . And in the midst of this, a *Roman centurion* confesses

they saw what had taken place, returned home beating their breasts.

There were also women looking on from a distance, among whom were Mary Magdalene, and Mary the mother of James the younger and of Joses, and Salome. When he was in Galilee, they followed him and ministered to him, and there were also many other women who came up with him to Jerusalem.

Since it was the day of Preparation, and so that the bodies would not remain on the cross on the Sabbath (for that Sabbath was a high day), the Jews asked Pilate that their legs might be broken and that they might be taken away. So the soldiers came and broke the legs of the first, and of the other who had been crucified with him. But when they came to Jesus and saw that he was already dead, they did not break his legs. But one of the soldiers pierced his side with a spear, and at once there came out blood and water.* He who saw it has borne witness—his testimony is true, and he knows that he is telling the truth—that you also may believe. For these things took place that the Scripture might be fulfilled: "Not one of his bones will be broken." And again another Scripture says, "They will look on him whom they have pierced."

When it was evening, there came a rich man from Arimathea, named Joseph, who also was a disciple of Jesus. He was a member of the council, a good and righteous man, who had not consented to their decision and action; and he was looking for the kingdom of God.

---

that Jesus was the Son of God. Even in death, Jesus affects *everything*. Religion, creation, death, even the soul of a man, who may have ruthlessly killed hundreds if not thousands. . . . And are these crazy things because of Creation's reaction? Or are they the Father's lament for His Son? For lament, is naked aggression, and God exposes Himself as the curtain of the Temple is torn.

*For the skeptics who reason Jesus could have still been alive when he was buried in the tomb, believing that Jesus had only passed out on the cross, the Swoon Theory, a spear piercing his heart literally destroys this argument. Jesus was *dead* when he was buried. Additionally, the spewing of blood and water is known as pericardial effusion, a fluid membrane forming around the heart as a result of heart failure.[20]

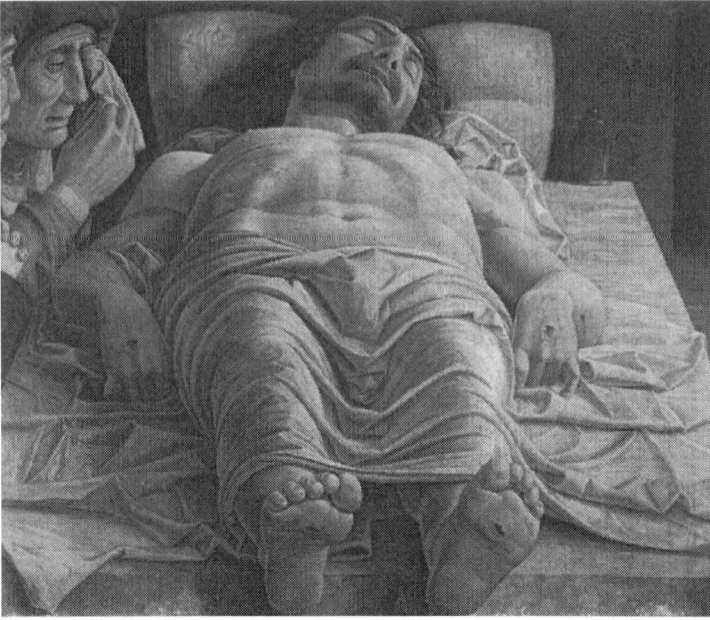

He took courage and went to Pilate and asked for the body of Jesus. Pilate was surprised to hear that he should have already died. And summoning the centurion, he asked him whether he was already dead. And when he learned from the centurion that he was dead, he granted the corpse to Joseph. Nicodemus also, who earlier had come to Jesus by night, came bringing a mixture of myrrh and aloes, about seventy-five pounds in weight. And Joseph bought a linen shroud, and taking him down, they wrapped him in the linen shroud as is the burial custom of the Jew, and laid him in a tomb* that had been cut out of the rock, where no one had ever yet been laid. And he rolled a stone against the entrance of the tomb. Mary Magdalene and Mary the mother of Joses saw where he was laid. Then they returned and prepared spices and ointments.

The next day, that is, after the day of Preparation, the chief priests

---

*The baby who was born in a manger, was also he, who was buried in a tomb that was not his own. He could have chose to have been born to royalty, lived as a king. Yet, he chose to be the humblest amongst us. Chose to be the God, who would serve man.

and the Pharisees gathered before Pilate and said, "Sir, we remember how that impostor said, while he was still alive, 'After three days I will rise.' Therefore order the tomb to be made secure until the third day, lest his disciples go and steal him away and tell the people, 'He has risen from the dead,' and the last fraud will be worse than the first." Pilate said to them, "You have a guard of soldiers. Go, make it as secure as you can." So they went and made the tomb secure by sealing the stone and setting a guard.

On the Sabbath they rested according to the commandment.

NOTES

1. Fig. 1: Da Vinci, Leonardo. *The Last Supper.* 1498. Santa Maria delle Grazie: Milan, Italy.
2. "Passover - Pesach: History & Overview." *JewishVirtualLibrary.org.* 2017. Web. 17 Oct. 2017.
3. Fig. 2: Blake, William. *The Last Supper.* 1799. National Gallery of Art: Washington, D.C.

4. Fig. 3: Michael D. O'Brien. *Christ in Gethsemane.*

5. Fig. 4: Blake, William. *The Agony in the Garden.* 1799-1800. Tate Britain: London.

6. Strobel, Lee. *The Case for Christ: A Journalist's Personal Investigation of the Evidence for Jesus.* Grand Rapids, MI: Zondervan, 1998. Print. p. 194-195.

7. Fig. 5: Blake, William. *Judas Betrays Him.* 1803-1805. Tate Britain: London.

8. Richardson, Don. *Peace Child.* Minneapolis, MN: Bethany House, 2014. Print.

9. Fig. 6: Blake, William. *Jerusalem The Emanation of the Giant Albion*, Plate 78. 1804. Yale Center for British Art: New Haven, Connecticut.

10. Chekhov, Anton Pavlovich and Constance Garnett. *The Tales of Chekhov: The Lady with the Dog and Other Short Stories.* New York: Macmillan Company, 1917. Print. p. 173-174.

11. Fig. 7: Adriatikus. "Jesus Christ Fragment." 2008. *Photograph.*

12. Strobel, p. 195-196.

13. McLarty, p. 305-306.

14. Idleman, Kyle. *Not a Fan: Becoming a Completely Committed Follower of Jesus.* Grand Rapids, MI: Zondervan, 2016. Print. p. 160.

15. Fig. 8: Vecelli, Tiziano. *Christ Carrying the Cross.* 1565. Museo Nacional del Prado (Prado Museum): Madrid, Spain.

16. Fig. 9: Blake, William. *Christ Nailed To The Cross The Third Hour.* 1800-1803. The Morgan Library and Museum: New York.

17. Strobel, p. 196-200.

18. Fig. 10: Blake, William. *The Soldiers Casting Lots for Christ's Garments.* 1800. Fitz-william Museum: Cambridge, England.

19. Fig. 11: Blake, William. *The Crucifixion: 'Behold Thy Mother'.* 1805. Tate Britain: London.

20. Strobel, p. 201-202.

21. Fig. 13: Mantegna, Andrea. *The Lamentation Over the Dead Christ.* 1470-1474. Pinacoteca di Brera (Brera Art Gallery): Milan, Italy.

22. Fig. 14: Blake, William. *Sealing the Stone and Setting a Watch.* 1800-1803. Yale Center for British Art: New Haven, Connecticut.

23. Fig. 15: Eric Feather. *Cross React*

CHAPTER 21

JESUS, THE SAVIOR, PART 2:

THE RESURRECTION:

SURPRISE!

I t was my last weekend in Rolla, a very bittersweet moment indeed. On one hand, I would be returning to Searcy, to Harding. Getting to reunite with friends I hadn't see in three months. Getting a chance to dive more deeply into my studies. Beginning my last thirty-two weeks of schooling before graduating. . . . But I would also be leaving Rolla. Leaving friends I had known for years at camp, and leaving new friends who I was just getting to know. It's hard in life, when you give up something good, for something as equally good.

That weekend, I was invited to the house of the Wilsons, to both celebrate a delayed sixteenth birthday party for Dalton, and to shoot off a few leftover fireworks from the Fourth. Invited to join a family for cake! I mean, very blessed, to join a family in a night of fun, laughter, and celebration!

***

JESUS WON A mighty victory at the cross! A feat worth celebrating every day. But, his death upon that cross, would have meant nothing if he did not rise again. For every man dies, but how many are

410

able to resurrect themselves from the grave?*

All four Gospels record this miraculous event. Yet, they each do so very differently. Some even suggest, that there are contradictions between the Gospels. So of course, the teens and I had to investigate. I read aloud the account of Matthew, before splitting the class into three groups. One to compare and contrast Mark's Gospel to Matthew's, another Luke's, and the other John's. I think they had ten or fifteen minutes to make a list of similarities and differences, before we discussed what all three groups had found. Here,

---

*It's a mystery, of where Jesus was or what he was doing during those three days while his body was in the grave. He had told the thief on the cross that he would be with him in Paradise, (Luke 23:43), but Peter also mentions Jesus ministering to the spirits of those who had lived during the time of Noah (1 Peter 3:18-22), and Jesus' words in Revelation 1:17-18, "Fear not, I am the first and the last, and the living one. I died, and behold I am alive forevermore, and I have the keys of Death and Hades," lead some to believe, that Jesus literally went to Hell to retrieve those keys.

is some of what we discovered:

Now after the Sabbath, toward the dawn of the first day of the week, Mary Magdalene and the other Mary went to see the tomb. And behold, there was a great earthquake, for an angel of the Lord descended from heaven and came and rolled back the stone and sat on it. His appearance was like lightning, and his clothing white as snow. And for fear of him the guards trembled and became like dead men. But the angel said to the women, "Do not be afraid, for I know that you seek Jesus who was crucified. He is not here, for he has risen, as he said. Come, see the place where he lay. Then go quickly and tell his disciples that he has risen from the dead, and behold, he is going before you to Galilee; there you will see him. See, I have told you." So they departed quickly from the tomb with fear and great joy, and ran to tell his disciples. And

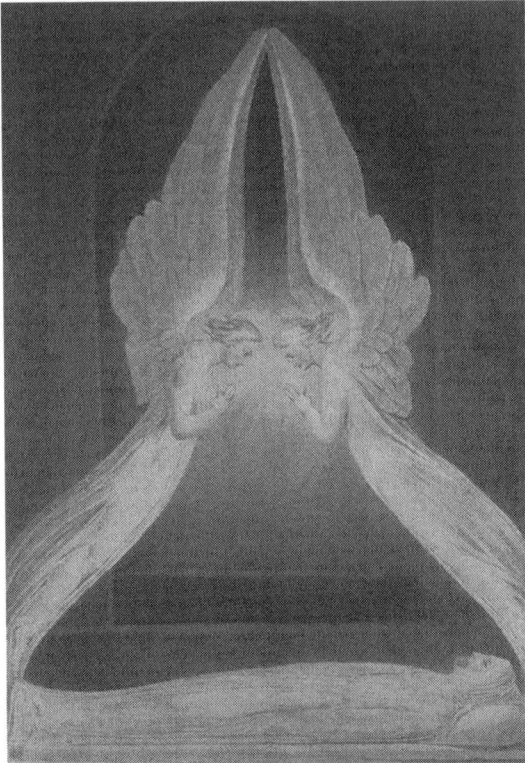

412

behold, Jesus met them and said, "Greetings!" And they came up and took hold of his feet and worshiped him. Then Jesus said to them, "Do not be afraid; go and tell my brothers to go to Galilee, and there they will see me." (Matthew 28:1-10)

Like a phoenix, Jesus had risen from the grave! And in all four accounts, his empty tomb was first discovered by women, they who become eyewitnesses of this discovery. Before diving into the differences of these accounts, let me point out that this incident is weird in itself. Jesus' death and resurrection begins the era of Christianity. However, if you're revamping a religion, or starting a new one in the ancient world, you would not want to do so on the word of a woman, especially a woman like Mary Magdalene, who had once been possessed by seven demons (Luke 8:2). A woman's

word was worth nothing, compared to that of a man's. But God doesn't choose who man deems qualified, but qualifies whom He deems worthy. Therefore, this detail is actually evidence that Christianity is true, and not just some made up religion.

However, how many women were at the tomb?

According to Matthew, there were two, "Mary Magdalene and the other Mary." In Mark, there are three, "Mary Magdalene, Mary the mother of James, and Salome" (16:1), Luke says there were at least five, "Mary Magdalene and Joanna and Mary the mother of James and the other women with them," (24:10), and John only mentions Mary Magdalene (20:1).

Also, in comparing numbers, there's a difference in the number of angels present: in Matthew and Mark (16:5) there is one, in Luke there are two (24:4), and in John, Mary at first, only sees an

empty tomb (20:1), before two angels appear after Peter and John leave the tomb (20:12)

So, do these differences mean that the Bible contradicts itself?

Not necessarily. Firstly, just because Matthew only mentions two women, doesn't mean there weren't others there, too. Every author must choose what details to include or exclude within his story. A story would go nowhere if a writer tried to include every single detail, even within a single setting. Think of it, how long would it take you to describe *everything* around you at this very moment? And compared to the core of the story, secondary details aren't as important.

Secondly, though each Gospel was written by the Spirit, the Spirit also wrote each Gospel through the creativeness of a man. Men with different agendas and different Gospels, appealing to different groups of people.

Thirdly, since the Spirit chose to work with man, each of these four men have different writing styles and literary techniques. For example, Matthew sometimes uses two as a symbolic number for witness, since in the Jewish culture, two or three witnesses were needed to convict someone for a crime (Deuteronomy 19:15, Matthew 18:16). Other examples of Matthew's use of two, include two men who were demon-possessed (8:28-34), while it is a single man who called himself "Legion" within Mark's (5:1-20) and Luke's (8:26-39) accounts, and Jesus healing two blind men at Jericho (20:29-34), while he only heals a man by the name of Bartimaeus in Mark (10:46-52).

Lastly, as pointed out by Lee Strobel in his book, *The Case for*

Christ, it's actually a good think that the Gospels have different details instead of being the same, actually providing more genuineness and proof that they were not just some made up stories.[6]

What? You're joking right?

No, no I'm not. Think about it; if each Gospel was exactly the same, it would be more proof that they were created by collaboration instead of being a historical event. If the Gospels were more similar, it would actually be proof that their authors were plagiarizing each other. For example, let's say you were at a friend's house. And while you are there, you and him accidently break his mom's prized vase. However, instead of telling his mom the truth, you both decide to be dishonest and to lie that it wasn't a football that had been thrown inside the house and shattered it. Therefore, you collaborate on a coherent story, making sure you both remember the same details in exactly how the vase met it's fate, in preparation for his mom's interrogation.

Or, as another example, you can have two teens sitting in the same Bible class, experiencing the same lesson; however, both of them will remember different details that stood out to them, and reversely, also not remember details that didn't stick out to them. Or, they could also remember the same details but differently. This phenomenon held true when I was working on my second book, *Tales of the Soul: Joplin May 22*. While I was reading different accounts of the Joplin Tornado, some described that the tornado sounded like a roaring jet engine, while others say it sounded like a train, or a *giant* lawnmower. And some mentioned that there was hail after the storm, while others never did. So would missing a small detail like this, make one account a lie, and the other the truth?

> While they were going, behold, some of the guard went into the city and told the chief priests all that had taken place. And when they had assembled with the elders and taken counsel, they gave a sufficient sum of money to the soldiers and said, "Tell people, 'His disciples came by night and stole him away while we were asleep.' And if this comes to the governor's ears, we will satisfy him and keep you out of trouble." So they took the money and did as they were directed. And this story has been spread among the Jews to this day. (Matthew 28:11-15)

In Matthew's account, he mentions that the angels told the women to inform the disciples of what they had witnessed at the tomb; however, he neglects to tell us of the women delivering this message to the disciples (Luke 24:8-9, John 20:2), of Peter racing to the tomb (Luke 24:12) and being outran by John (John 20:3-9), of Jesus appearing to Mary Magdalene (Mark 16:9-11, John 20:11-18), or that he had appeared to two disciples on the road to Emmaus (Mark 16:12-13, Luke 24:13-35), or of Jesus appearing to his disciples in the upper room (Luke 24:36-49,* John 20:19-23†).

However, what Matthew does mention that the other Gospels do not, was that the guards who were supposed to be guarding the tomb, went and told the chief priests of what they had seen. They were then bribed to spread the lie that the body was gone, because the disciples had stolen it, in exchange for their lives. Protection from meeting the death penalty in failing to guard the tomb.

---

*When Jesus first appears to his disciples, they are afraid of him, thinking he was a ghost. However, to demonstrate to them he had truly risen, and wasn't just some animated spirit seeking revenge for his death, but that he was still flesh and blood, Jesus had the disciples touch his hands and feet, and he also ate some broiled fish. This is *crucial*, for it proves Jesus was still both man and God after his resurrection, still having a body—a glorified body, but a body.

†John's Gospel is the only one that mentions Jesus being pierced by a spear after his death. His Gospel is also the only one that mentions the episode of 'Doubting Thomas.' For some reason, Thomas had been absent when Jesus had first appeared to the other ten. Therefore, he did not believe them, when they told him of what they had seen. Perhaps believing they were attempting to pull a poor April Fools joke on him, demanding a sign in exchange for his faith, "Unless I see in his hands the mark of the nails, and place my finger into the mark of the nails, and place my hand into his side, I will never believe" (20:25).

Thomas, is the only disciple who had the chance to believe like us. To believe in the resurrection of Jesus without physically seeing him. Sort of like a friend telling you to trust him, and put to your hand into a coyote jaw-trap. Saying that it won't bite off your hand. But that intimidating metal trap, creates doubt of what your friend is saying is true. (However, if the trap was designed to snap off the leg of an animal instead of holding it, wouldn't it be able to get away before the hunter could return for it? Though the speed and pressure of the trap could leave a nasty bruise on your wrist, and be careful not to get your fingers caught—make a fist. Otherwise, it could break them.)

Like many of us, Thomas wanted evidence of Jesus' resurrection. However, though he doubted, notice the other disciples didn't excommunicate him for it. In fact, he is still with them eight days later when Jesus shows himself again, this time, with him present. (Can you even imagine, how awkward those eight days must have been?) And though we normally thinking of him as 'Doubting Thomas' (though we don't think of Simon as 'Denying Peter'), look at what he says to Jesus: "My Lord and my God!" (John 20:28). If Jesus had not been the Son of God, Thomas would have committed the worse crime imaginable in the Jewish eyes, blasphemy. For he proclaimed Jesus to be 'God.'

418

(Another man who almost killed himself instead of being executed by his Roman overseers, also believing he had failed in guarding, was the Philippian jailer, who thought his prisoners had escaped during a great earthquake (Acts 16:27).) However, the foundation for this lie falls flat for several reasons:

1. Perhaps the most obvious, was that the body could not be found. A man's corpse is kind of the best evidence that he's actually dead. The Sanhedrin could have stopped Christianity in it's tracks, if they could have supplied Jesus' dead body. As McLarty points out, *everything* hangs on the Resurrection. This being one reason why my youth minister has pointed out, that perhaps, we should start wearing the tomb around our neck? The cross is *significant*; however, it would have been worth nothing, if Jesus never rose from the grave.

2. There are too many witnesses who see a living, breathing Jesus. Not only did he appear to the women at the tomb, to the eleven in the upper room, and to the two disciples on the road to Em-

maus, but also to his brother, James (1 Corinthians 15:7),* to *five hundred* people on another occasion (1 Corinthians 15:6), and to all who witnessed him ascend into heaven on top of a mountain [as well as to Saul (Acts 9:3-6)].

3. If the disciples had stolen Jesus' body, and if they had collaborated together to fabricate this lie, all eleven of them would not have died for it in excruciating deaths. A man may die for a lie—if he believes that it's the truth. But only an insane man would die a torturous death for a lie that he created. And the odds of eleven men doing so, is not in favor of Jesus' resurrection being fabricated:

Peter (according to tradition), was crucified on an upside down cross, believing he was unworthy to die in the same manner of his Lord.

[**Paul** is believed to have been beheaded in Rome by many, while others believe he actually got to leave Rome alive, travelling to Spain as he had wanted to, and spreading the Gospel there.]

Andrew was scourged and crucified.

James (the son of Zebedee) was beheaded with a sword (Acts 12:2).

John, according to some accounts, was boiled alive in oil, before he was banished to the island of Patmos. There, he lived peacefully to an old age, and where wrote the book of Revelation.

---

*Though James was the brother of Jesus, he was not always a believer (John 7:5), many speculating that he reminded a skeptic until Jesus personally appeared to him after his resurrection. For what would you think, if your brother claimed to be the Savior of the World? However, James became an *important* figure within the Church: being present in the upper room on the day of Pentecost (Acts 1:14), becoming a leader of the Jerusalem church, and even writing an epistle within the Bible. And look at how James begins his letter, "James, a servant of God and of the Lord Jesus Christ, To the twelve tribes in the Dispersion:

Greetings" (James 1:1).

To call oneself a "servant" of his brother, takes amazing humility.

Phillip was scourged, thrown in prison, and crucified.

Bartholomew is said to have either been beaten and then crucified, or skinned alive and then beheaded.

Thomas was run through with a spear.

Matthew was stabbed in the back with a sword.

James (the son of Alphaeus) was beaten, stoned, and then clubbed on the head.

Thaddeus was crucified.

Simon was crucified.

And **Matthias** was burned alive.*

Now the eleven disciples went to Galilee, to the mountain to which Jesus had directed them. And when they saw him they worshiped him, but some doubted. And Jesus came and said to them, "All authority in heaven and on earth has been given to me. Go therefore and make disciples of all nations, baptizing them in the name of the Father and of the Son and of the Holy Spirit, teaching them to observe all that I have commanded you. And behold, I am with you always, to the end of the age." (Matthew 28:16-20)†

And so, Matthew ends his Gospel, with Jesus giving the Great Commission—a fantastic theme verse for any mission trip, both foreign and local. For Jesus said to *go* out into *all* the world. Not just to Africa, but America, China, Searcy, Rolla—into all the world.

---

*Additionally, according to history and church tradition: the Gospel writer, Mark, was dragged by horses through the streets of Alexandria till he died, Luke was hanged, and Jude (Jesus' brother) was shot with arrows.

†Only Matthew and Mark record Jesus giving the Great Commission (Mark 16:14-20). Also, if we did not have Luke's Gospel, we would not have an account of Jesus' Ascension (though Mark does briefly mention it (Mark 16:19); however, it's also debated if this verse was later added to Mark), and Luke writes about it twice. Once at the end of his Gospel (Luke 24:50-53), and again at the beginning of Acts (1:6-11).

For *everyone* has a need for the Savor. Matthew leaving us a command, to be active participants of the Kingdom.

AS WAS POINTED out by Team 3, John's is the most unique of the four Gospels, having more material that is not included within the other three. Such as John stating the theme for his book, "but these are written so that you may *believe* that Jesus is the Christ, the Son of God, and that by *believing* you may have life in his name (20:31)," Jesus appearing to seven of his disciples while they're fishing on the Sea of Galilea, helping them to catch a *bounty* of fish (just as he had, when he had first called Peter, Andrew, James, and John (Luke 5:1-11)) before he sits and has breakfast with them,* consisting of bread and fish (21:1-14); Jesus asking Peter to, "Feed my sheep" (21:15-19), Peter questioning if John will die before Jesus returns again (21:20-24), and John alluding that Jesus had performed *many* more miracles than what are recorded within the Bible: "Now there are also many other things that Jesus did. Were every one of them to be written, I suppose that the world itself could not contain the books that would be written" (21:25).

"Why do you think, that Jesus asked Peter three times, 'Do you love me?'" I asked the class.

"Because Peter had denied him three times," quickly answered a teen.

"Yes. It's believed, that Jesus was redeeming Peter, and seeing if his disciple was truly committed to him. Also notice, that just as each time Peter had denied Jesus his emotions had grown, to the

---

*Jesus and his disciples sit around a charcoal fire (John 21:9). The only other place where John mentions a charcoal fire ἀνθρακιὰν (anthrakian), is in 18:18, where servants and officers are warming themselves, where Peter joins them, and makes his third denial (18:25-27).

point of him invoking a curse upon himself and swearing, so too does his emotions elevate each time he answers Jesus, 'Lord, you know everything; you know that I love* you.'"

For the great Redeemer had come to redeem all things. Especially, those whom choose to follow him. Though Peter had denied Jesus, he was still used by God, becoming a head apostle within the Church. And even being the one to boldly deliver a sermon to the multitude, on the day of Pentecost (Acts 2:14-41).

***

AFTER THE FIREWORK show had ended, it was nearing time to drive home and to call it a night. But before that . . . something pretty cool happened. Micah, the Wilsons' second to youngest, and recently dubbed nine-year-old, went out into the yard, and grabbed a fragment of one of the exploded rockets. He then ran back to me and handed me the rocket, saying, "Here. Have this. So you don't forget me before you come back."

So many mixed emotions came from that small gesture: warm fuzzies from this gift that had been bestowed upon me, by one of the boys who I could wrestle with, spin around, talk about Legos, and playfully tease about liking girls; a pinch of sadness that I was leaving, and a hint of disbelief that Micah would think that I could forget him (though I understand how someone his age could think that).

"Thank you," I told the young boy, as I accepted his gift, before

---

*What's also really cool about this passage, is that two times Jesus asks Peter, "ἀγαπᾷς με;" ("Agapas me?"). 'Agape,' is the highest form of love in the Greek language—a selfless love for *everyone*, seeking their interest over your own. And Peter answers, "φιλῶ σε." ("Philo se.") 'Phileó,' being a love of deep friendship, a brotherly love, loyalty. Peter, perhaps, greatly loving Jesus, but in his grief, could not yet love him with agape, which is why Jesus asks him a second time. But, the cool thing about Jesus, is that he meets us where we're at. For when Jesus asks Peter the third time, "Do you love me?", he asks Peter by saying, "φιλεῖς με;" ("Phileis me?"). (Repetition and three, seams to be an effective teacher for Peter. For in Acts 10:9-16, Peter is given a vision of a sheet filled with all kinds of animals. And the Lord tells him three times to, "Rise, Peter; kill and eat.")

wrapping him in a hug. "And don't worry, I won't forget you, man. And I'll be back next summer," I promised him.

To this day, I still have the bottom of that rocket, currently standing on my window seal in my dorm room. And Micah's gift, reminds me of the gift that Jesus left for us, so that we wouldn't forget him until he returned, the Holy Spirit. The Helper who guides us and gives us comfort, until the day, of the return of the King.

NOTES

1. Fig. 1: Blake, William. *The Entombment*. 1805. Tate Britain: London.
2. Fig. 2: Blake, William. *Christ in the Sepulchre, Guarded by* Angels. 1805. Victoria and Albert Museum: London.
3. Fig. 3: Blake, William. *Angels Rolling away the Stone from the Sepulchre*. 1805. Victoria and Albert Museum: London.
4. Fig. 4: Blake, William. *Mary Magdalen at the Sepulchre*. 1805. Yale Center for British Art: New Haven, Connecticut.
5. Fig. 5: Blake, William. *The Three Maries at the Sepulchre*. 1800. Fitzwilliam Museum: Cambridge, England.

6. Strobel, p. 213-217.
7. Fig. 6: Blake, William. *Christ Appearing to the Apostles after the Resurrection.* 1795. Tate Britain: London.
8. Fig. 7: Blake, William. *The Ascension.* 1805-1806. Fitzwilliam Museum: Cambridge, England.

Epilogue Dos

Jesus, who is he? I mean, when you hear the name 'Jesus,' what is the first thing you think of?

There is nothing wrong with a white Jesus. No, he was probably not white when he lived here on earth. But the beauty of the Gospel, is that it's truly heterogenous. You do not have to be a Jew nor an American to be a Christian. You do not have to be able to speak Hebrew or Greek or to read Latin or Arabic. You do not have to be male, or a Republican, or white. The Gospel is truly for *all* peoples, and can be adapted to minister to all.

Jesus, is the same. The color of his skin does not matter. Yes, he came from the lineage of David, and yes he was a Jew . . . but he did not come as the Jewish Messiah. He came as the Savior of the world.

All people were created in his image. Americans, Africans, Chinese—all peoples have their roots within Christ's garden. Jesus' skin color does not matter for salvation. And part of the beauty of not knowing what Jesus truly looked like, allows him to be adapted, to be relatable. However, his character, his teachings, *him*, should *not* be changed to fit our molds.

His character must remain his. For as Christians we're supposed to be like him, not him like us. Otherwise, you could invent a Christ who's pro crack.

His teachings must remain his. For they are the words we're supposed to follow. Otherwise, we could twist them to support a prosperity theology.

And he must remain him. For there is *no* other like Jesus. The God who humbled himself to be born as a man. Who lived amongst us, as one of us. He who was a son, a brother, a friend, a teacher. The Lamb, who loves *you* so much, that he willingly gave himself up to be sacrificed by his creation upon the cross, so *you*, whom he loves, may be saved. He who was buried in the tomb, but on the third day, was raised from the grave. For not even death could hold him. He who left to prepare a place for us. And he, who will one day soon, return as the triumphant Lion.

This,

is,

JESUS!!!

ACKNOWLEDGEMENTS

Much thanks is needed in crafting a book just as this. Many hours were spent sweating and toiling, like a smith hammering over an anvil. Sparks flying as the hammer clangs, refining and shaping crude metal into shape and form. Yet a smith can grow weary and sometimes dishearten, needing the encouragement of others to continue to forge and to form. Not to mention, that many of the materials he used were not his own, but given to him by others, who took part in the forging. Therefore, it is only proper, to thank those who assisted in giving this book form.

***

THANK YOU FIRSTLY, to the **Rolla Church of Christ**, for allowing me to be your summer intern. For being so generous, loving, and encouraging. If it wasn't for you all, this book would have never been written in the first place. . . . Thank you!

Thank you **Ty Kalisz**, for your sermons on the Good Shepherd and on Esther, which have had a great impact upon both chapters within this book. Thank you **Theo** and **Kelly Theobald**, for your support, and for the opportunities you have given me through the Lord's Library. And thank you **Sabrina** and **Jenifer Davis**, for being my proofers, and catching so many of my mistakes.

Thank you **Tye Zola**, my mentor and youth minister, who has taught me so much about the Bible, and about living for our Savior.

Thank you, **Dr. Oden** and **Dr. Robertson**, for teaching BIB 409: Critical Issues in the Old Testament and New Testament, which has sparked many conversations within this book, such as the one concerning the Book of Enoch. Thank you **Dr. Youngblood**, for your Hebrew guidance, and your inspiring insights on the Old Testament—especially concerning the book of Jonah, and **Dr. Bury**, for your Greek tutelage, especially for supplying me information in the use of *Ego eimi*. Thank you **Dr. Rice**, for your insights on the Gospel of Luke, especially concerning the theme of Divine Reversal, and thank you **Dr. Daggett** and **Dr. McLarty**, for teaching me so much about the Gospel of John, and for allowing me to quote from your book, Dr. McLarty. Thank you, **Dr. Manor**, for allowing me to use photographs taken from the Linda Byrd Smith Museum of Biblical Archaeology.

And thank you, **Dr. Hunt**, for introducing me to the 'wounded foot motif' in your ENG 415: Mythology and Folktales, and for having me read the stories of little Krishna.

Lastly, but certainly *not* least, I would like to thank the artists and others, who have graciously allowed me to use their own artwork, or personal property, within this publication:

Atif Saeed, for your *Angry Lion* photograph. **Jon Ross**, *The I Am Statements of Christ*, **Michael D. O'Brien**, *Christ in Gethsemane*, **Eric Feather**, *Christ Feeding the Five Thousand* and *Cross React*, **Keith Kampschaefer**, *Superboat XLVIII*, **Andrew M. Wright**, the cylinder seal depicting The Descent of Inanna, and **Mark Mir** and

Dr. Wu, for permission in using the Oriental Nativity scenes.

***

AFTER *MUCH* WORK, the clanging stops. The hammer is laid down, as the smith lifts up the object he had just made. A smile of pride cannot leave his face, as he gazes at the art he had created. A most precious treasure, crafted by the fingers of many hands.

79741050R00271

Made in the USA
Columbia, SC
07 November 2017